CREATING CAPACITY FOR ATTACHMENT

Dyadic Developmental Psychotherapy in the Treatment of Trauma-Attachment Disorders

Editors

Arthur Becker-Weidman, PhD

Deborah Shell, MA, LCMHC

Collaborators

Craig Clark, MA, LMFT

Dafna Lender, MSW, LCSW

Jessica Mroz, MSW, LCSW

Miranda Ring, PsyD

Phyllis Rubin, PsyD, CCC-SLP

Robert Spottswood, MA, LCMHC

Contributors

Susan Becker-Weidman, MSW, LCSW

Scott L. Blackwell, PhD

Karen Doyle Buckwalter, MSW, LCSW

Beth Green, parent

Jody R. Hanson-Walker, parent

Daniel Hughes, PhD

Karen A. Hunt, parent

Joseph McGuill

Michelle Robison, MSW, LCSW

Published by:

Wood 'N' Barnes Publishing & Distribution
2717 NW 50th
Oklahoma City, OK 73112
(405) 942-6812

Cover Design by Blue Designs
Copyediting & Design by Ramona Cunningham

Printed in the United States of America
Oklahoma City, Oklahoma
ISBN#1-885473-72-9

This book is dedicated to my daughter, Samantha.
It is because of her that my work and interests turned to the
nature of attachments. She has taught me so much
about love, family, and relationships.

I would like to acknowledge the support and help of my spouse,
Susan, and my children, Emily, David, and Samantha, who
taught me about being a parent. In addition, I also
acknowledge the families I have worked with,
who have taught me what it takes to heal.

ARTHUR BECKER-WEIDMAN

For Art, Craig, Dafna, Dan, Jess, Miranda, Robert, and Phyllis:

Sometimes a moment stands out from the others around it, hard to ignore, and once overlooked, the opportunity to discover its meaning is lost. Such a moment flowered in my brain one warm August evening while the eight of us who wrote this book were seated together at a restaurant in Maine. We'd become a bit raucous, as was our way following a day of serious supervision. Not rude, not too disturbing, but definitely uproarious and a little silly. There were a few airplanes with messages flown from one end of the fish-laden table to the other, and one, which I commanded in flight, asked, "What about a book?" I knew this was the moment. This was the group to do it. Sitting all around me was a unique complement of practicing therapists. I was overwhelmed by excitement knowing how each would bring their rich life experiences to the fore. Although diverse in age, gender, and geographic location, we had all been working with the same challenging population, and here we sat, smack in the middle of a week of advanced Dyadic Developmental Psychotherapy training with Dan. The moment was captured, and here is the result.

This group of therapists has been phenomenal. Each worked hard alone, and then together, melding a common vision. As co-editor, Art's extensive research base, training, and clinical experience – coupled with a generous spirit – helped provide the essential foundation for this book. We met again the following year, the same eight therapists with Dan for our week of advanced supervision in Maine. While apart, we kept up a close connection through e-mails. In an effort to convey actual working models of Dyadic Developmental Psychotherapy-influenced treatment in alternative placements, we invited several experienced therapists to describe the scope of treatment with children at their residential treatment facilities. Additionally, the testimony by parents describing their experience of treatment rounded out this effort.

Dan's guidance, suggestions, and insights further advanced our understanding as we worked through each chapter. Ultimately we developed and produced this text, which is intended to provide an accurate and readable description that we hope will be a valuable tool for therapists who want to learn about Dyadic Developmental Psychotherapy inside and out. Thanks, Dan, for bringing this moment, and us, together.

Much love,
Deb

Table of Contents

The Development of Dyadic Developmental Psychotherapy

DANIEL HUGHES

When this model of treatment is being fully used, the therapist engages in a very active use of self in the treatment sessions. Full engagement, evident in playfulness, acceptance, curiosity, and empathy becomes present in spontaneous and unique ways. For the therapist to have a transforming impact on the client, the client must also be having an impact on the therapist. –Daniel Hughes

In 1985, I was attempting to provide treatment for a nine-year-old foster girl who presented with many emotional, behavioral, and social difficulties. I had noticed that she had manifested similar difficulties in her previous three foster homes and that in each case, the problems did not become evident until she had been living in the home for about three months. I commented on that fact to her and asked her if she wanted any help. She quickly replied that she did want help. Not hearing such a response very often, I replied with enthusiasm: "Great! What would you like help with?" Her response was deliberate and thoughtful: "Could you help me to move every three months?"

This girl's request left me speechless. I struggled to understand her view of her world. What did "family" mean to her? What were her motives for such a request? Why did she not know what she was missing? Most importantly of all, how could I help her to attain what I thought was in her best interests—a stable, permanent, home—when she saw value in attaining the opposite.

My clinical training did not prepare me for a girl who wanted to move to 30 or 40 foster homes before turning 18. In graduate school and during my clinical internship, I had been exposed to psychodynamic, cognitive-behavioral, and family-systems theories and their related therapeutic interventions. None of these seemed to explain this girl's wish, nor how I might have an impact on her wish and her subsequent development.

In 1986, I chanced to attend a workshop in Maine that was being given by a pediatrician by the name of Vera Fahlberg. She spoke with great enthusiasm about attachment theory and research. While I had previously heard about this theory, I had never taken much interest in learning more about it, and it had not been part of my graduate school education. (I had received my PhD in Clinical Psychology in 1973.)

What she said sparked my interest in learning more, and I turned to the literature. I was shocked to discover the depth and comprehensiveness of the research. This truly was not some fringe theory without research backing. It was evident that my lack of knowledge about attachment theory and research represented a giant gap in my training and knowledge. As I began to study, however, my irritation over what I did not know was quickly replaced by my excitement over what I was learning. I was beginning to understand why a nine-year-old girl might want to move every three months. I was beginning to understand what she had not experienced and what she did not understand: the meaning and value of a secure attachment.

For the next several years, I learned about John Bowlby and Mary Ainsworth. I discovered the research of Alan Sroufe, Dante Chichetti, Mary Main, and Patricia Crittenden, among others. I began to understand how abuse and neglect create a legacy that can greatly impair a young child's ability to feel safe, to trust others, to enter into reciprocal, enjoyable interactions with attachment figures, to seek comfort and support under conditions of distress, and to proceed along pathways that facilitate their overall psychological development. I began to understand why some children who had been exposed to intrafamilial trauma had such difficulty achieving resolution of the traumatic event while others did not. I was learning a great deal about attachment but was much slower to learn how to assist children who had been traumatized and whose attachment behaviors were contradictory and too disorganized to proceed along healthy developmental paths. They seemed to be living with skilled foster parents, but they were not able to permit their foster parents to "parent" them. And I was not of much assistance.

In 1989-90, two experiences helped me to begin to develop new ways of providing psychological treatment for foster and adopted children and their families. The first experience involved two visits to The Attachment Center in Evergreen, Colorado. This was the only program that I was aware of at the time that spoke of treating "reactive attachment disorder." This program offered a form of treatment at that time that was quite controversial and was known as "holding therapy." It involved adopting a much more active stance in treatment than I had ever considered. The stance involved providing high levels of confrontation with regard to the children's defenses and behaviors as well as a high degree of nurturance for their traumatic roots and current fears. The foster or adoptive parents were actively involved in the treatment and in providing a home structure that was congruent with the treatment itself.

My response to the treatment program at The Attachment Center was one of strong ambivalence. They were working with children who had severe emotional, behavioral, and social difficulties, and I knew that the traditional approaches of treatment that were available to me would not be helpful for them. They were taking a very active stance and were directly addressing the child's past traumas and current difficulties. It immediately seemed to me that an active stance might be necessary since the more nondirective and play-centered approaches of treatment that I had been using were not effective. It also seemed that if I were able to sufficiently engage the child to successfully address the child's traumatic experiences and current difficulties, I might be able to help him or her to resolve and integrate these experiences into a more coherent sense of self. They also frequently found ways to assist the children in noticing the quality of care that they were receiving in their foster or adoptive home.

My response was ambivalent because I did not believe that the highly confrontational interventions could facilitate a sense of safety that I thought to be necessary if the child were to be open to exploring past traumas as well as new ways of relating with his or her foster/adoptive parents. I also did not believe that many of the interventions I saw were congruent with the attachment theories and research that I had been studying for the previous four years. While I could see the value of a more directive, active stance that facilitated the child's readiness and ability for greater emotional awareness, attachment behaviors, and communication skills, I did not concur with central features of the interventions that were being used.

My second experience served as the impetus for developing new interventions to achieve the goals just mentioned. I read *The Interpersonal World of the Infant* by Daniel Stern. This book made me aware of the moment-to-moment, dyadic interactions between parent and young child that facilitates their attachment, the child's emerging sense of self, as well as the development of associated emotional, social, cognitive, behavioral, and linguistic skills. I was able to see that the very active stance intuitively taken by parents is necessary for so many areas of their child's development. I became entranced by the concepts of attunement, vitality affect, cross-modality matching, and intersubjectivity. I could see how these parent-child experiences led to safety, attachment security, discovery of self and other, exploration of the world, and an integrated sense of self. They represented the means whereby young children first acquire these skills.

After reading Stern's book, I now had a general template for assisting foster and adopted children to move beyond their experiences of loss, abuse, and neglect and develop a secure attachment with their foster and adoptive families. I would use the same interventions that have been used for centuries by parents worldwide. These interventions were not based upon confrontation and obedience but rather on attaining a reciprocally enjoyable and congruent parent-child "emotional dance." One might have to modify the means whereby the child is taught this dance, but our first goal is to successfully develop this dance.

A year or two later, I became aware of a form of therapy that also took the parent-infant playful interaction as a guide for therapeutic interventions. This treatment, known as Theraplay, was developed by Ann Jernberg in Chicago. It involves the therapist's active use of self in forming an enthusiastic and playful engagement between the therapist and child. The treatment is primarily nonverbal and experiential, focuses on the here and now, and involves the therapist taking a very directive stance to lead the child into various interpersonal experiences that are representative of experiences common to parent-child interactions. Theraplay continues to evolve as a treatment modality through the active direction of Phyllis Booth and others, and now involves a component in which the child's parent is shown how to facilitate the same interactions with the child that are occurring between the therapist and child.

In attempting to describe what I thought to be the key factors in the treatment relationship, I again looked to the parent-child dance and described what seemed to be central features of those interactions. From this, I began to speak of "the attitude," which I still see to be central in the therapeutic relationship as well as in the relationship that the therapist attempts to facilitate between the child and his or her foster/adoptive parent. "The attitude" consists in four factors: playfulness, acceptance, curiosity, and empathy (PACE) which are seen to be the active ingredients in developing and maintaining the dance.

I was convinced that if I were to assist children with serious difficulties becoming engaged in secure attachment relationships with their new caregivers, I would have to replicate this early parent-child dance. However, I struggled with how to lead children into such an emotionally intimate relationship when they had previously been abused or neglected in parent-child relationships. Many of these children were very oppositional and defiant. They resisted the great majority of parent-led interactions. Many of them manifested features consistent with the attachment disorganization classification. These children show an intense need to control all aspects of their environment, including their relationships. They were and are very unwilling to relinquish their desire for control.

Turning again to the parent-infant dance, continuous reciprocal movement from following to leading to following were evident in the parent-infant interactions. The parent would be quick to follow the child's lead as to focus of attention, affective state, and apparent intentions while nevertheless active in co-regulating the affect as it emerged and co-creating the meaning of the interactions. When the child manifested signs of distress, the parent accepted the distress, and co-regulated the affect, and co-created meaning about it before considering leading the child into a new activity.

This process, which relied so heavily on accepting the child's current affective state and making sense of it with the child, reminded me of the Utilization Principle to which I had been exposed many years earlier when studying the work of Milton Erickson. A central feature of Erickson's unique model of hypnotherapy involved accepting whatever "resistance" was being manifested by the client and utilizing that behavior in the service of the therapeutic goal. When the therapist accepted the resistance, the client had very little left to resist and so was much more likely to follow the lead of the therapist into a state of very receptive therapeutic engagement.

In a similar manner, when the child worked to avoid both the therapeutic engagement and the themes that were being introduced, the therapist could "utilize" whatever act of avoidance was being manifested by the child, accept it, co-regulate the associated affect, and co-create its meaning. This act of acceptance of whatever behavior was being expressed by the child proved to hold the child within the therapeutic engagement with affect often characterized by playfulness and/or empathy. Within the state of acceptance, the child often was more willing to enter into "meaning making" about both the resistance and the original focus of the interaction. The therapist maintained a tone of non-judgmental curiosity about the meaning of the child's intentions, behaviors, and past experiences of abuse and neglect.

Still, many children manifested more intense resistance than I had anticipated. Having taken measures to insure that the child felt safe, I was surprised at the intensity of the child's intention of avoiding any exploration of his current behavioral problems or past traumatic experiences. The child appeared to be relaxed, he or she had control over the pace of the exploration, the parents who were present conveyed understanding and support, and still many children remained reluctant participants to the therapeutic process.

At about this time—1995—I discovered the comprehensive work of Allan Schore, *Affect Regulation and the Origin of the Self*. In his book, Schore brought together an extensive body of research in the areas of neuropsychology, early childhood development, infant mental health, and psychoanalytic concepts. He covered both normal, early-childhood development and developmental variations that resulted from abuse and neglect. His theoretical formulations and conclusions from such a wide range of studies were truly remarkable.

One of Dr. Schore's areas of focus that I found to be the most helpful for the treatment model I was trying to develop was his consideration of the role of shame in early childhood neurological, emotional, cognitive, and social development. He demonstrated how, as the infant enters toddlerhood, she enters into a neuropsychological state of shame when limited by her parents. He showed how this is a normal aspect of early childhood and represents the first means of socialization of the young toddler. In normal parent-child relationships, the parent observes the distress of the state of shame caused by the limit, and quickly co-regulates the affect and repairs their relationship, while still limiting the behavior. The shame remains small and quickly dissipates, but it has an important role in activating states of inhibition and impulse control.

However, in homes characterized by abuse and neglect, the young child experiences "pervasive shame" that does not dissipate. The limit itself may well have been abusive, triggering overwhelming negative affect that could not be regulated. The parent was likely to also have abandoned the child in that state, not attempting to regulate the affect or repair the relationship. If a young child is holding an expensive camera and it is taken from him, his experience of shame will be small if the parent explains why it is being taken, comforts his distress, and helps him to direct his attention to something else. However, if the parent screams at the child, slaps him, and then refuses to talk with or comfort him, that child is certain to enter into a deep, long-lasting state of shame that will be very difficult to regulate. That child will be at risk of not being able to explore well nor seek comfort when in distress. With repeated experiences of similar degrees of shame, he is likely to conclude that he is stupid, bad, and/or unlovable and to hesitate to try to meet his most basic interpersonal needs.

Schore's description of pervasive shame brought deeper understanding and empathy for the children's intense resistance to exploring either their misbehavior or past experiences of abuse/neglect. Pervasive shame would also contribute to our understanding of these children's strong resistance to affirmations of worth, affection, comfort, and enjoyable, validating experiences. If treatment was to be able to successfully engage children and then maintain this engagement while focusing on negative states, it would have to recognize the power of shame, co-regulate it, and reduce its intensity. Only through dealing with the child's shame can the therapist hope that the child will become willing to become engaged in the process of reducing the negative affective and cognitive states of his life.

that was then this is now
shame
coregulation
pleasure

Schore's work also led me to explore in greater depth the need to help abused and neglected children become more capable of experiencing and integrating states of pleasure and joy. Just as negative affect needs to be co-regulated, so too do states of positive affect. Therapy cannot just focus on trauma and loss. It needs to provide children whose lives have been so negative with co-regulated experiences of positive affect. This focus on pleasure and joy led me to the work of Colwyn Trevarthen regarding primary and secondary intersubjectivity. Trevarthen demonstrates in detail how the infant and young child develops the original sense of self, other, and the world through the affective/cognitive responses that their attachment figures have toward them and their world. Bringing these insights into therapy and parenting for abused/neglected children, one can see the need for the child to be able to have a positive impact on his therapist and foster/adoptive parents. Yet, this may be difficult when the child's frequent misbehaviors and disorganized attachment behaviors may activate a negative response from the adults in his or her life. This dilemma is solved if the therapist and parents are able to persistently gaze upon and respond to "the child under the behaviors." Rather then confusing the symptoms for the child, the therapist and parent need to be responding to the underlying motives, perceptions, thoughts, and feelings that led to the behavior. Looking "under the behavior," they are likely to see fear and doubt, shame and discouragement, confusion and mistrust, as well as courage, hope, and a deep desire to become attached to their parents and to feel worthy of such attachments.

As the year 2000 approached, I became increasingly aware that while the focus on ways of engaging and treating the abused and neglected child was crucial in facilitating developmental change, frequently it was not sufficient. While the foster and adoptive parents were always active participants in the treatment process, adequate attention was not always given to maximize the impact of their participation or to understand the difficulties that they were having in parenting their children. These parents had often been, and continue to be, blamed for their foster/adopted child's many symptoms, and I had erred in "protecting" them from that blame at the expense of insufficiently addressing any difficulties that they were having in providing the high level of parenting that their child needed.

Over the past five years, I have become more aware of the powerful role of the parents' own attachment histories on their ability to help their child to resolve their attachment histories. Their child's behaviors secondary to abuse, neglect, or insecure/disorganized attachment behaviors often activated similar issues in the parents' attachment histories. As a result, the parents were able neither to remain regulated in the presence of their child's behaviors nor to help the child to create new meaning about a situation and modify his or her behavior. Thus, it became

parents own attachment hx

increasingly evident that the treatment had to include an exploration of the parents' attachment histories and assistance in addressing any unresolved aspects. The research of Mary Dozier, Miriam Steele, and their colleagues makes this point very clearly.

Along with addressing any unresolved areas of the parents' attachment histories, it also is important to address issues more related to the current family situation. The foster and adoptive parents may also have to explore issues of grief and loss, shame, anxiety, anger, and depression secondary to the extensive difficulty that they encounter in their attempts to raise a very challenging child. These difficulties can become severe after many months or years of continual failure with decreasing hope for progress.

Along the way other theorists, researchers, and clinicians have had an influence on this treatment approach. This includes the work of Dan Siegel, Diana Fosha, Susan Johnson, Mary Dozier, Peter Fonagy, and the Circle of Security Project, among others.

As the model continues to evolve through the work of thoughtful, sensitive, and skilled clinicians throughout the US, Canada, and the UK, it will need to develop into a more standardized form of training for both parents and therapists so that it can more easily be replicated and studied. Training now consists of providing a foundation in attachment theory and research, followed by a formal presentation of principles and strategies of treatment that follow from this foundation. Videotapes of treatment sessions are presented and discussed in detail. The training participants also engage in role-play exercises in which they take the roles of therapist, child, and parent. In the advanced groups, the therapists initiate discussions of their successes and struggles in implementing this model. They also show and discuss videotapes of their work.

What is evident upon reviewing the videotapes of many therapists is that this model of treatment is able to be replicated by therapists of various theoretical backgrounds, personalities, ages, and genders. While each therapist is unique and her specific manifestation of the model is also unique, the principles and interventions are still able to be utilized in a replicable fashion. Just as there are common elements of parent-child interactions among very unique parent-child dyads, so too in therapy are the common elements able to be present among highly individualized therapist-client relationships.

When this model of treatment is being fully used, the therapist engages in a very active use of self in the treatment sessions. Full engagement, evident in playfulness, acceptance, curiosity, and empathy, becomes present in spontaneous and unique ways. To have a transforming

T= Co-regulate emerging affective states
co-create new meanings ⟹ resolution
⟹ integration

impact on the client, the client must also be having an impact on the therapist. Her engaged presence with her clients is likely to appear quite similar to her engagement with her own children if she is a parent.

TS / *wn* The therapist who is most fully able to utilize this model has developed her own coherent autobiographical narrative. She is likely to be autonomously attached herself and to have resolved any traumas or losses in her own attachment history. As a result, she is consistently able to remain present and responsive to her clients when they are facing unresolved or disorganized aspects of their own attachment histories. Having resolved any similar features in her own history, she is able to remain with her client psychologically, ready to co-regulate emerging affective states and co-create new meanings that will facilitate resolution and integration.

From among these therapists, I have received a large amount of feedback that this model of treatment has consistently produced more significant treatment results than have the previous forms of treatment they employed. Through active use of self, the therapist is able to follow the client into unresolved areas, lead him when necessary, and communicate therapeutic presence in a fully affective/reflective manner. These results are evident to the many therapists who have taken this attachment-focused perspective and joined their clients in this transforming inter-subjective journey. At this point in time there is a need to establish an "evidence base" for Dyadic Developmental Psychotherapy, including more standardized treatment and training protocols. The recent study by Arthur Becker-Weidman serves as an important beginning of this process. Further efforts are now being made in hopes of expanding the empirical foundation for this work.

As this process unfolds, I expect the following factors will prove to be the "active ingredients" in this attachment-focused, narrative-making model of family therapy. These factors all facilitate the ability to develop and maintain a rhythmic emotional dialogue that enables the co-creation of coherent narratives for our clients.

1. NONVERBAL VERBAL COMMUNICATION. For toddlers, verbal communication flows naturally from nonverbal communication. For all of us, nonverbal communication is the primary means we use to give expression to our inner lives as well as to become aware of the inner lives of others. The therapist needs to be sensitively aware of the nonverbal expressions of family members, help to make these expressions verbal, and help to create congruence between the nonverbal and verbal.

2. FOLLOW-LEAD-FOLLOW. The therapist is not distracted by the nondirective/directive debate, but rather follows the lead of the family member, joins, and when necessary leads into related areas that are being avoided, while then following the client's response to that lead. This process parallels the parent-infant dance.

3. CONNECTION-BREAK-REPAIR. In therapy, as in all relationships, there are frequent breaks in the felt sense of connection due to many factors. The therapist notes the breaks, accepts them, understands them, and facilitates interactive repair. Breaks are not to be avoided but rather are utilized for their meaning and as the source of new change opportunities in the relationship and the self.

4. AFFECT/REFLECTION BALANCE AND INTEGRATION. Meaningful dialogue contains a blend of affect and cognition, conversation and reflection, which holds the interest of the participants and co-creates the meanings of the narratives. The therapist is aware of the affect/reflection components of the here-and-now expressions and facilitates their balance, congruence, and integration.

5. ATTITUDE OF PLAYFULNESS, ACCEPTANCE, CURIOSITY AND EMPATHY. These factors provide the momentum for the therapeutic, transforming quality of the dialogue. The therapist actively conveys through these qualities that all memories, affective states, and events can be accepted, understood, and integrated into the narrative. Breaks are easily repaired, and the flow within nonverbal/verbal, affect/reflection, lead/follow proceeds within a sense of safety and with an openness to the discovery of new aspects of self and relationship.

6. PARENT-CHILD ATTACHMENT CLASSIFICATION CONGRUENCE. The therapist works toward facilitating congruence between the parent and child with both moving toward security/autonomy. The lead in the movement is most often the parents, but this is not a linear process, and the progress is reciprocal.

Other factors may also certainly be identified as being "active ingredients" in the effectiveness of the treatment. I believe, however, that they will not displace these six features, but will more than likely complement and enhance them.

Introduction

ARTHUR BECKER-WEIDMAN & DEBORAH SHELL

"If affect-laden experiences can be made less frightening in the therapeutic environment—that is, if patients can be helped to feel safe enough to feel—then they can reap profound benefits, for within core affective states are powerful adaptive forces and processes with tremendous therapeutic potential." –Diana Fosha, The Transforming Power of Affect

Dyadic Developmental Psychotherapy is an approach to treating children who have trauma-attachment disorders. It is a relationship-based approach (dyadic), and it is based on attachment theory, which is a developmental theory (developmental). Chapter One describes the underlying theory of this therapy, and Chapters Two, Three, and Four describe treatment under varied conditions. Other chapters in the book describe the therapist's use of self, present material for and by parents, and provide resources.

This book is the product of an extensive collaboration among eight of the authors (Art, Deb, Craig, Dafna, Jess, Miranda, Phyllis, and Robert). How we each got here is a long story; we come from varied backgrounds and life experiences. Although all eight original collaborators had extensive previous training in Dyadic Developmental Psychotherapy with Daniel Hughes, PhD, this endeavor originated during a particular week-long advanced training at Colby College, Maine during the summer of 2003. Over the course of the following year and a half, we developed this book, mainly through correspondence and another gathering in Maine during the summer of 2004. As the work progressed, we invited special contributors whose expertise and enthusiasm using Dyadic Developmental Psychotherapy blended with and deepened our own experiences. The chapters written by parents and therapists working with children in out-of-home placements have broadened the scope of this book. Our mutual bond lies in a deeply felt desire to help heal children and their families who have been traumatized and have severe disorders of attachment. This book grows from these common interests and experiences and the realization that there has not been enough available information for clinicians about helping children who have trauma-attachment disorders.

The foreword is written by Daniel Hughes and offers an overview of attachment theory and the development of Dyadic Developmental Psychotherapy as a therapeutic approach to healing.

The children, teens, and youth we will be focusing on are those who have experienced extensive and pervasive trauma during the first few years of life. The children come through the child welfare system, private adoptions, and international adoptions. While the details of their maltreatment vary, a common thread is that these children have experienced some significant and pervasive disruptions in the primary caregiver-child relationship. Maltreatment has caused the primary attachment relationship to be disordered and disorganized to such an extent that these children are highly defended, difficult to reach, and have either no capacity or a limited capacity to form authentic, meaningful, affectional ties with caregivers. As a result, many usual forms of treatment are ineffective with these children. Dyadic Developmental Psychotherapy evolved as an approach to treat such "untreatable" children.

Many of these children have extensive histories of physical abuse, neglect, sexual trauma, and emotional abuse. Others experienced serious and painful medical conditions that interfered with the normal developmental process of forming attachment relationships with their primary caregivers (Minde, K., 1993). In these instances, the attachment system was disrupted by such things as prematurity that necessitated extensive stays in Neonatal Intensive Care Units and painful medical interventions during the first years of life. You will read about children who were raised in orphanages and, while having all their basic needs met, did not have responsive and reciprocal affectional experiences with a primary caregiver. The effects of being raised in an institution in which the caregiver-infant ratio is 1:10 or higher are as devastating as physical abuse, maybe more so. Reactive Attachment Disorder and Post-Traumatic Stress Disorder, Complex Type, are the most common clinical diagnoses for these children. Many of these children, because of the previous neglect and lack of stimulation, may have other comorbid conditions such as Sensory-Integration Disorders and a variety of Neuro-Psychological dysfunctions. In addition, a significant percentage of severely maltreated children who come through U.S. foster care also have Bipolar Disorder I. Approximately 2% of the population is adopted, and between 50% and 80% of such children have attachment disorder symptoms (Carlson, Cicchetti, Barnett, & Braunwald, 1995; Cicchetti, Cummings, Greenberg, & Marvin, 1990).

The cost to society of not treating such children is enormous. Many of the families that enter the child welfare system have extensive multigenerational histories of abuse and neglect. We know from research that a child's state of mind with respect to attachment is best predicted by the mother's state of mind with respect to attachment. If the primary caregiver has unresolved trauma or has been raised in an abusive or neglectful home, then the child is at grave risk of perpetuating this intergenerational cycle of violence. Children who have experienced maltreatment are also at grave risk of developing severe personality disorders. Many of these children are violent (Robins, 1978) and aggressive (Prino & Pyrot, 1994) and as adults are at risk of developing a variety of psychological problems (Schreiber & Lyddon, 1998) and personality disorders, including antisocial personality disorder (Finzi, Cohen, Sapir, & Weizman, 2000), narcissistic personality disorder, borderline personality disorder, and psychopathic personality disorder (Dozier, Stovall, & Albus, 1999). Neglected children are at risk of social withdrawal, social rejection, and pervasive feelings of incompetence (Finzi et al., 2000). Children who have histories of abuse and neglect are at significant risk of developing Post-Traumatic Stress Disorder as adults (Allan, 2001; Andrews, Varewin, Rose, & Kirk, 2000). Children who have been sexually abused are at significant risk of developing anxiety disorders (2.0 times the average), major depressive disorders (3.4 times average), alcohol abuse (2.5 times average), drug abuse (3.8 times average), and antisocial behavior (4.3 times average) (MacMillian, 2001).

These children present with a variety of symptoms and behavior patterns. Generally, these are children who do not trust because their experiences have taught them that adults are not reliable caregivers and that the world is chaotic, unpredictable, and nonresponsive. Most of the symptoms presented by these children can be seen as expressions of this working model of the world and relationships.

In Chapter One you will read about the theory behind the practice of Dyadic Developmental Psychotherapy. Dyadic Developmental Psychotherapy has as its core the maintenance of a reciprocal, responsive, and affectively attuned relationship between therapist and child, between caregiver and child, and between therapist and caregiver. This is the central therapeutic mechanism and is essential for treatment success.

Chapter Two describes the logistics of a Dyadic Developmental Psychotherapy Session and Chapter Three will give you the flavor of an actual session. Dyadic Developmental Psychotherapy is based on attachment theory and is an attachment-facilitating and attachment-based treatment. Dyadic Developmental Psychotherapy was developed to heal children who are largely unresponsive to usual treatment approaches, such as nondirective play therapies, behavioral therapies, cognitive-behavioral therapies, and other family and individual therapies. These are the children who often are misdiagnosed with multiple conditions such as Oppositional Defiant Disorder, Conduct Disorder, Attention Deficit/Hyperactivity Disorder, and who have been unresponsive to treatment. Dyadic Developmental Psychotherapy focuses on maintaining an affective connection with the child. Through an authentic emotional tie with the child and with empathy, the clinician helps the child face and integrate the emotions, memories, and meanings of experiences that traumatized the child.

That which is split off is integrated and loses its power to corrupt and distort relationships in the present. Dyadic Developmental Psychotherapy is an experiential approach that focuses primarily on process.

In Chapter Four you will meet children being raised in homes of "good-enough" parents. You will find a description of therapy with families that have the capacity to create a healing PLACE (being playful, loving, accepting, curious, and empathic, as described in Chapter One) for these children. The methods and techniques described in this chapter have broad applicability.

Chapter Five describes work in a more difficult circumstance—work with parents who have their own unresolved trauma. Therapy in these instances presents special challenges, as one must help the parents heal in order to get them ready to help the child heal. These circumstances take even more patience and persistence. It is vital that the elements of PACE (being playful, accepting, curious, and empathic, as described in Chapter One) be applied to both parents and children.

Chapter Six describes work with children who are placed in institutional settings such as Residential Treatment Centers, Residential Treatment Facilities, and Group Homes. Many children are placed in institutional settings for safety reasons and will be returned to their homes upon discharge. When this is the case, therapy must involve both the residential staff and the family. However, when there is no permanent home for the child, then work must proceed differently. An extensive section describes two such remarkable programs at Villa St. Maria and Chaddock. These programs use Dyadic Developmental Psychotherapy as their treatment model, and have achieved some remarkable successes.

Use of self is an essential dimension of Dyadic Developmental Psychotherapy. The therapist and parent's use of self is critical to effectively applying Dyadic Developmental Psychotherapy. In much of what is done, it is how one intervenes that is often more important than the actual intervention itself. Chapter Seven discusses this aspect of the work.

Chapter Eight provides some practical tips for those who work with children diagnosed with Reactive Attachment Disorder. This includes teachers, case managers, youth workers, and wrap-around staff.

In Chapters Nine and Ten we have material specifically for parents. Since a critical resource for healing children with trauma-attachment disorders is the emotional availability of a primary caregiver, we provide information, techniques, and methods for parents to use in implementing a healing PLACE. Avoiding power struggles and maintaining an authentic, empathic, and supportive emotional relationship with these children is very difficult. Chapter Nine will help parents discover some useful and effective approaches to this problem.

Chapter Ten is written by parents of children who have been successfully treated with Dyadic Developmental Psychotherapy. It provides inspiration and practical information for families of children with attachment disorders. You will read about two domestic adoptions and one adoption from Russia. One family was treated primarily with a two-week intensive while the other two received weekly treatment. While each family is unique, you will find some common themes in their stories.

Chapter Twelve lists resources that therapists, parents, child-care workers, and others may find useful in working with these children. The resource lists include books, games, music, and much more. The resources have been compiled from the "bag of tricks" of each of the contributors and others in the field who practice Dyadic Developmental Psychotherapy.

For most readers, Dyadic Developmental Psychotherapy is a new subject. Having several authors provides a rich and deep presentation of the material, albeit at the risk of a certain amount of repetition.

Our intention is to provide the reader with a deep understanding of the process and content of Dyadic Developmental Psychotherapy in a variety of settings and under a variety of conditions. This therapy has shown effectiveness in helping families with adopted and foster children and those with trauma-attachment disorders. We hope that parents and professionals will find this material useful in their quest to help these children.

CHAPTER 1

Dyadic Developmental Psychotherapy: The Theory

ARTHUR BECKER-WEIDMAN

"Attachment to a baby is a long-term process, not a single, magical moment. The opportunity for bonding at birth may be compared to falling in love—staying in love takes longer and demands more work."
—T. Berry Brazelton, Touchpoints

CHAPTER INTRODUCTION

In this chapter we will describe the theoretical basis for Dyadic Developmental Psychotherapy. Dyadic Developmental Psychotherapy is rooted in Attachment Theory. The practice of Dyadic Developmental Psychotherapy and its methods are derived from the basic principles and tenets of Attachment Theory.

There has been a substantial amount of confusion and controversy about the diagnosis and treatment of Reactive Attachment Disorder (O'Connor & Zeanah, 2003). Attachment therapy, holding therapy, and other terms are often used interchangeably, as are Reactive Attachment Disorder, Attachment Disorder, and related terms, which only adds to the confusion. Dyadic Developmental Psychotherapy is not a "holding therapy" as defined by O'Connor & Zeanah (2003). They describe, "holding therapy" as being based on "rage reduction" techniques and state that, "the holding approach would be viewed as intrusive and therefore *nonsensitive* and counter therapeutic" (italics added) (p. 236). Dyadic Developmental Psychotherapy has as its core, or central therapeutic mechanism for treatment success, the maintenance of a contingent collaborative and affectively attuned relationship between therapist and child, between caregiver and child, and between therapist and caregiver.

A few definitions are in order. *Attachment* is a general term that describes the state and quality of an individual's emotional ties to another. *Attachment behavior* is any type of behavior that causes a person to attain or to retain proximity to a preferred individual and that results in an increased sense of safety and security. It is initiated by a perceived separation or a perceived threat of separation from the attachment figure. *The attachment system* is an internal working model or blueprint of the world in which the self, significant others, and their relationships are represented and which are then acted upon. *Trauma-attachment disorder* is a term used to describe the multiple and complex effects of early chronic maltreatment (physical and emotional neglect; physical, sexual, and emotional abuse) on the developing child. The continuing effects of early maltreatment operate on many domains including cognitive, emotional, psychological, and neuro-biological, for example.

John Bowlby developed attachment theory in the 1950's. Unlike other theorists at the time, Bowlby believed that his clients suffered from real loss and trauma. Bowlby broke with psychoanalytic theories that viewed patients' disorders as being based on fantasy. Many other theories of child development are based on the study of adult psychopathology. Attachment theory is based on the study of the normal development of healthy attachments and views the deleterious effects of trauma and loss as problems resulting from disruption of the normal attachment process. Attachment theory is rooted in ethology and posits a biological and evolutionary basis for attachment. "Attachment is a 'primary motivational system' with its own workings and interface with other motivational systems" (Bowlby, 1975). Attachment behavior is organized cybernetically, meaning that it becomes activated when certain conditions exist and stops when other conditions apply. Attachment behavior is activated by fear, pain, or fatigue. The behavior activated is directed toward achieving closeness with the mother so that the fear, pain, or fatigue is eliminated and a sense of safety, security, and comfort is achieved. A primary goal of the attachment system is the creation of a secure base from which the child can explore the outside world and to which the child can return to refuel and be nourished physically and emotionally.

The essential marker of a healthy and secure attachment is the ability to tell a coherent story about one's life, regardless of how difficult that life may have been. Those with an insecure attachment (anxious, ambivalent, or avoidant) and those with a disorganized attachment have difficulty. Their narratives are dismissing of their past and lacking in details, are overly detailed and stuck in the past, or lack coherence and consistency and contain verbal oddities such as talking about a deceased person as if that person were still living.

Secure attachment is characterized by infants who are able to use the parent as a secure base and who then can explore the environment. They are distressed during separations from the parent and are able to be comforted upon reunion.

The importance of early experiences on later development can be seen in the work of Tizard (1977), who confirmed Bowlby's theories that the time between six months and four years of age is critical for the capacity to form stable relationships. She found that children adopted after the age of four years remained antisocial in school behavior despite their having formed close and loving bonds with their adoptive parents. Furthermore, ample evidence for the intergenerational transmission of attachment problems can be found in the work of Mary Main (1990), Erik Hesse (1999), and others. The best predictor of a child's state of mind with respect to attachment is that of the parent(s) (Main 1991). Parents' early childhood experiences critically influence their capacity to respond to their child in an attuned and sensitive manner. Children whose mothers respond sensitively to the child's signals and who provide responsive comfort are children who respond most appropriately to others' distress. These children grow up to become parents who respond sensitively to their children. For example, Wolkind, Hall, and Pawlby (1977) found that mothers who had a disrupted family of origin (had a history of separation from one or both parents before the age of 11 years of age) spent nearly twice as long, on average, out of sight of their babies. In addition, these mothers spent significantly less time holding, looking at, and talking to their infants.

Once established, patterns of attachment tend to persist and be self-perpetuating by creating an internal mind-set or internal working model of the self, the other, the world, and relationships. These internal working models are the lenses through which relationships and behavior are viewed. The raw data of sensory input is filtered through these internal working models so that meaning is developed. The person responds to their perceived meaning of the behavior experienced, not to the raw experience. It is in this manner that internal working models perpetuate the established pattern of attachment that develops in the first few years of life. So, while initially the pattern of attachment is a property of the relationship, by the end of the first two or three years of life the pattern becomes a property of the child. There are substantial research findings that support this. For example, Main and Cassidy, 1988, found that the pattern of attachment assessed at 12 months of age is highly predictive of the pattern at six years of age.

These internal working models are created by repeated experiences of relationship with the primary caregiver. The model of self evolves from the experiences the child has with the parent and reflects the parent's image of the child as expressed in behavior. These models then govern how the child feels about himself and each parent, and how the child expects others to treat him.

Shore (2003, pg. 33) states, "Early failures in dyadic regulation therefore skew the developmental trajectory of the corticolimbic systems that mediate the social and emotional functioning of the individual for the rest of the lifespan." Iowa demand is to say that if **untreated**, then the child's development for the rest of the lifespan is skewed. Interventions can change the trajectory of the skewed developmental pathway and move the child closer to a normal developmental pathway. The brain, and in particular the corticolimbic systems and the orbital frontal cortex, is a plastic organ subject to environmental influences. In this manner the outside environment continues to influence the internal environment, exerting positive or negative influences. The effects of these influences are mediated by the structure and integrity of the child's current neuropsychobiological systems. In other words, current environmental and relationship influences are filtered through the lens of internal working models, which the neuropsychobiological systems created by early body experiences with the caregiving environment.

In summary, internal working models and the effects of past experiences on the developing child's neuropsychobiological systems create continuity and a proclivity to respond in certain ways. On the other hand, new experiences can create change in these systems.

The central therapeutic process of Dyadic Developmental Psychotherapy is attunement. Attunement is an affective process in which two people are in emotional sync, communicating verbally and nonverbally in a responsive and affectively sensitive manner. The archetypical model of an attuned relationship is the connection between a responsive and sensitive mother and her infant. This is not to discount other relationships. There is a hierarchy of attachment figures, the mother being the most important. Using attachment terms, the therapist creates a secure base in therapy so that the client begins to experience enough safety to allow himself to reexperience dissociated, disturbing, shameful, and feared emotions with the therapist. The therapist creates this secure base by becoming attuned and responsive to the client. The therapist must also facilitate the creation of a coherent autobiographical narrative and allow for emotional processing. As will be described later, a coherent autobiographical narrative represents the integration of primarily right hemispheric implicit and affective memories with primarily left hemispheric linear language processing. It is the integration of the "facts" (left hemisphere) of the story with the emotional (right hemisphere) components that allows for a coherent autobiographical narrative, which is a hallmark of a healthy and secure attachment.

Bowlby (1988) described five therapeutic tasks of the therapist, which are central tenets of Dyadic Developmental Psychotherapy.

> THE FIRST TASK, PROVISION OF A SECURE BASE, is essential for the provision of a space within which the client can explore relationships in the past and present, relive traumatic experiences with another rather than alone, and thereby achieve a healthier integration of self. Experiencing painful emotions and reconsidering the meaning of events and relationships may be impossible alone, but becomes possible when done with another.

THE SECOND TASK, EXPLORING CURRENT RELATIONSHIPS, expectations, and the meaning assigned to the behavior of others that guides his responses, enables the client to begin uncovering the biases that are creating problems for the client.

THE THIRD TASK, EXPLORATION OF THE THERAPIST-CLIENT RELATIONSHIP, allows for the exploration of working models in the present, here-and-now setting.

THE FOURTH TASK, EXPLORING HOW THE PAST IS STILL ALIVE AND ACTIVE IN THE PRESENT, is an integral component of the second and third tasks. It enables the client to reexperience past traumas in a direct manner rather than maintaining the split-off and largely unconscious aspects of past traumas and working models. The secure base established by the therapist allows the client and therapist to effectively contain the emotions and avoid dysregulating the client. By co-regulating the client's affect, the therapist enables the client to experience emotions that have been too painful or threatening to experience alone.

THE FIFTH TASK, ENABLING THE CLIENT TO RECOGNIZE VARIOUS WORKING MODELS of self, others, relationships, and meanings, while based in facts from early experiences with the parent, are not applicable now because the circumstances are different.

From these tasks we can see that the therapist must maintain an active stance of affective engagement with the client in order to co-regulate the client's affect and avoid dysregulation. The use of self is vital to this process, as strong emotions will be evoked in the client and in the therapist. Use of these emotions and a highly developed reflective function are essential if the therapist is to avoid becoming enmeshed in the client's negative working models, thus reenacting the past in the present. The avoidance of shaming experiences in therapy and the repair of the inevitable ruptures in the relationship that occur are all healing experiences. In fact, much of Dyadic Developmental Psychotherapy is about creating healing experiences. The process, much more than content and words, is central to the therapeutic endeavor.

The therapist provides the safe conditions within which healing can occur. This is done primarily by accepting the client's affect and meanings. The basic Dyadic Developmental Psychotherapy therapeutic process is creating a healing PACE: being playful, accepting, curious, and empathic. For parents, the framework within which they must operate is to create a healing PLACE: being playful, loving, accepting, curious, and empathic.

The Development of Attachment

The attachment system is a biologically driven system that evolved to ensure survival. Attachment behavior functions to maintain proximity with the caregiver so the child survives. In times of stress or threat, the attachment system is activated and proximity-seeking behaviors emerge. One's basic pattern of attachment and the working models that encode are developed within the first few years of life. The human infant is born in a markedly helpless state. Unlike other mammals, the human infant cannot ambulate or feed itself at birth and requires continual care if the infant is to survive.

WHY IS ATTACHMENT SO IMPORTANT? Difficulties in attachment cause a variety of problems. Healthy and secure attachment is necessary for the development of full intellectual potential. Children raised in a maltreating environment, which is nonresponsive or only marginally responsive to the child's needs, develop a working model of the world that is random, chaotic, and not attuned to their needs. They develop a working model of the world in which their efforts make no difference. As a result, they often do not put effort into academic activities and test poorly because they give up before they find the answer. Healthy and secure attachment promotes the development of the ability to think logically. Cause-effect thinking develops when a child has a relationship with the environment in which the environment is responsive to the child's needs, and the child's actions produce consistently reliable responses from the world. Other positive outcomes of a healthy and secure attachment include a broad range of affect regulation, the development of emotionally meaningful relationships, the capacity to effectively manage fears and anxieties, and the ability to manage stress and frustration without becoming dysregulated.

Initially the child requires continual care for the child's needs to be met. Food, temperature regulation, and stimulation all come from the primary caregiver. Infants communicate their needs by crying. The responsive caregiver notices the infant's cries and responds by meeting the need for food, stimulation, comfort, or by alleviating discomforts. In fact, this is the beginning of language. Gradually, the infant learns that if s/he cries one way, food will be provided, while if s/he cries in a different way other discomforts will be removed. The parent and child in their contingent and interactive, responsive relationship learn to recognize and respond to each other in a sensitive manner. The cycle begins with the infant expressing a need, the caregiver responding to this need, the infant experiencing relief or gratification, and then the cycle beginning again. This normally happens hundreds of times each week and thousands of times in the first year. As a result of this interaction, sometime during or by the end of the first year, the infant develops a sense of basic trust:

- Trust that the world is safe,
- Trust that the infant's needs will be met,
- Trust that the infant can effectively influence the world,
- Trust that the parent is reliable and good, and finally,
- Trust that the child is good.

The theme of the child's second year of life is "wants." In Erik Erikson's scheme, this is the phase of shame versus autonomy. During the second year of life, a primary task of the caring and responsive parent is to set appropriate limits for the child as the child begins to explore the world. In this manner the parent keeps the child safe, while facilitating the child's exploration of the environment. During the toddler years, parents frequently use the word "no" as limits are set. In order for the child to progress from experiencing shame to experiencing guilt, a pro-social shift, there must be repeated repair of the relationship disruptions that the parent's limit setting normally causes. The "shame cycle" begins with the child and caregiver being in sync or in a state of emotional attunement. At this point the child experiences the parent's approval. The child then engages in some activity of which the parent disapproves. The parent sets a limit and the child experiences shame. One can see this in toddlers who respond to a "no" or a scolding by covering their eyes, turning away, or hiding. The child experiences shame and affect that is painful and causes the child to want to hide or disappear. The attuned parent then repairs the relationship by reengaging the child and demonstrating, through the parent's behavior, that the child is lovable and cared about. The child makes amends, feels good, and the cycle renews. As this occurs, hundreds of times, these experiences enable the child to move from feeling a sense of shame to being able to experience guilt; in other words from feeling that the child is bad to feeling that the child is good, although the child's actions may at times be unacceptable to the parent. Once this occurs, the child is able to experience guilt. One way to think about the distinction between shame and guilt is that shame is about who you are, while guilt is about what you do. Shame is an isolating emotion, which leads to wanting to be alone or hiding. Guilt, while it may create a variety of other problems, is a very pro-social emotion, resulting in the person feeling engaged and connected. When an individual feels guilt, that person wants to fix what it is they have done wrong, or make amends.

DISORDERS OF ATTACHMENT HAVE MANY CAUSES. Maltreatment, including emotional and physical neglect and emotional, physical, and sexual abuse, are the most obvious and common causes of attachment difficulties. Chronic maltreatment, or its equivalent, is, by definition, inconsistent with responsive attuned child care. The chronic nature of the maltreatment creates the distorted internal working models of self, other, and relationships that become a pervasive and enduring trait of the person. The chronic nature of the maltreatment results in the child having repeated and significant experiences that confirm a world view that is chaotic, untrustworthy, unpredictable, and unresponsive. There can be other causes of attachment difficulties. For example, if the birth mother is under extreme stress and is ambivalent about the pregnancy, then her stress hormones will affect the developing fetus. The brain is a delicate organ and chronic stress can cause actual changes in brain structure and function. Prenatal stresses can result in a child that may be a "difficult" baby. Add stressed parents—maybe a single parent—to this and one has a potential recipe for early attachment difficulties. Other "red flags" to consider when assessing for attachment problems include sudden separations from the caregiver, maternal depression, frequent moves into and out of foster care, multiple and inconsistent caregivers, institutional and orphanage care, and premature birth coupled with extended neonatal intensive care or early chronic painful conditions, such as repeated surgeries to correct birth defects.

Institutional care of infants and children, while providing for the physical need for calories, often is quite emotionally neglectful. The mean birth weight of 252 consecutive referrals from Russia was 2,509 grams while 48% had low birth weight (under 2,500 grams). Twenty-seven percent of the children were premature. The average alcohol consumption in Russia is 38 liters of 100-proof vodka per adult per year. This breaks down to 23 ounces per person per week, or about three shots per day. Prenatal alcohol exposure was present in 91% of the referrals. In my experience, a large number of older children brought from Russia for "summer camp" experiences with pre-adoptive families have significant neurological difficulties and attachment disorders. They exhibit controlling behavior with peers and caregivers, difficulties with affect regulation and impulse control, disturbed problem-solving abilities, impaired ability to defer gratification, difficulties with transitions, and other difficulties with higher cognitive functions commonly described as executive functions.

Many of the symptoms of attachment disorder tend to group themselves in clusters that define different subtypes. There are a number of ways to describe attachment. Mary Ainsworth (1978) described the following categories: secure attachment and two types of insecure attachment, anxious and avoidant. Mary Main & Erik Hesse (1990) added a fourth subtype, the disorganized subtype. The three subtypes described by Mary Ainsworth are organized responses to maternal behavior. The disorganized subtype is seen when the parent, who is supposed to be the secure base, is also the source of threat. In these instances, the child does not develop an organized attachment strategy. The disorganized subtype is most likely to develop into Reactive Attachment Disorder. Elizabeth Randolph (2000) developed a scheme to describe attachment disorders using four categories: avoidant, anxious, disorganized, and ambivalent. Her categories are unrelated to those of the research categories developed by Ainsworth, Main, and Hesse.

Many psychiatric disorders have overlapping symptoms. Differential diagnosis requires the consideration of etiology and looking at the symptoms in the context of the child's past history and current social environment. For a child to have an attachment disorder, the child does not need to have all of the following symptoms. Similarly, a child who exhibits one or two symptoms does not necessarily have an attachment disorder. This is a listing of behaviors.

SYMPTOMS OF ATTACHMENT DISORDERS

1. My child teases, hurts, or is cruel to other children.

2. My child can't keep friends for an age-appropriate length of time.

3. My child doesn't do as well in school as she could do even with a little more effort.

4. My child pushes me away or becomes stiff when I try to hug, unless he wants something from me, in which case he can be affectionate and engaging.

5. My child argues for long periods of time, often about meaningless or silly things.

6. My child has a large need to control everything.

7. My child is hyper-vigilant.

8. My child acts amazingly innocent, or pretends that things aren't really bad or a problem when caught doing something wrong.

9. My child does dangerous things such as running away, jumping out of windows, or other potentially harmful actions. My child seems oblivious to the fact that she may be hurt.

10. My child deliberately breaks or ruins his things or others' things.

11. My child doesn't seem to feel age-appropriate guilt when she does something wrong.

12. My child is impulsive. My child seems unable or unwilling to stop doing something he wants to do.

13. My child teases, hurts, or is cruel to animals.

14. My child steals, or shows up with things that belong to others with unbelievable, unusual, or suspicious reasons for how she got these things.

15. My child likes to sneak things without permission, even though he could have had these things if he had asked.

16. My child doesn't seem to learn from mistakes, consequences, or punishments. (She continues the behavior despite the consequences.)

17. My child makes false reports of abuse or neglect. My child tries to get sympathy from others, or tries to get us in trouble, by telling others that I abuse, don't feed, or don't provide the basic necessities.

18. My child seems not to experience pain when hurt, refusing to let anyone provide comfort.

19. My child does not usually ask for things. My child demands things.

20. My child lies, often about obvious or ridiculous things, when it would have been easier to tell the truth.

21. My child is quite bossy with other children and adults.

22. My child hoards, sneaks food, or has other unusual eating habits (eats paper, raw sugar, nonfood items, package mixes, baker's chocolate, etc.).

23. My child often does not make eye contact when adults want to make eye contact with him.

24. My child has extended temper tantrums.

25. My child chatters nonstop, asks repeated questions about things that make no sense, mutters, or is hard to understand when talking.

26. My child is accident-prone (gets hurt a lot), or complains a lot about every little ache and pain (needs constant attention).

27. My child acts cute or charming to get others to do what she wants.

28. My child is overly friendly with strangers.

29. My child has set fires or is preoccupied with fire.

30. My child prefers violent cartoons, television shows, or horror movies (regardless of whether or not I allow him to do this).

31. My child was abused/neglected during the first year of life, or had several changes of primary caretakers during the first years of life.

32. My child was in an orphanage for more than the first year of life.

33. My child was adopted after the age of 12 months.

In infants there are several high-risk signs that suggest further assessment and the possibility of attachment difficulties. These red flags are:

- Weak crying response or rageful and/or constant whining

- Tactile defensiveness

- Poor clinging and extreme resistance to cuddling: seems "stiff as a board"

- Poor sucking response

- Poor eye contact, lack of tracking

- No reciprocal smile response

- Indifference to others

- Failure to respond with recognition to mother or father

- Delayed physical motor skill development milestones (creeping, crawling, sitting, etc.)

- Flaccid body

In my experience, children often present with a constellation of symptoms that largely reflect the pattern of maltreatment. For example, many, but not all, children who have spent considerable time in an institution are superficially engaging and present "as-if" children, with little authenticity. These children often respond with whatever answers they think are correct at the moment. Children with significant experiences of emotional neglect often appear devoid of affect. In many instances, they are unable to identify feelings beyond simply "good" or "bad," much as an infant experiences the world. Other children may be more angry, violent, and aggressive. In all instances there are several commonalities among all these "subtypes." First, all these children experienced significant and chronic maltreatment. Second, these children exhibit difficulties with affect regulation, frustration tolerance, and impulse control. Third, these children lack a sense of basic trust. Fourth, they have internal working models in which they experience themselves as defective, unloved, and unlovable. It is not unusual for these children to act out actively or passively when living in homes in which intimacy and closeness are an intrinsic part of daily life.

When left untreated, children with severe trauma-attachment disorders, such as Reactive Attachment Disorder, are at high risk of becoming adults with severe personality disorders. The most common adult sequelae of Reactive Attachment Disorder will be Antisocial Personality Disorder, Borderline Personality Disorder, Avoidant Personality Disorder, and Dependent Personality Disorder, among others. Attachment theory provides a framework for understanding human behavior in the social environment and for thinking about various other mental disorders. Bowlby (1988) describes a number of mental health problems, such as depression and anxiety disorders, as stemming from various difficulties with the primary attachment relationship early in life.

NEUROBIOLOGY OF ATTACHMENT

The intersection of neurobiology and attachment theory has opened up some exciting areas of research and theory that have profound implications for treatment. Early experiences have profound and long-lasting effects on the brain and on personality, behavior, emotions, and development. The brain is a "dyadic" organ in that it develops in relation to another brain and the physical and social environment within which it is located. Brain development is experience-dependent. How stimuli is perceived, interpreted, and acted upon depends, to a large extent, on prior experience. Internal working models of the world develop from patterns of interactions and early attachment experiences and are encoded within the brain. This section will briefly describe some of the key elements of the Neurobiology of Interpersonal experience and implications for treatment.

The brain is divided into two hemispheres that function differently. The right hemisphere operates primarily in a holistic manner and is largely responsible for social cognition, psychosocial development, affective memory and experience, and the perception and storage of interpersonally related information. The left hemisphere is largely language based and "linear or logical" in its functioning. The right hemisphere is dominant during the first three years of life. As language functions develop, the left hemisphere becomes the more dominant hemisphere.

The right hemisphere is most involved in attachment-related experiences. The orbital-frontal cortex (the area immediately behind the eyes) plays a central role in integrating limbic system responses with the neo-cortex. The limbic system is primarily involved in emotions, motivation, and goal-directed behavior. The neo-cortex is primarily involved in higher cognitive functions such as planning, judgment, and related functions. The connections between the orbital frontal cortex and the limbic system and neo-cortex enable the neo-cortex to exert a moderating and modulating effect on the limbic system's emotional responses. The amygdala is a part of the limbic system and is primarily responsible for fight/flight/freeze responses. Stimuli from the eyes and ears are directly processed by the amygdala before the neo-cortex is involved.

The parasympathetic nervous system slows down bodily functions while the sympathetic nervous system speeds up bodily functions. The hypothalamus is primarily responsible for the physiological regulation. It is also involved in stress responses. The hippocampus is primarily involved in memory.

> The key areas of the brain that are molded by attachment experiences and that regulate attachment, affect, and cognition are the following:
>
> 1. Right Hemisphere
>   a. Orbital Frontal Cortex
>   b. Limbic System
>   i. Amygdala
>   c. Para-sympathetic nervous system
>   d. Sympathetic nervous system
>   e. Hypothalamus
>   f. Hippocampus

Early interpersonal experiences have a profound impact on the brain because the brain pathways responsible for social perception are the same as those that integrate such functions as the creation of meaning, the regulation of body states, the regulation of emotion, the organization of memory, and the capacity for interpersonal communication and empathy (Siegel, 2002). Stressful experiences that are overtly traumatizing or chronic cause persistent elevated levels of neuroendocrine hormones (Siegel, 2002). High levels of these hormones can cause permanent damage to the hippocampus, which is critical for memory (McEwen, 1999). Based on this, we can assume that psychological trauma can impair a person's ability to create and retain memory and can impede trauma resolution.

Internal working models that develop during the early years of life are stored primarily in the right hemisphere and operate outside of conscious awareness. Working models are internal representations of the world, relationships, self, and other that act as schemas or lenses, filtering and interpreting experience and sensations. Internal working models are primarily implicit-procedural in nature. Explicit memories are located in the left hemisphere and are memories that are experienced as remembering, such as when you recall your high school prom or last Thanksgiving. Implicit-procedural memories operate outside of conscious awareness, such as occurs when driving a car or one's basic orientation to strangers. Internal working models guide one's orientation to the world and one's approach to experience. These are the schemas that operate outside of awareness and guide behavior so that conscious thought is not required for each interaction. The right hemisphere is also the primary location for the processing of social-emotional information and orbital frontal cortex function in relation to the limbic system, facilitating attachment, face recognition, affect regulation, and various active and passive coping functions.

One of the essential components of mental health is a coherent autobiographical narrative and the ability to regulate one's level of arousal, including affect regulation. Autobiographical narratives represent the integration of left hemispheric explicit memories with right hemispheric affect and implicit memories. Trauma interferes with this integration and with the development of a coherent sense of self with a past, present, and future.

Early experiences create pathways in the brain that, depending on the quality of the experiences, either facilitate healthy, functional, and integrated mental states or result in rigid response patterns and dissociated and non-integrated mental states. The effects of early experiences and maltreatment on brain development and later functioning provide the link between these early experiences and later behavior. The effect of maltreatment on the brain is the reason that these early experiences have such a profound and lasting impact on social-emotional functioning.

Maltreatment causes inefficient affect regulation because the various neurological systems involved in affect regulation are not properly integrated. The way the brain is wired, impulses from the eyes and ears reach the amygdala before these stimuli are processed by the neo-cortex. In other words, we react before we "know" what we are reacting to. If past experience has chronically excited these pathways, then the brain will be chronically exposed to various stress hormones and neurotransmitters. The more the fight-flight pathways in the limbic system and amygdala are used, the easier it becomes to trigger those pathways. Over time, chronic maltreatment causes a stressful response trait to become an enduring state. The child remains in perpetual high alert, hyper-aroused, and hyper-vigilant. Furthermore, there is evidence that these stress-related hormones and neurotransmitters interfere with memory and new learning. This may explain some of the learning problems that maltreated children experience. In addition, chronic trauma can cause an over-pruning of connections between the amygdala and the orbital frontal cortex so that amygdala-driven states are expressed without cortical inhibition or involvement. In this case, responses will tend to be rigid and lacking the flexibility that is characteristic of cortex-mediated responses involving planning and judgment and other higher functions. This disconnect between the limbic system and higher cortical functions may be seen as a basis for dissociation and other pathological responses such as those found in PTSD. The higher corticolimbic areas would be inefficient and ineffective in regulating affect and in providing responses that are more functional.

Chronic neglect in institutions may create the opposite effect, where the child is in a hypo-aroused state. The chronic lack of stimulation may create such deficits that the child does not develop a discrete sense of danger. This may be the reason such children appear to have no "fear" of strangers and willingly go to anyone around. These effects of trauma and dissociation can be viewed as a lack of integration among key brain functions.

Other effects of maltreatment include difficulties with perceiving social cues, problems with motivation, and other symptoms associated with attachment disorders. Each of these problems may be seen as the outcome of maltreatment's effects on brain development and functioning.

The attachment relationship is one of the major influences on the limbic system, orbital frontal cortex, and right-hemisphere development. Chronic maltreatment in infancy leads to failure of various regulatory functions. Chronic maltreatment by a caregiver with a disorganized state of mind with respect to attachment is the best predictor of disorganized attachment in the child (Main & Hesse, 1990). A birth mother's attachment classification before the birth of her child can predict with 80% accuracy her child's attachment classification at six years of age (Main & Cassidy, 1988). Finally, recent research by Dozier (2001) found that the attachment classification of a foster mother has a profound effect on the attachment classification of the child. She found that the child's attachment classification becomes similar to that of the foster mother after three months in placement. These findings strongly argue for a non-genetic mechanism for the transmission of attachment patterns across generations and for the beneficial impact of a healing and healthy relationship. Children who have experienced early physical and sexual abuse show Electroencephalograph (EEG) abnormalities in frontal temporal and anterior brain regions (Teicher & Glod, 1996). Chronic exposure to a hyperactive stress system alters the development of the prefrontal and orbital frontal cortex, causing fewer synapses and fewer neurons to develop.

Chronic maltreatment creates a profound regulatory failure that results in disturbed limbic, hypothalamic, and autonomic function. It is the dysregulation in these systems that is expressed as the affect dysregulation at the core of trauma-attachment disorders. The child experiences a profound inability to process and regulate stress, emotions, and relationships. One sees hypersensitivity of key sympathetic and parasympathetic pathways so that it is as if the child's emotional accelerator and brake are both being applied at the same time. As discussed earlier, the basis for this dysregulation is that the chronic stress of chronic maltreatment causes structural changes in the brain, resulting in fewer synapses and neurons in key brain regions required for affect regulation.

A misattuned caregiver can create a dysregulated and dysregulating environment, which over time will result in the child's developing a disorganized attachment (Main et al.). Such caregivers induce extreme levels of arousal in their children by providing too much unregulated stress and arousal (abuse) or too low a level of stress and arousal (neglect). Without interactive repair, the child's negative emotional states last for long periods of time and become internalized as part of the working model of self. A child with such an internal working model of self will experience him/herself as an unwanted, unworthy, unloved and unlovable, bad, defective person. The form of attachment that is most closely associated with these experiences is disorganized attachment. Disorganized attachment is associated with the caregiver's frightened, frightening, or disoriented behavior with the child (Main & Hesse, 1990). During the Adult Attachment Interview (Hesse, 1999) these parents usually show patterns of unresolved trauma or grief. Their narrative accounts of childhood are disoriented and disorganized, lacking consistency, coherence, and exhibiting odd and strange discontinuities, such as referring to a dead person in the present tense as if still living.

Avoidant Attachment (infant pattern; Ainsworth et al., 1978) and Dismissing Attachment (adult pattern; Main & Hesse, 1990) can be defined by impairment in the sympathetic circuits and overuse of inhibitory biased ortitofrontal systems. Under stress, a passive coping strategy of regulation is overused.

Resistant-ambivalent (infant)/preoccupied (adult) states of mind with respect to attachment can be defined as impairment in the parasympathetic circuits and the overuse of excitatory biased orbital frontal systems. Under stress, active coping strategies of regulation are overused.

Dyadic Developmental Psychotherapy approaches are based on these findings from the neurobiology of interpersonal experience. Since the best predictor of a child's state of mind with respect to attachment is that of the parent, work with the parent is a crucial element of Dyadic

Developmental Psychotherapy. Furthermore, since the attachment system is a mutually co-regulated system, treatment has to involve the whole system: parent and child.

These neurobiological findings have other implications for treatment:

1. Attunement is a key healing component of treatment. Maintaining attunement with both parent and child is essential for successful treatment to occur. When parents have their own unresolved trauma that may interfere with their attunement with their child, it becomes imperative for the therapist to actively demonstrate and model attunement with the parent. If the parent cannot do what the therapist models, then the child will be unable to develop empathy or reflective capabilities.

2. Repetitions of the Attachment Sequence: experience of *intense affect–disengagement–reattunement–interactive repair*. This means the therapist/parent will coregulate *intense affect* (for example, when the child is being corrected for misbehavior, s/he may experience shame), which may cause *disengagement* (may manifest as angry defiance, verbal or physical threats), followed by *reattunement* (child accepts empathic response that validates the underlying emotion, reducing shame), and *interactive repair* (child accepts support and makes amends). This teaches that the individual, at the core, is valuable and lovable, worthy of reconnection.

3. Another essential dimension of treatment is the co-regulation of affect. Since children with trauma-attachment disorders exhibit chronic and severe difficulties regulating affect, both positive and negative, the parent and therapist regulate the child's affect until the child has internalized this skill. This is a process that usually occurs as part of normal development during infancy. When infancy is characterized by chronic maltreatment, co-regulation of affect does not occur and the child is easily dysregulated.

4. Trauma often causes various memories and emotions to be split off and dissociated. One result of successful treatment is the development of a more coherent autobiographical narrative with appropriate affect. The presence of a coherent autobiographical narrative may be evidence of a healthy integration of right and left hemispheric functions and processes.

5. Interventions, while often verbal, are primarily initiated to create experiences that provide attunement, co-regulated affect, and demonstrate deep respect, empathy, and caring. The therapy is primarily experiential.

6. Trauma is revisited in order to integrate the cognitive and affective components. What was overwhelming when experienced as a young child and without support can be tolerated and integrated within a supportive therapeutic relationship.

Factors that Resolve Trauma

There are five factors (from Siegel, 2001) that are important for the development of a healthy and secure attachment and that are also critical for the resolution of trauma.

1. Contingent collaborative communication
2. Reflective dialogue
3. Interactive repair
4. Coherent autobiographical narrative
5. Affective communication

CONTINGENT COLLABORATIVE COMMUNICATION refers to responsive dyadic communication. Each response is guided by and in reference to the proceeding communication. Contingent collaborative communication involves eye contact, facial expressions, tone of voice, body gestures, and the timing and intensity of response. It is synchronized interaction. It is the coupling of emotional communication between parent and child and the development of a system of co-regulation. This communication helps create a coherent core self. This type of reciprocal communication facilitates healing trauma by providing a supportive context within which a sense of safety and security can develop. Contingent collaborative communication creates an environment within which the individual feels supported, understood, and, on an affective level, joined with another. One element of trauma that is particularly dysregulating is the sense of isolation and aloneness that occurs. Contingent collaborative communication is one element that diminishes this sense of aloneness.

REFLECTIVE DIALOGUE, generally referred to as the reflective function, involves a sense of self and other as discrete, independent objects. Reflective dialogue involves communication about one's own internal state of mind, and comments and observation about the other. In one sense, reflective dialogue is a stream-of-consciousness communication in which the individual shares internal thoughts, experiences, and emotions with another. It is through this sharing that a child comes to learn how to make sense of his or her own internal experiences. Reflective dialogues create meaning for the child so that the child can make sense of experience. Children learn about their own emotions, and their own value, by seeing themselves reflected in their parents' eyes.

The healing dimension of INTERACTIVE REPAIR is that it reduces shame. Furthermore, it helps a child progress developmentally from a shame-based identity to the experience of healthy and appropriate guilt. Interactive repair refers to the parents' actions to repair the relationship and to emotionally reconnect with and reestablish an attuned relationship with the child after there has been a breach in the relationship. Typically, the breach in the relationship is caused by some action on the part of the child. The breach may be caused by the parent setting a limit. The disruption in the relationship that occurs typically leads young children and toddlers to experience a sense of shame. The cycle of experiencing positive affect following negative experiences teaches the child that negative emotions can be tolerated and resolved. Over time, as the healthy parent reestablishes attunement, the child begins to experience him or herself as intrinsically good, although as one who occasionally does "bad" things. It is this movement from feeling that one is bad to feeling that one is good, but does bad things, that is at the core of the developmental step from shame to guilt.

People with a healthy and secure state of mind with respect to attachment have PERSONAL NARRATIVES THAT ARE COHERENT, consistent, and integrated, reflecting an integration of right and left hemispheric functions and an integration of emotional and linear memories or episodic and procedural memories. Children who have experienced chronic trauma frequently have disjointed, split, and dissociated autobiographical narratives. While the emotional sequelae of the trauma is clearly active in the child's behavior, the child is not aware of its impact. Revisiting the trauma in detail so that the emotions are experienced in the safe and secure setting of the therapy session and in the home allows for the integration of affective and episodic memories and the conscious awareness of how these events and feelings are operating in the present. This awareness provides an important healing dimension to treatment. Once dissociated elements are integrated into a coherent autobiographical narrative, the child is able to manage the underlying affect and engage the reflective function to select an appropriate and self-advancing response.

Finally, EMOTIONAL COMMUNICATION, which is largely nonverbal, is at the core of the healing experience and at the core of all experiences that facilitate the development of a healthy and secure state of mind with respect to attachment. Emotional communication is the verbal and nonverbal interchange between two persons. There is always an implicit or nonverbal dimension. In addition, there may be a verbal and explicit dimension. Without this, no healing can occur. The sharing of affective experiences on both the nonverbal and verbal levels creates attunement and helps the child to feel safely held, understood, and accepted. Communication that does not have this emotional dimension to it, while useful for sharing information, is not healing since at the core of the difficulties experienced by these children are distortions of interpersonal relationships, affect regulation, and the integration of affect. Emotional communication facilitates the integration of affect since communicated affect is shared and will not be as overwhelming as it may be when experienced alone. In addition, emotional communication facilitates the development of a more coherent autobiographical narrative by making explicit what may have been dissociated or implicit.

DYADIC DEVELOPMENTAL PSYCHOTHERAPY

Dyadic Developmental Psychotherapy is a treatment developed by Daniel Hughes, PhD, (Hughes, 2003, Hughes, 2002; Hughes, 1997). Its basic principles are described by Hughes (2003):

- Both the therapist and the caregiver are attuned to the child's subjective experience and reflect this back to the child without value judgment. The therapist and caregiver help the child regulate affect and co-construct a coherent autobiographical narrative.

- The focus of interactions between therapist, parent, and child is not on behavioral intervention, but rather reflects the intersubjective sharing of experience and co-creation of meaning as it unfolds within the therapy session.

- The therapist has primary responsibility for maintaining a healing PACE (playful, accepting, curious, empathic) during the therapy session, and the parents have primary responsibility for maintaining a healing PLACE (playful, loving, accepting, curious, empathic) in the home.

- The inevitable misattunements and conflicts that arise in interpersonal relationships are directly addressed and resolved using interactive repair.

- Caregivers are taught to use attachment-facilitating interventions to resolve conflicts as well as to increase enjoyment of interpersonal interactions.

- Focus is given to both the caregiver's and the therapist's own attachment strategies, as they may affect the interpretation of the child's expressed (acted-out) experience.

- A variety of helpful, non-coercive, attachment-friendly interventions are utilized and may include Theraplay®[1], cognitive-behavioral strategies, sensory-integration, and narratives.

Dyadic Developmental Psychotherapy is a unique treatment that integrates elements such as empathy, attunement, acceptance, development of a coherent autobiographical narrative, psychodramatic reenactments, interactive play, role-playing, and nonverbal processes. This integrated strategy is utilized to revise negative internal working models, develop a coherent autobiographical narrative, and foster the development of a secure and healthy attachment.

Since early trauma disrupts the normally developing attachment system by creating distorted internal working models of self, others, and caregivers, Dyadic Developmental Psychotherapy directly addresses the rigid and dysfunctional internalized working models that traumatized children with attachment disorders have developed.

Utilization of techniques that maintain a healing PACE in therapy and a healing PLACE at home provide the creation for a secure base. Developing and sustaining an attuned relationship within which contingent collaborative communication occurs helps the child heal. Coercive interventions such as rib-stimulation, holding-restraining a child in anger or to provoke an emotional response, shaming a child, using fear to elicit compliance, and interventions based on power/control and submission, etc., are never used and are inconsistent with a treatment rooted in attachment theory and current knowledge about the neurobiology of interpersonal behavior.

Current findings on neurobiology with regard to factors that resolve trauma strongly suggest that effective treatment requires an affectively attuned relationship. Siegel (1999, p. 333) stated, "As parents reflect with their securely attached children on the mental states that create their shared subjective experience, they are joining with them in an important co-constructive process of understanding how the mind functions. The inherent feature of secure attachment—contingent, collaborative communication—is also a fundamental component in how interpersonal relationships facilitate internal integration in a child."

This has implications for the effective treatment of maltreated children. For example, when in a therapeutic relationship the child is able to reflect upon aspects of traumatic memories, and experience the affect associated with those memories without becoming dysregulated, the

---

[1] When working with children with attachment problems, Certified Theraplay® Therapists and Trainers often combine Theraplay® and Dyadic Developmental Psychotherapy. As information about Dyadic Developmental Psychotherapy (and other effective models for treating attachment-trauma problems) has become more available in the past decade, combining these therapies is more common.

child develops an expanded capacity to tolerate increasing amounts of affect. The child learns to self-regulate. The attuned, resonant relationship between child and therapist and child and caregiver enables the child to make sense (a left-hemispheric function) out of memories, autobiographical representations, and affect (right hemispheric functions).

This treatment seeks to repair the negative working model of such children, using experiential methods that have several important and overlapping dimensions: modeling the healthy attachment cycle, reducing shame, safe and nurturing physical contact that is containing, reexperiencing the affect associated with the trauma in order to integrate the experience and not dissociate, and the interpersonal regulation of affect. Maintaining an affectively attuned relationship with the child enacts these dimensions. Accepting the child's affect—and more importantly the motivation behind the behavior or affect, which is based on early experiences of trauma that created the child's current working model expressed in the present—is central to effective treatment and resolution of attachment difficulties. Using curiosity and acceptance to uncover that deeper meaning is an important element of Dyadic Developmental Psychotherapy and the creation of a new meaning for the child in the present. These dimensions are also addressed through the use of eye contact, touch, tone of voice, cognitive restructuring, psychodramatic reenactments, and repeated implementations of the first year (needs) and second year (shame) attachment cycles. As a result of treatment, children can:

1. Affectively internalize their adoptive or foster parent's love, structuring, and nurturing, resulting in increased ability to tolerate affect without becoming dysregulated or dissociated, and

2. Develop a more coherent sense of autobiographical memory, increased trust, and increased self-esteem.

Treatment of the child has a significant nonverbal dimension since much of the trauma took place at a pre-verbal stage and is often dissociated from explicit memory. As a result, childhood maltreatment and resultant trauma create barriers to successful engagement and treatment of these children. Treatment interventions are designed to create experiences of safety and affective attunement so that the child is affectively engaged and can explore and resolve past trauma. This affective attunement is the same process used for nonverbal communication between a caregiver and child during attachment facilitating interactions (Hughes, 2002; Siegel, 2001). The therapist's and caregivers' attunement results in co-regulation of the child's affect so that is it manageable. Cognitive restructuring interventions are designed to help the child develop secondary mental representations of traumatic events, which allow the child to integrate these events and develop a coherent autobiographical narrative. Treatment involves multiple repetitions of the fundamental care-giver-child attachment cycle. The cycle begins with shared affective expe-riences, is followed by a breach in the relationship (a separation or discontinuity), and ends with a reattunement of affective states. Non-verbal communication, involving eye contact, tone of voice, touch, and movement, are essential elements to creating affective attunement.

Overall, successfully treated children will use their caregivers as a secure base for comfort from which they can explore their world. Behaviorally, such children exhibit lower levels of aggression, delinquent behaviors, thought disorders, depression, anxiety, and withdrawn behaviors. Through the healthy internalization of the caregiver, the child comes to trust the caregiver and experience a desire to please the caregiver. This is the beginning of conscience and morality.

DYADIC DEVELOPMENTAL PSYCHOTHERAPY DIFFERS FROM OTHER APPROACHES

There are several elements of Dyadic Developmental Psychotherapy that distinguish it from what might be termed traditional, optimal, sound clinical work with children, although it certainly shares many elements in common with sound casework practice. For example, attention to the dignity of the client, respect for the client's experiences, and starting where the client is are all time-honored principles of social work practice and good therapy. These are also the essential tenets of Dyadic Develop-mental Psychotherapy practice.

Dyadic Developmental Psychotherapy focuses extensively on the non-verbal experiential level of interaction as a way of addressing negative internal working models and as a way of creating a safe and secure base from which the child can explore past trauma. There is a greater empha-sis on nonverbal processes rather than on verbal content. Cognitive-Behavioral, Behavioral, Task-Centered Casework, and many other meth-ods do not focus as significantly on nonverbal processes for their pri-mary therapeutic intervention methods.

PRACTICE

Although the logistical practice of Dyadic Developmental Psychotherapy may vary somewhat according to the particular therapy environment, the following describes how therapy is conducted at The Center For Family Development, an upstate New York treatment center. Two-hour sessions involving one therapist, parent(s), and child are typical. Two offices are used. Unless the caregivers are in the treatment room, the caregivers are viewing treatment from another room by closed-circuit TV or a one-way mirror. The usual structure of a session involves three components. First, the therapist meets with the caregivers in one office while the child is seated in the treatment room. During this part of treatment, the caregiver is instructed in attachment parenting methods (Hughes, 1997; Gray, 2002; Thomas, 1997).

The caregiver's own issues that may create difficulties with developing affective attunement with their child may also be explored and resolved. Frequently, the caregiver's autobiographical narrative is a focus of discussion. Effective parenting methods for children with trauma-attachment disorders require a high degree of structure and consistency, along with an affective milieu that demonstrates playfulness, love, acceptance, curiosity, and empathy (PLACE). During this part of the treatment, caregivers receive support and are given the same level of attuned responsiveness that we wish the child to experience. Quite often caregivers feel blamed, devalued, incompetent, depleted, and angry. Parent support is an important dimension of treatment to help caregivers be more able to maintain an attuned, connecting relationship with their child. Second, the therapist, often with the caregivers, meets with the child in the treatment room. This generally takes one to one and a half hours. Third, the therapist meets with the caregivers without the child.

Broadly speaking, the treatment with the child uses three categories of interventions: affective attunement, cognitive restructuring, and psychodramatic reenactments. Treatment with the caregivers also uses three categories of interventions: first, teaching effective parenting methods and helping the caregivers avoid power struggles; second, addressing the parent's autobiographical narrative as this influences the parent's interactions with the child; and third, maintaining the proper PLACE or attitude. The caregivers provide a high degree of structure to provide safety for the child. Within this structured world, the caregiver maintains a high degree of affective attunement that is nurturing and that repeatedly enacts the attachment cycle of engagement, disruption, and interactive repair (Siegel, 2001; Schore, 2001).

The treatment described in Figure 1 (on page 32) adheres to a structure with several dimensions. First, behavior is identified and explored. The behavior may have occurred in the immediate interaction or at some time in the past. Second, using curiosity and acceptance the behavior is explored and the meaning to the child begins to emerge. Third, empathy is used to reduce the child's sense of shame and increase the child's sense of being accepted and understood. Fourth, the child's behavior is normalized. In other words, once the meaning of the behavior and its basis in past trauma is identified, it becomes understandable that the symptom is present. Fifth, the child communicates this understanding to the caregiver. Sixth, finally, a new meaning for the behavior is found and the child's actions are integrated into a coherent autobiographical narrative by communicating the new experience and meaning to the caregiver.

An example of such an interaction is the following:

Child (C): "I hit my mom last night." [looks down and away]

Therapist (T): "What happened?"

Mom (M): "I told her it was time to stop playing and put her toys away."

T: [to child] "What happened?"

C: "She took my favorite doll and put in on the bookshelf and told me to stop playing ... she never lets me play."

T: "Wow, I see how you got so angry when your mom asked you to pick up your toys. What made you angry about that?"

C: "She's always mean to me and never lets me play. I hate her."

M: "Do you really feel that way, sweetie?"

C: [looks at Mom with a sad face and mumbles] "Yes."

T: "You thought she was being mean and didn't want you to have fun or didn't love you. Maybe you thought she was going to take everything away and leave you like your first mom did, like when your first mom took your toys and then left you alone in the apartment that time."

C: "She took my bestest doll and was going to keep it or get rid of it and I was so scared I'd never get it back and I got mad and I hit her and then bit her leg and now she's going to get rid of me; I heard her talking with the social worker this morning."

T: "Oh, wow! You were really scared! Oh, I can really under-stand now how hard that must be for you when Mom said to clean up. You really felt mad and very scared. That must be so hard for you."

C: "Yes, I get scared a lot."

T: "Mom, did you know she was so scared?"

M: "No, I didn't. Oh, honey, I just put your doll on the bookshelf so it wouldn't get stepped on while we cleaned up."

C: "Really?"

M: "Yes. I just called the social worker this morning to reschedule our appointment. You're my little girl. I love you ..."

Dyadic Developmental Psychotherapy

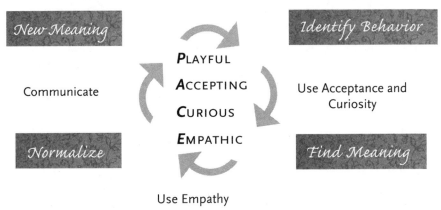

FIGURE 1

Past traumas are revisited by reading documents and through psychodramatic reenactments. These interventions, which occur within a safe, attuned relationship, allow the child to integrate past traumas and understand past and present experiences that create feelings and thoughts associated with the child's behavioral disturbances. The child develops secondary representations of these events, feelings, and thoughts that result in greater affect regulation, and a more integrated autobiographical narrative. By co-regulating the child's emerging affective states and developing secondary representations of thoughts and feelings, the capacity to affectively engage in a trusting relationship is enhanced. Caregivers enact these same principles. If the caregivers have difficulty engaging with their child in this manner, then treatment of the caregiver is indicated.

Dimensions of Practice

THE FIVE BROAD DOMAINS: The practice of an attachment-based therapy, such as Dyadic Developmental Psychotherapy, comprises the following.

1. Secure Base

2. Exploration
3. Protest, Assertiveness, and Loss
4. Internal Working Model
5. Reflective Function

Without a SECURE BASE, there can be no exploration or healing. The creation of a secure base in therapy or at home is the foundation on which all other activities and further growth depend. A secure base requires consistency, reliability, emotional attunement, and relationship repair. Normally, children seek their secure base when there is some threat. Children who experience attachment-trauma disorders require the creation of a secure base through active interventions by the therapist and through attachment-based parenting methods. Over time, these external structuring and nurturing interventions become internalized as an internal representation of the external relationship.

When the child or client feels safe and secure, then EXPLORATION is possible. This is analogous to the toddler's exploration of his/her environment when feeling safe and in the presence of a secure base. There is a reciprocal and inverse relationship between secure base behavior and exploration. During times of stress, secure base behavior increases and exploration behavior decreases.

Another important domain of practice is "protest." PROTEST or anger occurs in response to threats of separation or abandonment. These issues must be addressed at both the beginning and ending of each session. In addition, this will be an important domain for parenting interventions, particularly in the early stages of treatment.

The capacity to cope with LOSS is an important one for healthy function. Dyadic developmental psychotherapy has as an essential component: the working through of losses at various levels. These losses include the loss of the birth family and relatives, the loss of the family that might have been, and the loss of a childhood that should have been.

As described earlier, INTERNAL WORKING MODELS are schemas that guide behavior, are based on early prior relationships, and are primarily rooted in procedural memory. Internal working models are rooted in implicit procedural memory, as opposed to explicit episodic memory, and they can be difficult to identify. However, the operation of internal working models can be inferred from behavior. Since all behavior is adaptive, "odd" or "strange" behaviors are windows into the operation of internal working models. These less-understood behaviors suggest that an internal working model is functioning, based on past experiences, and no longer functional in the current environment.

The REFLECTIVE FUNCTION is simply the capacity to reflect upon one's feelings, thoughts, and relationships. It is the capacity to reflect on one's own state of mind, and on the states of mind of others. The reflective function requires the ability to maintain itself, others, and relationships as internal representations that can be maintained in awareness. The reflective function evolves from the parent's reflecting, amplifying, and identifying the child's affect and state of mind and the parent's affect and state of mind.

Eight Elements of Each Session

Each psychotherapy session utilizies the following elements in varying proportion depending upon the stage of treatment and the assessed immediate need of the client.

1. Forming and maintaining the therapeutic relationship
2. Attunement
3. Emotional proximity
4. Challenge
5. Balance
6. Freedom of movement
7. The capacity to tolerate negative emotions
8. Reflective capabilities

1) Forming and Maintaining Relationship: The primary objective of Dyadic Developmental Psychotherapy is the healing of a child who has trauma-attachment disorders. Healing requires integration. Integration requires the exploration of split-off memories, experiences, and emotions. Exploration requires a secure base. A secure base requires forming and maintaining an alliance. Hence, forming and maintaining an alliance or relationship is the essential base from which all later work flows.

A significant amount of attention must be given to forming and maintaining the relationship. Early in treatment this often will be the primary and maybe even the only consideration. The development and maintenance of a relationship is the prerequisite for all other therapeutic interventions and strategies. This is usually accomplished by joining with the child and accepting whatever affect is generated. Regardless of what the child offers, the therapist accepts that and explores further. The PACE model can be your primary guide. By being playful and accepting and using your curiosity to explore the child's experience, a relationship is formed. Generally, a certain amount of time must be devoted at the beginning of each session to restoring and recreating the relationship.

2) ATTUNEMENT: Attunement may be described as empathic responsiveness. Through attunement the therapist is able to develop and maintain the therapeutic relationship, dyadically regulate the child's emotional state, and help the child avoid dysregulation.

3) EMOTIONAL PROXIMITY: Emotional proximity grows out of attunement. The development and maintenance of the therapeutic relationship requires emotional proximity. As the result of emotional closeness, a secure base develops. The essential means by which emotional proximity is achieved is the arousal of affect. As the result of your efforts to develop and maintain attunement, emotional proximity is enhanced.

4) CHALLENGE: After a beginning therapeutic relationship is formed and there is emotional proximity so that a secure base is developing, challenging interventions can be used. Challenging interventions are used primarily to destabilize negative internal working models. Through the exploration and then the challenging of these internal working models, the child will be able to develop a more healthy and secure attachment and a more positive core sense of self. Challenge is achieved using such techniques as interpretation, reframing, confrontation, and clarification. Parents use challenge after they have created a healing PLACE, and have accepted the child's emotions and perceptions that are underneath the behavior, and have real empathy for the child. At that point, then challenges to the child's view (see the previous example on page 30) can be accepted by the child as another point of view rather than as a discounting of the child's view.

It is vital that all challenges be done without anger. Challenging interactions are used to help a child understand, affectively, the distortions in the child's internal working model. If challenge is done out of anger or as punishment or in a shaming manner, then all that is accomplished is a reinforcement of the child's negative internal working model.

5) BALANCE: Balance refers to maintaining an equitable relationship between cognition and emotion and considering each attachment style's pattern of relating in order to remedy deficits. For example, when working with a child whose primary state of mind with respect to attachment is avoidance, there will be an emphasis on developing emotional closeness. With the ambivalent child, there will be an emphasis on developing perspective and maintaining emotional distance. With a disorganized type, there will be an emphasis on achieving integration and coherence.

6) FREEDOM OF MOVEMENT: Freedom of movement refers to the process of not allowing oneself to be boxed into a fixed position. The basic method by which this is achieved is the use of curiosity and acceptance. Asking questions for clarification is a method to avoid being boxed in.

Freedom of movement is also created by the rules and expectations of the therapeutic relationship. Rules, structure, place, consistency, and use of time enable you to have freedom of movement within this secure base. Essentially this demonstrates to the client that it is the freedom to choose that is liberating rather than the ability to control or cling.

7) NEGATIVE CAPABILITY: The capacity to tolerate negative emotions, uncertainty, and doubt is essential to this work. While the sight of a distraught or emotionally upset child may bring out the desire to quickly comfort that child, this may not be in the child's best interests. Cutting off negative feelings and trying to "comfort" the child too quickly may inadvertently give the message that strong affect is dangerous and intolerable. Furthermore it gives the message that you are not able to tolerate the child's experience, further reinforcing the child's sense of being bad and that affect is to be avoided. When the child is allowed to experience negative or disturbing affect within a secure and safe environment, the child can integrate the experience.

8) REFLECTIVE FUNCTION: The reflective function is at the core of and essential to the practice of Dyadic Developmental Psychotherapy. A strong, observing ego is necessary to do this work. The thinking mind and self-observation are key components of Dyadic Developmental Psychotherapy. Using acceptance and empathy, the therapist helps the child develop a new meaning that leads to new choices of action that can lead to healthier functioning. All of this requires a well-developed reflective function.

PROCESS OF TREATMENT

Dyadic Developmental Psychotherapy progresses through five stages. The stages are the following:

1. Initial Engagement (Initial Phase)
2. Maintaining the Working Alliance (Initial Phase)
3. Working Through (Middle Phase)
4. Integration (Late Stage)
5. Ending Treatment–Loss

1) INITIAL ENGAGEMENT: During the initial engagement you have four primary tasks: forming a therapeutic alliance, developing a treatment contract, forming initial theories of behavior or meanings to be explored, and creating a secure base. The paramount task is joining with the child by using acceptance and empathy so that the secure base is created.

The creation and maintenance of the secure base is accomplished by using acceptance of whatever the child offers and containment to keep the child safe. Cradling is one example of a technique that helps a child feel safe. The very structure of the session and rules (such as no hurts) also helps the child feel safe. Other methods of creating and maintaining the secure base involve the therapist's consistency, reliability, and constancy. At home, the parents' close supervision of the child also creates a secure base by not "letting" the child get into trouble or do things that would increase the child's shame. Being with the child at all times prevents many of the problem behaviors from occurring. For example, the child cannot steal if the parent is ever present. The use of attunement is another method for developing and maintaining the secure base in the initial phase of treatment. By maintaining attunement you are able to accept what the child offers and help regulate the child's affect and level of arousal. In addition, your attunement with the child enables you to have empathy by understanding the affect-driving behavior. Attunement enables you to regulate emotional proximity. So, for example, you would work on emotional closeness with the avoidant child, containment with the disorganized child, and perspective with the preoccupied child.

2) MAINTAINING THE WORKING ALLIANCE: Maintaining the working alliance becomes primary after engagement has occurred and there is a beginning level of attunement and secure base present. The primary task of this part of the initial phase is managing emotional proximity. There must be enough emotional proximity to promote the experience of affect, but not so much as to cause dysregulation. The primary tasks are maintaining attunement and affective engagement. The primary intervention strategies are attunement, curiosity, acceptance, and attachment-facilitating parenting.

3) WORKING THROUGH: The indication that one is in the middle phase of treatment and can begin the process of working through issues is that there is a beginning level of cooperation and engagement on the part of the child. At some point, you will realize that developing and maintaining engagement, secure base, and attunement have all become easier and that the child is more collaborative and cooperative. In other words, there are behavioral indications of trust. The primary tasks of this phase are the following:

- UNCOVERING THE PAST IN THE PRESENT. This involves repeated explorations of how the past is alive in present relationships. Feelings, perceptions, and beliefs that developed in the past maltreating environment remain active in the present.

- EXPLORATION OF WORKING MODELS. The past is uncovered in the present by exploring internal working models that are active in the therapy room or with the parent. As is evident, exploration cannot occur until there is a secure base. One must continually monitor the strength and health of the secure base so that the child can tolerate the potentially dysregulating affect that arises when the past is explored on an affective level.

- DEVELOPING THE REFLECTIVE FUNCTION. Once a secure base is established and exploration begins, then the reflective function will begin to mature and develop.

- FINDING MEANING IN BEHAVIOR. Because of the early maltreatment and resultant negative internal working models, the affect that drives behavior (the meaning of the behavior) may be opaque. Because your life experiences may be quite different from that of the child's, your ability to have empathy and know what the child is experiencing will be limited. It is for this reason that the PACE model of *playful, accepting, curious, empathic* is so important. One becomes an ACE therapist by *accepting* what the child offers and being *curious* about what the child thinks, feels, and experiences so that you develop *empathy*. Once you have empathy for the child (that experience of "Now I understand!"), then you are able to find the meaning in the behavior. An example of such an interaction is the following:

> *"Wow, I see how you got so angry when your mom asked you to pick up your toys. You thought she was being mean and didn't want you to have fun or didn't love you. You thought she was going to take everything away and leave you like your first mom did, like when your first mom took your toys and then left you alone in the apartment that time. Oh, I can really understand now how hard that must be for you when Mom said to clean up. You really felt mad and scared. That must be so hard for you."*

- BEGINNING EXPLORATION BEYOND SECURE BASE. This task summarizes what the working-through phase of treatment focuses on. As stated before, one continues with the primary tasks from previous stages and their associated intervention strategies, but to a lesser degree. The primary intervention strategies of this phase follow:

a. Review of history. A review of protective service reports, police reports, and other documents assists in exploring the factual and emotional events of the child's life. The review of documents and memories is undertaken to revive affect that is often buried, split-off, and evident in behavior but not cognition. The goal is to develop the reflective function so that the child has choices about how to manage the affect. In addition, what was unmanageable and intolerable as a lonely, alone, small child is tolerable in the present with the secure base of home and therapy.

b. Role-playing and psychodramatic enactments are another set of intervention strategies to bring the past into the present for examination and to bring to the fore affect related to internal working models.

c. Attachment-facilitating parenting can focus on increasing responsibility and freedom at home. Earned privileges based on what the child is ready to manage enhance a growing sense of competence and efficacy.

d. Strategies such as cognitive-behavioral interventions, interactive play techniques, EMDR (Eye Movement Desensitization and Reprocessing), and other interventions can all be useful now that the child is actively engaged in treatment and is collaborating and cooperating within the secure base.

4) INTEGRATION: In the later phase of treatment the primary tasks are:

- DEVELOPMENT OF A COHERENT AUTOBIOGRAPHICAL NARRATIVE. As the child explores how the past is alive in the present and revisits past trauma, a coherent picture of the child's life emerges. Themes and meanings emerge and from this mix of images, meanings, themes, feelings, and experiences; a coherent autobiographical narrative emerges.

- INTEGRATION OF TRAUMA AND A REDUCTION OF SPLITTING. As the implicit and explicit memories of trauma are experienced with the reflective function, integration of the implicit and explicit occurs. In effect, there is an integration of right- and left- hemispheric functions resulting in less splitting off.

- DEVELOPMENT OF A BALANCED VIEW OF SELF AND OTHERS, PARTICULARLY OF THE BIRTH FAMILY. A crucial task of this phase is the development of a more balanced affective experience of birth family. There can be an acceptance of the maltreating adults as flawed individuals who where neither all bad nor all good, but some mixture of both. This is a shift from an "either-or" view to a "both-and." As the child develops a coherent autobiographical narrative with a "meaning" to the child's life story, the child also develops a more balanced view of self.

- FURTHER ENHANCEMENT OF THE REFLECTIVE FUNCTION. This is a continuing task.

- At this point, parents reflect on current experiences and status and past actions. There is a nearly "normal" parent-child relationship and home life.

- There are a variety of intervention strategies, as described in the previous section, that can be used now.

5) ENDING TREATMENT: There is no final ending of treatment. Rather it is useful to think about a time when there is no need for further sessions. The primary tasks of this phase follow:

- Grieving losses, particularly the loss of the life not lived.
- Integrating treatment experiences into autobiographical narrative.

The primary intervention strategies include the following:

- Dialogues and reflective engagement about the therapy process. A review of past sessions, themes, events, and experiences assists in integrating therapy into the narrative. Furthermore, this reflection helps the family recognize the substantial gains made and to feel pride in what they have accomplished together.

- Frequently it may be useful to suggest to the child that, while no additional sessions are being scheduled, you want to continue to hear from the child by card, note, or e-mail.

For therapy to be effective, problematic affect has to be evoked, brought into awareness, and then set within a new context of meaning. Successful therapy requires affect arousal and assimilation of emotions into a new narrative.

The creation of a secure base requires a secure holding environment at home and in therapy. Secure holding is created in therapy by the structure and acceptance that facilitates the creation of a secure base. In addition, cradling, touch, and playful interventions can also create this sense of safety. Many children who have experienced chronic and severe maltreatment have a disorganized attachment and Reactive Attachment Disorder. Such children experience ambivalence and exhibit disorganized behavior in the presence of their parents—the secure base. The reasons for this have been previously cited in the work of Main & Hesse (1990); the source of safety is also the source of threat. This simultaneous activation of the fight/flight system and the attachment system results in disorganized behavior. Overcoming the fear of the secure base requires that the child be "held" securely. The literal sense of "holding" may mean cradling a willing child, or the practice of keeping the child physically near to the secure base (time-in) in order to reduce shame-induced acting out, and/or by use of PLACE and PACE. This secure holding may be figurative or literal, but it is not coercive in the sense of cradling with the intention of creating a reaction, nor is it done against a child's will. Depending upon the child and the nature of the conflict being addressed, cradling a child may reduce shame and habitual rejection of the child's secure base (the parent). However, successful treatment does not require physical cradling. The creation of a situation in which trust, safety, and security are possible and within which a coherent and consistent relational strategy develops can be accomplished by "holding" in a figurative sense, using PACE.

RESEARCH ON EFFECTIVENESS

There has been little empirical research on the effectiveness of attachment-based treatment for children with Reactive Attachment Disorder. The Center For Family Development completed a follow-up study (Becker-Weidman, 2005) of 64 closed cases of children who meet the DSM IVTR criteria for Reactive Attachment Disorder. Of these 64 cases, 34 had been treated with Dyadic Developmental Psychotherapy and 30 received "usual care," such as family therapy, play therapies, residential treatment, etc. The families that received "usual care," received this treatment with a variety of other providers, but not at Center For Family Development.

The study examined the effects of Dyadic Developmental Psychotherapy on children with trauma-attachment disorders who meet the DSM IV criteria for Reactive Attachment Disorder. A treatment group composed of 34 subjects and a usual-care group composed of 30 subjects were compared. All children were between the ages of five and 16 when the study began. Seven hypotheses were explored. It was hypothesized that Dyadic Developmental Psychotherapy would reduce the symptoms of attachment disorder, aggressive and delinquent behaviors, social problems and withdrawal, anxiety and depressive problems, thought problems, and attention problems.

Significant reductions were achieved in all measures studied. The results were achieved in an average of 23 sessions over 11 months. These findings continued for an average of 1.1 years after treatment ended for children between the ages of six and 16 years. There were no changes in the "usual-care" group subjects, who were retested an average of 1.3 years after the evaluation was completed. The results are particularly salient since 82% of the treatment-group subjects and 83% of the usual care-group subjects had previously received treatment with an average of 3.2 prior treatment episodes. An episode of treatment is defined as several treatment sessions directed at treating a specific diagnosis. This past history of unsuccessful treatment further underscores the importance of these results in demonstrating the effectiveness of Dyadic Developmental Psychotherapy as a treatment for children with trauma-attachment problems. In addition, 53% of the usual care-group subjects received "usual care" but without any measurable change in the outcome variables measured. Children with trauma-attachment problems are at significant risk of developing severe disorders in adulthood, such as Post-Traumatic Stress Disorder, Borderline Personality Disorder, Narcissistic Personality Disorder, and other personality disorders.

In a recent extension of that study, the families were recontacted and again completed the Randolph Attachment Disorder Questionnaire and Child Behavior Checklist. All of the control-group families had sought and continued in treatment, with an average of 50 sessions. Despite receiving extensive treatment, the usual-care control group actually exhibited an increase in symptoms over the 3.3 years since the original study was completed. We found a significant clinical and statistical increase in anxious and depressive symptoms, attention problems, rule-breaking behavior, and aggressive behavior, as measured by the Child Behavior Checklist.

About 42% of the treatment group received treatment after completing Dyadic Developmental Psychotherapy. Most of this continued treatment was for co-morbid conditions, such as bipolar disorder and Attention Deficit/Hyperactivity Disorder. The majority received medication management treatment. For this group we found continued significant clinical and statistical improvements nearly four years after treatment ended, as measured by the Randolph Attachment Disorder Questionnaire and Child Behavior Checklist; all scores remained in the "normal" range.

This study supports several of O'Connor & Zeanah's (2003) conclusions and recommendations concerning treatment. They state (p. 241), "Treatments for children with attachment disorders should be promoted only when they are evidence-based." The results of this study are a beginning toward that end. While there are a number of limitations to this study, given the severity of the disorders in question, the paucity of effective treatments, and the desperation of caregivers seeking help, it is a step in the right direction. Dyadic Developmental Psychotherapy is not a coercive therapy, which can be dangerous. Dyadic Developmental Psychotherapy provides caregiver support as an integral part of its treatment methodologies. Finally, Dyadic Developmental Psychotherapy uses a multimodal approach built around affect attunement.

This study suggests that Dyadic Developmental Psychotherapy is an effective intervention for children with trauma-attachment problems.

CHAPTER 2

The Logistics of Providing Dyadic Developmental Psychotherapy

ARTHUR BECKER-WEIDMAN

"The world is not comprehensible, but it is embraceable: through the embracing of one of its beings." —Martin Buber

Dyadic Developmental Psychotherapy is an approach that can be used with children, teenagers, and adults. As an approach to treating adults and couples, there are no special logistical factors to consider, and the principals discussed in this book can be easily adapted. However, when treating children and adolescents who are experiencing trauma-attachment problems, there are a number of logistics that are different from other approaches and that require consideration. Treatment of youth with trauma-attachment disorders takes place within the context of a relationship, which may include adoptive parents, foster parents, birth parents, or substitute care staff. Dyadic Developmental Psychotherapy is an affective dyadic approach to treating trauma-attachment disorders. The therapy focuses on the relationships, internal working models, the intersubjective sharing of affect, and reflective abilities of the child, the therapist, and the caregiver as well as the various relationships among those involved.

This chapter focuses on the logistics involved in providing Dyadic Developmental Psychotherapy for children and adolescents with trauma-attachment disorders.

BEGINNINGS

It is useful to begin with a thorough evaluation of the family, child, and caregivers. Children with trauma-attachment disorders have experienced chronic maltreatment. Such maltreatment can cause a variety of mental health, psychological, neuropsychological, psychosocial, developmental, and interpersonal difficulties. A thorough assessment of the child's mental status, comorbid conditions, and a screening of sensory-integration and neuropsychological issues is important. Evaluating the caregiver's state of mind with respect to attachment and the capacity to maintain an attuned relationship with a well-developed reflective function are other important factors to consider. While each practitioner may have a particular approach to assessment, a reasonably thorough assessment might include the following elements:

1. MEETING WITH PARENTS
   a. Gather history of child and relationships within the family.
   b. Assess the caregiver's reflective capacities, capacity to engage in primary and secondary intersubjective experiences, and attachment history.
      i. This can be done informally by observing the process of the interview and the parent's ability to be empathic and insightful regarding the mind of the child.
         • Are the parent's responses consistent, coherent, and concise?
         • Can the parent view experiences through the child's eyes and have theories of mind about the child that consider the child's past experiences and how these may be impacting on present relationships?
      ii. Alternatively, one can use more formal procedures such as the following:
         • Adult Attachment Interview.[1]
         • Insightfulness Assessment.[2]
   c. Review past records, including the following:
      i. Protective service reports: These reports provide you with some understanding of the extent of the maltreatment.
      ii. Police reports: Police reports can provide detailed and accurate descriptions of conditions in the home. This information can be very useful in formulating theories about the child's experience and for the development of role-plays and psychodramatic reenactments.
      iii. Previous evaluations: Social history, psychological, occupational therapy, speech therapy, medical, genetic, neurological, developmental, etc.
      iv. School records.
      v. Court documents.

2. PSYCHOLOGICAL TESTS AND QUESTIONNAIRES
   a. Primary.

---

[1] Hesse, E. (1999). The Adult Attachment Interview. In J. Cassidy & P. Shaver, (Eds.), *Handbook of Attachment*. New York: The Guilford Press.
Main, M., & Hesse, E. (1990). Parents' unresolved traumatic experiences are related to infant disorganized attachment status. In M. T. Greenbert, D. Cicchetti, & E. M. Cummings, (Eds.), *Attachment in the preschool years*. Chicago, IL: University of Chicago Press.
[2] Oppenheim, D. & Koren-Karie, N. (April, 2002) *Insightfulness Assessment Interview Protocol*. Unpublished manual, Center for the Study of Child Development. Isreal: University of Haifa.
Oppenheim, D., Goldsmith, D., & Noren-Karie, N. Maternal insightfulness and preschoolers' emotion and behavior problems. *Infant Mental Health Journal*, In Press.

    i.   Child Behavior Checklist: Parent, Child, and Teacher versions.

    ii.   Vineland Adaptive Behavior Scales: Many children who have experienced a chronic history of maltreatment are developmentally delayed. This instrument can provide results that are useful with schools and parents. Parents often find it very helpful to have an instrument that shows the developmental delay of their child. It helps the parent appreciate that, while the child may be physically one age, the child is functioning at a much younger age.

    iii. Randolph Attachment Disorder Questionnaire.

    iv. Caregivers' autobiography. This information can be useful in understanding the caregiver and what aspects of parenting may be easier and more difficult for the caregiver.

    v.   Behavior-Rating Inventory of Executive Function.

    vi. Sensory-Integration Screener.[3]

    vii. Attachment Story Completion Test.[4]

    viii. House-Tree-Person Projective Test (both achromatic and color).

    ix. Child Apperception Test.

  b. Secondary. These methods may be added, depending on the purpose of the evaluation and age of the child and the parents' issues.

    i.   MAPI

    ii.   MCMI-III

    iii. Ainsworth Strange Situation

    iv. Structured observation and play session

    v.   Trauma Symptom Checklist

    vi. Adult Attachment Interview[5]

    vii. Connors Rating Scales

3.   SESSION WITH THE CHILD

  a. The main purpose of meeting with the child is to evaluate how the child relates to others and the child's capacity for reflective engagement, and to begin to assess internal working models. I use a semi-structured interview to accomplish this in which the process of what occurs is the primary focus. Incorporate the following elements into this session:

---

[3] See checklist at www.Center4FamilyDevelop.com for an example.
[4] Bretherton, I., Ridgeway, D., & Cassidy, J. (1990). Assessing internal working models of the attachment relationship. In M. T. Greenberg, D. Cicchetti, & E. M. Cummings (Eds.), *Attachment in the preschool years.* Chicago: University of Chicago Press.
[5] Hesse, E. (1999). The Adult Attachment Interview. In J. Cassidy & P. Shaver, (Eds.), *Handbook of Attachment.* New York: The Guilford Press.

    i.   House-Tree-Person Projective Test (both achromatic and chromatic). This is a good way to begin as many children are quite "therapy savvy." How the child manages this semi-structured situation is as important as the drawings that are produced.

    ii. Attachment Story Completion Test.

    iii. Review of history.

    iv. Child's understanding of the child's behavior.

    v. Ask four questions:
- What have you done that you are most proud of?
- What is the worst thing you've done?
- What is the best thing that ever happened to you?
- What is the worst thing that ever happened to you?

    vi. From a set of primary colors, ask the child to pick colors for mad, sad, glad, and scared and write these at the bottom of a page. Then ask the child to draw a big heart and to fill in the heart with the proportion of each feeling that the child usually has most of the time. The response to this is often accurate and helpful.

4. SESSION WITH THE CAREGIVERS: to review assessment and diagnosis, and to make treatment recommendations and referrals (such as to an SIPT Certified Occupational Therapist for sensory-integration issues or to an neuropsychologist for an evaluation). Also discuss the treatment recommendations and how treatment may proceed.

    a. During this session, if the family wants to engage in treatment, provide several resources about attachment-facilitating parenting.

    b. Briefly describe Dyadic Developmental Psychotherapy and set a time to begin parent training.

THE FIRST SESSIONS

The first one or so sessions, during which we discuss parenting principals, methods, and options are usually with the parents. Often it will work best for the family and child if the child is removed from school and at home with the primary caregiver. This allows for a safe, secure, and contained environment within which the attachment-facilitating parenting can be enacted. Many of these children function at the developmental level of a toddler; and thus, keeping the child home to focus on building the attachment relationship is often most effective. The therapist can provide a letter to the school indicating that it is an essential and necessary part of treatment for the child to be home with the parent. Furthermore, explain that the parent should not home school the child at this point. Often these children will make schooling and school work a battle, and it is important to remove as many obstacles to the parent-child relationship as possible. The school district can provide a tutor. In New York, a tutor is provided two hours a day, five days a week. I have found that in the last 10 years, I have only had two or three children who actually had to repeat a grade.

Parents can be enormously creative in finding ways to stay home with their child. The federal Family Medical Leave Act allows a parent to take up to 12 weeks a year off to care for an ill family member. This is one helpful resource. I frequently complete the necessary paper work for the working parent, which the parent can get from their company's Human Resources Department. Families make shift changes so the mother can be at home with the child, change working hours, and/or engage in other very creative ways of making this work. Finally, many children have an adoption subsidy. The evaluation we provide is frequently used as the basis for changing the subsidy to a special rate, which can also help a family allow the primary caregiver to stay home with the child.

STRUCTURE OF SESSIONS

My experience is that it works best when sessions are two hours in length, typically once a week. During a typical session I will meet with the parents for 20 to 30 minutes alone while the child is in the other office. The two offices are connected by closed-circuit TV so that we can monitor the child. During this part of the session we discuss the week and how the parents are doing. If a parent is experiencing difficulty, this time is extended. During the next 60 to 90 minutes the parents and therapist meet with the child, or the parents remain in the other room observing the session on the TV or through a one-way mirror. At the end, we "debrief" with the parents, discussing the session and what was observed and the parents' experience of the session.

One can do this therapy with one office; however, that does mean having the parents in each session, and there are important clinical reasons for which you may want a parent to observe a session. For example, you may have concerns about a parent being too harsh or critical, or the parent may become too anxious about having their child "behave" for you. In these instances it can be useful for the parent to observe your work. One can always ask the parent to just sit quietly in the room and observe, but they will generally be more relaxed in a second room. In addition, if you are able to work with a colleague, having an observation room allows the colleague to comment on the session.

Therapists often ask about how one bills for such a setup. Certainly one can bill one hour as a family session and one hour as an individual session, using the child's and/or parents' insurance. However, it is probably better to work with the insurance company to have your approach reviewed and approved so that you bill one CPT procedure code for the session at some agreed-upon rate. If the mental health coverage is managed by an NCQA accredited company, they may want to review your approach with their Technology Committee or have you talk with their child psychiatrist. In these instances it is very important that you have a good collection of articles about treating children with trauma-attachment disorders to present, as well as empirical data to support the effectiveness of Dyadic Developmental Psychotherapy. My group, The Center For Family Development, has been very successful at developing special contracts with various insurance companies and Departments of Social Services for the provision of Dyadic Developmental Psychotherapy in a two-hour session using two offices.

Unfortunately, some therapists practice in mental health clinics in which productivity is measured not by the number of clinical hours, but by the number of patients seen. In these instances I have seen that the therapist is discouraged, or even prohibited, from having two-hour sessions and sometimes is encouraged to have 30-minute sessions. One cannot do Dyadic Developmental Psychotherapy in a 30-minute session. There is just not enough time to engage the client, create the secure base, and then begin exploration. In these instances, it is probably most ethical to not treat trauma-attachment disordered children. One may even be at risk of malpractice claims if one provides ineffective treatment or treatment in a manner known to be ineffective when there is an effective treatment available. But, that is a question for your attorney.

EQUIPMENT

Having a one-way mirror between the two offices can be very useful because then you can have the camera in the observation room, which allows for focusing in and out. In our setup we actually have one camera in the observation room shooting through the mirror and a second camera in the therapy room, at a different angle, so that we can see everyone's face during sessions. In another set of offices we have a camera connected directly to a VCR and TV in the observation room, with the cables going through the wall, and that works fine as well.

The type of equipment that you can use:

1. A surveillance color camera with a zoom lens is an inexpensive alternative to buying a consumer video camera. The camera can be connected to a VCR, which is then connected to a TV.
   a. If you want to have the capability of doing split-screen taping, you will need a second camera and a video mixer, which can be expensive—around $1,000.

2. Sound is very important. After much trial and error I have found that consumer microphones available at local electronics stores are inadequate. It is worthwhile investing in a "phantom-power" boundary microphone (around $100 to $150) connected to an audio mixer ($100 to $150). Any good commercial audiovisual store can provide you with the video and sound equipment necessary, along with the cabling and wall mounts.

CREDENTIALING, POLICIES, PROCEDURES

In addition to being a licensed mental health provider, it is very helpful to have demonstrated credentials as one who can provide treatment to trauma-attachment-disordered children. So, for example, becoming a registered clinician with The Association for The Treatment and Training in the Attachment of Children[6] is one way to demonstrate that one has met a minimum standard for training and has appropriate policies and procedures in place.

Finally, there is the matter of various releases and informed consent. Following are examples of releases and an informed consent documents that one can use. You may want to create your own and then have a local attorney review your documents.

---

[6] See the list of registered clinicians at www.ATTACh.org for examples of policies and procedures.

PERMISSSION TO VIDEO/AUDIO RECORD THERAPY SESSIONS

Agency or Practice Name: _____
videotapes therapy sessions during the two-week intensive, at other times, and in other therapy sessions, at the discretion of the therapist. I understand and agree that any taping of treatment sessions or taping of me/us and/or my child/children in a treatment home, or in treatment, is for use in supervision and/or clinical staffing of my case. I also understand and agree that (Practice Name)_____
will maintain confidentiality in handling any tapes. I understand and agree that these tapes are not part of the clinical record.

_____
Parent/Guardian signature   (Date)

_____
Parent/Guardian signature   (Date)

_____
Witness signature   (Date)

I/we, _____
(Print Parent/Guardian's name)

hereby give my/our permission for The Center For Family Development

to produce and use pictures, slides, film, video tapes, and audio of tapes

of me/us and my/our child, _____
(Print Child's name)

for the purpose of familiarizing others with this work and for purposes of

training and professional education.   No full names or other identifying

data will be included.

_____

Parent/Guardian signature   (Date)

_____

Parent/Guardian signature   (Date)

_____

Witness signature   (Date)

Child's Name: _____

Date of Birth: _____

I/we do hereby seek and consent to participation in the outpatient treatment program for children with trauma-attachment difficulties provided by The Center For Family Development. The model of treatment used is Dyadic Developmental Psychotherapy.

The treatment model is based on the principal that children develop in a relationship and that the nature of the parent-child relationship is central to a child's healthy development. When a parent is attuned to the child's subjective experience, makes sense of those experiences for the child, and then communicates those understandings back to the child, then the child's view of him/her self can change and develop. Children with early histories of chronic maltreatment have not had dyadic interactions that facilitate growth and healthy development. The effective treatment and parenting of traumatized children must be based on creating experiences that we know to facilitate healthy attachment. The principals and methods that follow are not an exhaustive listing, but do provide an understanding of this approach.

I have been advised that specialized attachment interventions are family-focused and may include evaluations, assessments, individual counseling, adjunctive therapies, and supplemental services. An individualized treatment plan will be developed with my/our input, and clinical services will be provided in accordance with that plan.

These services may include the following specific interventions depending on the individualized treatment plan. All services provided are based on the best clinical judgment of The Center For Family Development staff and consultants. However, we understand and recognize that there are no guaranteed outcomes, cures, or certainties about the effectiveness of any treatment intervention, despite the best clinical judgments, assessments, and treatment plans.

Services May Include Any or All of the Following:

- Principals.
  1. Eye gaze, tone of voice, touch, movement, and gestures are used to communicate acceptance, safety, curiosity, playfulness, empathy, and love. These interactions are never used to threaten, intimidate, or coerce a child.

     Cradling of a child is done to help a child feel safe, loved, and secure. It may be used to help a dysregulated child become regulated when other interventions are not working. The primary goal is to ensure that the child and others are kept safe. The intention is to sooth a child in the same manner that one may sooth a frightened, overstimulated, or cranky toddler.
  2. Decisions and actions are undertaken to provide opportunities for success.
  3. Opportunities of fun, joy, laughter, and enjoyment are provided throughout the day.
  4. Symptoms and problems are contained and the underlying affect accepted. The intention is to reduce shame. It is based on an understanding that these behaviors are based on the child's history of maltreatment and were adaptive responses to horrific environments. As the child's trust and sense of being accepted increase, the child's self-esteem will improve and gradually symptoms, avoidance, and controlling behaviors will diminish.
  5. Resistance is accepted and contained, not shamed.
  6. The parent's capacity to self-regulate is the model for the child. Therefore, it is important that parents are willing to explore their own attachment histories in order to be better able to help the child.
  7. The child's cognitive understanding of the reasons for the child's problems helps the child develop a more integrated and coherent autobiographical narrative, which is an important element of health. Understandings are not excuses.
  8. Parents must work hard to maintain empathy for the child. Each child is doing the best that child can do, given the child's history.

- Contracting with the child and parents.
- Treatment planning and modification.
- Education of the child and parents.
- Processing the child and family's trauma.

- Processing and working through the grief and loss experienced by the child and family.

- Cognitive restructuring of the child and parents to challenge and re-pattern thought processes that interfere with healthy reciprocal relationships.

- Therapeutic cradling of the child by the parents and/or therapist(s) focusing on nurturance and the attunement process.

  This is an across-the-lap nurturing cradling, as one would hold an infant. At The Center For Family Development we do not use wraps, compression holds, or holds that utilize provocative stimulation, i.e. screaming and/or painful stimuli. Therapeutic cradling is not the same as restraint. Restraint techniques are solely for the purpose of maintaining the immediate safety of the child and others and do not resemble therapeutic cradling and are not a part of Dyadic Developmental Psychotherapy.

- Interpretation "color commentary" of the child's life and decisions focusing on describing and expressing feelings while expanding the range of feeling that the child can recognize and utilize.

- Validation of the child's feelings while broadening the emotional options available to the child.

- Psychodrama, psychodramatic reenactment, and role-playing of prior significant events and trauma.

- Training the child and family to use empathy, nurturing, and reciprocity.

- Teaching the parents how to create a healing PLACE by being playful, loving, accepting, curious, and empathic.

- Helping parents understand and address their own family-of-origin issues and attachment history in order to become more effective.

- Strategic interventions utilizing paradoxical prescriptions.

- Modeling behaviors, expression of feelings, and alternatives.

- Reparation for hurt and wrongs done in the past and present.

- Interrupting the child's behaviors.

- Talking for the child.

- Talking about the child.

- Consequences for child's behaviors (natural and logical).

- Elements of therapeutic parenting as described in *Building the Bonds of Attachment* and *Facilitating Developmental Attachment* by Daniel Hughes, PhD; *Attaching in Adoption* by Deborah Gray; and *Parenting from the Inside Out* by Daniel Siegel. Note that not all elements in these texts are used by The Center For Family Development.

- Eye Movement Desensitization and Reprocessing.
- Written assignments.

THE FOLLOWING ARE INTERVENTIONS THAT WE DO NOT USE:

- Holding a child in anger and confronting the child.
- Holding a child to provoke an emotional response.
- Holding a child until the child complies with a demand.
- Shaming a child or eliciting fear to get compliance.
- Poking or provoking a child in order to get a response.
- Coercing a child to engage in long or painful physical activities in order to get compliance or a response.
- Wrapping a child, lying on top of a child, "rebirthing," or similar techniques.
- Interventions based on power/control and submission.
- "Firing" a child from treatment because of non-compliance and punishing a child at home for being "fired" from treatment.
- Sarcasm or laughter at a child about the consequences being given the child.
- Interventions that are based solely on compliance; "Basic German Shepherd Training."
- Blaming the child for one's own rage.
- Labeling the child's behaviors or symptoms as meaning that the child does not want to be part of the family and then making the child "suffer" the consequences by:
  - Sending the child away to live elsewhere until he complies.
  - Putting the child in a tent outside until she complies.
  - Having the child eat in the basement until he complies.
  - Making the child stay in the her room until she complies.
  - Making the child sit motionless until he complies.

I am aware that the practice of therapy or counseling is not an exact science and no guarantees have been made to me as to the result of treatment or services provided by The Center For Family Development.

I have been advised that my participation in this program is entirely voluntary and I may terminate treatment at any time.

I authorize The Center For Family Development to videotape any treatment conducted during the therapy.

I acknowledge that I have had the services listed above and my client rights explained to me as well as videotaping expectations for participation in treatment, and have had the opportunity to have any questions answered. I have received a copy of my Client Rights Statement.

Parent/Guardian Signature   Relationship to Child   Date

Parent/Guardian Signature   Relationship to Child   Date

Parent/Guardian Signature   Relationship to Child   Date

Parent/Guardian Signature   Relationship to Child   Date

Witness/Therapist Signature   Date

Witness/Therapist Signature   Date

CHAPTER 3

A Dyadic Developmental Psychotherapy Session

ARTHUR BECKER-WEIDMAN & DEBORAH SHELL

"An adult who loses a spouse can manage without a close connection to another person for a period of time; a child who loses a parent can't exist alone emotionally without significant cost." —Hope Edelman, Motherless Daughters

This is a transcript of an actual session. Although sessions vary in terms of content explored, this session clearly illustrates how basic Dyadic Developmental Psychotherapy principles are practiced and may be utilized regardless of the particular issues discussed. The therapist maintains a PACE environment, so that a comfortable conversation evolves between Mary, her parents, and the therapist.

Mary and her great-aunt and guardian, Mrs. Owens, have had a conflictual relationship. After her first two years growing up with neglect and domestic violence, Mary came to live with Mrs. Owens' family. She continues to struggle with developmental delays and language processing problems. While referring to her great-aunt and great-uncle as "Mom" and "Dad," Mary still has difficulty allowing Mrs. Owens to care for, nurture, and/or show physical affection for her.

Descriptions of the components of a Dyadic Developmental Psychotherapy session are italicized. This is the second session with Mary, 15, and her great-aunt caregiver.

ART'S SESSION TRANSCRIPT AND COMMENTARY:

My sense is that Mary would like to feel loved and cared for; she just doesn't believe she deserves it. So my first remarks to her are indirect encouragers to help her with the risk.

Art: [sitting in chair alongside couch] "Why don't you sit there? [gestures toward couch; Mary sits down on couch cushion next to "Mom" and looks straight ahead]

"Or, you know what would be easier, why don't you take your shoes off and sit on your mom's lap? I think that would be easier for you, and you can put your feet up on the couch and stretch out. [Mary hesitates, then takes off shoes]

"Go ahead, sit on your mom's lap."

Mary: "Okay." [she hesitantly climbs onto Mom's lap]

My sense is that while hesitant, Mary actually wants to be closer with Mom. If Mary had objected, I would have then asked her to sit next to Mom, maybe lean on her, or let Mom put her arm across her shoulder. At this point I want to keep Mary engaged and remain attuned to her underlying affect.

Art: "Is that okay? There, lean back. That's right. Go ahead and sit right on her lap." [Mary repositions herself on Mom's lap]

Mary: [to Mom for reassurance] "Will I hurt you? I'm kind of heavy."

Mom: "That's okay. You're fine; come on my lap." [Mom helps position Mary in her lap, cradling her, with Mary's arm comfortably under Mom's arm and around Mom's middle, to maximize closeness and eye contact]

Mom and I had previously discussed the importance of showing Mary physical affection as one way of demonstrating that Mary is loved and lovable.

Art: "That's all right. Put your arm around your aunt, your mom."

Mary: "Did you used to hold Sarah like this?" [Sarah is Mom's older daughter]

Mom: "I used to, when she was a little baby. But now it would be hard; she's six feet tall!"

Art: [scratches his chin] "I wonder."

Now I want to begin to explore how the past may be alive in the present—perhaps dictating the meanings Mary makes about the present—and how past experiences continue to affect Mary. I see this as a way of beginning to help Mary. I hope she will finally experience herself as blameless for her abandonment and neglect, and feel truly loved by her great-aunt in the present.

Art: "Did your mom [great-aunt] ever hold you this way?"

Mary: "Who?"

Art: "Your mom. Did she ever hold you like this?"

Mary: "Maybe."

Mom: [nodding] "A lot."

Art: "How old were you when you first came to live with your mom?"

Mary: "Two."

Art: "Oh. You were really, really little. And before that, whom did you live with? Where were you before you lived with your mom and dad?"

Mary: "A lot of people. A lot of places."

Art: "But primarily who did you live with?"

Mary: [Names several relatives and friends of birth mother. Mom nods along.]

Art: "Did you live with your birth mom at all?"

Mom: "Sometimes."

Mary: "I did?"

Mom: "Mm hmm."

Art: "Oh, okay. Now, Mary, have you actually seen little tiny babies that are six or eight months old?"

I'm thinking I'd like to engage Mary in a discussion of babies–what they need, how they are supposed to be treated, and how all this affects the child (how their treatment affects them). My thought is that this will help her see that she was not treated well and that may help explain how she feels now. I want to help develop some threads that we can use to weave her a new autobiographical narrative. I hope that we can co-create a new meaning of her early years, from being simply a not-wanted, abandoned child, to being a child who was first mistreated and then eventually placed in a loving home. I am hopeful that we can weave the first threads of that new narrative today. As Mary becomes increasingly involved, I feel a strong sense of attunement with her. We are emotionally in the same place at the same time. This leads me to feel comfortable pushing her emotionally a bit further.

Mary: [names a cousin who she thinks is four months old; Mom nods]

Art: "Yeah, four months, that's a little, little baby. So what do babies need?

*In order to co-create a new narrative and develop new meanings, I have to
elicit these from Mary, not give them to her. I ask questions so that the story
that emerges is her story, her words. In addition, by asking questions and
then accepting her responses, I am demonstrating that I accept her, her feelings, and her experience. This acceptance will allow Mary to go deeper.
Finally, this approach allows us to maintain an intersubjective sharing of
affect, and we are beginning to turn a primary intersubjective experience into
a secondary representation, which is the basis for the narrative.*

Mary: [thinking a little] "Attention ... to be held like this ... and
             hugged a lot."

Art: "And what else do they need?"

Mary: "Food."

Art: "Yeah, they need food, they need a lot of things, diapers changed,
             they need lots of stuff like that." [pause while Mary thinks] "How
             do babies let you know that they need all of that?"

Mary: "Cry."

Art: [nods, strokes his chin] "They cry. And the little baby, when
             she's hungry, or wet, or cold or just needs to be picked up, what
             does the mom do when the baby needs something? When the
             little girl needs something, what's the mom supposed to do?"

Mary: "Love her. Rock her."

Now I will try to summarize our dialogue and move into affect and meaning.

Art: "So, Mom is supposed to pick her up and figure out what she
             needs, and rock her if she needs to be rocked, or cuddle her if she
             needs to be cuddled, or feed her if she needs to be fed. She cries,
             and then the mom's supposed to come, and she picks her up and
             figures out what's wrong and takes care of it. So if that happens a
             lot, if every time the baby needs something her mom comes and
             makes it better, how do you think it makes the baby feel?"

Mary: "Happy."

Art: "And if that happens a lot, and for a long time, how do you think,
             then, the baby starts to feel about herself? What kind of kid do
             you think she feels like?"

Mary: "Like she's loved."

Art: "Yeah, like she's loved. Like she's a good kid, a loveable kid. So every time she needs something, she starts to feel like she's okay, and she's loved and 'I'm a good kid and good things are happening to me.'" [pauses, strokes his chin]

"Did that happen for you when you were a baby?" [pause]

"Do you think every time you needed something, every time you cried, someone came and took care of you, when you were four months old?"

In this section I talk slowly with frequent pauses. This keeps Mary involved and listening to my every word. I find this can be a useful method of engaging the child and moving into a deeper experience of attunement and intersubjective sharing of affect. At this point I feel like we are in a deep state of attunement and intersubjective sharing of affect. My focus is only on Mary. The rest of the room has largely disappeared and I experience a deep and strong connection with Mary.

Mary: "I don't know ... where was I?" [looks at mom]

Mom: "Well, just any time you were with your parents." [implying: "Did they take care of you?"]

Art: "What do you think? Do you think that happened for you? Every time you cried people came to see what you needed?"

Mary: "When I came to my mom ... she did it ... now."

Art: "But, then you were 22 months old. Before that, when you were living with [birth] Mommy and moving around? Who helped you then?" [Mary doesn't answer; looks questioningly at mom.]

Art: [pausing] "When you look in your mom's eyes ... can you see her with the glasses? Yeah, okay."

I am wondering if the glasses they both wear are needed to see or if they will be an obstacle to connecting with Mom. I don't really know, so I ask her and Mom.

Art: [pausing] "So, look in your mom's eyes. Can you see her eyes well? With your glasses on can you see her eyes?" [Mom gently takes Mary's glasses off and places them on the table.]

Next I want to move the deep sharing between Mary and me to being between Mary and Mom. I feel that Mary is ready to connect with Mom and that Mom will be able to be present for Mary. What I decide to do now is have Mary tell her mom how she might have felt as a toddler. I will ask Mary to say some things to Mom. I feel confident that at this point if I ask Mary to say something that isn't right, she will correct me because I've been so accepting of her experience.

Art: "Good. So, look in your mom's eyes, and I'd like you to tell her, 'I don't think anyone really took care of me when I was a baby.' Tell her that." [Mary looks into Mom's eyes for a moment and starts to cry; Mom snuggles her up and holds her very close, rocking her, and patting her back]

I now feel Mary's sadness and Mom's sadness that Mary was so alone, scared, and mistreated. I decide to both allow this to unfold and to try to deepen it by having Mary say more. I am hopeful that Mary will be able to experience these very deep and profound feelings AND think about these feelings, i.e. put into words what is her experience at this moment and her experience back then. This is an example of the reflective function.

Mary: [crying] "I don't think anyone took care of me!" [now sobbing]

Mom: [crying] "You know I love you, I love you. And you know we're going to be all right."

Mary: [through tears] "Right."

Art: [pauses, then softly] "Can you tell your mom, 'I wanted someone to take care of me.'"

At this moment I did not want Mom's reassurances to cut off Mary's expression of profound grief, sadness, and isolation. So, I ask Mary to say to her mom what I believe Mary to be feeling now and what I believe she may have felt then.

Mary: "I wanted someone to take care of me ..." [She cries; Mom rocks and pats her neck and shoulder.]

I feel better here. Mom is behaviorally accepting Mary and her affect without having to "make it better." This is very important. If Mom can tolerate Mary's affect, then so can Mary. And if Mary can tolerate this strong affect, then she can integrate it into a coherent narrative. I sense that Mary is able to do this and am confident that she will; this encourages me to go deeper.

Art: "Can you say to her, 'I was really, really alone and scared.' Look in your mom's eyes and tell her how alone and scared you were."

Mary: [broken sobs] "I felt alone and scared."

Mom: [rocking Mary] "I bet you did."

Mary: "I'm really glad you took me in."

Now that Mom has accepted Mary's affect, Mary is able to move beyond the primary experience of the affect into weaving another thread of her narrative.

Mom: "I'm glad too."

Mary: "And I love Dad, too."

Art: "It must be so hard for you ... to be a little baby and be hungry or scared or cold or needing something and cry and not have someone come and pick you up, not have someone make you feel special and love you ...."

"That must have been so hard for you as a little baby .... That must have been so hard for a baby girl."

Mary: [thinking, wondering] "But ... I don't remember it."

Art: "No, but I think your body does. It's so hard for you now. You have such a hard time now. It's hard for you to sometimes believe that your mom and your dad really are taking care of you. Maybe that's why sometimes you argue with them so much, 'cause you don't think they're really taking care of you. You were just a little baby ... nobody came when you cried ... maybe it felt to you like nobody cared .... [pause]

"Can you say, 'Mom, it felt like nobody cared about me.'"

Mary has experienced some profound emotions with her mom, who has accepted Mary's affect. I now want to begin to bring in more of the reflective function to integrate past with present. This new thread of her narrative redefines her current problems as stemming from these past experiences and not reflecting any badness in her or any negative sense of self. This is the normalizing and new meaning dimension of the "cycle" of Dyadic Developmental Psychotherapy.

Mary: [looks sad, lifts head to look into Mom's eyes] "Mom, it felt like nobody cared about me or loved me!" [fresh tears spill over]

Mom: "Sorry." [Mom cries, hugs, rocks, pats Mary.]

Art: "What kind of kid would that make you feel like, do you think?"

Mary: [sadly, through tears] "An unloved kid. A bad kid."

Art: "Tell your mom that. How did that make you feel as a baby?"

Mary: [sadly, to Mom] "I felt like I was a bad kid."

Art: [Gets tissues and both wipe their own eyes. Art asks Mom to wipe Mary's eyes.]

At this juncture I am thinking that I want Mom to do something to enact her feelings for Mary, to demonstrate that she loves Mary and will take care of Mary. Wiping Mary's tears seemed like a way to do this.

Mary: [to Mom] "Do you want me to wipe your eyes?"

Art: "Moms wipe their own eyes and moms wipe their babies' eyes." [pauses, sighs] "You probably didn't have anyone to do that for you when you were a baby, either, wipe your eyes when you were crying. That must have been sad and hard for you .... And so, for two years you went like that! Boy, two long years."

Mary: [to Mom] "I'm really happy that you took me in, and Dad."

Art: "Do you think your mom, now—you're almost sixteen now, and it's fourteen years later and a lot of things have happened in that time, and some not so good—so, do you think your mom is *still* happy that she took you in? What do you think? [Mom continues to rock and pat Mary.]

"How can you tell that she's still happy after all these years and with all these problems, how can you tell she's still happy she took you in?"

I am hoping that Mary is experiencing her mom as loving her and caring for her and making her feel loveable and loved. So I decide to ask Mary if she can tell if her mom is still happy about making Mary her child.

Mary: [softly] "Because she cares about me, she's holding me."

Art: "Mm hmm. That sounds right. Boy, after all these years she still loves you; she's always loved you. I know she's your aunt, but she's really been a mom to you."

I sense that we've done enough deep emotional work and that it is time to move to the cognitive level, to lessen the emotional dimension. This is an example of dyadically regulating the child's affect. We are now reflecting on the experience and expanding Mary's reflective function. We are becoming more cognitive so that Mary has the experience in treatment of successfully experiencing profound affect without becoming dysregulated. In fact, she experiences profound emotions very deeply and is able to become closer to her mom because of this. This will make it more likely that she will continue to be able to do this work in future sessions. As a side note, I feel comfortable with strong affect and with profound sadness. My own history of loss and having come to terms with that has allowed me to be able to tolerate others' sadness, sense of aloneness, and grief.

Art: "What's a mom supposed to do?"

Mary: "Love you, take care of you, help you with problems, hold you ...."

Art: "Can you say to her, 'You've done all the things a mom's supposed to do'?"

Mary: [looks into Mom's eyes] "You've done all the things a mom's supposed to do!"

Mom: [wiping Mary's eyes] "Thank you!"

Mary: "You're welcome." [Mom and Mary hug, rock, rest comfortably together.]

Art: "All the things a mom does for a baby, a mom does for a little kid and a mom does for a big kid. They make sure they have clothes, make sure everything's okay."

Mary: "Help with problems at school, take care of them."

Art: "Hmm. So, what would you like to say to your mom, now? Look her in the eye and what would you like to say to her right now?"

Mary: [looks into Mom's eyes] "I love you."

Mom: "I love you, too."

Mary: [through tears] "I love Dad, too."

[Mom wipes Mary's eyes]

Art: [to both] "Do you get to do this much at home?"

Mom: [looks thoughtfully at Art] "We sit on the couch and we started to hold hands more ... hug every once in a while ...."

Art: "What do you think, could you maybe work this into the routine, once a day find some time to sit like this? What do you think, Mary, do you think once a day your mom and you could sit together like this and cuddle like this?"

I want to find a way to integrate this experience into their life at home.

Mary: [pulls away a bit, then says to Art] "Can we be watching TV while we're doing it?"

Art: [shakes head] "No. If you're watching TV then you're not looking at each other and being there with each other. Watching TV might be good for another time, but to be there with each other, talk with each other, hold each other, you don't want distractions. So what do you think, could you let your mom do this every day? How would that be for you?"

Mary: "Okay."

At this point I am wondering to myself if I've pushed Mary too far and if the idea of being with Mom at home in this way might be too much. So, I have to ask her what 'okay' means.

Art: "Okay like when you go to the doctor to get your shot?"

Mary: "No!"

Art: "So, what kind of 'okay' do you mean?"

Mary: "Like, okay, I would like that!"

Art: "Oh! 'Okay' like you feel *good* about it!" [pauses, then to Mom] "How long has it been since you and Mary have sat like this?"

Mom: "A long time. *Long* time."

Art: "Mary, can you remember the last time you sat on your mom's lap?"

Mary: "No, but I know she must have done it when I was six or four or two."

Art: "So it's been a really long time. It's a good thing to do. Probably when the other kids aren't around."

Mary: "Yeah."

Art: "Some special time for you and Mom. So that would be a good thing I think, if you and Mom could spend some time together. That would probably help. It sounds, Mary, like a lot of things should have happened when you were just a little, little baby— things that didn't happen."

Mary: "It's not Mom's fault."

Art: [nods] "When you were with [birth] Mommy and you were moving around and she would give you to different people to take care of you and they didn't know you very well, for those two years it sounds like you didn't have anybody to be with you all the time. You'd be with Mommy, Aunt Cindy, birth mom's friends ... you kept moving and had all these strange people taking care of you. That must have been really hard! So, this could be a kind of way your mom now could do some of the things she would have done if she'd gotten you when you were first born. I wonder how you'd be different if your mom got you just when you were born?"

I am now thinking that as a teen she may be able to think about a life that wasn't but that might have been .... I wonder if she can consider how her life would have been different. I also am thinking that this might be another way for Mary to "realize" that this mom is different from all the other "moms" she's had.

Mary: [thinking] "I'd probably be like Paul. [another of great-aunt's birth children] He doesn't argue so much ...."

Art: "So, if you were born to *this* mom you wouldn't argue with her or be angry with her? Mmm. How do you think things would be different if you'd been with her since you were born? How do you think you'd feel differently if you'd been with her since the time you were born?"

Mary: [lifts head slightly to look at Art] "Less anger."

Art: "I could really understand that, as a little, little girl, you'd be angry that people didn't come when you were hungry, cold, or needed to be picked up, and I could see how you could have come to your mom at two and been angry about a lot of things. Nobody took care of you the way you needed to, the way you should have been. So, you'd be less angry now ... yeah, that's probably true [nods head]. So do you want to work on all these things over the next few months?"

At this point, I think we are getting ready to end and I want to know if Mary wants to continue this work. I'd like her to feel some measure of control over her therapy ... the pacing will develop between us and include her. I want to communicate to her that I value her and will respect her capacities and abilities at the moment.

[Mary nods]

Art: "Okay, good! Anything else you want to say to your mom?"

Mary: [looks at Mom] "I love you!" [starts to get up from couch]

Art: [gestures to wait]: "Why don't you give your mom one big hug ..."
          [they hug]

Mary: [to Art] "Thank you."

Intersubjectivity is achieved when the therapist's active awareness of
Mary's affective experience is stated and understood; this allows new
meaning (and empathy) to unfold. Oftentimes the child and parent have
misinterpreted each other's meaning. Co-creation of meaning is achieved
through PACE, and can help both parent and child to view each other in
less negative terms. For example, instead of a parent interpreting a child's
aggressive behavior as "mean," and responding from a negative interpretation, the parent can be helped to see how the child may be protective of
her/his self by subverting underlying fear into aggression. If the parent
sees a "frightened" child instead of a "mean" child, the parental response
is more likely to be in accordance with what the child really needs, and to
help the child to feel more secure. Most likely, the child has also given
negative attribution to the parent's behaviors; therefore, a goal of therapy
is to co-create meaning in order to help the child change his/her interpretation of the parent's honest attempts to nurture. Often the child can't
easily tell the difference between abusive and nurturing parenting, and so
when the nurturing parent says "no," the child reacts as if the child has
been deprived of a basic need. The child may misinterpret the parent's
limit setting as representing another example of how the parent does not
care about the child, but only cares about the parent. In addition, the limit
setting may be misinterpreted by the child as another experience validating
the child's experience of self as unloved, unlovable, and as intrinsically
bad. If a parent is taught to recognize the underlying meaning of a child's
behavior (as a response to a *perceived* threat), instead of reacting to the
behavior, the parent might say, for example: "Did you think I wasn't taking
good care of you when I *turned off the TV/told you no more candy/asked you
to change your sheets/ left you home with a babysitter/* etc."

Mary is "stuck" in a very regressed state. She reacts to her great-aunt's
nurturing attempts as if she was the one who neglected her when she was
little. The parents have not been aware of how little she feels, and how
afraid she is of abandonment. A new interpretation would be to view her
controlling behaviors as a desperate attempt to prevent further loss.
Through this lens, the parents can provide the particular nurturing she
needs and be sensitive to situations that she may interpret as threatening.
Through empathy and acceptance, a person feels truly understood and
attached to another human being.

CHAPTER 4

Dyadic Developmental Psychotherapy in Practice

JESSICA MROZ & PHYLLIS B. RUBIN

"I don't believe that children can develop in a healthy way unless they feel that they have value apart from anything they own or any skill that they learn. They need to feel they enhance the life of someone else, that they are needed. Who, better than parents, can let them know that?" —Fred Rogers, Mister Rogers Talks with Parents

Dyadic Developmental Psychotherapy invites parents and children to look into each other's hearts in ways that many people do not know is even possible. It offers an opening that allows the child to attach emotionally to his current parents and that allows the parents to really see and attach to the child they have. This chapter will describe how we help children and parents open their hearts to each other.

It is not only the children who may be surprised by the Dyadic Developmental Psychotherapy approach, but also parents, who are bringing the child to therapy in hopes of behavioral change. Dyadic Developmental Psychotherapy prescribes a therapeutic way of parenting and thinking that can be hard for the most receptive of parents. Parents often want us to come down hard on the child and get the child to conform to their expectations. Dyadic Developmental Psychotherapy is based on an attachment perspective in which parental emotional availability and responsiveness are the keys to change. We teach parents how to attune to and provide empathy to their child. In response to the parent's emotionally available and responsive attitude, the child becomes attached to the parent and, as a result, the behaviors improve. It's a dance of attachment whose major ingredients are not the usual and predictable consequences with which some parents feel most comfortable. Dyadic Developmental Psychotherapy requires parents (and therapists) to learn new ways of interacting with the child and new ways of responding to the child's problem behaviors. Once learned, this new way can open up the relationship between parent and child and deepen the attachment bond.

DOING DYADIC DEVELOPMENTAL PSYCHOTHERAPY

Before we describe Dyadic Developmental Psychotherapy in detail, we need to make a statement about the role of the parent or special caregiver. Dyadic Developmental Psychotherapy actively involves the child's parent in the treatment process. "Parent" could mean birth parent, adoptive or foster parent, guardian, or group-home therapist. We believe that the parent has an essential function in helping the child heal from past hurts. There is enormous therapeutic value in the parent being present to bear witness to the child's experience and to convey empathy for the child's situation and acceptance of the child's feelings. The parent provides the ultimate corrective experience for the child by adopting the powerful attitude of PLACE: Playfulness – Love – Acceptance – Curiosity – Empathy. We will talk more about these qualities in the next section on "setting the stage."

In contrast to therapy in which the therapist works with the child alone, therapy with the parent present and participating in the treatment creates a more integrated experience for the child. Many traumatized children live fragmented lives and will separate and deny parts of themselves. As a result, they often have distorted thoughts about how others feel and think about them. Without the parent present to dispel those thoughts by sharing their view of and feelings about the child, a therapist who sees a child individually may unwittingly reinforce the child's distortions. Only when the parent is there to look into the child's eyes and convey genuine love and understanding will the child be able to leave negative self- and other-perceptions in the past, and begin to develop healthy ones in the present.

We will now describe how the therapist sets the stage for Dyadic Developmental Psychotherapy in the beginning and deepens the treatment as it progresses, and discuss issues in ending therapy.

SETTING THE STAGE IN THE BEGINNING

In the beginning of treatment, the therapist:

- Maintains the attitude of PACE.
- Stays attuned to the child while managing the flow of therapy.
- Finds opportunities to bring up the child's trauma, abuse, and disruption history.
- Attempts to discover the meanings the child has given to life experiences and co-creates new meanings with the parent and child.
- Creates opportunities for parent and child to feel close and enjoy one another.
- Supports the parent as the primary protector, caregiver, and nurturer of the child.
- Demonstrates to the child and parent that no topics are off-limits and that trauma and pain will be dealt with in an honest, truthful, and empathic manner.

We have already mentioned that we want parents to use the attitude of PLACE. In this section we will describe how the therapist achieves an attitude of PACE. PACE is simply PLACE without the L, which stands for Love. The other letters stand for the same qualities mentioned earlier. We believe that Love represents deep feelings of warmth, tenderness, devotion, and enduring loyalty and is the purview of the parent, not the therapist. A therapist can feel affection, concern, and care for a child client, but not love. Thus, for the therapist, we will now describe PACE. PACE is not a set of qualities that you do in a sequence; rather, these are qualities that you integrate into your therapy session as needed to keep the child and parent engaged in the process of healing.

PLAYFULNESS

The family has come to you because of a problem. Often playfulness is one of the first things to disappear from a relationship because negativity, frustration, and worry have set up shop. Parent and child can appear jaded, depressed, and even cold. The therapist's job is to give parent and child hope, the hope that joy can be part of their lives together. Without the possibility of joy, there will be little reason for the child or parent to respond to your efforts. Being playful allows you to see if you can warm up the child, the parent, and the relationship.

Some of your first interactions with the child are likely to be light and playful. This can be a way of engaging the wary or defensive child on an emotional level, in a nonthreatening manner. Meeting the child for the first time, you might comment on how strong the child's handshake is, or how quick the child's eyes are, looking all around to scope the place. You could then, quickly, turn hyper-alert eyes into a game where you try to see if you can guess what the child is looking at as the child's eyes move.

> Therapist: "Oh, you're looking at the table, now the clock, now my nose. No? I'm wrong? Man, you are really fast, kiddo! You won!"

Or, for a later session when you know the child better:

> "My nose! How dare you look at my nose? Something wrong with it? Don't tell me. Better not tell me or I may have to give you that donut over there just to keep you quiet. You wouldn't want a donut, now would you? Naw! How about a tickle instead of a donut. You'd rather have a tickle, wouldn't you?"

To be playful, you must be able to feel harmlessly mischievous, sometimes even silly, and be willing to act younger than your age. Playful challenges are not serious, and egos (the child's or the adult's) should not be hurt. Playfulness should be fairly transparent to the child through your facial expression, body posture, and use of healthy touch. Gentle teasing may or may not be playful depending on the child. Non-playful teasing is cruel, hurtful, and damages fun and trust. In contrast, pure playfulness helps the child to relax, to see you as someone who could possibly bring relief, and to feel you are safe. It helps you and the child build a therapeutic relationship that can withstand the approaching explorations into painful areas of the child's life. Examples of playfulness are described in the section on how the therapist creates opportunities for parent and child to feel close and enjoy one another.

Acceptance

One of the most important messages we want the child (and parents) to hear is that we accept the child and all the feelings and motivations for the child's behavior. This may be a new experience for both parents and child. Past treatment providers may not have been understanding of behaviors and accepting of the underlying feelings, but instead may have attempted to change the child through behavior management techniques. When a child experiences someone's complete acceptance of his feelings and understanding of behaviors, the child will more likely be open to exploring the roots of behaviors and feelings.

> "No wonder you hide in your room all day. You didn't think your foster mom knew how to take care of you when you were feeling sad. If I thought that, I would hide in my room too."

The child should not feel that the therapist and parent are simply trying to elicit change or convince him/her to feel and behave differently. That type of approach is likely to produce only temporary changes at best.

Curiosity

The key to being experienced as accepting is to adopt a *curious stance* to problems. Being curious requires the therapist to have a genuine interest in the child's experience, thoughts, and feelings, and what these mean to the child. One must be able to take real delight in the child. A curious stance, particularly when facing hard topics, protects the child from feeling paralyzing or rage-triggering shame. It helps assure the feeling of acceptance, even as the most self-depreciating feelings begin to rise, and keeps the processing going. Some ways of conveying curiosity include:

- Open your eyes wide and lift your eyebrows.
- Have a puzzled tone of voice.
- Show (and feel) no anger.

- Sound incredulous but not sarcastic.
- Express confusion.
- Above all, don't take anything personally.
- Thank the child for sharing thoughts and feelings with you.

The therapeutic value of maintaining a curious stance is unsurpassed. Curiosity helps turn off the child's internal, abuse-sensitive alarm system—the flight, fight, freeze reaction. The seven behaviors (above) that signal the presence of curiosity, when truly done without anger or personal investment, are antithetical to an angry/disappointed/punitive reaction that could set off the child's alarm system and cause emotional dysregulation. When the therapist is able to stay curious in the face of provocative behaviors, the child is likely to stay better regulated and be able to continue exploring hard topics. Without curiosity, you are more likely to lose the child through avoidance or withdrawal (flight), anger (fight), or a confusing combination of both when the child has the look of a deer frozen in the headlights (freeze). Curiosity helps to promote the child's openness and the trust that there will be no humiliation, rejection, anger, or punishment. It hints that the child's efforts will be welcomed, accepted, and understood. Curiosity gives the child hope to remain engaged in the hard process of sharing past experiences.

EMPATHY

Empathy is the ability to "sit" with another's feelings. It means being able to feel what the other is feeling, but not be overwhelmed. Being aware of the therapist's empathy may be a new experience for the child. When a child expresses a strong negative feeling or shows obvious signs of discomfort, it is probably more common for people to say, "Don't worry," or "You're okay"—comments that don't reflect the child's experience. When you begin to touch hard stuff, you can provide empathy by acknowledging, "It's really hard to think about that." Or you can verbalize what the child is feeling or may have felt in the past.

> Therapist: "You look so sad right now. I think that's how you felt when your parents left you alone every night. You were so alone, so alone."

The parent may have difficulty with empathy. Struggling to care for a child with significant attachment-trauma problems, the parent may be feeling overwhelmed and ineffective. Because of this, the parent may resort to behavior that would, with a more normal child, be uncharacteristic of this parent. When the therapist accepts the parent and empathizes with the struggle, the parent will be more likely to begin to display the same attitude toward the child.

Lew was a 17-year-old adopted child. He came to live with his mother at the age of two and a half years, not showing the signs of attachment we hope to see develop when a child becomes part of a healthy family. There were problems with eye contact, the presence of superficial smiles, and indiscriminate friendliness that were not recognized at that time as possible signs of trouble. Lew would often sink into silence and depression, avoid eye contact, complain a lot (like any adolescent), and was no longer the smiling, appreciative, and easier child of his first years with his mom. Mom came to sessions worn out, frustrated, and feeling like she was certainly unloved. All she saw from Lew's demeanor was indifference and sometimes hostility toward her. Now Mom was starting to doubt that she would be able to parent Lew in the ways he needed. Maybe she wasn't a good parent for Lew after all.

Lew's therapist empathized with how hard it is to parent a child with a history of abuse, neglect, and repeated loss. Such a child can get scared of loving, and maybe Mom was picking that up and getting scared of loving her son as well. Mom had experienced the loss of that cute, smiling, two-year-old who had made her feel like a good mom. Now she was left with a very needy adolescent whose job it was to push against her limits while still avoiding eye contact and not showing much love. The therapist agreed it was hard to show love to someone who seemed like he didn't want it. It was hard to take a chance, and would take a lot of energy to do so. Hard to risk being hurt again. Maybe Mom didn't have energy left?

Mom: "Well, I'm not giving up on him yet. I still love him."

When the session was over, Mom had regained hope because she was able to reach out to Lew despite his avoidance, and Lew responded with, not surprisingly, eye contact and smiles.

The therapist stays attuned to the child while managing the flow of therapy.

Stay attuned to the child, remaining aware of the child's responses on all levels (verbal as well as nonverbal), and shifting the interaction or content of the session based on the needs of the child. If the child states emphatically, "I don't want to talk about that!" do not take this as a signal to shift course nor as a signal that the child has been harmed by pursuing—or continuing to pursue—this topic. At the same time, do not demand or insist that the child discuss the difficult content. Instead use this as material for the present moment in the session. Thank the child for expressing these feelings. Comment on how hard life has been for the child and how much hard work it takes to feel safe and protected. Congratulate the child on the good job being done. Wonder aloud about times when the child was not able to tell people "no," maybe when the child was just a small baby and needing very much for adults to provide protection. As the therapist, you may sense that the child needs even more of a break in the content and will give that break—in content, but not in emotional connection. Engage the child in a playful exchange, delighting in and enjoying the child's presence. Playfully tease the child or encourage the parent to be playful as well. Congratulate the child for letting the therapist and parent know that a break was needed. Do all of this while confidently remaining in the lead of content and interaction within the session.

> Marie was a seven-year-old girl adopted from an orphanage in Poland. She came to her adoptive family at 16 months of age. Marie also had medical needs to be addressed when she first arrived in her adoptive home. She was very independent and always wanted to do things for herself from the beginning. When Marie's adoptive mother met her, she was holding her own bottle. As soon as she could walk, she was moving away from others. During therapy sessions, Marie frequently began to tell her therapist and mother what to do. The therapist often did not respond directly to her demands and did not enter into a power struggle with Marie. She did, however, initiate a playful exchange with Marie.

The therapist finds opportunities to bring up the child's trauma, abuse, and disruption history.

The resolution of trauma entails the integration of split-off experience. In order to achieve this, help the child to develop a coherent autobiographical narrative. Facilitate this process by making connections between the child's current behaviors, feelings, thoughts, and the past deprivation or disruptions of healthy, loving parenting. Even if the trauma is out of awareness because of dissociation or because the child was so young at the time, making the connections between current "bad" behaviors and past experiences helps the child make sense of the behaviors and lessens the child's feelings of overwhelming shame and of just being a bad kid. As in the next example, making these ties can be the vehicle for opening up areas to explore, or for touching and then validating forgotten pain.

Rose was a four-year-old girl adopted from Russia. Smart and quick, she was the boss of her mother and ran the show in a very cute but demanding way. Having been to the therapy room before, she came in for her first Dyadic Developmental Psychotherapy session to look for a stuffed dog that had been moved from the back of the couch. When she finally found it, she hugged it and said she missed it and wanted to take it home with her. Looking up at her therapist with wide eyes, she continued to repeat that she really loved this dog and wanted to take it home. She would take good care of it, she said. Kids are often allowed to take stuffed animals home for a week. But something about this child felt different. It might have been the feel of blatant demandingness—like if she gave a good enough argument and elicited enough therapist guilt, she'd get what she wanted. Nothing in her voice and nothing in her face signaled any feeling other than pure entitlement: "I want, so I should have." Something told her therapist not to agree to her wishes, that there was a lesson to learn from this.

Therapist: "No, Rose, the doggie has to stay here."

Rose: "But I want him, and if you don't let me have him, I'll be mad."

Therapist: (knowing that Rose was adopted from an orphanage) "Rose, the doggie has to stay with his mommy. He can't go with you just because you want him. He shouldn't be taken away from his mommy."

Rose: "But I want him!"

Therapist: "But dogs and little children shouldn't have to leave their mommies. He has to stay here with me."

At that point, Rose began to cry, first angry tears, then tears of sadness and a bit of hopelessness. Already in mom's lap, the therapist had Mom hold her in a very comforting way. Rose held on, crying into Mom's chest. As she cried, the therapist kept saying that no doggie or child should have to leave their mommies and that no one should just take him away. She cried harder, turned her head outward and sobbed. Mom had never heard such sobs and felt them to be real. The therapist wondered out loud if this is how she had cried when she was in the orphanage.

> *The therapist attempts to discover the meaning the child has given to life experiences and co-creates new meaning with the parent and child.*

Throughout this sequence, utilize empathy, acceptance, and curiosity, and speak for the child as necessary (Hughes, training handout). The following case example illustrates this process and the basic treatment cycle of Dyadic Developmental Psychotherapy in Figure 1 on page 32.

Andrew is an 11-year-old child who, at the time of the following therapy session, had been in his current foster home for approximately nine months. Mr. and Mrs. Randall intended to adopt both Andrew and his younger sibling. Prior to his placement with this family, Andrew had been in several other foster homes, many of which were also intended to be pre-adoptive in nature. Andrew was removed from his birth mother at the age of seven after inconsistent care, including abuse and neglect and being left with various family members, some of whom were also abusive. Andrew was also abused in several of his previous foster homes.

The day before the therapy session, there were visitors in Andrew's foster home. Andrew was familiar with these adults and interacted with them positively until his mother needed to take about 10 minutes to speak with them and was not available to interact directly with Andrew. Mrs. Randall suggested that he look at some books while she spoke with the guests, directed him to the bookshelf, and made a few suggestions. Andrew became anxious and began to run around the home. Mrs. Randall recognized that Andrew was having a difficult time accepting that she could not focus her attention on him at that moment. She explained to him that she only needed a few minutes, empathized that she knew this was hard for him, and again directed him to the books. When this again did not work and Andrew continued to run around, Mrs. Randall decided that Andrew needed some focused physical activity, which was often quite effective with him. She suggested that Andrew run outside in the backyard to the tree at the far end of the yard and back to the house a few times. Andrew did as his mother suggested, but then began throwing rocks at the house and then opened the door and began swearing at his foster mother. Mrs. Randall was not able to finish her conversation with the visitors and spent the rest of the afternoon attempting to calm Andrew.

STEP 1: THE THERAPIST IDENTIFIES THE BEHAVIOR.

Choose a recent incident in the child's life to explore during the therapy session. The incident (or problem) represents an interpersonal disruption in which the child feels shame and reacts to his own internal meaning that he places on the behavior of others. Another target for exploration can be around the parent having given the child a consequence. This often brings up feelings in the child about the parent and in the parent about the child.

Begin this conversation in a non-judgmental, playful, and engaging manner. Attempt to get the child talking and feeling relaxed about this exchange. When making the switch to the difficult conversation of the child's behavior, continue to convey acceptance by not changing tone.

> Therapist: "Andrew, I heard that yesterday you had some visitors at your house."
>
> Andrew: "Yep. Mom's friends."
>
> Therapist: "That's right. Mr. and Mrs. Johnston. I heard you had some fun when they were over."
>
> Andrew: "Yeah. Mr. Johnston showed me a magic trick. He's cool. And Mrs. Johnston brought my favorite cookies."
>
> Therapist: (mirroring Andrew's pleasure) "Andrew, that's great. Sure sounds like you had a good time." (playfully) "Hey are you going to show me that magic trick? I love magic tricks."
>
> Andrew: (laughs) "It's too hard!" **[Healthy attunement in process: therapist and child are emotionally in sync.]**
>
> Therapist: "Hey, that's okay .... I hear Mr. Johnston's a pretty good magician .... So Mr. and Mrs. Johnston come over a lot, don't they? Sometimes they bring their kids with them too, and you like to play with them, right? You have a lot of fun when they come over. That's great! Hmm ... but then it seems that something happened that you weren't having fun anymore." (very curious) "I'm guessing you weren't having fun because you swore at your mom."
>
> Andrew: (head down, sad facial expression) "Yeah, I got mad." **[Attunement disruption: Andrew's head is down, signaling some dysregulation, the anticipation of feeling shame and emotional disconnect from the therapist.]**

Attempt to discover the underlying belief held by the child that drives the
child's behavior. Explore a hypothesis in a curious manner, speaking in an
emotional, exaggerated tone. Wonder aloud for the child, and begin to
draw the connections between what the child did and why that may have
happened. Guess at what the child may believe about himself, others,
or the world. Assess the accuracy of the guess based on the child's
responses in the moment during the session. Watch the child's nonverbal
behavior, observe changes in breathing, eye contact, and muscle tension.
When the child's belief is revealed, the child often becomes quiet and
intent, less resistant, and no longer protests or behaves in a silly manner.
The child may also look away or bury his or her face in the parent, particularly if there is an experience of shame associated with the event or belief.

> Therapist: (mirroring Andrew's affect and words) "Yeah, you
> got mad. So I was thinking about that. I was thinking, 'I won-
> der why Andrew would get so mad after having such a nice time
> visiting with the Johnstons? I wonder why he would get so mad
> that he would swear at his mother?'"
>
> Andrew: (remains quiet, breathing deeply, looking down at his
> hands in his lap, while picking at his cuticles)

Andrew is likely experiencing shame at this moment. He feels that he
got mad and swore at his mother after having such a nice time because
he is "a bad boy." He may be feeling that he is always a bad kid and he
didn't deserve the nice time he had to begin with. While he may be fear-
ing where his therapist will go with this conversation, he may not be
"acting out" as he normally would when experiencing shame because he
feels understood by his therapist through her accepting manner and
tone. He feels that he may be understood in a new way, and that he isn't
going to be reprimanded for his behavior. **[Attunement disruption continues: Andrew shows signs of anxiety and shame.]**

> Therapist: "Hmm ... I was thinking that maybe you felt confused
> yesterday. After having such a nice time with Mom and the
> Johnstons, when Mom said she needed to talk with them with-
> out you, maybe you felt like she was saying they didn't want to
> be with you."
>
> Andrew: (breathing remains the same, head remains down,
> appears to be listening intently to his therapist)
>
> Therapist: "Maybe you felt like Mom was saying they were just
> too busy to keep playing with a little boy; they had adult things

to do and didn't have time for little boys. Maybe when Mom said she needed to talk with the Johnstons without you, you were thinking, 'They don't even want to be with me. They probably wish I wasn't even here.'"

Andrew: (eyes look teary, head remains down) **[Attunement disruption continues.]**

Therapist: "And you kept trying to get Mom's attention. You kept trying to remind her you were there! And then she told you to go outside and run! I wonder if you were thinking, 'Hey, I don't want to go outside! I want you to pay attention to me!'"

Andrew: (glances up at therapist and then over at mother and back down again, he then shifts in the seat, bares his teeth, and growls at his mother) "She made me mad!"

Therapist: (matching Andrew's affect and tone) "That's right! When Mom told you to go outside you felt so mad! You felt like she was just telling you to go away! That made you mad! It felt to you like Mom just wanted to get rid of you!"

Andrew: (looks at therapist with wide eyes, groans, and dramatically drops his head down onto the couch next to mother)

Therapist: (leans forward, touches Andrew's arm, and speaks in a soft voice, looking into Andrew's eyes) "When Mom sent you outside, you thought she was saying she just wanted you to go away from her. You thought she just wanted to get rid of you."

STEP 3: THE THERAPIST EMPATHIZES WITH THE CHILD'S BELIEF.

When the underlying belief has been sufficiently identified, the next step is empathizing with that belief. Without stating that the belief is true, express to the child how hard it must be to feel that way.

Therapist: "It must be so hard, Andrew, to think that your mom just wants you to go away. To think that your mom might have wanted to get rid of you."

Andrew: (curls up his body, looking like a much younger child)

Therapist: "Oh, that's so sad, Andrew. So sad to think mom just wanted to get rid of you. Maybe it feels just like all the other moms. All those moms were nice to you. And then they got rid of you. They told you to go away." **[Attunement disruption continues: Andrew feels disconnected from his mother.]**

STEP 4: THE THERAPIST NORMALIZES THE CHILD'S BEHAVIOR WITHIN THE CONTEXT OF THE BELIEF.

Validate the child's feelings and behavior, emphasizing that they are a natural result of the uncovered belief. It is important that *the child's belief should not be validated.* We do not want to send the message to the child that we agree with the belief, particularly because these beliefs are most often based on negative self-images and strong feelings of shame.

> Therapist: "Well, no wonder you got so mad at your mom. You thought she was saying she just wanted to get rid of you just like all those other moms. No wonder you got so mad and swore at her .... Makes sense to me .... If I'd had so many moms and thought this mom wanted to get rid of me, I'd feel pretty scared, Andrew, and having that *scared* feeling might make me mad." **[Attunement disruption continues: Andrew is feeling rejected by his mom, stirring up shameful anger and fear.]**

STEP 5: THE THERAPIST EXPLORES THE DEEPER IMPLICATIONS OF THE CHILD'S INNER BELIEF.

Explore the child's belief at a deeper level. Verbalize the implication behind the child's belief. State aloud what it would mean about the child, others, the world, if the child's belief were true.

> Therapist: "How sad, Andrew. If this mom wanted to get rid of you just like all the other moms, that would mean ... no one wanted you, Andrew. That would mean no one knew how to take care of you, Andrew."
>
> Andrew: (begins to cry and moves away from mother) **[Attunement disruption continues.]**

STEP 6: THE THERAPIST EMPATHIZES WITH THE IMPLICATION OF THE CHILD'S BELIEF.

> Therapist: (reaches out again to Andrew, hand on his arm) "So sad, Andrew. You've had way too many moms. Too many moms for any boy. So sad. It must be so confusing, Andrew. You must just not know what to do with this." **[Attunement disruption continues: Andrew is in the depths of despair now, feeling alone, unwanted, and far away from emotional connection.]**

This is the opportunity for the parent to provide some empathy for the child and his or her feelings. Even though the parent was there and heard the previous conversation, the therapist and the child repeat for the parent what they discussed. The parent then has the opportunity to empathize with the child's belief and the implications of the belief. The parent stays with the child through the sadness, without trying to convince the child not to feel the way s/he does. After the parent has empathized with the child, the parent will have the opportunity to gently correct the child's belief by communicating what the parent experienced, felt, and meant to communicate. In this manner, the misinterpretation by the child, the behavioral manifestation of the child's negative and distorted internal working model, is corrected. **[Repair of healthy attunement with parent.]**

> Therapist: (leaning in so that she can look at Andrew's eyes and speak softly) "Andrew, I think we need to tell your mom about how you were feeling. What do you think?"
>
> Andrew: (sneaks a glance toward mom and covers his head)
>
> Therapist: "I wonder what mom might say ...."
>
> Andrew: "I don't want to talk about it."
>
> Therapist: "I'll help you out with talking to Mom. I have an idea. I'll say the words for you and you can just watch mom's face and eyes and see what she says."
>
> Andrew: (sits up, moves to the far end of the couch, sneaks glances at his mother)
>
> Therapist: (places a hand on Andrew's arm to help him feel connected and to help him stay with them) "So, Mom, Andrew and I just had a really important conversation here. And Andrew and I learned something really important about what he was feeling yesterday. We want to share that with you."
>
> Mrs. Randall: "Well, I can't wait to learn something more about Andrew's feelings too."
>
> Therapist: "Okay, Andrew, I'll talk to Mom for you. Are you ready? Don't forget to watch Mom's eyes." (turns to Mrs. Randall, keeps a hand on Andrew's knee) "Mom, yesterday I got really mad at you."
>
> Mrs. Randall: (nods) "I know. You sure were mad at me."

Therapist: "Well, Mom, I got so mad because I got scared. When you stopped paying attention to me when the Johnstons were over, I was mad because I wanted to you to pay attention to me. And then you told me to go outside, and I thought you just wanted to get rid of me. Mom, sometimes I get scared thinking you just want to get rid of me just like all those other moms I had. Sometimes I'm scared you'll just think I'm a bad boy and want me to go away like all those other moms."

Mrs. Randall: "Oh, Andrew. That makes me so sad that you were feeling that way. You've had too many moms, Andrew. It makes *me* mad that all those other moms got rid of you. No wonder sometimes you think I just want to get rid of you." **[Repair of attunement in process.]**

Therapist: (still speaking for Andrew) "Well, do you want to get rid of me, Mom?"

Andrew: (looks expectantly at mother)

Mrs. Randall: "Oh, no Andrew! Your dad and I love you very much and we're going to keep you with us. We're not getting rid of you, Andrew. You've had a lot of moms, and that's just so scary. But no way! We are not getting rid of you!"

Andrew: (giggles and hops up on his knees on the couch) **[Attunement repair continues.]**

Therapist: (keeps her hand on Andrew to help him stay, and continues to speak for him) "But, Mom, why did you stop paying attention to me? Why did you send me away, outside?"

Mrs. Randall: "Well, Andrew, sometimes I have to talk to other people or do other things and then I can't be with you right at that minute. But, I do not want you to go away from our family. How hard that must be for you to think that." (She puts her arm around Andrew, draws him in closer to her.)

STEP 8: THE THERAPIST CO-CREATES NEW MEANING FOR THE CHILD'S BEHAVIOR.

Therapist: "So when Mom had to talk with the Johnstons and couldn't pay attention to you, you started running all around the house, then when Mom sent you outside you threw rocks at the house and swore at Mom. You were scared and thinking mom wanted to get rid of you like all those other moms. My goodness, that's why you were running around and swearing! You were upset and really scared that you would have to leave Mom and Dad. Now I understand!"

Mrs. Randall: (cuddles Andrew closer, he relaxes and sighs) **[Attunement repair successful.]**

Therapist: "Next time you feel that way, can you tell Mom right away, 'Mom I'm feeling bad—or scared inside. Something's not right.' Then Mom can help you try to figure it out."

The therapist creates opportunities for parent and child to feel close and enjoy one another.

We know that feeling close and sharing joyful experiences build human bonds. In fact, positive parent-child play is a requirement for secure attachment. The persistent inability of parent and child to play together signals the demise, or potential demise, of the relationship. To build attachment, the therapist must know how to be playful so as to help parents lighten their children's hearts and bring hope to their struggle to get out of trauma-based interactions. And when Dyadic Developmental Psychotherapy is underway, play can provide a break from the hard trauma work by nurturing and rejuvenating the soul.

PLAY TO BRING SOME RELIEF FROM THE HARD STUFF
Take opportunities to give the child a break during the session. Many times the parent can be involved in creating this break, bringing the parent and child closer together. The therapist may comment to the parent, "Have you noticed how many freckles your son has? I wonder if you could count those freckles." The therapist may be more direct, noticing the child squirming and appearing to need a break and the parent with his or her arm around the child. "Why don't you just snuggle a minute there with your mom. Mmm, that feels good. Mom knows just the right way to hug you and hold you."

Or the therapist might engage in playful competition with the parent.

Therapist: "I think I'll keep your boy here with me today."

Parent: "No way. He's mine and I'm taking him with me."
(A light, playful and gentle tug of war with the child ensues, in which the parent, of course, wins.)

Therapist: "Boy, you sure aren't going to let him go."

STORIES AND MUSIC

Use stories and music to promote closeness between parent and child. There are a variety of children's books with attachment themes. Reading such a book to their child, allows the parent to create the intimate connection described in the story while they are sitting close and gazing at or touching one another. Music can also be a helpful medium for evoking strong emotions. After parent and child have worked hard together to process past traumas, overcome challenges to their relationship, and experience some repair, music can even further deepen the moment and help to integrate the experience for both parent and child. Such a touching moment, with parent and child sitting together, the parent holding the child while listening to an evocative song that expresses loving emotions, often surprises the most defensive of parents when they feel their heart softening to their child. One of our client's adoptive parents said that this was the first time her newly adopted daughter had let her get close enough to cuddle her. Some children need concrete tools in order to enhance closeness with their parents.

> Jenny was an eight-year-old child adopted from China. Jenny came to her adoptive parents at eight months old. Jenny felt as though she never had any nice times with her adoptive mother. She was very stuck in this feeling, and despite the intense work that occurred in her treatment and her mother's reassurances, Jenny continued to express this feeling, saying, "I never get to do anything nice with Mom." Jenny's therapist and mother continued to do much hard work with Jenny around her feelings of shame, abandonment, profound loss, and sadness. Jenny's therapist decided that Jenny needed tangible evidence that she and her mother had many special times together right from the beginning of her adoption. During therapy, the therapist and Jenny's mother helped Jenny develop a "Jenny and Mommy" book. This book was separate from Jenny's lifebook or general photo album and only focused on Jenny and her mother's relationship. Jenny's mother brought in photographs of the two of them from the time Jenny came to live with the family. Jenny, her mother, and the therapist looked through the pictures and noted the closeness shown in the photos, commenting on how her mom was holding her, the way they looked into one another's eyes, and the way they smiled, laughed, and played together in the photos. The photos were then placed in the book with comments and descriptions. If they did not have a photo for an event, they drew a picture. Sometimes during sessions, when Jenny and her mother shared a special moment, the therapist took a Polaroid® picture and placed that into the book with the date and description. After the book was started, there

were occasions when Jenny would be feeling sad and ask for the "Jenny and Mommy" book to look through so she could "remember nice things" with her mother.

The therapist supports the parent as the primary protector of the child.

Provide education to parents on issues that relate to child development, attachment, and trauma, and help them understand the importance of increasing attunement and decreasing shame in their efforts to help their child heal. Communicate to the parent that the parent is the one person who knows the individual child the best and also is the one who is most essential to that child's healing. This attitude is also conveyed to the child. Frequently turn to the parent during a session to check in with the parent about how he or she is feeling about the child, the difficult experiences the child has lived through, the hard emotions the child is presently experiencing, and so on. Make sure the child observes the check-in with the parent and hears the parent's response. The therapist may also convey this message to the child in a playful manner with such statements as "Gosh, Mom, you sure know your boy so well!" or, to the child directly, "I'm sure glad your mom was with you when you were having such sad feelings. She's really a smart mom and knows just what you need." The child needs to experience the parent as the comforter and healer whenever possible. It is crucial for both parent and child that the parent take on this essential role. It empowers the parent who the child will then experience as capable, protective, and comforting–in other words, the child's safe haven. Then, the parent's positive experience of being the child's safe haven ("Wow! I'm an effective parent and my child needs me.") will evoke feelings of love and increase the parent's devotion to the child. Feeling more competent, the parent will likely initiate similar healing and supportive interactions when the child needs them at home.

The therapist demonstrates to the child and parent that no topics are off-limits and that trauma and pain will be dealt with in an honest, truthful, and empathic manner.

Children who have experienced early trauma often experience a profound sense of shame. This feeling of shame can be triggered by certain events and any negative affect. Children with such histories often feel overwhelmed by their own intense negative affect and may have fears that no one else can handle or manage those feelings. The therapist should begin early in the treatment to demonstrate his or her ability to handle such feelings. Accept the multitude of emotions the child experiences and make no attempt to eliminate those emotions. Shame often leads the child to attempt to avoid difficult topics and negative affect. It creates a relational break manifested by resistance. Accept the child's resistance and empathize with why it would be a difficult topic for the child to discuss. Do not, then, stay away from the subject, but realize that it may be time to give the child a break in the difficult work and become more playful in order to repair or heal the relationship before returning to the shame-inducing topic.

When children have experienced severe trauma, the adults in their lives often avoid discussing the trauma with them. Believing they are protecting the child, these adults are unwittingly supporting the child's distorted belief that he or she should actually feel shame about those experiences and that it is not acceptable to talk about the trauma. In addition, the child may learn that adults are not emotionally able to handle such topics and conclude that she is alone when attempting to understand the trauma.

> Veronica was a 13-year-old child adopted through the child welfare system. She had been adopted after spending about 14 months in the pre-adoptive foster home, and treatment began about two months after her adoption was final. Veronica had lived with her teenage birth mother and several siblings until they were removed from the mother's care for neglect when Veronica was about two years old. Veronica and her siblings remained in care, moving among relatives until they were returned to their birth mother when Veronica was five years old. The children were again removed from the birth mother when Veronica was seven years old, after a younger sibling, a boy named Jordan, was drowned in the bathtub. The perpetrator was suspected to be the birth mother, but she was never prosecuted. Veronica lived in three foster homes after the second removal before being placed with her adoptive family.

> During the four years between the time Jordan died and the time Veronica entered into treatment with her therapist, no one had spoken directly with her about her brother's death. No one had shared with her the known facts, asked her how she felt about it, or helped her honor the memory of her sibling. During the course of Veronica's treatment, her therapist began to speak with her about her brother. The therapist helped her remember special things about Jordan and, together with Veronica's foster mother, they wrote a poem about Jordan and drew pictures of

his life. The therapist, Veronica's mother, and Veronica lit a candle in memory of Jordan and concluded the session with a prayer offered by Veronica's mother.

Therapist: "Veronica, do you know how Jordan died?"

Veronica: (begins to cry, shakes her head) "No, and I'm not supposed to tell anyone."

Therapist: (in an accepting tone) "Veronica, if you don't know, how could you tell anyone?"

Veronica: (crying harder, head in her hands) "I don't know." (barely audible) "I don't know."

When Veronica's brother died, Veronica had been away for the weekend with an aunt. She returned to the home to see Jordan taken away in an ambulance. Her older brother and sister had told her not to tell anyone what had happened, but Veronica actually never knew what had occurred.

Veronica's mother gently placed her arms around Veronica's shoulders and softly stroked her hair and kissed her head. The therapist allowed space for Veronica to be comforted by her mother. Then after both her mother and therapist empathized with how hard it would be keeping a secret you did not know, the therapist asked Veronica if she would like to know more.

Therapist: "Veronica, would you like your mother and me to tell you what we know about how Jordan died?"

Veronica: (nods her head and sits up, still leaning her body against her mother)

The therapist and her mother honestly and gently tell Veronica that Jordan drowned in the bathtub. He was only three years old and may have been left alone to take a bath without an adult watching and slipped under the water, but no one knew for sure.

Veronica: (looks at her mother) "I thought so. I thought my birth mom did it. Sometimes she used to put Jordan in the tub under the water when he was being bad."

Veronica's mother reported that Veronica was calmer following this session and soon began talking openly about what had gone on in the home with her birth family and in other foster homes. She began to spontaneously bring up these issues in her home as well as during sessions.

The therapist should ensure that the implied feelings during a session are made explicit for the child and parent. Take every opportunity to make a parent and child aware when they are connecting with one another. "Do you feel your mother loving you through the touch of her hand on your back?" Now the child is less able to dissociate and distance herself from the parent's touch and the present moment.

Veronica had spent the first several sessions crying when the therapist identified some of her underlying beliefs and when empathy was expressed for those feelings. The therapist attempted to help Veronica and her mother connect by encouraging her to look in her mother's eyes when the foster mother expressed empathy for Veronica's experiences and feelings. Veronica spent many sessions unable to do this. The therapist empathized with Veronica's need to protect herself by not looking at her mother and pointed out other ways in which the mother's love was being expressed, like the feel of her hand and the sound of her voice. Then the therapist congratulated Veronica on letting in mom's love in those ways.

In the fifth session, Veronica finally said, "Sometimes when my mom says she loves me, I think she's lying." The therapist praised Veronica for shar-ing her feeling and worked to move to a deeper level. When the therapist encouraged Veronica to look at her mother while Mom empathized with her feelings, she still could not do so. But again, the therapist made ex-plicit to both Veronica and her mother the ways in which her mother was loving her and expressing her feelings to her in that moment, and again congratulated Veronica for taking in her mother's love in those ways.

Prior to the eighth treatment session, Veronica's mother told the therapist that Veronica's birth mother would tell her things like "I just don't know what to do with you, baby. I just don't know what you need." And so Veronica's mother feared that Veronica believed that no one knew how to take care of her and admitted that sometimes she herself would ask Veronica "How can I help you?" Even though she meant it to be empathic, it may have reinforced to Veronica that no one knew what she needed. During the session, the therapist took an opening to explore this.

Therapist: "I wonder if you think no one knows how to take care of you. Not this mom, not your birth mom, not any of the moms you've had."

Veronica: (begins to cry, nods her head)

Therapist: "That's so sad, Veronica. That is so sad to think that no one knows how to take care of you. That must feel so lonely and scary." (turns to the mother) "Mom, you know sometimes Veronica just feels no one knows how to take care of her, that no one knows what she needs."

Mother: "Veronica, that makes me so sad to think that you feel no one knows how to take care of you. You must feel so scared when you're feeling that way. I want to work real hard, Veronica, to show you I know how to take care of you. I love you very much, and I do know what's best for you. I know that's hard for you to believe since you've had to move so much and no one so far has really known how to take care of you. But, I'm going to do it. I love you, and I'm going to take care of you."

Therapist: "Wow, Veronica. Mom just said some really special things to you. I'm going to ask her to say them again, and I want you to look right at Mom's eyes to see if she really means the words she's saying."

Veronica: (looks in her mother's eyes and maintains a loving gaze while mom repeats her words; the two hold hands)

Therapist: (softly) "Veronica, what did you see? Did Mom mean those words she said? Did her eyes show love?"

Veronica: (with tears glistening in her eyes, but still maintaining the gaze with her mother, nods her head)

Therapist: (bringing out the significance of this experience, speaks in an excited whisper) "Veronica! I am so happy for you right now. You did it. You looked into your mother's eyes and you saw her love." (turns to Veronica's mother) "She did it, Mom. She looked into your eyes and saw your love."

Veronica: (smiles, looks down, then looks back at her mother)

Mother: (touches Veronica's shoulder, looks into her eyes) "Yeah, I saw that. She looked in my eyes and saw my love." (She pulls Veronica close for a hug and a kiss on the top of her head.)

> *The therapist attends to the here and now for information about the child's feelings, beliefs, and experience.*

Not only do we use past experience as targets for exploration, but we also notice and talk about the child's reaction to us, the parent, and to the experience of therapy. Withdrawn, avoidant, bossy, hyperactive, suspicious, or overfamiliar behaviors (naming just a few) toward the therapist or a parent in a session can trigger questions or comments about the child's inner world or way of coping with stress.

For example, in her first session, a child reaches out to give the therapist a hug.

> Therapist: "Oh my! You must think I'm just like your mother! You've had so many, any lady is the same. Goodness. We'll have to help you learn that hugs are just for moms."

Another example is Terrance, who still bends his head down and shrugs his shoulders when asked a question about himself even though we are past the beginning sessions of therapy. While the therapist used to guess the answer and Terrance would nod or shake his head, it was time now for him to put his thoughts and feelings into his own words and "own" them. But he avoided it.

> Therapist: "Terrance! You can't talk to me? You can't answer? Are you still worried about telling me what you're thinking?"
>
> Terrance: (shakes head, looks away)
>
> Therapist: "Goodness! This is really hard for you. I wonder what makes it hard for you to talk to me. Maybe you think I won't like you anymore if you tell me you're mad at your father. Maybe you think I only like polite, nice kids. Or maybe you're afraid of saying the wrong thing and then I'll think you're stupid. Wow! You really must worry about what people think of you. Better not say anything. Let everybody else talk for you. Then they can still like you because they don't really know the real you."

Then there is Jamie, who came into sessions loud, boisterous, and controlling. He searched through drawers for toys, tried to control the topics of discussion, and blustered his way through the session. At one point, when he was talking particularly loud and tough, the therapist responded in kind, matching his angry tone. Jamie hesitated for a second and then laughed.

> Therapist: "Are you trying to be so loud so that it scares me away? Maybe I won't bother you if you sound so mean and angry? Mom, too. Maybe she'll leave you alone and not bug you if you keep talking so tough. Maybe that's what you want."
>
> Jamie: (immediately quiets to a normal voice)
>
> Therapist: "I bet, Mom, that Jamie needed to talk tough when he lived with his birth family. That way, all those strangers who

came to his home might not bother him. It kept people away. I wonder if Jamie really wants to keep you and me away just like those strangers."

Deepening the Treatment

As therapy progresses, the therapist's role broadens to deepen the treatment. The therapist:

- ◼ Helps the child gain access to and experience strong/genuine feelings (grief, loss, anger, rage, fear, helplessness, loneliness, shame).

- ◼ Helps the parent stay emotionally connected to the child while the child experiences strong feelings.

- ◼ Helps the hurting child seek and gain comfort from the parent.

- ◼ Helps the child regulate strong emotion.

- ◼ Gives homework that promotes connection throughout the week.

- ◼ Helps parents use consequences that promote connection.

- ◼ Helps the child develop a new narrative of his life.

- ◼ Helps the parent become aware of and remove blocks to being emotionally connected and responsive to the child.

The therapist helps the child gain access to and experience strong/genuine feelings.

Trauma work involves confronting not only the traumatic event but also the feelings that accompanied the original event (James, 1989; Archer & Burnell, 2003). This can be very painful work. A person who suffers from Post-Traumatic Stress Disorder avoids and defends against overwhelming feelings at all costs. When a child is abused or neglected, the overwhelming feelings of being alone, helpless, violated, rejected, forgotten, or attacked are warded off, denied, or repressed. One sees this in blunted affect, avoidance of topics or situations, and by the unexplained behavioral eruptions at unpredictable moments that surprise the family and sometimes the child. Children who have experienced trauma may put on a happy face, laugh, or smile and look cheerful to the casual observer. Parents may describe their child as happy and good-natured. Healing will not be possible without unlocking and releasing these avoided feelings.

Dyadic Developmental Psychotherapy merges trauma and attachment work when the child experiences strong affect in the presence of the parent and with the parent's emotional support. The therapist, then, must work to reach the affect; that is, the therapist does not only not avoid the hard stuff, but actively works to achieve an intersubjectivity of the experience that allows for the co-regulation of affect, and allows the child to feel the old experience in all its complexity and depth without dysregulating (i.e., experiencing overwhelming emotion).

Ten-year-old Tanya was adopted from China at two years of age. It was thought that her birth family left her in a park in cold weather when she was only a few months old to hopefully be found and cared for as is the way for may Chinese families who have too many daughters. She then lived in an orphanage until adopted. Her parents sought therapy because Tanya, who could be so agreeable and happy outside of home, was prone to highly ambivalent interactions at home in which she would ask for help, then reject it with a raging tantrum. Tanya entered the room all smiles, looking sweet and shy. Her responses were, "okay," "fine," "sure." There was no sign of a tempest brewing, but the therapist had a sense that she was checking him out and carefully hiding any true emotions. As Tanya was lying in her adopted mother's arms so that she could see both Mom and therapist, the therapist began to talk about her early life.

Therapist: "You had a hard life. There you were, a little, little baby, just wanting your mom and dad to take care of you. And your mom did take care of you, just like moms should do. But one day, something awful happened. Your mom bundled you up and took you away from home to a strange place. It was a park. She put you down and left you there. And it was cold. It was winter. Gosh, and you were just so little! You didn't know what was happening except your mom was gone and you were all alone and very cold. You must have wondered, 'Where's my mom? Where's my mom?' You might have been very scared. Babies shouldn't be without their moms. Babies shouldn't be left alone in the cold. Their moms shouldn't leave them. You were so alone."

Tanya: (looks intently at the therapist with tears running down her cheeks, and Mom looks at Tanya with tears running down her cheeks)

Therapist: "That was so sad. No mom and all alone. And then you went to another strange place with strangers and a lot of children and still no mom. Where was your mom? You must have been thinking, 'I don't want to be here. You're not my mom! I want my mommy! Where is she? Mommy, I want you. Come back!'"

Tanya: (now sobbing and Mom is also sobbing, but Tanya is looking at the therapist and Mom is looking at Tanya)

Therapist: "Tanya, look at Mom. Why is she crying? She wasn't left. You were left! Why is Mom crying?" (Tanya is crying so hard that the therapist decides to ask Mom the question for her.) "Mom, why are you crying?"

Mom: "Children shouldn't be left. You are so wonderful. How could your mom leave you? How could she do that? I would never to that to a child. Never!" (mother and child hold each other while sobbing)

Mom told the therapist afterward that she had never seen Tanya sob like that. This was the first time she let out deep feelings of loss and abandonment.

Sometimes, a child wards off all negative affect, reversing or denying the "bad" ways he feels about himself, birth parents, prior caregivers, or new parents. In other words, the child's overwhelming sense of shame causes the child to hide his feelings.

Wally lived on and off with his young, disorganized, and irresponsible mother until he was four years old. His birth mom would periodically leave him with other relatives who themselves showed at best questionable and at worst inadequate parenting ability. When he had needs, he would be laughed at, made fun of, and otherwise humiliated and rejected for having normal needs for comfort and protection. Finally, relatives were called to rescue this child who entered their home afraid to talk or do much of anything. He was withdrawn and fearful and had few self-help skills. As the family worked together in therapy, he was reluctant to let himself feel mad at his new mom, his new dad, or at his therapist. With a frightened look on his face, he shook his head "no" when asked if he was feeling mad, or briefly acknowledged some anger only to smile and say that now it was now okay. He was also very reluctant to verbalize his thoughts. And when he began to sense that a bad feeling was coming up, he would reach for his mom's lap to get immediate comfort and protection from having to feel more. Mom was an excellent nurturer, and responded as most moms would by holding him and soothing his anxiety.

The therapist discussed with his parents the importance of Wally's allowing negative thoughts and feelings to come out, and they agreed to support this goal. When Wally showed avoidance and discomfort at the topic of discussion, the therapist helped Wally express his disavowed thoughts and feelings. Wally avoided eye contact and squirmed, overwhelmed by his fear to experience such feelings of shame. He moved himself into Mom's lap, while the therapist continued to put into words Wally's unspoken feelings. The therapist's voice got softer, saying that this was really hard for him and that the therapist knew he really wanted the feelings to go away. The therapist continued to encourage him to say how mad he was that the therapist kept talking about hard things. But still he was mute. The therapist continued speaking for him, words she believed he was feeling. "I'll bet you're thinking 'I don't want to talk about this any more!'" Since Wally had learned to appease adults, and avoid harm with politeness and deference, it was frightening for him to try to say how he actually was feeling. After much reassurance that his feelings were okay, and that he would not be harmed if he said how he felt, he was eventually able to nod that he would like the therapist not to talk about such hard things. Within the safety of his mom's lap, his quiet alert state let everyone know that he was taking it all in, unable yet to speak, but aware and listening. The therapist continued to connect past with present, acknowledging how hard it was to say how he really felt, since he used to be hurt by grown-ups when he did tell them what he needed. Wally had been avoiding his negative feelings all these years. As a small child, he couldn't be mad at his caregivers. He would have been ridiculed, humiliated, or emotionally abandoned. Numbing his feelings was a logical way to cope in the past, but was neither healthy nor appropriate in this family now. Wally needed the corrective experience of acceptance, attunement, and empathy for saying to us and feeling what he couldn't as a young child.

The therapist helps the parent stay emotionally connected to the child while child experiences strong feelings.

Your job, as therapist, will be to model for and help the parent stay emotionally "with" the child while the child is in the grip of strong emotions like Wally's, without you yourself becoming dysregulated. If you cannot tolerate strong affect, then you will not be able to help the family. The parent's role is crucial here. It is a corrective experience when the victim does not feel alone physically or emotionally, but instead feels "held" while in the pain of past or present. This experience is a requirement in both trauma and attachment therapy. Feeling this pain within the context (within the "arms") of a safe relationship is part of creating a secure base for the child. Being held and regulated by a caring adult (co-regulation of emotion) is the precursor of future self-regulation.

Allan Schore (2003) states that the inability to regulate intense emotions is one of the most damaging and far-reaching effects of early relational trauma. Being able to regulate one's emotions means being able to experience intense affect and coping with it in a productive fashion. It means delaying one's response in order to take in information. In the face of strong emotion, a regulated individual will think before acting. Dysregulation manifests as disruptive behaviors that discharge emotion, such as yelling, blaming, hitting, grabbing, spanking, and threatening, to name a few. These are antithetical to achieving a secure bond.

> Mom feels her insides start to tighten in the session when Tommy gets mad about her limits and says, "I hate you. You're not my real mom anyway. I'd be happier if I'd stayed with her. I hate living with you!"
>
> Mom might have been tempted to respond in kind: "You are so ungrateful! I do everything for you. Your birth mom did nothing, and I'm wearing myself out to be a good mom to you. You don't know how good you have it. If you think she's so great, go back to your birth mom and find out."
>
> But Mom doesn't say any of that. Instead, she takes a breath and remembers that it is normal for kids to get mad when parents set limits. She was there once herself. She also remembers that adopted kids happen to have a birth mother to hold over the adoptive mom, hoping to evoke guilt and a counterattack, and that as an adoptive mom, she is susceptible to feeling preempted by the birth mom and more insecure as Tommy's mom. Then she remembers telling her own mom long ago in anger that she "wasn't fair" and wished she had another mom because other moms let their daughters do what they want to do. Then Mom remembers that all her son needs at this moment is to know that she will not be destroyed or devastated by his anger, that she will still be his mom, and that they can survive this tense moment in their relationship. Mom softens. She has regulated her emotions and will, in turn, be able to help Tommy regulate his.

To help parents stay connected, the therapist models the following with the child: maintaining eye contact, physical contact, emotional attunement, acceptance for feelings, matching of feelings, and offering comfort with messages of safety.

The therapist must stay emotionally regulated. To help parents connect with their child directly, the therapist may put an arm around the parent's shoulder, offer comforting words to the parent, and reassure that the child's feelings are those of the past projected onto the present, distorting the child's current experience. Some parents will need help to get quiet in the face of their child's pain and to just allow their child to feel. They don't have to say anything if they are cuddling their child. The child will feel their presence, and, at this time, it is often the feel of the parent's presence as witness that will touch them more than words. Often the parent begins to have feelings too. We support parents crying *with* their children, and sometimes *for* their children if the child is blocked from feeling. No one should be suppressing strong emotion that could bring people closer together.

The therapist helps the hurting child seek and gain comfort from the parent.

When the child is feeling emotional pain, encourage physical contact and comforting. As the child and parent go through an attachment sequence, there will be a point at which the child will feel deeply an uncomfortable emotion that the child prefers to avoid: loneliness, shame, rejection, fear. This is the child's most vulnerable moment. It is also the moment the child most needs the parent. Although this may also be the moment most difficult for the parent, staying connected is crucial. The child needs to feel that the parent is present while s/he is feeling such pain. The child needs to feel the parent's love even though the child may be feeling shameful, disgusting, bad, or worthless. The parent's touch and loving gaze will begin to undo the child's negative self-concept. "If Mom and Dad still love me, even while I'm feeling so disgusting and vile, then maybe I'm not really so bad after all." The child is likely to need repeated experiences of unconditional love before s/he begins to feel and to truly believe that s/he is valuable and lovable.

Giving comfort at this critical moment does not mean reassuring the child that s/he is lovable or that "it's okay." The parent needs to allow the child's negative feelings to continue and to resonate with those feelings. In other words, to achieve an attuned state within which affect is shared and meaning develops, therapist and parent maintain empathy and let the child's emotions just "be." It is a time for sensitivity, patience, and great respect for the child's pain. Sometimes parents cry, and that is just fine. Pain shared is more manageable than pain borne alone.

The therapist helps the child regulate strong emotion.

Infants learn to regulate affect when they experience attunement from a regulated adult. It is the therapist's state of self-regulation while staying attuned to the child that will help the child develop the capacity to maintain affective self-regulation. When the child experiences the strong affect described in the previous sections, the child must be supported through it by an emotionally regulated therapist and parent. We regulate a child's emotions in a variety of ways. Regulation is maintained by the therapist and parent when they stay emotionally connected to the child while the child is in the grip of strong feelings; the child in emotional pain needs to receive comfort from the parent and therapist throughout the entire session. During the attachment sequence, maintaining emotional connection through interactive play and humor can be a natural way to take a break from hard topics. Humor can prevent the tension from becoming overwhelming. Or, we might tell the child to take a deep breath before continuing with hard work. Switching from face-to-face exploration of a topic to psychodrama, drawings, or other forms of expression can reduce tension. Sometimes a massage helps, and parents can be taught, after a demonstration on themselves, to gently massage the child's arms and hands.

Some children will need help with positive emotions. They get too giddy and silly when having fun, so overexcited and nervous that they are not really having a positive experience at all. The therapist may need to slow down the pace and exude calmness, patience, and the competence to take charge of an escalating situation. Verbal reassurance and/or physical closeness can help regulate and calm escalating emotions. The therapist's calm emotional state will help the child regulate.

The therapist gives homework that promotes connection throughout the week.

Creative homework assignments can help parent and child maintain emotional connection between sessions and give them practice at having positive experiences with each other. Assignments can involve play, touch, nurturing, using nonverbal signs to communicate, surprises, songs, and more.

> Leslie and her mom seemed to have little time after school and after work to share pleasure together. The therapist challenged them to a competition: Who could initiate the most "special

moments" that had to involve touch, eye contact, and either play or nurturing?

When children do not seem to be getting much healthy, warm touch from parents, the therapist may coach the parents to find any excuse and grab any moment to tousle their child's hair, beep a nose, squeeze shoulders, give a fast hug-and-release (before the child can reject or avoid it), touch a hand, or any of the myriad of other avenues to warm, affectionate physical connection. This should never be done in a teasing or suggestive way, of course. The therapist should check in the next session to see how the homework went. Asking the dyad to show you how they sang the song or fed each other can be a good idea until you are confident the parent can lead the interaction in a healthy way. More good homework ideas can be found in *I Love You Rituals* (Bailey, 2000) and *Theraplay* (Jernberg & Booth, 1999).

The therapist helps parents use consequences that promote connection.

The therapist will also help parents develop consequences that are relational. That is, consequences which have meaning to the relationship and have the potential to bring parent and child closer together. For example, instead of "time-out" or "grounding," a child who needs his parent to take time away from other responsibilities to deal with his problem may have to "give time back" by doing a chore for Mom or Dad or helping to make dinner, clean up the table, fix what was broken, or other comparable task. For a child with attachment issues, "time-in" can be highly meaningful. Time-in means more time with Mom or Dad; staying close by and in clear view while parents are doing their chores. Not only is the child in clear view of the parent, but the parent is in clear view of the child, which meets the child's attachment need to be able to check in with the parent and maintain connection. Rather than being separated from the parent when the child disappoints, the child with attachment issues needs closeness. The child should be helped to repair any breaks in relationships whenever possible. Relationship breaks may occur with a parent, a sibling, or another family member—even a pet. The child should be helped to ask the offended party what might help increase the feeling of trust and caring. Or the child can be asked to think of what can be done for the hurt party that would help that person feel better, and to also feel better about the child.

Through the process of Dyadic Developmental Psychotherapy, the child develops a new narrative of his/her life, thereby resolving abuse or trauma and earning a secure attachment. There are a variety of techniques that a therapist can use to facilitate this goal.

CREATING STORIES ABOUT THE CHILD'S LIFE

The therapist helps parents create stories that reveal to the child parts of the child's life or the life the child should have had. The telling of these stories can promote the attachment process and also shift the child's beliefs about himself and others from negative to positive. We have found this to be an extremely valuable bonding experience for both parent and child. The typical leading line for this narrative is, "If you had been my baby when you were born, I would have ..." and the parent describes all the care, attention, and love the child would have received from day one. It is an opportunity for nurturing and allowing the child, if he or she wants, to be a baby in his mother's or father's arms, helpless, vulnerable, and pure.

> Mother: (Mikey's mother holds him, cradled in her lap.)
> "Mikey, if you had been my baby, I would have held you in my arms just like this, and looked at you and looked at you. I would have never been able to take my eyes off of you. I would have taken such good care of you. If you were wet, I would have changed you. And when you were hungry, I would have fed you warm milk from a bottle. I would have held you close and watched you while you were drinking your milk ... and, when you looked at me, I would be smiling right back at you. When you were tired, I would gently put you in your crib and cover you with a small blanket. And I would be there when you started to roll over, and I would be so excited to see you do that. Then I would be so happy when you started to sit up by yourself. My little baby is sitting up! I would be telling everybody that you could sit up all by yourself. I would play peek-a-boo and pat-a-cake with you, and count your toes and fingers. I would give you a bath in the sink because you were so little. Oh, and I would be taking pictures of you all the time, in your handsome clothes. I would take pictures of you eating with your fingers, and maybe getting your first taste of cake all over your face and hands! I would take a picture of you learning to drink from a sippy cup. I would be so proud! And then you would start

crawling, and then walking. Oh, I would be so excited and proud. I'd take you to the doctor for checkups and find out how much you had grown and how many teeth you had. And I'd brag to my friends about you. And you would recognize my favorite songs and lullabies because I'd sing them to you every night. And I'd give you a kiss good night every night. I would take such good care of you. I would always pick you up if you were sad or if you got hurt, and I'd kiss you to make you feel better. Oh, I would be so happy to be your mother! And I would be so happy you were my son!"

Some children feel less threatened if the parent tells the story in the third person, for example, "If Mikey had been with me when he was a baby, I would have held him in my arms just like this and looked at him ...." Or others may do well if the parent tells the story in the third person while sitting across from the child holding a baby doll and caring for the doll. For other children, any direct experience of intimacy is too frightening, as in the following case of Lucy.

> Lucy was a seven-year-old girl adopted from an orphanage in Romania at the age of five. When the therapist and Lucy's mother attempted to have her lie in her mother's arms for a claiming narrative during a treatment session, she became very dysregulated, and the focus of the rest of the session was on helping her calm and return to a regulated state. The following week, mother and therapist conducted an alternate variation of this technique. They made it into a game. First they "played" that Lucy was a baby alone in the crib in the orphanage. Then they "played" as if she had been her mother's baby. While she "napped" in the play crib, her mother ingeniously pretended to receive a phone call from a friend. She then proceeded to tell that friend all about her beautiful baby, Lucy. She elaborated on Lucy's beautiful hair and skin and how she enjoyed counting her 10 toes and 10 fingers. She told her friend how Lucy giggled and smiled at her that day and how just being with her, playing with her, feeding her and changing her was such a joy. In the following week's session, when Lucy's father was present, her mother and therapist were delighted when Lucy asked, "Can we play that game again about me being your baby?" Once again, they created the scene. This time when "baby" Lucy napped, mother and father together gazed at their lovely daughter and spoke to one another about the joys of caring for her.

PSYCHODRAMA

Bobby's parents used psychodrama to show him how he should have been protected from abuse as a young boy.

Bobby had been maliciously mistreated by his parents' friend who had been staying with them. Although his parents knew of this some time after it happened, Bobby brought it up in therapy years afterward. The therapist pointed out to his parents that when a child repeatedly brings up a traumatic event, it usually means it has not been resolved. The therapist told the parents that Bobby needed to feel they were on his side as he lamented about how he was treated, and that they needed to feel as angry as—or angrier than—he toward this friend and her actions. His parents agreed to participate in a drama in which the friend was accused and tried by a judge and lawyer (played by the therapist), and Bobby and his parents insisted and fought for the maximum penalty against the friend for Bobby's emotional abuse. At the therapist's urging, the parents became more and more expressive and emphatic in voicing to "the court" their outrage at what the friend had done. After being loud and demanding to the court in defense of Bobby's needs, his parents became quiet and serious. They told Bobby they were so sorry that the abuse happened by a friend and under their roof, that such a thing should never happen to children and that it was not his fault. They told him they would make sure it would never happen again. And they told him that they loved him, and hugged him quietly. Bobby never brought up the topic again.

TIME LINES

Making a visual picture of the child's life can help the child better understand some of the realities of the child's past. You can use computer paper, or separate pages or cards that can be laid out in a row. Draw a line that starts at birth and mark out each year of the child's life. Use a different color for each placement, even for being with birth mother if only for a day. Then write down whom the child was living with in that placement, why the child moved, and any other information known about what happened then, including things that happened to the child. You can also include how the child felt about that placement by drawing a face with an emotion or by using stickers depicting different feelings. Seeing the parts of one's life can make an impact in ways that words might not. For example, for a child who has been in this current placement for a relatively short time, providing a visual picture could be enlightening:

Therapist: "Look how long you were living in that home. No wonder you've been having a hard time knowing that you won't lose this mom. You've only been in this home for a short time, see? But you were in this other home for much longer."

Another opportunity for visualizing a child's life would be to use pictures of the child at different ages. After making copies of the pictures, lay them out chronologically, and write on the pictures where the child was living and with whom, and what happened there.

DRAWINGS

Drawings can bring to life the dynamics of how the child relates to others. A picture with a wall between parent and child, or a wall around the highly guarded child, can evoke the sadness of separateness and fear. It can lead to an exploration of how the bricks of the wall got there, what the bricks represent, and what it would take to lower and eliminate the wall. You could talk about what is not happening because the wall is there. And you can help the child and parent practice ways to slowly take down the bricks.

You can draw a picture of the child's heart and write in it what makes it hurt. Or you can have the child and parents draw a picture together.

PHOTOS, LIFEBOOKS, VIDEOS

We suggest that parents preserve and keep any mementos of the child's past life. Photos or videos of the child with prior caregivers, birth parents, or orphanage staff (or even just the building) can be invaluable for eliciting the child's history and feelings about the people, places, and events of her life.

Dena's mom had the video of when she got her from the Chinese orphanage. One by one, each baby was brought out to the new parents and transferred from caregiver to the parent's arms. When transferred, Dena started to cry and continued screaming throughout the little ceremony marking this adoption day. No other baby was crying. Dena's screams were poignant and painful to hear. We talked about how terrified she must have been to be given to a perfect stranger who looked so different from any caregiver she had ever known.

There are agencies that can provide you with pictures of certain locations in other countries. Having a picture of the place where the child was abandoned can make the past more real and bring up deeper feelings.

Adoption or Trauma Storybooks

You can also use published books of adoption or trauma stories to evoke feelings and discussions about the child's life. It is sometimes easier to read the story of another person than to talk about one's own painful life. Many good stories are listed in the resource section of this book.

Reviewing the Records

Sometime during the course of therapy, a reading of the child's legal, medical, or child protection services records is important. These are the documents that confirm the facts of the child's life. They can provide a springboard for more exploration of trauma and family disruption. Some programs begin the therapy process with a reading of the records (Archer & Burnell, 2003). It is sometimes better to prepare the child to hear the painful truth. In therapy sessions prior to beginning the review, the therapist and parent should show much empathy toward the birth mother, father, or family. Hearing the "bad news" is easier when it comes from a person who is not seen as harshly judging the neglectful or abusing adults.

Recapping the Session

Summarizing a session before ending can help the child integrate the content and the emotions. The therapist is creating a narrative that the child can hold onto, retell silently or to others, and make part of his/her life story. Developing the summary together at the end of a session, when emotions are no longer high and the child is regulated, makes it more likely to be received, integrated, and remembered. What you are doing is taking a primary experience and helping the child develop a secondary representation of that experience, thereby developing the reflective function.

The therapist helps the parent become aware of and remove blocks to being emotionally connected and responsive to the child.

We all have "buttons." Some of us have many—and more intractable ones—than others. Sometimes the therapist will see or feel that the parent is having trouble with one or more of the elements of PLACE. The parent may maintain emotional distance from the child, have trouble giving empathy, or find it hard to take a curious stance toward problems. The child will read the nonverbal communication from the parent as:

- My parent is not available to me now.

- My parent has gone from me.

- My parent doesn't love me.

- My parent doesn't understand me.

- My parent thinks I'm bad.

- I'm on my own with no one to help me.

- I've ruined my chances with my parent.

- My problems are too big for my parents.

- I am too hard for my parents to take care of.

- My parents want to get rid of me.

- I am hopeless.

- I am worthless.

- No one cares about me.

When such interactions happen, opportunities are lost for improving the relationship between child and parent and for resolving trauma. The more times such experiences happen, the more danger there is that the child will find maladaptive ways to gain protection from painful feelings evoked by the statements listed above. These coping mechanisms solidify attachment and trauma problems, rather than heal them.

When we see blocks to a parent's being therapeutic with their child, we must address this by telling the parent how much the child needs PLACE and exploring what the barriers to providing it might be.

> Shasti was a 14-year-old girl, who had come into foster care with this mother at age six and later was adopted. Shasti never adjusted to or accepted her new mother as her mom. She kept herself distant and aloof. Previous therapy had focused on behaviors only and not on the emotional connection between Mom and child. Now, years later, Shasti was a huge disappointment. Mom came to this therapist feeling that she would never have the relationship with her daughter she had hoped for. She was tired, angry, and critical of Shasti. Although the therapist worked with Mom to help her understand what early neglect and trauma do to a child's ability to relate and trust, and similarly tried to help Shasti soften to her mom, they both remained distant and suspicious of each other. There was no chance that Shasti would risk softening if Mom remained so guarded and critical. In time alone

with Mom, the therapist brought up this impasse and began exploring Mom's own attachment history in which she had been the source of disappointment for her own parents. It was only after Mom could acknowledge her own painful childhood feelings that she began to warm up to Shasti and accept her pain.

Ending Therapy

There will be a time to evaluate whether therapy should end. You will know that trauma and attachment issues are being resolved when:

- The child claims the parents as his/hers and feels a clear sense of security and belonging.
- The child can talk about feelings.
- The child is more comfortable being nurtured by the parent.
- The child can talk realistically about family and adoption.
- The child has a realistic view of the child's own life history.
- The parent can maintain the attitude of PLACE.

When the child claims the parents, the child will no longer reject the parents when they impose strong limits. While the child may of course be angry or argumentative about limits or consequences, the child will not as easily shift to wishing to go back to the birth parent. It is normal for foster or adopted children to periodically feel the loss of the birth parent or prior caregivers, regardless of the strength of their attachment with the new parents. Acceptance of the new parents as parents means that the child asks for help and advice and can make use of the parents' support. It also means that the child can have fun and enjoy good times with these parents. The therapy has created a secure base from which the child can explore the child's inner and outer worlds.

Another indication that it is time to end occurs when the child can talk about feelings, both negative and positive. The child won't be afraid to express opposition to the parent for fear of being rejected or abandoned. Neither will the child hide feelings of sadness, guilt, or fear. In being able to express feelings, the child will be showing that the parents are experienced as a secure base. Breaks in their relationship, when they occur, will be brief and repaired.

The child must be comfortable being nurtured appropriately by the parent. The style of nurturing will, of course, change as the child matures. Yet the parents should be a source of comfort and safety to the child.

You want to see the child readily accept the parent's arm around the shoulder, warm hugs, and loving gaze, and the child should be able to respond in kind. Physical contact between parent and child should feel comfortable and natural.

The child should be able to talk realistically about family (past and present) and adoption. With help, the child should develop ways to talk about these topics that are comfortable and that do not evoke shame.

It is very important that the child be able to talk about painful life experiences in ways that are realistic and with emotional regulation. When a child is able to do this, it signifies the achievement of an earned secure attachment with respect to relationships. It means that the child's past is integrated into a healthy sense of self; it has a place in the child's life but no longer controls it or causes overwhelming shame.

In addition to evaluating the child's attachment to the parent, you also want to assess the parent's ability to maintain the attitude of PLACE because it is this ability that will better ensure that the family will sustain the progress made in therapy.

Does achieving the above criteria mean that the child is "cured"? Past trauma is often never completely cured. Yet it can be increasingly well-integrated into the person's sense of a healthy self. Parents using PLACE can continue to solidify the child's progress on their own. Most often, when all or most of the above criteria are met, then a decision that we have "done all that can be done now" will be made with the knowledge that trauma issues—and sometimes attachment issues—can resurface across time. Because of this, endings should involve normalizing future "tune-ups"—return visits to assess how things are going, what issues have come up, how the parent and child have handled them, and whether the child is able to use the parent as a secure base. The spacing of tune-ups can vary. Initially they can be every two to three months, decreasing after that if things are going well, until yearly tune-ups are adequate.

How do you end therapy? As in any other course of therapy, you start talking about ending first with the parent and then with the child and parent together. You can talk about how this course of therapy went, describing how things were with the child and the family when therapy started and comparing it with what the family has achieved at the end. You will want to appreciate and admire examples of when the family is working well, not just when they are cooperating but when they actually handle a problem effectively. And you will want to have them talk about how they will handle things when future difficulties occur. Practicing may be helpful here. Have the family actually practice phoning you as though it were a time when the parent or the child feels stuck. Play should be part of the ending, too, as well as delighted conversations about how much Dad or Mom and son or daughter have now achieved the look and feel of parent and offspring. Share joy in the birth of this family. It is a profound accomplishment that will affect lives for the better far into the future.

CHAPTER 5

Dyadic Developmental Psychotherapy Working with Unresolved Parents

DEBORAH SHELL

"Children are sensing machines. They know before they have words who we are, whether they can express their anger in front of us, whether they can feel sad with us or joy, and above all, whether they can confide in us." —Dr. Arthur Janov, The Biology of Love

Parents who have experienced traumatic events face a special set of challenges when attempting to parent an abused child. The child's behaviors may trigger the parent's own set of defensive responses, thereby challenging the parent's ability to accurately interpret and respond to the child's need. This issue may be especially germane when attempting attachment therapy, since many of the families referred by social services to seek help through Dyadic Developmental Psychotherapy may themselves harbor unresolved trauma. Some of the more problematic configurations include family-of-origin kinship placements, replacement with birth parents following lengthy foster care separations, parents who are recovered alcoholics or drug addicts, incarcerated birth parents, or foster parents who lacked prior knowledge of the child's history and whose long-term commitment may waiver. Without recognition of personally vulnerable areas of reactivity, parents may inadvertently increase fear in their children, thereby limiting or even preventing attachment development.

When a parent lacks the ability to affectively attune to the child, a cascade of events is set in motion. Whether the inability to accurately assess the child's needs and to respond accordingly is due to parental trauma that resulted in depression, addictions, or issues with domestic violence, the result to the child is the same (Fosha, 2000). Simply put, a parent helps to regulate positive and negative affect by interacting with the child and simultaneously interpreting and giving meaning to shared experience. When a child is deprived of intersubjective experience that both validates and connects, the child is left bereft of a reflected sense of coherent self and lacks an internalized working model of effective interpersonal interaction. Occasional misattunement isn't the issue; it is the frequently inconsistent and inaccurate responses to a child's experience that create problems in attachment. The child's perceived threat of separation from an attachment figure triggers attachment behavior. Normally, when the child's attachment behaviors are most activated, the parent resolves the child's need by attending to the child in ways that comfort and reassure.

Problems in attachment occur when the parent does not consistently respond in ways that resolve the child's stress.

A useful tool for assessment of parental attachment process is The Adult Attachment Interview (Main and Hesse, 1990). Researcher Mary Main found that the best predictor of a child's state of mind with respect to attachment is the parent's. An unresolved attachment style may make it difficult for a parent to remain emotionally and cognitively present when the current situation reminds them of the unresolved person or experience (Hughes, handout). Developed for use as a research tool, the interview's use of questions relating to family-of-origin experience affords additional opportunities to identify and explore areas of potential vulnerability.

A child healing from the trauma of past experiences with abusive caregivers needs a healthy family to provide the counterpoint of stable relationships without threats, violence, or inconsistent responses to the child's needs. Traumatized children present pervasive, provocative, and persistent behaviors, which were learned in the family of origin as defense against the deeply hurtful and damaging effects of maltreatment. Situations fostered by such hurtful environments often result from generations of inappropriate parenting, and it's no wonder that an inability to provide for the physical and emotional health of a child is often also the experience of the family-of-origin caregivers. As many perplexed and disappointed adoptive parents know, simply placing a child in a healthy environment won't automatically change ingrained responses to perceived threats. A child placed with a family whose responses are also complicated by unresolved parental trauma finds it even harder to learn better ways of relating, or worse, reinforces negative beliefs about the nature of caregiver relationships.

As discussed earlier, the effects and responses to trauma reside deep within the brain, in the autonomic nervous system, which almost instantaneously accesses survival mechanisms seemingly without cognitive interpretation. Learning to live and function without these defenses takes a lot of practice! Since the amygdala processes information from the senses in such a way that interpretations of the caregiver's tone of voice, body posture, pupil dilation, and speech cadence can precede cortical interpretation, a child may react defensively even though the intended interaction between parent and child was inherently benign.

We know that even the healthiest environment with all the love in the world won't automatically reverse a child's defenses or deeply ingrained negative internal working models, and to the dismay of many adoptive parents, the child's behavior may worsen. From the child's point of view, one reason to avoid intimacy may be fear of vulnerability. Dependency requires trust. Another reason could be that the child's negative self-image, based on prior experience and/or perceptions of rejection, triggers defenses that fit better with prior experience, i.e. "I'm really a worthless piece of trash and I'll have to work harder to prove this to you, until you treat me the way I'm supposed to be treated."

As therapists, we try to convince parents that the way they respond to their child makes a big difference in whether or not a new kind of relationship, built on trust, will form. The hardest concept to teach is how to respond in ways least likely to reinforce beliefs taught in the family of origin. For example, in a birth home where a child's needs were neglected, the message given by the parent to the child was "You're not worth the effort." If the child was handled roughly in anger, or physically hurt when wet, soiled, hungry, or crying, the message was "Your needs are not valid." Each time the child was moved, the message "I care for something/someone else more than you," and "You're not worth keeping" reinforced a negative self-concept. Most children with such histories believe emotionally they are the cause of their fate. They believe if they had somehow been better babies and children, then they would have been kept.

Some neglected and abused children have so little experience being cherished and loved that they don't even know what healthy relationships are. They don't respond to the most rudimentary interactions in ways that indicate a shared understanding of positive intersubjective experience. Such children may appear normal to an inexperienced social worker, but on the inside, they are so bereft of internal working models of healthy interpersonal experience that once placed in a normal home (not chosen for therapeutic value), they act out and fail to meet expectations that require some prior experience with healthy working relationships. In effect, they create emotional distance because that feels safer than intimacy.

Most of the children brought to us are unable to fit into normal family life without special parental training. Much like the square-peg-in-a-round-hole analogy, children without healthy relationship experience aren't able to slide into family life, and will try to make everyone else square, too!

In my caseload, more parents than not have adopted children with Reactive Attachment Disorder and didn't know it. Many parents with such children suffer from unresolved trauma from their own negative family-of-origin experiences and don't know it until they try to parent their own adopted, Reactive Attachment Disorder child and find it difficult to enact the attachment-facilitating parenting methods we discuss. Others have children in Social Rehabilitative Services custody for reasons of abuse and neglect and are now attempting reunification. These parents are vulnerable to effects of the unresolved trauma issues of their own lives,

which resulted in choices to abuse drugs or alcohol, engage in promiscu-
ous relationships, or allow unstable living situations. They are also reactive to the effects such parenting choices have on their children.

When doing therapy with parents whose unresolved trauma interferes
with the development of healthy relationships, it is necessary to spend
time working through the stages of Dyadic Developmental Psychotherapy with the parent, before attempting to focus mainly on the child.
Try to collaborate with the parent to identify issues the parent struggles
with while developing a framework around how those issues impact
effective responses. In other words, join with the parent and accept their
experience. Helping a parent to personally discover the effects of attunement by my attunement to the parent's underlying emotion (not their
behavior) can help illustrate how the parent can learn to become more
accurate when interpreting his or her child's underlying emotional need.

Polyvagal Theory (Steven Porges, Psychological Science Agenda, 15, 9-11,
2003) describes three neural circuits that regulate behavioral reactivity.
Basically, we're less likely to hear/understand human voice when afraid.
The Parasympathetic nervous system reacts as a primary response to
perceived threats, so when working with a parent who may interpret
probing as threatening, the first priority is to build trust. Not easily accomplished with a parent who lumps the therapist together with authority figures whose power is resented. Parents need to hear the therapist
while they are in as relaxed a state as possible since this is when new
learning can occur. This can be accomplished by expressing curiosity
about and acceptance of their underlying emotion. Tone of voice, the
rhythm and cadence of the therapist's speech, posture, and facial expression are all directed toward demonstrating acceptance of the parent.

Unresolved trauma can make people slippery and seemingly unpredictable. When considering a parent's challenging behaviors (i.e. hitting,
yelling, threatening, emotional blackmail), use Dan Hughes' handout
describing interventions that are not found within the Dyadic Developmental Psychotherapy model of therapeutic treatment or model for
parenting. Going over this with the parent can help depersonalize (i.e.
"These responses are not helpful for children learning to trust"), as well
as to normalize more appropriate responses ("Many parents have
learned to say this, instead"), providing a way to explore in more detail
how to respond more appropriately. Role-play works well for this, with
the therapist taking on the role of abusive parent. Then they can talk
about how the parent felt when treated disrespectfully. Not all parents
are able to recognize by reading handouts, articles or books how they
may perpetuate abuse cycles, partly because most unresolved trauma
seems to defy insight and stays hidden behind blind spots, which are

difficult for people to recognize in themselves. This is one reason that individual work with the parent to address the past trauma and integrate the split-off affect, memories, and experience is often a part of treatment. Discussion generated from a list of detrimental responses can be a nonthreatening therapeutic tool that precedes closer examination of unresolved issues. The pace and therapeutic focus are tailored to fit the specific needs of each parent.

Honesty follows trust. The saddest cases involve those parents who remain fearful, distrustful, and continue to present "as-if" responses to my questions and observations. Without emotional safety, children rarely take the risks of intentional dependency. They continue to demand control, sabotage, and rage. If we can talk openly about the vulnerable times, when a parent has reverted to abusive responses (without blaming the child), then healing progresses for them both.

CASE STUDY ONE

Rose & Traci: A parent personalizes her child's behavior.

Case study one describes one mother's personalized interpretations of her adopted daughter's behavior, as a result of her own unresolved trauma. This mom's internal working models caused her to filter her child's behaviors through a lens that prevented accurate interpretation of her daughter's underlying emotional needs. Interestingly, this mom's trauma-influenced responses had minimal affect on her birth children. They did not reactively respond to mom's issues because issues of abuse and neglect weren't cogent for them the way they were for their adopted sister. The adopted child's own history, and current behaviors enacting that history in the present, triggered the mother's unresolved and split-off trauma. Mom's birth children were sustained by their overall experience of adequate affective-attunement through the course of their lives, while the adopted daughter had no such bank to draw from.

Rose and her pre-adoptive daughter were referred to me by the state Social Services agency due to fears that the placement might fail if the child's behaviors didn't improve. Traci was almost seven years old when she and Rose arrived in my office for help. Rose had a list of behaviors she wanted me to know about and fix. Her biggest concern was why, after Traci had been with them for nearly nine months, she had become so unreasonable and mean. Rose had known about Traci's case and SRS's search for an adoptive home for a year before she was placed with the family. Rose "chose" Traci because the case reports said she was well behaved, agreeable, and sweet while in the previous foster home. Rose longed for such a little daughter. Traci was now hitting, scratching, spit-

ting, and urinating more than ever. With fingers shaped like pistols, she'd run through the house knocking things over while threatening to kill her brothers, sister, mother, father, and herself. She used foul language at the table. The entire household was on edge. Rose and her husband were concerned that their other children would be permanently affected. Everyone was angry with Traci, and not a day went by that she wasn't punished.

It was obvious that Rose and Traci were not in a connected, attuned state during that session, and Traci looked as if she fully expected to be scolded by me. Rose looked as if she hoped I would back her up and tell Traci what a naughty girl she was and threaten her with (?!) to make her mind. Rose sat bolt upright in the chair facing me, arms folded in front of her, not looking once at Traci. Rose cried several times, wiping her eyes with tissues, saying she didn't know what to do or what would happen. Traci was expressionless, limp; she looked straight ahead or sometimes sideways at Rose, out of the corner of her eyes. When it was time to leave my office that day, Rose ordered Traci to get up. Traci refused, so Rose grabbed her arm, jerked her up and pushed her out the door. "You're listening to me, young lady!" She walked ahead of Traci down the hallway, grabbing her again in the parking lot when she refused to get into the car.

Now, when I am referred a new case, I arrange to meet the parents first without the child in order to avoid such a scene, which risks reinforcing to the child that she is truly bad. However, in this case it was valuable to me to actually see how Rose parented. Her lack of shame regarding her roughness let me know something about her disciplinary beliefs and strategies. She seemed to associate her stress with frustration that her usual parenting tactics weren't working, that something was wrong with this child, and all she knew to do to remedy this was to become harsher. It is important to recognize and treat the parent's issues first, so they will be given a chance to reorganize their responses without repeating harmful practices in session. I'm always on guard when working with unresolved parents. They can become emotionally reactive to the same subjects their child hasn't yet learned to integrate. It isn't productive to have the parent or the child in a dysregulated state; sometimes a therapist must stop to assess whether or not this is happening, or if it is about to. I don't want either to feel emotionally unsupported. Dan Hughes' dictum prevails: "Don't overestimate the parent's ability to accept a child's vulnerability" (Hughes, 11/4/2003). If I'm surprised by a parent's shaming words (or looks), my first response is to speak for the child from an emotional perspective. Sometimes this awakens the parent enough for them to do corrective reassurance. I may change the focus entirely if the parent hasn't been properly prepared to respond empathically or if they become dysregulated and reactively abusive. Subsequent sessions (without the child) will focus on exploration of the parent's underlying emotions that drive the behavior. Using PACE, I gently challenge the parent's unhelpful methodology while also attempting resolution of traumatic issues so that the parent can attend to their child without the burden of blinding reactivity.

In subsequent therapy sessions with Rose, I began to explore the myriad emotions that drove her parenting behaviors. She was somewhat rough with all her children; her farm upbringing was reflected in how she approached adversity concretely. She described her mother and father as loving, yet bitter tears welled up when Rose described childhood disappointments such as the loss of toys, pets, and eventually the family farm following a devastating fire. Her siblings were more privileged, and she was aware of not being her family's favored child. She had only herself to blame, what with being so forgetful, a poor student, and female. Her childhood was fraught with harsh physical punishments for misbehavior and sexual molestation at the mercy of itinerant farm help. Girls weren't valued unless they could do a man's work. Her husband, although loving, wasn't the type to help much with the children, and this adoption was her idea and responsibility. She convinced him by saying it would make her happier, and he did want that. She promised to handle most of Traci's caretaking; after all, she wasn't talking about an infant, and there would be no diapers or bottles to bother. It sounded not unlike the way a child might try to convince her skeptical parents to allow a new puppy. Although she didn't feel it with Traci, Rose said she felt bonded to her other children from birth, and they seemed to understand her roughness as part and parcel of mom.

Our discussions also began to reveal periodic struggles with depression, the unwelcome host to paralyzing emotions, deeply connected to the primal wounds of rejection and inadequacy. Rose's adopted daughter had triggered painful memories rooted in Rose's childhood experiences and were now brought to life daily. With no escape and no preparation for a more effective interpretation of Traci's behaviors and their underlying issues, Rose responded as if her whole being had been judged, deemed inadequate, and rejected. She interpreted Traci's behaviors as if they were about Rose only, instead of also being Traci's response to underlying defenses against another rejecting relationship. Interestingly, rejection and inadequacy were the banes of both of their lives, deeply wounding beliefs about themselves that they played out for each other every day.

I was beginning to think that our sessions were helping Rose to integrate some of her unresolved trauma and could see increased evidence of attunement, so I was surprised when she called to inform me that there had been a report made about her to Social Services. "It was during a basketball game; this woman gave me dirty looks the whole time. I'm sure it was her who called. I was keeping *Traci* close to me, you know, like you said to do. She'd been bad all day, hadn't eaten her supper like I told her, and she was hungry. Complained the whole time in a very loud voice that I was starving her. Well, I wasn't going to give in to her. She had to sit right next to me and think about what she did. This woman sitting next to us snuck her something to eat while I went to the bathroom. Can you believe it! *Traci* said I was mean for taking it away. That woman doesn't know what I put up with!"

I gulped for air. Sometimes parenting a reactive child can bring disapproving stares or worse, but this time Rose's rigidity had gotten in her way. What might have been a bonding experience became another opportunity for Traci to reinforce her negative beliefs about herself and mothers. How could I help Rose understand that developing attachment wasn't about how thoroughly she consequenced every negative behavior, but instead, how well she could use every opportunity to demonstrate her subjective understanding? She seemed to think that having fun at a basketball game opposed the goals of teaching Traci to rely on her mother's good advice. Traci's difficulty at supper didn't need to drag into the evening activity. Thoughtfulness, demonstrated by the provision of a snack, could have helped Traci to join with her mother as well as the other spectators in their intersubjective experience of the game. When teaching a child how to love, the importance of providing opportunities to feel part of mother, family and community is as much a necessary ingredient as is appropriately timed limit setting.

As we know, even if Rose had prepared a snack, it's possible that Traci would have rejected such ministrations. Even if Rose had responded with empathy instead of reactivity and anger, it's possible that Traci would have persisted with solicitation of strangers' sympathies. But, by showing how to get over disruptions quickly, and by offering many opportunities for interactive repair, over time it would have become less likely that Traci would refuse enticing offers to belong, have fun, and enjoy shared moments of pleasure. These are the moments that whittle away negative beliefs and consequently reduce non-compliant behavior.

The good news was that Rose had the resources Traci hadn't developed yet, and was able to learn to view her daughter's behaviors as expressions of misguided beliefs about Traci, not herself. We talked about how Traci learned by her past experiences to view herself as unlovable. Rose lamented, "I feel like a bad mother. I do nice things and she doesn't like it." Rose was looking for approval from virtual strangers, who she sensed based their judgment of her on the way Traci behaved. Unresolved trauma about Rose's self-worth interfered with her ability to respond to Traci's needs in a non-reactive manner.

We worked on correcting long-held negative beliefs and introduced new ways of valuing herself. With Rose's permission, I videotaped several sessions, which allowed us to view Traci's responses to Rose's parenting interventions. Rose and I watched together and processed our observations of how Traci recoiled when Rose moved close in front of her face, raised her voice, and pointed her finger to illustrate a point. During our first viewing together, Rose focused on Traci's misbehavior. I commiserated with her, saying how hard it must be to love this girl so much and want her to participate joyfully in family activities, etc. I struggled to help her see what I saw. Traci's behaviors were the surface indications of how she felt underneath; she didn't know how to have fun and didn't feel like she belonged. Still, Rose didn't get that even though well-intentioned, her way of communicating care for Traci came across, and was interpreted, as the opposite. Even when Rose was expressing affection, Traci visibly stiffened as the too-rough pat on the leg was applied. Slowly, I helped her relate the in-your-face attempts at discipline to Rose's treatment by caregivers when she was a child. "When Dad spoke, we kids listened!" We discussed how, given Traci's experiences with physical abuse and neglect, she misinterpreted Rose's well-intentioned affection as well as her attempts to discipline. Slowly, through coaching during therapy sessions as well as by a trained, post-adoption case-manager's interventions in the home, Rose began to practice more helpful responses to Traci's frequent dysregulation. This, in turn, afforded more frequent harmonious interactions and the development of trust.

It was difficult for me to help Rose realize that Traci often didn't understand the underlying positive intentions of her mothering requests (e.g. take a shower so you smell nice, put a barrette in to keep your hair off your face, play outside on a nice day, wear the warmer boots for sledding). I wanted Rose to learn to recognize her daughter's confusion and subsequent dysregulation by watching Traci's responses, and to be comfortable addressing this with her daughter as it happened. I began to do this in sessions; if I sensed Traci's misinterpretation of mom's intentions, I'd say, first to Rose, "I wonder if Traci thought you were punishing her when you told her to play outside." Then I'd wait for Rose to be curious and ask Traci if "that's why you threw the toy, because you thought I was being mean to you," or something along that line. If she didn't, then I'd say it. I might also say to Rose, "I wonder how you could let your daughter know you were really caring for her when you asked her to___." This would usually elicit a response from Traci, such as Mom wants her to smell nice, have pretty hair, get fresh air to be healthy, etc. "because she loves me." If I could remind Rose to give an affectionate hug when Traci said "the right things," then Traci's confusion would resolve and we'd see her soften and become congruent with her mother. With lots of modeling on my part, how to recognize and respond to

Traci's attachment behaviors eventually helped Rose to become more adept at attuning to her daughter's underlying emotions.

Three years later, Traci still struggles to manage many triggers that result in dysregulation. Through exploration, we were able to understand that deliberate, early-morning peeing on the bed probably related back to the years when Traci was left alone and untended, while her birth mother recovered from a night of drinking. Rose has come to understand what such bizarre behaviors are likely to mean, especially when Traci is feeling neglected. More often than not, she has learned to respond in ways that effectively derail Traci's attempts to prove herself unlovable.

Working toward the resolution of Rose's own trauma allowed the relationship between her and her daughter to progress out of a cycle of harmful interactions. Rose's tenuous beliefs about her own worthiness, based on her own unresolved trauma, had to be addressed before she was able to perceive and respond to her daughter's underlying emotional needs.

When unresolved trauma interferes with a parent's ability to attune to the underlying emotion and respond in ways that validate the child's experience, the relationship is further damaged. In more simplistic terms, if a child is thirsty and needs hydration, giving her pretzels doesn't help her feel understood, nor does it reduce her thirst. Although parents may try to stop challenging behaviors by punishing a child who has no other built-in resources from which to draw, truly compliant behavior derives from feeling connected with and belonging to the parent. As described throughout this book, connections are built through shared experiences in an environment of emotional safety.

Uncovering a parent's unresolved trauma requires utilization of relationship-building techniques and begins with development of a therapeutic alliance. Knowing a parent's history exploring with them beliefs about parenting, discipline, and the value of key relationships in their own lives can provide opportunities to expose unresolved trauma while also helping them identify how they may be inadvertently re-traumatizing their child because of their own very negative experiences with similar emotions.

CASE STUDY TWO

Joan & Vera: The parent's own trauma requires resolution.

Case study two illustrates a mother's need for trauma resolution work to address unresolved issues that interfered with her best intentions. The child's somewhat hysterically expressed fear of abandonment triggered mom's own unresolved abandonment issues, and they reacted to each other in horribly re-traumatizing interactions.

Joan was referred by an acquaintance of hers who had worked with another attachment therapist with good results. Prior to meeting me, Joan requested that I speak with the therapist she'd worked with for several years, to obtain his approval first. That accomplished, we met for an intake appointment to discuss concerns regarding her daughter, Vera. Joan described horrendous scenes, both of them yelling, screaming, crying, and threatening one another until they were too exhausted to fight, only to clash again and again. Joan cried while describing the years of hurt feelings she'd endured. "I can't take it anymore." It sounded as though Joan didn't feel safe in her own home, tormented as she was by her eight-year-old daughter.

We spent several sessions exploring attachment histories, while I tried to build an alliance with her. She didn't seem to relax or feel safe from session to session. She called after each one and again several times before the next. Once, she waited not quite five minutes for me in the waiting room and was furious. Her intense response to slight mishaps indicated fear of being taken advantage of, as well as a warning not to disrespect her. Joan presented more like a battered wife than a young child's mother. She seemed to have no authority in her home. She described Vera as controlling, mean, angry, and threatening to her, but very nice to everyone else, including her father. She said Vera would punish her "later" if Joan did something Vera didn't like when they were out in public or visiting one of Joan's friends.

I used the Parent Profile as well as other handouts to explore with Joan how she approached her daughter's behaviors while also gently probing into beliefs about her own emotional process. I wanted to know how Joan valued herself and whose standards she measured herself against, seemingly coming up short every time. How did she express anger? What were the most painful issues of her childhood? What were the salient issues of her adult life? She revealed pervasive reactivity to the trauma of her childhood experiences. Such personalized, and therefore misattuned, reactivity interfered with her ability to respond in helpful ways to her daughter's distress. Joan interpreted Vera's acting out as if Vera were the caregiver who punished, tormented, and controlled Joan. What a dance these two acted out!

Vera's history included being left swaddled inside a laundry basket on the doorstep of an Eastern European orphanage at approximately one month. At one year she was moved to a facility for toddlers, where she was cared for until her adoption by Joan at nearly two years. Joan flew to the orphanage to receive her new daughter and met the caregiver in charge of the orphaned toddlers. She helped Joan to become acquainted with Vera and taught her how to calm her when she cried. Joan demonstrated with a pillow how she was shown to rock Vera's little behind until she cried herself to sleep. From this and other suggestions given to Joan, we surmised that Vera had not been an easy baby to soothe, nor were there enough arms available in the orphanage to properly hold and carry a fussy infant. We talked about the effects of this, in terms of maternal emotion regulation and the normal way babies are biologically primed to experience trust and love. One morning at the orphanage, Joan visited the babies' quarters. Babies were kept in cribs lining one wall of the cement block building. She asked an attendant why the babies wore so many diapers at a time. This kept them drier between infrequent changes, she was told. In my office, Joan imagined how Vera spent her first year of life in such a sterile environment. She missed the positive effects of having a mother to notice and tend her needs. Although kind and caring, the orphanage caretakers had many other babies and toddlers to soothe, and Vera's needs often went unmet.

Vera was two and a half by the time of her adoption and had four prior "mothers." In my office she was nearly uncontrollable. She seemed intensely reactive to the situation of our talking quietly together, and my curiosity was piqued. In subsequent sessions, I was able to explore the implications with Vera and her mom. It seemed that having Mom talk to me was recreating some dynamic from her past. I guessed that this was an all-too-familiar scene prior to her being handed over to another mom. At this remark, Vera regressed before our eyes, turning back into that orphaned two-year-old who whimpered, sucked her hands, and rocked herself in absolute misery. For the first time, Joan was able to connect the hysterical behaviors her daughter displayed with real fear of another abandonment.

Our problems were far from resolved, however. Vera reacted instantaneously to perceived rejection by Mom and would resort to hands-on aggression in her efforts to prevent Mom from what Vera interpreted as undeniable disregard. Vera, like most children, assumed the reasons for previous abandonment were due to maternal rejection of her. Didn't Joan back up Vera's thesis every day by saying what a horrible child she was to get in her mother's face like that?

And wasn't Vera ferocious in her rage! Mom was so reactive to Vera that she would shut herself in the bathroom, begging her daughter to stop. Vera would rage on, terrified of mom's inability to take charge. The emotional blackmail would come later, neither speaking to the other, with looks that stung the heart.

Although Joan had received previous therapy, she was still traumatized by her own unresolved issues. I wasn't comfortable working solely with her since her reactivity toward me sometimes interfered with our alliance. I was concerned that possible confrontation could damage the attachment work with Vera, and I wanted to continue to be a resource to them. It was clear that Joan desperately needed better coping skills to manage her own quick-to-boil temper. And once again, Joan had become angry with me. Her own frustration at home manifested as disillusionment. She blamed me for not being able to resolve their issues soon enough. I was definitely off the pedestal. Even though I could have done more work with Joan, at this juncture I was tired and losing enthusiasm. I knew this would not be a good situation for building trust, so I referred Joan to an individual therapist for trauma work and invited her back, with Vera, once she had a better handle on her ability to cope with the triggers that resulted in her own reactive tantrums. This was a friendly parting.

After about six months, with occasional calls in between to report improvements in behaviors toward each other, we resumed sessions that included Vera. Joan continued to be mistrustful and inconsistent with regard to her feelings about me, and this played out a few times when she thought I was disrespecting her by not calling back soon enough. I noticed how my stomach jumped when I heard her voice on my answering machine, never knowing whether or not she was going to be reactive. After I'd apologized for whatever infraction she thought I'd purposely done to hurt her, she could recognize these fears as remnants from her past.

Joan began to own behaviors that undermined Vera's trust in her ability to parent. She was using more positive self-talk to reinforce confidence in her ability to respond supportively to Vera's underlying emotions. We had several discussions about how to approach her daughter first, before Vera began to feel alone and react with controlling tactics. This would demonstrate to Vera that Joan was a capable and sensitive mother.

Joan stopped seeing her individual counselor after several sessions, saying she didn't feel a connection. Nevertheless, Joan seemed in better spirits and wanted to work with me again. To my surprise, Vera mirrored her mom's renewed energy and made a leap forward. Vera became more trusting in sessions with me and seemed to believe that my role was indeed to keep her and her mother together. This allowed us to talk about and validate Vera's experiences of losing three mothers, learning a new language, and being an inexperienced mom's first and only child. In sessions, Vera became more expressive to her mother and verbalized how it felt when mom yelled and what helped her to feel safe and loved.

Once Joan recognized how unresolved trauma interfered with her ability to parent her daughter, there was no going back. I'm convinced that when Vera tries to replicate her deeply rooted beliefs of inherent unworthiness, Joan will (sooner than later) recognize Vera's behaviors as reactive (to them both) and will sidestep harmful engagement, which used to increase their mutual terror.

By far the most challenging cases for therapists involve parents recovering from severe unresolved trauma that resulted in lifestyle choices so detrimental to their children that they were placed in foster care. There are cycles of recovery for such parents, and before working toward reunification, I insist on clarification of motives to gauge emotional safety for the child. If the parent hasn't had sufficient treatment for substance abuse, domestic abuse, or other mental health concerns such as depression, schizophrenia, or other psychosis, then that must come first. The parent's ability to develop insights into the workings of trauma's effects is necessary prior to committing to attachment work. This translates into parental recognition of the effects of abuse, as well as relinquishment of denial regarding parental responsibility for unsafe situations endured by their child. I can offer a safe forum in a non-judgmental environment to parents who may not have had an opportunity to discuss issues that led to family disruptions. While I'm not here to judge a parent's choices, this doesn't preclude recognition of the effects of such choices.

I can help validate parental emotions that were driving forces behind disruptive choices through the use of Dyadic Developmental Psychotherapy practices such as affective attunement and empathic responsiveness. I can use PACE to develop trust and build an alliance that permits explorations of unresolved trauma. I can teach nonviolent ways of responding to a child's reactivity to family disruption. But it doesn't always work.

CASE STUDY THREE

Giselle: Intergenerational effects of poverty, trauma, and mental illness.

Case study three describes the generational effects of poverty, mental illness, and bad luck.

Giselle was born in Quebec during the early eighties and moved to New Hampshire with her mother and three of seven siblings when she was four. Although vague about with whom the others stayed or how they eventually found their way in the world, she reported that her lineage could be traced to the The Filles du Roi, or King's Daughters. These were courageous young women enticed by favorable incentives at state expense to emigrate to, and populate, the colony of New France as wards of King Louis XIV. Their ranks hailed from the orphanages of Ile-de-France and Normandy; some were prostitutes, and a smaller number were dowried upper-class Filles de Qualite, Daughters of Quality. As Giselle expounded upon her lineage, I wondered at the difficulties those orphaned girls faced, aside from incentives to produce large numbers of children. Many had experienced grave situations in which unresolved trauma could have resulted in difficulty raising emotionally healthy off-spring. Many had not had mothers to form attachments with and had little experience to draw from when caring for their own babies. Many were poorly prepared for the harsh climate and frontier life. Quick marriages to frontiersmen and gratuities awarded to families of 12 or more achieved the goal of populating the country. I pondered the generational effects of such new beginnings.

Giselle already had three children taken away for substantiated abuse and neglect. The telltale physical effects of cocaine abuse revealed reddened gums and many missing teeth. Dark circles surrounding her deep-set eyes only increased a look of haunted grief. She described her years in foster care, when her mother was hospitalized and eventually died, leaving the younger children orphaned. At 14, a sternly Christian, paternal aunt adopted her. She recalled her father as illiterate and violent and remembered overhearing her French-speaking grandmother telling others how he'd return home every year or so to father another child. She doubted all her siblings were the result of his affections, however, and heard he'd been murdered in a dispute involving drugs. Giselle ran away to Vermont at 16, pregnant and alone.

She sat dry-eyed, retelling her story without emotion. She talked about her life as if it were someone else's. The baby was taken shortly after birth, and soon thereafter she was reunited with him in a foster home. "They hated me," she said. "Nothing I did ever pleased them."

I asked if it was adolescent behavior they objected to, since she became a mother so young. She became thoughtful and said, "It was probably true what my aunt had always said about me: I really wasn't mother material." After all, when her twin girls were born prematurely, she relinquished parental rights without a fight. What kind of mother does that? From the sound of things, she'd suffered severe postpartum depression, resorting to a familiar solace of self-medication with illegal drugs. I still wasn't sure whether she was motivated to keep her fourth child out of guilt or a desire to raise him and be his mother. Giselle was sitting with me in my office because she wanted to get her first child back, as well as to keep her fourth, a six-month-old, red-haired boy named Jason, whose father promised to marry her.

We read the Social Services case-plan review for both children. Most likely she'd be able to keep baby Jason if she continued to provide stable living conditions and stay clean. Later on I observed her with Jason and saw some hope for their relationship. His birth had occurred during a fairly stable time. Giselle had completed inpatient drug abuse treatment during the pregnancy, and despite a low birth weight, Jason was otherwise healthy. She lived in a facility for unwed mothers during the first three *months postpartum until she secured her own apartment through help from two social welfare agencies. Jason was the only child who remained with her from birth. We talked a great deal about attachment and the effects he'd enjoyed because of all the things she had done for him. I categorized his needs as both physical and emotional while relating how he'd learned to trust and love her as a result of her care. One of the most beautiful scenes I was privileged to witness occurred at a case review attended by 10 professionals and the baby's parents. Jason was perched on Giselle's lap, grinning toothlessly at all of us gathered around the table. Suddenly he turned to face her, looked into her eyes and kissed her chin. Pure affection, adoration, and love manifested between them.*

Social Services was allowing home visits between Giselle and her first son, Luke. He'd been around. Having blown out of five foster homes, two of them pre-adoptive, he then spent a year at a residential treatment center for challenging children. He was diagnosed with the usual ODD, ADD, and recently, RAD. Medication took the edge off, and since deemed successfully treated, he was now available for release either to Giselle or a currently unidentified adoptive home.

Giselle reported that although visits had initially been good, they'd recently turned sour. It turned out she wasn't being entirely truthful about how she was handling things. I'd gotten a call from the visit supervisor who described Giselle as passive, almost shell-shocked. When Luke demanded different soup she opened another can. She seemed to retreat as he tested her strength. Things got worse. He began to have explosive outbursts, threw objects, swore, and banged the floor and walls. For the first time I saw Giselle cry. What if the other tenants complained to their landlord? Her attachment to baby Jason was solid enough for her to understand what was at stake.

We agreed to decrease Luke's visits home while increasing therapy time. Most sessions with Luke included the baby. Giselle often couldn't find a sitter and frequently combined sessions with other errands that needed doing in the city. The stepfather never came to sessions at all. Giselle's manner with Luke was mostly patient and understanding. On the rare occasion that Jason wasn't there, she would rock and sing to Luke, who quickly regressed to nonverbal states. I tried to get them into more interactive play, so Luke could see and feel his mother responding to him as the seven-year-old he was. Giselle seemed to lose herself during these times, and couldn't keep up without a lot of coaching from me. Appropriate as she was in my office (with my coaching), at home she wasn't able to handle everyone's needs coming at her. Luke and Giselle were so much alike! Same ocean-blue eyes, honey-gold, curly hair. They also shared a very low frustration tolerance and confusion when overstimulated; difficulty in prioritizing seemed to manifest in destructive anger for both. Giselle went inside of herself, frozen and fearful of hurting her child or herself; Luke acted out in violence.

Time was running out for the case plan and Social Services wanted in-home visits to resume. We tried shorter-duration visits with telephone calls between and put in place a behavior plan so Giselle would have backup if she wasn't able to manage Luke's aggression. Again, things went okay for the first few weeks, but Luke's anger intensified. He was becoming increasingly challenging in the foster home. Patience was waning. During one of the last visits, Luke smeared his feces on the walls. When he was restrained for throwing objects at the windows, he vomited purposefully. His reactivity was more than Giselle could handle.

She admitted feeling as though a great weight had been lifted following her decision to relinquish. As sad as she was at not being able to mother Luke, she understood where her own limits stood and did not want to risk losing her sanity or Jason. "He's the one thing I seem to be doing right," she said through fresh tears.

As weak as she had been when Luke needed her to be strong, she showed remarkable ability during good-bye visits. I traced both of her hands and both of Luke's on felt and placed one of each together. They chose the colors and made two small pillows, one for each, with their names embroidered below the sewn-on hand tracings. They stuffed each other's pillows "with love." The pillows were meant to commemorate their relationship, and to honor it even while accepting that new parents would be necessary, too. Luke clung to his first mother, legs wrapped around her waist, begging her not to let him go. I could sense his terrible fear of the unknown. With resolve, she spoke well of the pre-adoptive home he'd be moving into, and said she'd see him again when he was older. They parted.

In the two years since, Giselle has managed to lose and find work several times, changed residences twice, and married Jason's father, who got his driver's license back and is training to become an assistant manager. They are expecting another baby. She attends a program for recovering addicts, and from the looks of things, has managed to stay clean. I received a few frantic calls when she thought Jason was going down the same path as Luke. The baby had become a willful and stubborn toddler. She attended parenting classes as part of the Social Services requirement for return of custody and made some new friends with other young mothers. Hopefully she's learning the necessary skills to handle her child's emergent autonomy without seeing it as a threat to her own. She often thinks about Luke and wonders whether or not she made the right decision. But, so far guilt hasn't paralyzed her ability to effectively mother Jason.

To date, Luke hasn't fared as well. The pre-adoptive home returned him after he threatened a neighbor child, and he was placed back into residential treatment. Soon he'll be moved into a therapeutic group home with more stable staff and maybe a chance to build a relationship with one of the caregivers.

This mother's failed attempt at reunification was a sad experience. I felt she could almost do it. Maybe I was feeling the same possibility as other service providers before me, who also kept trying. Had Luke been freed for adoption earlier, his chances to heal would have been so much greater. Too many issues complicate Luke's chances, and now the wounds of trauma may be carried into another generation.

Dyadic Developmental Psychotherapy is based on attachment theory and the premise that people are biologically primed to thrive in relationships. With this in mind, it is helpful to know that every encounter we have with clients adds to their (and our) intersubjective experience. Concepts of each other and ourselves are not static. While we explore with a parent the salient issues that shaped beliefs upon which they now base decisions, we are also influencing their interpretation and giving new meaning to daily experiences. The possibility for change doesn't stop, and with careful, genuine, and supportive exploration of unresolved trauma, parents can become better equipped to proactively manage triggers with less reactivity. As they heal, they heal their children.

One of the most common challenges seems to be a parent's difficulty recognizing the underlying emotional message expressed in their child's behavior. The following describes core assumptions to keep in mind regarding the underlying motives of caregivers/parents struggling to parent their children and may assist the therapist in identifying what lies beneath any given parental response.

My Core Assumptions about Certain Behaviors of Parents
Unpublished Papers, by Daniel Hughes, PhD

A parent may present with:

Chronic anger, harsh discipline, power struggles, not asking for help, not showing affection, difficulty sleeping, appetite problems, ignoring the child, remaining isolated from the child, reacting with rage and impulsiveness, lack of empathy for the child, marital conflicts, withdrawal from relatives and friends, chronic criticism.

Yet, the motives under the behavior will likely be:

- Desire to help the child develop well.
- Love and commitment for the child.
- Desire to be a good parent.
- Uncertainty about how to meet the child's needs.
- Lack of confidence in ability to meet the child's needs.
- Specific failures with the child associated with more pervasive doubts about self.
- Pervasive sense of shame as a parent.
- Conviction of helplessness and hopelessness.
- Fear of being vulnerable/being hurt by the child.
- Fear of rejection by the child as a parent.
- Inability to understand why the child does things.
- Inability to understand why self reacts to child.
- Association of child's functioning with aspects of own attachment history.
- Feeling lack of support and understanding from other adults.
- Felt sense that life is too hard.
- Assumptions that child's motives/intentions are negative.
- Feeling that there are no other options besides the behavior tried.

My Core Assumptions About Certain Behaviors of the Child

The child may present with:

Arguing, complaining, controlling, rages, withdrawal, not asking for help, not showing affection, banging head to fall asleep, screaming over routine frustrations, constant chattering, avoiding eye contact, lying, stealing, gorging food, socializing indiscriminately.

Yet, the beliefs/motives under the behavior will likely be:

- Conviction that only self can/will meet own needs.
- Never feeling safe.
- Pervasive sense of shame.
- Conviction of hopelessness and helplessness.
- Fear of being vulnerable/dependent.
- Fear of rejection.
- Feeling "invisible."
- Inability to understand why s/he does things.
- Need to deny inner life because of overwhelming affect that exists there.
- Inability to express inner life even if s/he wanted to.
- Fear of failure.
- Fear of trusting happiness.
- Routine family life is full of associations to first family.

- Discipline is experienced as abuse/neglect.
- Inability to be comforted when disciplined/hurt.

I help parents connect with the underlying emotional meaning of their child's behavior because this frees them to respond with empathy and support. Rarely is it necessary to teach supportive responsiveness if the parent's own issues are validated and somewhat resolved, yet it's all too easy for a parent to become periodically blind to the origins of their child's reactivity. This is an example of how unresolved traumas are split-off and continue to operate outside of conscious awareness. For example, every few months one of the mothers I work with comes in alone, without her child. Most of the time what's needed is a reminder about her adopted child's abusive experiences. Once we go over her child's history, sometimes in graphic detail if necessary, to help her recognize how appalling his circumstances were and the inevitable effects, she's able to stabilize and more accurately interpret his needs and respond with empathy.

CASE STUDY FOUR

Lynn & John: A parent discovers the powerful effects of acceptance and empathy.

An adoptive parent's unresolved trauma may become recognizable during the work of parenting. Taken as an opportunity to explore and heal emotional wounds that otherwise fester without resolution, the act of intersubjective understanding can unleash powerful empathic responses. Case study four illustrates such a journey toward health.

Lynn, the mother of a newly adopted, barely verbal four-year-old, gained important insights into her own isolation and loneliness by learning what is and isn't normal social development for toddlers and young children. Her biracial son, John, was still very skeptical about trusting mothers, as demonstrated one day when he fell and scraped his elbows bloody. Instead of either waiting for mother to come over to him or running to her for comfort and help, he did what he'd learned to do from prior experience with inconsistent caregivers. He ran away. No mind for traffic, pedestrians, dogs, just away from people!

In my office he could tolerate only moments of connection, and then he'd run to the opposite wall, posing in manly-looking postures, with arms folded, his hip jutting out. His body seemed to say, "Don't either of you mess with me." Then he'd slump to the floor, pull a toy from his pocket, and engage in isolated play facing away from mother and me. Lynn and I talked a great deal about how John was born perfectly healthy and expecting to have someone he could depend on. His current working hypothesis about the negative value of mothers developed out of harsh experiences that proved relying on a mom was dangerous. John stopped trying to find out if some moms are more reliable than others. By his experience, the time to experiment with new moms wasn't when he was hurt and really needed someone.

I modeled how to act with him, so that even if he didn't know yet how to have a mother who cares, we would show him by caring anyway. We fussed over him if he was hurt and gave language to the feelings he expressed through his body language, just the way a properly attuned mom would have been doing for him all along. I would let him play by himself in the corner for a few minutes, then run over and scoop him up, swing him in a circle, and on count of three, toss him into mom's arms. He loved this, but didn't ask for more. We had to show him there was more! John wasn't at ease interacting with people, so I wanted to show him some of the benefits. One day, on his way to play alone in the corner, I grabbed him onto my lap in the swivel chair and spun around in circles. I was becoming dizzy and stopped, when John yelled out loud, "Green light!" I pushed the chair around again until he yelled, "Red light!" Watching him actively participate in interactive play brought tears to his mother's eyes. He could tolerate and even enjoy the closeness as long as he had some control. His mom could adapt these games at home to help John learn, day by day, that this mom cared for him. Since he seemed so uncomfortable with people, she needed not to leave him alone, as was her inclination.

Lynn told me that she was also healing and hadn't realized before the power of a relationship to mend a broken heart. Through her new insights regarding the underlying issues her son struggled with, especially intimacy, she recognized her own isolationist tendencies. Leaving him alone in his misery wasn't good for him, she now knew. Her husband had not left her alone, either, when she didn't know how to go to him with her hurt feelings, sadness, or frustration. He taught her how to use his love, just the way she was showing her little son how to use hers.

These are some of the powerful ways relationships can help move us along the continuum of health. Relationships are what make Dyadic Developmental Psychotherapy. Most defenses manifesting in challenging behaviors are attempts to squelch underlying shame rooted in unresolved, fear-inducing emotions. Since Dyadic Developmental Psychotherapy works within the natural processes of healthy attachment, through the genuine sharing of affect and acceptance of all emotions, it is possible to dismantle the toxic effects of unresolved trauma and free people to experience each other in more authentic and validating ways. This builds trust and intimacy. An emotionally safe space for parents to speak subjectively about their feelings can help integrate split-off trauma, resolve shame, and allow more accurate interpretation of their children's affective needs.

Dyadic Developmental Psychotherapy in Impermanent Settings: Therapeutic Foster Care, Group Homes, Residential Treatment Centers

CRAIG W. CLARK, KAREN DOYLE BUCKWALTER, MICHELLE B. ROBISON,
SCOTT L. BLACKWELL & JOSEPH McGUILL

"If mistreated children are not to become criminals or mentally ill, it is essential that at least once in their life they come in contact with a person who knows without any doubt that the environment, not the helpless, battered child, is at fault." —Alice Miller, The Untouched Key

CHAPTER INTRODUCTION

In this chapter, we will explore the practice of Dyadic Developmental Psychotherapy in alternative placements for children who cannot live with birth or adoptive families. The alternatives for these children include residential treatment centers, group homes, children's shelters, and therapeutic foster families. In each of these settings, children are faced with numerous challenges and losses that adversely affect their ability to achieve developmental milestones. The fundamental building block that is most often disadvantaged is their ability to form secure attachments with their caregivers. The U.S. Department of Health & Human Services statistics for the year 2001 indicate that the total population of children in foster care, residential treatment, or group homes is approximately three million.[1]

This population that is destined for inclusion in residential treatment centers (RTC), foster care, and group-home facilities are children who have not been able to adjust to life with their birth family or in a foster or adoptive home. Their behavior is such that they are deemed unsuitable for the foster-adopt system. Group homes are more local facilities that provide homes for children whose behavior does not permit them to be housed in a foster or foster-adoptive home. These children live in houses with several other children with supervision provided around the clock by staff, who are usually college-age and unlicensed, although

---

[1] U.S. Department of Health & Human Services, Administration for Children & Families. FFY 2001 CCDF Data Tables and Charts.

trained to some degree. Therapeutic foster families provide homes to children who are judged to be capable of living in a family milieu, and who require a higher, more therapeutic level of care than is usually provided in foster care. Sometimes children are placed temporarily in these homes while reunification with their birth family is processed through the court. Other times, children may be placed in long-term foster care and/or adoptive placement. Current law requires that counties follow concurrent planning guidelines, which will provide options for both short-term and long-term or permanent placement. Permanent placement could either be in the form of returning to the birth family, long-term care, or adoption.

The choices that are made for these children have profound long-term influences and determine how these children mature into adult life. We know through the work of Bowlby[2], Ainsworth[3], and others that children must have nurturing contact with a primary caregiver from birth through the first three years of life in order to best succeed in forming a healthy and secure attachment. If this opportunity is disrupted through maltreatment, then the child grows to mistrust others and feels that his or her needs will not be satisfied. The child welfare system may have other goals and objectives that interfere with the normal process of forming a healthy and secure attachment. For example, the use of temporary foster placements until a "permanent" foster placement can be made may result in several moves for a child. Consequently the priorities for rules, staff, and program approaches do not always allow for the type of relationships to form between staff and child that would naturally or therapeutically promote the establishment of a healthy and secure attachment relationship. Often the child's needs for food, shelter and a safe place to live preempt the child welfare system's ability to therapeutically address the child's innate emotional needs. There are two residential treatment centers in the United States that utilize attachment-based therapeutic models, specifically Dyadic Developmental Psychotherapy. We will see how these two institutions, Chaddock in Quincy, Illinois and Villa Santa Maria in New Mexico, work with severely disturbed youth using Dyadic Developmental Psychotherapy. This approach will be contrasted with therapeutic approaches practiced in group homes, therapeutic foster families, and in facilities that use a behavioral model of treatment, as most residential treatment centers generally use.

---

[2] Bowlby, John (1988). *A secure base: Parent-child attachment and healthy human development*. USA: Basic Books
[3] Ainsworth, M., Blehar, M., Waters, E., & Wall, S. (1978). *Patterns of attachment: A psychological study of the strange situation*. Hillsdale, NJ: Lawrence Erlbaum.

Using Dyadic Developmental Psychotherapy in a Residential Treatment Center

KAREN DOYLE-BUCKWALTER & MICHELLE B. ROBISON

OVERVIEW AND HISTORY

Founded more than 150 years ago by the Methodist Episcopal Church, in the last century and a half Chaddock has served as a college, an orphanage, a boys school with a military curriculum, and since 1982, a home for abused, neglected boys and girls. Today, Chaddock is an $8.2 million organization offering a full array of residential, community-based and educational programming for children, birth through age 21, and their families. Based on a 30-acre campus in Quincy, Illinois, Chaddock is nationally accredited by the Council on Accreditation of Services for Children and Families, Inc., as well as the United Methodist Association of Health and Welfare Ministries. In addition, Chaddock's on-campus special education school is accredited by the North Central Association of Colleges and Schools.

As evidenced by its rich history, Chaddock is committed to adapting its programming to respond to the emerging or unmet needs of children and their families. The most recent programmatic shift has been toward providing more specialized treatment, primarily for adoptive and foster children and their families, using attachment theory along with the most current brain research to guide our clinical treatment practices, as well as the management of our milieu.

Since the early 1990's, the treatment at Chaddock has been strongly influenced by the work of Dr. William Glasser and his treatment model, Reality Therapy/Choice Theory. Since Reality Therapy/Choice Theory is not a behavior modification approach and adheres to the tenants that "relationships are the primary agent of change" and that "all behavior is purposeful," a move toward a model based on attachment was more consistent with Reality Therapy/Choice Theory rather than a departure from this philosophy, and as such was a natural next step for the agency.

Although many adolescents were making great strides in their treatment at Chaddock using the Reality Therapy/Choice Theory philosophy, there were some clients who just did not seem to respond to the treatment. These were youth with whom not even the most seasoned therapists and milieu staff could forge a relationship, which was critical to success in the Reality Therapy/Choice Theory model. There was one young man in particular who proved to be the turning point. He was a 16-year-old who had been in the treatment program for several months. He was in a cottage (a dorm-type structure where the children at Chaddock live) managed by one of the most experienced cottage managers on staff. She was a 13-year veteran who seemed to always have a sixth sense about what was going on with the children in her cottage. She came to me one day and said, "My cottage is in total chaos, and I cannot figure out what is going on and how to get things back into the right rhythm. But one thing I know, when I walk in the door into the chaos each day, there is Tom sitting on the couch with a really calm but slightly smug look on his face while all the other kids are bickering and arguing." She later figured out that behind the scenes in very subtle, what some would call sneaky ways, Tom was stirring up all the other kids. We now know this is a very common dynamic that occurs particularly with the more quiet, passive children with attachment difficulties. Whatever dynamic the children created in their home, they often recreate in the cottage with the staff who are in the parent role, and with the other children who are in a sibling role to them. It became clear to us that adolescents, such as this young man, needed more "attachment-specific interventions."

The focus of the remainder of this chapter will be describing how our attachment-based program, known as Integrative Attachment Therapy, works and uses Dyadic Developmental Psychotherapy. Before we began to incorporate Dyadic Developmental Psychotherapy into our attachment work at Chaddock, we had already been using Theraplay® both in our outpatient and residential services. We have found that with younger children we may use Theraplay as the primary, and sometimes only, mode of treatment. However, Theraplay is not a technique where children and adolescents have the opportunity to process their trauma and begin the development of a more coherent autobiographical narrative. Thus we have found that Dyadic Developmental Psychotherapy and Theraplay can be used as complementing therapies, particularly in the earliest phases of treatment.

Treatment Team Members and Roles

The Integrative Attachment Therapy Treatment Team at Chaddock will have input from many individuals who have been involved historically with the child being referred. This may include therapists, psychiatrists, physicians, social workers, adoption workers, caseworkers, guardians ad litem, private attorneys, family advocates, local probation or parole bodies, and the courts. In addition, a variety of Chaddock staff members will be involved in the child's treatment at Chaddock. This includes the psychiatrist, nurse, teacher, therapist, family services coordinator, cottage manager, program coordinator, attachment counselor, chaplain, and the family's hometown therapist. From this group of individuals the Chaddock Core Treatment Team, a multi-disciplinary team, is developed and meets on a weekly basis to discuss and provide for the individualized treatment of the child. The Chaddock Core Treatment Team consists of the therapist, family services coordinator, cottage manager, program coordinator, attachment counselor, chaplain, and teacher.

DYADIC DEVELOPMENTAL PSYCHOTHERAPY IN A RESIDENTIAL SETTING

The specific approach of Dyadic Developmental Psychotherapy may utilize the following interventions: engagement and leading, contracting, attachment sequences, challenge, information and education, psychodrama, paradoxical interventions, illustrated stories, children's books, stuffed animals, and music, all used in the same manner that they would be in outpatient therapy except that the role of the parent is assumed by the child's attachment counselor. The central principals are:

1. Developing attunement,

2. Developing primary and secondary intersubjectivity,

3. Developing an integrated autobiographical narrative, and

4. Integrating past trauma into the narrative and exposing the operation of internal working models and how these are distorting current relationships (Hughes 1997, p.93).

When families visit, they are then a part of the therapy sessions. The major difference is not in how the techniques are used in therapy, but in the supports that are incorporated in the entire residential treatment environment. The child-care workers who assume the parent role act as parent surrogates within the Dyadic Developmental Psychotherapy model by implementing PACE, and then, in turn, provide this information to the parents during milieu observation opportunities.

MILIEU THERAPEUTIC WORK

One of the ways that an attachment-based residential program differs from a traditional residential treatment program is that the child's relationship with the milieu staff is viewed as the primary agent of change rather than the child's relationship with the therapist. One of our slogans is *"the magic happens on the floor,"* meaning that the quality of day-to-day relationship with the child-care workers, who function like a parent with the child, is the crucible for healing for the child (*Facilitating Developmental Attachment*, Hughes, p. 93). The milieu staff focus on the here and now, and the therapist, in therapy sessions, focuses on the past. Hughes (1997) writes that, "given the trauma which these children have experienced, it is critical that past trauma be understood and explored with the new caregiver within the context of the child's new life" (*Facilitating Developmental Attachment*). If they are not, the effects of the trauma will tend to distort his current relationships and make it very difficult for him to seek help from his new parents (in our case child-care workers). Child-care workers have respect and sensitivity for the past in dealing with the child but do not do focused trauma work in the milieu. Rather, they employ the Dyadic Developmental Psychotherapy attitude of PACE (Hughes 1999, p. 302). Often when the child is struggling in his day-to-day experiences and relationships, his attachment counselor, if she is not already the one working with him, needs to be brought into the interaction with the child. Since this attachment counselor attends therapy with the child, she is able to provide an even greater degree of empathy and support for the child's current struggles.

MILIEU MANAGEMENT

Another way that an attachment-based residential program differs from a traditional residential care program is how the milieu is managed. Since the program is not a behavior modification or a cognitive behavioral program, there is not a level or point system. Rather, what a child is permitted to do is based on the status of the child's relationship with the caregivers at any given point in time, as well as how anxious the child is (often exhibited by controlling and hypervigilent behavior and many questions directed at staff members). The program, which is run on the rhythm of the environment as opposed to the system or structure running the program, was developed to enhance the opportunities to focus on attunement and relationship. Attunement is a core principal of the Dyadic Developmental Psychotherapy model. In a traditional residential program, the structure of the program, such as Level 1, dictates the amount of freedom and activities for the day. In an attunement-based program that uses the Dyadic Developmental Psychotherapy model, the child-care staff have the unique opportunity to provide the children with what they need based upon their assessment of the relationship and what the child can handle. This allows the child-care worker to create a dyadically regulated relationship much as a mother has with an infant, rather than rely on an external structure to regulate the child. It is important to emphasize that nurturance is provided to the children regardless of the their behavior. This is based on the belief that children must have opportunities to experience nurturance not because they earn it but because that is what they need and deserve.

One of the ways that we remember the importance of nurturance is through the use of the mantra **"When you increase structure, you must increase nurture."** This is another basic component of Dyadic Developmental Psychotherapy. Paradoxically, child-care workers know that by increasing their nurturance of the child regardless of the child's behavior, they will offer an experience inconsistent with the child's internal working model, which may lead to an increase in the child's use of defenses and distancing behavior. The goal is that the child-care staff will be attuned enough to the child to notice small changes in behavior that will prompt the staff to intervene by using two primary interventions with the child, these being "time-in" and time in the "white room," which is a safe, neutral environment. The most restrictive type of intervention involves the seclusion room, which is only used as a last resort when the child becomes a threat to himself or others. Even during this time, a child-care worker is standing outside the door and using his voice to convey that he is present and available to the child.

In situations where this resistance becomes aggressive and/or out of control, the child-care workers utilize the interventions of "time-in." The goal is to always have the presence of a caregiver available during these times of affect dysregulation, but when children who have the impulse control and regulation capacity of a younger child and the physical body of an adolescent dysregulate, safety and security become the primary concerns. At this point it is necessary to secure physical and emotional safety for the child, other children, and staff through the use of the seclusion room. Although we would prefer to hold these children as we would an out-of-control/aggressive toddler, their physical size and strength prevent us from doing so. The best that we can do in these situations is maintain a physical presence for them outside the seclusion room and end the period of seclusion as quickly as possible.

USE OF RITUAL AND CEREMONY IN PROVIDING CLOSURE AND COHERENCE

As we continue to progress in our journey of learning how to help these children heal, we have found that infusing rituals and ceremonies throughout the program is very important. Celebrations may include the one-year anniversary of coming to Chaddock. Rituals may involve preparation for discharge and marking important events in the child's life, such as the loss of a loved one, birthdays, and adoption days.

Celebrations around admission dates occur to symbolize progress and accomplishment, as opposed to defeat and failure. For example, one situation occurred with a client whose anniversary date was coming and he was extremely angry, scared, and sad all at the same time about this date. He wanted to go home, but yet he knew this was not an option. He saw other children leave who had come after him, which disappointed him. He saw his anniversary as a failure. When he was given the information that we would be celebrating his success of being here for a year, it was amazing to observe the transformation of his outlook on the situation. He began telling others of his success at Chaddock and the fact that he was still here, as opposed to seeing his stay as being another failure. Although the celebration was extremely overwhelming and created a great deal of psychological dissonance for him, especially after it was over, he was able to see himself as having success, which for this child was extremely difficult to do.

Rituals are also used during the separation/transition phase of treatment. Preparing for discharge is often difficult for all involved, including the child, the other children in the cottage, the family, and the staff. Grief and loss issues come up throughout the treatment process, but become especially difficult as the child begins to consider moving on from treatment into a new situation. Channeling grief and sadness in positive ways, through good-bye letters, good-bye sessions, and letting-go ceremonies has been effective in assisting the child to view the loss of their relationships in a very different manner from their pervious experiences.

These experiences help create a coherent autobiographical narrative and allow for the integration of past trauma into current experience through the use of primary and secondary intersubjectivity. In this manner, meaning is created, and more healthy and flexible behaviors and options become available.

Issues Unique to a Residential Care Setting Using Dyadic Developmental Psychotherapy

Increased Degree of Parent Trauma and Burnout
One can assume that if the parent-child relationship and family dynamics have become so problematic that the child needs to enter a residential care facility, the parents and other family members will likely present as angry, overwhelmed, tired, depressed, and depleted. Parents experience a form of secondary PTSD as a result of living in what they sometimes call a "war zone" or "being a prisoner in their own home." These parents often have a need to tell the same stories about their children over and over again. It is as though they are desperate to get professionals who may have misunderstood their situation for years to finally understand their story. Unfortunately, this sometimes leads people who do not understand parent trauma to think that the parents are negative and difficult people who have nothing good to say about their child. Such people unknowingly exacerbate this scenario by trying to point out positive qualities and strengths in this child, a technique that most social service professionals are trained to utilize. Unfortunately, using this

method with a traumatized parent adds insult to injury and further convinces the parent that they are not being understood.

Another way the parent's degree of burnout and trauma impacts progress in treatment is during Chaddock visits and home visits. One of the first things that we explain to parents before they place their child at Chaddock (during what we refer to as a "preplacement visit") is the reality that we do not cure children. Our goal is to decrease the intensity, duration, and frequency of the difficult behaviors the child engages in. Parents will usually agree with and understand this premise in theory, but when they are confronted by one of the child's challenging behaviors they are often devastated that the child is not cured and that "everything is the same as before." This is a dynamic that is also explained by understanding parent trauma issues. When a child behaves in a way that has wounded the parents hundreds of times before, the effect is similar to the experience of a flashback in trauma victims. Even though it is only one incident of the behavior to the parent, who has a PTSD response to this specific behavior, one infraction has the same overwhelming, painful feeling that 100 infractions had in the past. It is essential that the parent have support from their hometown therapist to deal with these feelings and this experience. Parents need to decide, through the resolution of their own traumatization and continued work with their own therapist, what they can live with. How "good" does the child need to be? What is acceptable? It is also important that the hometown therapist work with the parents on developing a support system and a very specific plan for self-care to avoid further burnout.

This is where Dyadic Developmental Psychotherapy's emphasis on primary and secondary intersubjectivity and the creation of an attuned relationship becomes vital to successful treatment. The therapist reflects the parent's experience and accepts their affect. Because the therapist accepts the parent's affect and develops real empathy with the family, the family is enabled to accept their feelings, integrate those experiences into a coherent narrative, and move on.

LONG-DISTANCE PARENT WORK

Most of the children in our treatment program are from outside the State of Illinois, some coming from as far away as Alaska. Many people ask the question, "how can you do attachment work with a child when their parents are very far away? In particular, how can you use a therapeutic model such as Dyadic Developmental Psychotherapy, which requires involvement of the parent in therapy sessions and views the parent figure as instrumental in the child's healing process? How does one do Dyadic Developmental Psychotherapy work without the dyad?" We do acknowledge that it is always a better scenario if the child with attachment problems can remain in the home and benefit from Dyadic Developmental Psychotherapy provided on an outpatient basis. Placing a child in a residential treatment center, particularly a child that has already had repeated losses of their attachment figure, is far from the ideal situation. However, in some cases children are so severely disturbed and their behaviors so unmanageable that they cannot remain in a home setting. We believe that we have developed a model creating the best possible situation if a child must be removed from the home and placed in a residential treatment center. The child-care staff and child become the primary treatment dyad.

FAMILY VISITATION

Due to the long distances many parents live from Chaddock, their visits with their child become a critical component of working with the family. Parents are required to visit their children a minimum of once every six to eight weeks. Visits follow a progression from a very high level of staff involvement to increasingly lower levels of staff involvement, as the treatment team deems appropriate. Our experience has been that although the child's difficulties many times did not develop in the current family system (most of the children in our program are adopted out of the foster care system or from orphanages), family systems begin to organize around the symptoms of the child. By the time that the child's behaviors are serious enough to require residential treatment, often the parents and the child have become victim to a negative cycle that both parents and child perpetuate. In other words, even though the pathology of the child did not originate in the family system, the family eventually begins to engage in behaviors that perpetuate and sometimes exacerbate the child's initial symptoms. Few families can continue to maintain behaviors and affect that promote attachment in a child who is repeatedly attempting to sabotage the parent's efforts to build a loving and reciprocal relationship.

Initial parent visits occur entirely in the cottage with staff present. The treatment team explains to the parents that the goal of the first few visits is to allow the parents to begin to have fun with their child and observe how the child-care staff work with their child and other children in the milieu. It is a chance for the parents to observe the cottage staff using the attitude of PACE that Dyadic Developmental Psychotherapy describes—being playful, accepting, curious, and empathic in interactions with their child as well as with other children in the cottage. It is critically important that the negative cycle of the parent-child interaction begin to be interrupted in this early stage of treatment. Therefore, we ask that parents let the child-care staff handle any behavioral issues that their child exhibits during the visit. Many parents tell us that by the time their child enters our program they have become more like wardens or cops than parents. They feel tremendous grief and sadness about the loss of what they had hoped would be a loving and guiding parent role with their child. We ask parents to let us be the "wardens" during these early visits so they can relax and explore the possibility of having fun with and enjoying their child in a way that very possibly has not happened in a number of years, if ever.

Eventually, the parents are given the opportunity to take the child out of the cottage for short excursions such as dinner or a visit to the local mall. One of the cottage staff will accompany the parent(s) and child so staff can intervene if the child or parent begin to struggle. Even though the child may have significantly improved many of their behaviors, the anxiety of seeing their parent (the most intimate relationship they have) causes the old behaviors to emerge again. The cottage staff member who is with the family can intervene with a response that is different from what the parent has used, and this will often diffuse the situation, as well as allow the parent to see how an alternate response can be successful with the child. These visits allow us further opportunities to access difficulties the parent and child have reported as well as patterns between the parent and child observed in the Marschak Interaction Method assessment. These interactions provide valuable information that can be used in the therapeutic work with the family.

As the child improves and the parent has had opportunity to begin their own healing process, as well as to gain knowledge through working with their hometown therapist, completing therapeutic reading assignments, and participating in milieu observation, the treatment team will determine if it is time for the parent and child to venture out on their own without the support of the program staff. Their first outing together will be a similar activity to their first time off campus with the child, such as going out to dinner. However, this time there will not be a staff member with them. The parent is instructed to bring the child back to campus immediately if the child begins to struggle or if the parent feels too anxious. In this way the parent and child can come back and, with the support of the cottage staff or their therapist, process what is happening in the dyad. This provides an excellent opportunity for exploring the "shame-inducing experience" of the child, as is essential in the Dyadic Developmental Psychotherapy model, almost immediately when it is happening rather than at a time later in the week as is typically done in weekly outpatient therapy.

Through all of these steps in the progression of visits, we gain a deeper knowledge of the dance the child is caught in with the parent(s) and are able to design more specific interventions to address the family's difficulties. Eventually, when the parent and child have had success on short-term visits away from the campus, an overnight visit to a local hotel where the parents are staying can be planned. These visits have the same parameters in that the parent is to bring the child back to campus if either they or the child begin to struggle.

Finally, during the final separation phase of treatment, the child goes on home visits. During these home visits, the parent is instructed to have appointments set up with the hometown therapist so that therapy can begin occurring in their home community and so that the parents and child have local support available during the home visit. In addition, the parent is also given a written plan called an Individual Care Plan, which lists all of the problem behaviors of the child and the treatment team's recommended responses based on their experiences of what has been successful in managing the child while they have been at Chaddock. Finally, as another means of support, the Chaddock staff will call daily to check on how things are going with the visit, and the parent is encouraged to call the team if they need advice or assistance during the visit.

STAFF TRAINING

The paradigm shift to Dyadic Developmental Psychotherapy for residential treatment from a Reality Therapy/Choice Theory approach has been a long journey for us. One aspect that has been particularly arduous is convincing staff that the resistance phase of treatment described previously is to be expected and actually indicates the child is making progress. It is indicative that the child is no longer honeymooning and is beginning to show the team the difficulties that landed him in residential care to begin with. Children can often keep up this hypervigilance, which appears at times to be a manipulative charade, for many weeks or even months. We are pleased when the child moves on to the resistance phase. This allows us to begin to demonstrate to the child that we can work with, accept, and even embrace all the parts of him, not just the nice parts. However, many staff members, like parents, have the idea that controlling or squelching behavior is desired and preferable. Childcare staff need to be able to reframe the child's challenging behaviors as part of the defensive structure that is bound to become more prominent when we begin to touch on the child's core issues of trauma. They cannot personalize it and must trust that they will not be blamed by the administration for not appropriately dealing with or managing to keep the child's behavior in check.

Another challenge in training staff in an attachment-based model and Dyadic Developmental Psychotherapy is that attunement, attachment theory, and understanding of trauma dictate how to interact with a child rather than a specific set of rules or a predetermined structure. This makes the role of the child-care worker very complex in that each child in the milieu may require a unique response. Many staff find this unpredictable, constantly changing way of dealing with the children very anxiety-producing initially. Eventually, when they have internalized attachment theory and PACE, and can view the children through this lens, things become clearer. Philosophy dictates what to do, and the decision is much easier when you have internalized the philosophy. The state between trying to use "techniques" they see senior staff using while still not yet understanding the theory and rationale is a confusing and stressful time for staff because it appears that there is no consistency and no right way of doing things. Staff must be given a great deal of support from their team and their supervisor to be able to endure this uncomfortable phase of their training and development. Self-care among staff, just as with parents, needs to be emphasized. Even more experienced staff can burn out when dealing with the barrage of behaviors that eight to ten significantly disturbed traumatized children can throw at their caretaker. If staff are not taking care of themselves and working on their own issues, just as we ask parents to do, they cannot be effective and therapeutic with the children. We often remind staff and each other, *"If you don't work your issues, the kids will work them for you."*

SUMMARY

Through the incorporation of Dyadic Developmental Psychotherapy into Chaddock's Integrative Attachment Therapy Residential program, this intensive treatment has gained added depth, and thus effectiveness, in creating pathways for healing. The specific therapeutic interventions guided by Dyadic Developmental Psychotherapy principles allow the adolescents in the program to revisit and process their traumatic past in such a way that they feel safe and supported enough to venture through the dark recesses of their experiences to create a new picture of reality.

Interventions such as "the attitude" have given staff definitive tools to set clear, consistent expectations with these youth, thus freeing them to approach the child in a much more empathic, sensitive manner. This provides a new experience and new opportunities to build a framework for attachment with young people for whom traditional methods are simply ineffective.

Treatment that excludes parents is fleeting in its effectiveness. Educating parents in the fundamentals of Dyadic Developmental Psychotherapy and how to incorporate the attitude into their relationship with their child is a critical part of the puzzle. Traditional parenting strategies have proven unsuccessful with their children, and Dyadic Developmental Psychotherapy can provide a lifeline for parents to sustain their hope for a caring, reciprocal attachment with their child. Chaddock's Integrative Attachment Therapy program demonstrates that, more than a specific technique, Dyadic Developmental Psychotherapy provides a frame of reference that impacts every aspect of a program, from therapy to milieu experiences, parent, staff, and child.

Dyadic Developmental Psychotherapy in Residential Treatment

SCOTT L. BLACKWELL & JOSEPH MCGUILL

Alexi's early life would read like a Russian novel, but it is true. Alexi was born to a poor, homeless Russian woman who abused alcohol during pregnancy. Nothing is known of his first months of life, but at nine months of age, he and his sister were abandoned in a forest outside of a small Russian village. He and his sister were discovered and placed in an orphanage, where he lived until he was seven years old. While living in the orphanage that housed well over a thousand other children, he received no education and insufficient nutrition, and he was neglected and abused. When he was seven years of age, Alexi was rescued by a caring couple who brought him to their home in the United States. However, he immediately began having difficulties bonding with his parents and adjusting to life in a home and community. Alexi would become severely aggressive by screaming, throwing things, and threatening to kill himself and others when any limit was set. When confronted with stealing from home, Alexi would lie and run away. His parents desperately attempted to show him that they cared for him, but ultimately turned to professional help. Unfortunately, Alexi's behaviors escalated to setting fires, harming animals, and fighting with children at school. On one occasion, he stole a handgun from a store and expressed his wish to kill others at school, his parents, and then himself. By nine years of age, Alexi had been hospitalized on two occasions, placed on multiple medications, and was engaged in extensive outpatient psychotherapy, all with little sustaining effect. Over the next two years, Alexi participated in behavioral modification residential treatment on two occasions, two more hospitalizations, and referrals to the juvenile authorities for assault and battery and destruction of property. He was described as chronically suicidal and had made several gestures to harm himself. Four years of living with Alexi had left his parents feeling desperate and hopeless. Their marriage was in shambles, and they were wondering where to turn next.

Bill's mother was only 15 when she got pregnant after a brief encounter with a much older man. She had a history of emotional instability and was frequently homeless or temporarily residing with different men. She was known to abuse alcohol and drugs. After becoming pregnant with Bill, she attempted to stabilize her life with Bill's biological father. However, he also had a history of drug abuse and was frequently unavailable.

Due to their chaotic lifestyle, Bill was raised with a variety of relatives as his mother drifted in and out of his life until he was five years of age. Bill was just beginning kindergarten when his mother gave him a note to take to the store. An intelligent and perceptive boy, Bill had a feeling that his mother was in trouble and did not take the note to the store. Rather, he walked to a neighborhood police substation and told them he was worried about her. At the substation, Bill overheard the police scanner when the police arrived at his home. He listened as it graphically described the remains of his mother, who had killed herself with a shotgun blast to the head. Bill's troubled life then became even more chaotic. He was placed with various relatives who did not have much time for him. Soon, Bill was harboring frequent suicidal thoughts, banging his head to the point of bleeding, and complaining of frequent nightmares. Stealing, lying, destroying property, and fighting were common occurrences for him in school and in the community. Trials of outpatient psychotherapy were frequently interrupted, and inpatient hospitalizations resulted in only brief changes of medication. By 10 years of age, one of his caretakers expressed concerns that the family may need to relinquish their parental rights unless Bill could get the help he needed.

Simone's first four years of life were spent going from her biological parents' home to various foster homes. Her biological parents were frequently accused of neglect and abuse, which resulted in Simone's first foster placement when she was four months old. For the next two years, attempts were made to help her parents care for little Simone, but to no avail. Two-year-old Simone and all of her siblings were adopted by a single woman who meant well. However, Simone's adoptive mother relinquished custody of all the children four years later after being charged with severe physical abuse. Simone again lived in a variety of foster homes until adopted at age seven. At that time, Simone had little trust for adults and a great deal of anger. She exhibited severe temper outbursts, was a habitual liar, and showed little empathy after hurting other children at school. Intensive outpatient psychotherapy and several medications did little in changing Simone's behavior. Although she would behave for short periods of time, temper outbursts became more violent. The family tried inpatient hospitalization and intensive outpatient "attachment-oriented" therapy with little success. Simone could be superficially engaging, which led to her parents' questioning their parenting ability and feeling blame for their daughter's behaviors. However, problems at home continued to escalate, and Simone was placed in a foster home. Within two weeks, Simone's problem behaviors in the foster home led to her immediate removal.

These children and many others with similar histories of attachment disruption and trauma are often described as hopeless and incorrigible while their parents are emotionally, physically, and frequently financially drained. Although many mental health professionals may concur that outpatient psychotherapy, inpatient hospitalization, and other less restricted means of treatment have not been successful, they continue to harbor concerns with residential treatment. For example, many professionals argue that placing the child away from home, especially for an extended period of time, will break the bond between the child and his parents, which may contribute to the relinquishment of custody. Secondly, the family may become comfortable without the child in their home, which will interfere with the developing attachment between child and parents. Finally, many express concerns about the high cost of residential treatment in comparison to the more reasonable cost of continued outpatient psychotherapy, in spite of the poor results and possibly escalating crises for the child and family. These concerns fail to consider the following issues.

First, the bond or attachment between these children and parents are disturbed or pathological as exemplified by the escalating pattern of aggressively acting out, leading to excessive punishment and control. This bond may need to be "broken" before a more nurturant attachment can grow. Rates of relinquishment of adoptive children have been estimated to occur in up to 30% of adoptive families. Many of the families referred for residential treatment have already considered relinquishment; therefore the creation of a supportive, attuned attachment between parents and child would minimize the occurrence of parental relinquishment.

Secondly, the risk of the family becoming comfortable in their relationships without the child living at home is a significant concern. However, the overwhelming needs and behavioral difficulties of attachment-resistant children have significantly interfered with or disturbed many, if not all, family relationships. It is not uncommon that the parents report severe marital discord due to years of chronic crises while the child's siblings harbor resentment and depression as their own wishes and needs have been neglected. Placing a child in residential treatment allows the family to address neglected issues within their family so as to better prepare them for the needs of their child when he or she returns home.

Finally, the high cost of attachment-oriented treatment cannot be disputed. However, continuing ineffective treatment and the revolving door of repeated hospitalizations is not only costly in the short run, but extremely costly to the family and community. The child may require containment, often in correctional facilities, or extensive adult psychiatric services as he or she matures. Children with a history of disturbed attachment without effective treatment have a higher incidence of personality disorders as they repeat the disturbed attachment patterns in their adult lives while draining society in mental health and supportive services.

Therefore, attachment-focused residential treatment provides an important therapeutic service for many severely disturbed children and their families and should be considered when all other therapeutic services are deemed unsuccessful.

MODELS OF RESIDENTIAL CARE

To facilitate an understanding of how Dyadic Developmental Psychotherapy can be integrated into residential treatment, differentiation of the models of residential care is necessary. Acute hospitalization usually adopts a medical model in which the average length of stay ranges from one day to a few weeks. The goal of treatment in this model is crisis management or stabilization and returning the child to his home and community as soon as possible. A psychiatrist usually directs treatment, which is focused on medication and referrals for follow-up care. Therapy, if provided, usually consists of brief cognitive behavioral techniques to defuse the crisis while providing skills for management outside the hospital. Family therapy usually involves psychoeducation and occasional parent support groups. De-escalation of severe temper outbursts is usually through chemical or mechanical restraints or seclusion.

Most forms of residential treatment, including partial hospitalization, adopt a behavior-modification model. Length of stay may be for a few weeks to a few months, depending on the severity of symptoms and the constraints of insurance. The primary agent of change is the therapist, who oversees a behavior-modification program within the milieu and adapts the program to home. The focus of treatment is on behavioral regulation, which rewards "good behavior" with points and level systems and punishes "bad" behavior with response cost, time-out, and isolation. Therapy usually involves weekly individual psychotherapy and periodic family therapy to educate the parents about their child's psychiatric disorder and to help them create a behavioral modification program in their home. A child's acting-out behaviors are met with time-outs and physical restraints, as well as chemical restraints.

In contrast, residential treatment using Dyadic Developmental Psychotherapy requires an extended period of time, often nine to 18 months, with a focus on developing more safe and secure relationships and helping the child to regulate his or her emotions. The primary agent of change is the milieu or the living environment encompassing the relationships with the child-care workers. Through these relationships the child begins to learn to co-regulate stressing emotions with an adult, which is then practiced with their most intimate relationships within their families. Rewards through points and levels to change behavior are not used in this model, but rather "privileges" are given to a child based upon what the child needs, not what the child earns. In Dyadic Developmental Psychotherapy in a residential setting, attunement to the child's emotional state is fundamental. This is not to say that there are no limits for misbehavior within this model. Natural and non-punitive consequences frequently follow behavioral difficulties. Time-out or isolating the child from others is never used. Rather, co-regulation with child-care workers or the use of "time-ins" help a child trust that adults can care for them when upset or dysregulated. Suffice to say that all therapy is considered "family therapy" in this model. Individual therapy with the child is conducted with a child-care worker who not only provides support in the session, but may also be actively involved in role-playing or other therapeutic interventions. Issues in therapy are integrated into the milieu, where they can be incorporated into the child's everyday life. Dyadic Developmental Psychotherapy serves as an excellent model for residential treatment as reparative attachment sequences can occur countless times between the child and child-care worker, child and therapist, and child and parent.

MODEL OF MILIEU THERAPY

The Villa Santa Maria in Cedar Crest, New Mexico has integrated Dyadic Developmental Psychotherapy into its model of residential treatment for children. The Villa Santa Maria was founded in 1955 by the Reverend Monsignor Bernard M. Burns as a home for troubled children. Over the past four decades, the Villa has served hundreds of children and their families. What was originally conceived as a group home evolved into a multidisciplinary residential treatment center. In May, 1992, Villa Santa Maria was certified by New Mexico Children, Youth and Families Department to provide mental health services and rehabilitation for children. In 1998, the Villa's leadership and staff committed to implementing Dyadic Developmental Psychotherapy as our sole clinical approach. The Villa Santa Maria is a private, nonprofit charitable organization with no religious affiliation.

MILIEU

In a residential program that uses Dyadic Developmental Psychotherapy, the milieu is often seen as the most significant and powerful agent of change for the client. This is not meant to minimize the contributions of other aspects of residential life, formal therapy, and education, but to emphasize the importance of the intense primary care relationship in the client's emotional development. Regardless of which model a residential facility employs, undeniably it is the environment where the client will spend the majority of their time.

MODEL

Given the history of children with attachment disorders and the array of services they traditionally have received prior to residential treatment, it is imperative that an environment of safety and caring be established. In other words, a secure base must be established from which all other modalities can draw. The secure base enables the child to explore difficult feelings and histories with others in their treatment. To establish this culture, we approach the child in the milieu with the guiding message: *"We will take care of you."* We view the task of the milieu as one of building intense personal relationships with children who find it difficult to trust and often resist the care of others.

To begin, we limit the number of rules for the children in the milieu. Behavior modification systems, as seen in more traditional settings, have not been effective for these children who often demonstrate poor cause-effect thinking. In addition, behavioral models tend to focus more on behavioral aspects of the child rather than on relationships and their respective internal working models. The de-emphasis on points and levels prioritizes the interpersonal interactions between the caregiver and the child. Interpersonal interactions are the central focus when applying Dyadic Developmental Psychotherapy in a residential setting.

Oftentimes, parents and professionals believe that a list of rules, rewards, and consequences will provide structure, safety, and compliance. However, in children with compromised attachment, this is rarely the case. Interventions such as these would be effective if the child trusted adults to be fair and consistent and they believed themselves to be worthy of privileges, which is rarely the case.

THE MILIEU SETS THREE BASIC RULES

1. THE CHILD NEEDS TO ASK FOR EVERYTHING S/HE NEEDS AND WANTS.

Having the children ask for everything they need and want has important effects that are key elements in the care and treatment of the child. First, it promotes an interaction between the child and the caregiver and shows the child that an adult is here to take care of the child's needs. This creates a dependency on the adult caregiver, who must be nurturing, timely, and accurate in providing care. Second, this rule promotes safety and success with the premise that the caregiver will not do anything that would not be good or safe for the child.

2. WE MUST KNOW WHERE YOU ARE AT ALL TIMES.

The important message here is that if we don't know where you are, we cannot take care of you or keep you safe.

3. No hands on without permission.
The message to the child is "you will not be hurt and others will not hurt you." The message is that touch is an important and meaningful part of relationships and should not be harmful or indiscriminate.

Beyond these rules, which keep everyone safe, interactions with the child shift in response to what is best for that child at the moment. Interactions and communication with the child are flexible, stressing alliance and reciprocity in the relationship. This is how we implement a guiding principle of Dyadic Developmental Psychotherapy, maintaining attunement.

Finally, the children will be kept close at all times. The focus of the treatment with the caregiver is the *relationship*. It is these interpersonal relationships that are seen as the foundation for emotional and behavioral gains within the milieu setting.

Guiding Philosophical Concepts

- Children get what they need, not what they earn.

- Nuturance is a right of the child.

- Fairness is getting what you need, not the same amount or the same thing as another child.

- True change is based on the intense interpersonal relationship, and is not technique-driven.

- Everyone has permission to feel.

- All moments in the interactions with the child are seen as therapeutic opportunities.

- Care prioritizes alliance rather than compliance.

Treatment Concepts Important to Attachment-Driven Milieu

Attunement
The caregiver is present to the child's affective state at all times to meet the child's needs in a timely and accurate manner. In short, the caregiver lends himself to the child to help organize the child's internal feelings and to help clarify misunderstandings and misinterpretations.

RHYTHM CONTROL

Rhythm control is a regulatory process that helps to manage the pace and processing of the children's emotions and behaviors within the milieu. Rhythm management provides safety and promotes trust in the caregivers while facilitating attachment. Emotional and behavioral states are contagious as the child can enter yours or you can enter theirs. In the milieu setting, it is the adult's responsibility to set and manage the rhythms. The philosophy asserts: *"He who controls the rhythms controls the house."*

SUPPORTIVE CONTROL

All interventions are supportive in nature. Interventions are neither punishment nor consequences. The focus of supportive control is providing what is in the best interest of the child. Discipline and control are demonstrated as nurturance, not punishment. Alliance building is emphasized over compliance in the adult-child relationship. Supportive control should always move in a proactive manner. The application is to help children meet the expectations of the adult rather than react to situations that have occurred in a punitive manner. The intensity of all interactions with the child, if supportive and nurturing, will strengthen the relationship. Compliance only intensifies shame and is often perceived by the child as rejecting and abusive.

CLOSENESS

Children at the Villa are kept close at all times. Physical presence gives the children a sense of safety and relays the message that the adult caregiver is capable of being present, even during difficult times. This sense of safety or a secure base allows the child to explore the world around him with adult support. In addition, closeness promotes an interrelatedness and reciprocity in the healthy relationship.

At the Villa closeness is not negotiable. When a child is upset, she is brought even closer to the adult. In essence, the child has been given the message that when she is unable to self-regulate, the caregiver will help.

Isolation is never used in the milieu. Isolation serves only to distance the relationship between the adult and the child, supporting a sense that the child is "bad" and the caregiver cannot provide safety. In addition, isolation asks the child with poor impulse control to self-regulate, which is not a well-developed skill in these children. It is not a skill an infant develops on their own, nor is it a skill that should be expected of these children because of their chronological age and developmental level of functioning. It is tantamount to emotional abuse to leave these children alone with their anger, sadness, shame, and despair.

Isolation takes many forms that are unacceptable within the milieu. Although not exhaustive, these include sending a child to their room, isolation rooms, mechanical restraints, chemical restraints, time-outs, and social isolation of any kind.

It should be kept in mind that no amount of rules or structure provided can substitute for closeness.

STAGES OF TREATMENT

The child-care staff practice three developmental stages of treatment within the milieu that are based on Dyadic Developmental Psychotherapy: Trust of Care, Trust of Control, and Trust of Self.

TRUST OF CARE

Dependency on a healthy caregiver is emphasized. The caregiver serves to meet all of the physical and emotional needs of the child in a timely and accurate manner. Remember, the children ask for everything they need and want. Basic caregiving and safety are emphasized. We recognize the child's inherent biological need to be kept safe and close. The message is: "I can take care of you, I will take care of you, and I want to take care of you."

In the milieu, Trust of Care takes the form of such things as keeping doors locked, overt supervision, safe touch, proximity, smiling, unsolicited nurturing, actively repairing relationships, empathy, curiosity, acceptance, attunement, avoiding shaming and lecturing, rocking, surprises, playing with and not just watching children, an overall concern for the physical environment, and the creation of a healthy, mutual history together. Practical care includes combing the child's hair, clipping their toenails and fingernails, helping wash their face, and tying their shoes. The issue is not whether the child is capable of these tasks, as many obviously are. However, these activities are experienced as healthy caregiving and ease resistance to nurturance and intimacy. Using the theoretical framework of Dyadic Developmental Psychotherapy, these actions underscore that the child is loved and lovable, intrinsically good.

The consistent demonstration of these interactions creates a secure base that allows the children to trust that their caregiver is doing what is best for them. When problems arise, we have built a history of safe and nurturing caregiving. The care begins to take on qualities that feel good and are gratifying. In short, a healthy dependency is created, needs are met, and trust is built.

TRUST OF CONTROL

The caregivers demonstrate nurturant discipline and control. Limits are set to assist children in meeting expectations of the caregiver. We prevent the child from doing things that are not good for them. For the caregiver, the language of alliance is paramount over the language of compliance. ("I see you are having a really difficult time with that right now. If you need me, I can help you with that.") The intent is to help the child regulate behavior and emotions through the process of co-regulating.

Trust of Control is about the caregiver's ability to set limits, and as such, attunement will be broken. Within this context, emotional tensions may run high, and feelings and behaviors will need to be regulated; shame will arise, and relationships will need to be repaired. Discipline and control is followed by repair, thus reducing shame while helping to regulate behavior and teach self-control. This repetition of interactions and the cycle of repair contributes to the permanency of the relationship.

The emphasis and subsequent interactions for the child-care worker will always be presented in a context of supportive control rather than reactive control. The caregiver's interactions will be proactive rather than reactive.

TRUST OF SELF

During this phase of treatment, more trust and responsibility is given back to the child. The child has demonstrated the ability to self-regulate or can recognize dysregulation and seek adult care. The child demonstrates flexibility in their relationships and begins to feel and care about others. The child can repair relationships and move ahead successfully. We begin to see the child make efforts to reconnect and re-attune in ways that are internally driven. The development of remorse as opposed to shame begins to materialize.

The caregivers begin to adjust and transform the language and messages given to the child to match the child's newly acquired, internally driven efforts to reconnect and reattune relationship breaches. These messages can now be communicated and received as they are meant; they rely upon the relationship connection built between the child and caregiver. The child's now-genuine internal desire to feel close to the caregiver allows this shift. The message may be "I don't like it when you ..." (now the child can recognize behaviors as separate from core sense of self), as opposed to early treatment, when the focus is on "it's not good for you to ..." (then, the caregiver isn't expecting the child to be able to separate expressed behaviors from internalized sense of negative self).

In addition, opportunities for autonomy are increased. The children may attend public school, participate in community activities, receive extended home passes, and have increased responsibilities in the milieu. More choices, compromises, and negotiations are entered into with the child.

INTERVENTIONS IN THE ATTACHMENT-DRIVEN MILIEU

Before entering into a discussion of overt interventions, it is important to understand that the philosophy is the overriding intervention. Without the philosophy, interventions are meaningless. Specifically, Dyadic Developmental Psychotherapy defines that the shape of relationships are the catalyst and leverage that bring about change in the children, not the interventions themselves. In this particular model, the act of intervening and the manner in which that act is carried out are what is healing.

SEATS

Within the milieu, as a form of helping children with regulation, seats are utilized. The use of seats has taken on different meanings for different professionals. Here it is important to discriminate between different philosophical constructs.

WHAT SEATS ARE	WHAT SEATS ARE NOT
• Structured yet flexible	• Ridged
• Non-isolative	• Isolative
• Rhythmic	• Stationary
• Emotional/Cognitive/Physical presence with caregiver	• Emotional/Cognitive/Physical distance from caregiver
• Co-construction of meaning	• Primarily behaviorally focused
• Proactive	• Reactive
• Co-regulating	• Self-regulating

First and foremost, seats are used by employing the concept of supportive control. In other words, a seat is never given as a punishment, but as a proactive step to slow the child down before the child engages in behaviors that will not be good for them. Fundamentally, the task is to help the child gain self-control and process with the child what is going on in the moment to gain control of the rhythms.

Seats are never used to produce physical discomfort for the child with the intent that the child's behavior will be extinguished as a result of the adverse effects. A seat is a way to help children meet expectations, not punishment for unmet expectations of the adult.

Secondly, seats are viewed as time-ins rather than time-outs. Seats are a time when a child is experiencing emotional difficulty and needs the closeness of the adult to help regulate emotions and to attune to the needs of the child at the moment. The attunement takes on the properties of empathy, curiosity, acceptance, and an overall ability of the caregiver to be present with the child's pain.

The overall function of the seat is not to get the child to say the behavior will never happen again, as this would prove futile, but to help by "holding and containing" as the caregiver soothes and helps the child process their feelings. The message from the adult is "I understand, I can help, and I can be present with the difficult times as well as with the good times."

HOLDING

Philosophically, holding at the Villa is seen on a broad spectrum which includes cognitive, emotional, and physical aspects. Before entering into a discussion of holding, it is important to draw distinction between "holding therapy" and "therapeutic holds."

Holding therapy in the context of rage reduction is not the intended practice within the Villa milieu model. As described in Chapter One, which provides you with the basis for our approach, intrusive and coercive interventions are not a part of the model of treatment specified by Dyadic Developmental Psychotherapy. Within the milieu setting, the intent is not to provoke rage in the child in the hopes of forming a bond or bringing the child to the point of exhaustion in hopes of a calmer day. The intent of holding a child within the milieu is to provide a container for all to be safe: the child, the caregiver, and the other children in the program. This is holding in an emotional sense. Caregivers move from the concepts of escalate and de-escalate to the concept of co-regulate.

The co-regulatory aspects assist the child in gaining control over aggressive impulses. Initially this appears more in the form of external regulation, but ultimately, the child assimilates the rhythm leading to progress toward self-regulation. In short, the child forms the ability to identify and communicate their feelings and to control their own impulses and affective states.

All touch should be nurturing. It is important for the caregiver to match the vitality of the child's feeling states while being attuned to the intensity and shape of the affect. During this time, it is important for the caregiver to maintain an emotional connectedness, empathy, acceptance, caring, soothing, and an overall sense of relatedness to the child. No one should ever touch a child unless that person is regulated themselves.

When a therapeutic restraint for safety reasons is initiated, the end of a hold is often followed by a deep sense of shame for the child. Therapeutic restraints are not therapy. These are restraints used to protect a child from hurting himself or others. At this critical time, the caregiver will intimately process feelings with the child. It is critical that the shape of this process take on the qualities of interpersonal repair. The quality of the hold is measured by safety, the child's ability to process feelings, and his/her ability to engage in repair.

We always want to give the child the message that we can take care of and be present with their rageful emotions. We also want to give the message of hope. "I am really going to be excited for you when the day comes that you have the 'gift of self-control.'" But we will be with them until that day comes.

TRANSITION GROUPS

Transition groups are impromtu gatherings/meetings used whenever there will be a change in routine. Everyone involved will be asked to gather together to talk about and reflect on the change so that the effects can be talked out and shared, instead of being acted out. Transitions are an integral part of rhythm control. They are held whenever a change is made in the structured segments of the day. Before transitions are made, emotions and behaviors are regulated and needs are met. The transition groups provide the care, safety, and emotional regulation that is needed to move throughout the day. Ultimately, these transitions serve to instill in the child their own sense of internal control.

ROLE OF THE THERAPIST

The therapist provides three major functions at Villa Santa Maria: individual therapist, milieu consultant, and family therapist. Principles of Dyadic Developmental Psychotherapy guide the therapist in each role.

However, in keeping with the philosophy of Dyadic Developmental Psychotherapy, the child-care worker is present in the therapy sessions, and the worker's relationship with the child is frequently the focus of the session. The day-to-day interactions between child and child-care worker create a unique bond in which sequences of attunement/shame/reattunement occur in a naturalistic setting. Initially, therapy helps to create a link with the child's past experiences and their manifestation in current situations played out in the milieu. In addition, feelings or behaviors which have occurred in the milieu are brought into therapy to help the child learn to coregulate his/her emotions with a child-care worker, thereby increasing his/her trust that adults will provide safety, security, and consistency when the child is exploring painful emotions. At all times, techniques that maintain the healing PACE are used. The child is accepted for whatever s/he brings into the therapy session and guided to resolve past hurts and to enhance coherence in his/her life story. Finally, the child-care workers are integrated into therapy not only for safety, nurturance, and support, but also as active participants who may assist in role-playing to better resolve past traumas. If a child becomes dysregulated, child-care workers can help the child become co-regulated and calm in a safe and nurturant manner.

The therapist also provides a vital role as milieu consultant. Relevant information from individual and family therapy is shared with child-care workers to assist them in their understanding of the child and how such issues are expressed in the child's day-to-day interactions with others. In addition, the therapist may participate in activities such as play or meal preparation while observing the attachment sequences which reoccur countless times throughout the day. The therapist must have expertise in principles of attachment theory and its expression within the milieu. The therapist can then act as a consultant to the milieu as a whole as well as on specific issues with each individual child. Transference and counter-transference issues between child-care workers and children are explored on a regular basis. Although the therapists are assigned specific children for therapy, it is often said that *"all the children belong to all of us,"* which acknowledges that the children have relationships with all members of the treatment team. Therapists are kept apprised of each child's specific history and therapeutic progress.

Finally, the therapist provides family therapy with a child-care worker frequently present. The therapists are respectful of the primary relationship between parents and child. Children admitted to Villa Santa Maria have strong emotional ties to their families, both positive and negative, which influence almost all areas of their life. The family provides the unique personal history for the child through experiences, teachings, and a shared family heritage of genetic, cultural, and social influences. The primary significance of the family's role in the child's life is never questioned, but rather actively acknowledged and supported.

STAGES OF FAMILY INVOLVEMENT

Family therapy at Villa Santa Maria involves three sequential, but often overlapping stages. These stages are based on Dyadic Developmental Psychotherapy principals and practice. Each stage has its own goals and interventions that seek to successfully reunite the child with their family and community. The focus of treatment may change from parent-child interactions to the parent's own attachment histories to marital and sibling relationships and back again to parent-child interactions. The follow-ing is a description of the three stages of family involvement, which coin-cide with the overall stages of attachment-focused residential treatment.

STAGE ONE: TRUST OF CARE

The primary goal of the Trust of Care stage is alliance building. The family and staff at Villa Santa Maria are learning from each other rather than actively changing behaviors. The family is developing relationships with child-care workers, therapists, teachers, and medical personnel while Villa Santa Maria staff are gaining further information from the family through documents and observations to direct the treatment process. Parents par-ticipate in treatment team meetings to develop and review treatment plans. Parents of children placed in Villa Santa Maria may experience a variety of emotions including relief, guilt, anger, resentment, and loss, which are shared and explored through regular telephone contact and vis-its with their child's therapist. Through exploration, a parent can resolve these feelings, leading to renewed hope and excitement as their child progresses through treatment and prepares to return home. In addition, as the family is less consumed by the intense behavioral and emotional demands of their child, they may become aware of the needs of others within their family. Sibling or marital issues which have been overlooked or neglected can then become a focus of treatment.

Family involvement during the Trust of Care stage includes helping the family to reestablish enjoyment and attunement in their relationship with their child while understanding and empathizing with their child's fears of rejection and abandonment. Regular telephone contact is encouraged between family members and their child with brief dialogues between the parents and child-care workers. The therapist also establishes a weekly telephone interview with the parents in order to share information about the child's well-being and to obtain further diagnostic information. These telephone calls are an opportunity for parents to learn more about the treatment program at Villa Santa Maria, ask specific questions re-garding their child's care, and discuss any issues with the child's teacher or other staff members. If the child is taking medications, telephone contact with the child's psychiatrist will occur. Parents are encouraged to call their child on a weekly basis, not only to support their bond, but also to encourage their child to participate in the program and to relieve fears of abandonment by reiterating that the child will return home when he or she and the family are ready.

The child may harbor rescue fantasies, and he or she may attempt to manipulate the parents to prematurely remove them from the program, thereby avoiding or escaping their own internal struggles which led to placement. These rescue fantasies may result in comments to their parents that they have miraculously changed and are ready to return home or that the staff is not as helpful or caring as their parents. These behaviors can be quite painful for parents who struggle with their own guilt and anxiety. It is important for the parents to share their feelings and concerns when such interactions arise while encouraging their child to participate in the program and reassuring their child that they will return home when the time is right. Talking with child-care workers prior to and following telephone calls with the child helps to minimize the deleterious effects of these rescue fantasies.

In some situations, placement of a troubled youth at Villa Santa Maria will reveal the needs of other family members, which have been neglected due to the child's behavioral and emotional difficulties at home. Although family therapy during visits is helpful for many families, it is insufficient to meet the needs of all the family members. Individual counseling or marital therapy with providers who use Dyadic Developmental Psychotherapy may be needed. The therapist will refer the family to a therapist in their home community and then communicate with that therapist to integrate the treatment approaches.

Family visits to Villa Santa Maria are not only encouraged, but are crucial for successful treatment. Visits, which involve family therapy, time spent within the milieu, and psychoeducation with an expert in child development, occur every four to six weeks. In addition, visits may include brief passes for the child and the family to help reestablish their enjoyment with each other. Within the milieu, parents are offered the opportunity to observe their child in relationship to child-care workers, which leads to discussions regarding parenting practices, communication skills, and discipline methods. Milieu visits may last up to four hours at a time and may include engaging in daily activities such as meal preparation, chores, and recreational activities. Through such observations, the parent's trust that staff members are able to care for their child increases. Finally, participation in the milieu will also encourage an understanding of the attachment model in preparation of skill acquisition in stage two, Trust of Control.

STAGE TWO: TRUST OF CONTROL
The focus during the Trust of Control stage is on change. Trust between the family and Villa Santa Maria has developed, and a clear treatment plan for the child and the family has been established. During this stage, the focus of change is on the current behaviors and interactions of the child and on helping the parents develop confidence in their ability to parent their child. Family members may also be helped to accept and prepare for conditions which are likely to persist. For example, a child's neurological and developmental difficulties may more clearly emerge as his/her behavioral or emotional problems diminish.

The focus on current behaviors is not to say that past experiences are not important during this stage. Using supportive reenactment while maintaining co-regulation with their parents, the therapist may encourage the child to remember or experience past traumas, losses, or difficulties. Supportive holding techniques are often used during this stage to help the child remain connected to his parents while experiencing painful feelings. Holding techniques involve the child's sitting on the parent's lap or being calmly rocked. Child-care workers present in family therapy may model more effective co-regulation practices for the parents. Although past traumas may be reexperienced, the primary focus in the middle stage is on reparative interactions between the child and parents rather than simply gaining information or developing insight.

Change for the child and family is through skill acquisition. The child is participating in an intense treatment process in which he or she is developing new psychological and relational skills. Skills may include identifying and communicating feelings, self-regulation, enhanced conflict-resolution skills, and relationship skills such as learning to empathize with others. Parents are also faced with developing new skills that parallel the child's progress and treatment. These new parenting skills help to replace past responses of anger, futility, and hopelessness with feelings of competence and renewed investment in their child. Dyadic Developmental Psychotherapy offers an excellent model for learning and practicing effective parenting skills.

Visits continue during this stage of treatment. The length of the visits may increase. New behaviors or interactions may lead to enthusiasm as well as anxiety as it is anticipated that the child will demonstrate some behavioral difficulties on passes. Therefore, short visits that build on success with family therapy sessions before and after passes are preferable to lengthy or extended family passes. Family therapy sessions may last for several hours as patterns of attunement/shame/repair/reattunement are actively stimulated and resolved. Parent education may also include discussions of normal development, communication skills, supportive control, discipline practices, and school and academic functioning as well as attachment issues pertinent to their child. Visits within milieu are usually shorter during this stage as the family is able to spend more time together away from the direct supervision of the milieu.

Crises are anticipated, but are interpreted as an opportunity for growth and change during this stage. Crises may reflect a child's anxiety prior to a pass or behavioral difficulties to test their parent's commitment to using the new parenting skills. Crises are therefore an opportunity to strengthen the parent-child bond and to help each of them deal productively with emotional upheaval. Child-care workers are immediately available to support the family during such crises.

STAGE THREE: TRUST OF SELF
The goal during the Trust of Self stage of family involvement is on reintegrating the child back into his family and community. The family continues to be actively involved with the treatment team, and discharge planning intensifies, including solidifying follow-up treatment and school placement. The behavioral changes made by the family and child are consolidated while the staff identifies the specific services that the child and family will need at home, such as follow-up outpatient family therapy, medication management, special education, or other services. Difficulties in transition are anticipated, and the family is supported in handling behavioral difficulties and regressions which may arise as the child prepares to return home. During the Trust of Self stage, the family continues weekly telephone calls and visits. In addition, passes to their home, which may involve seven to 10 days at a time, will help the child and family become more comfortable in their new interactions while exploring details about follow-up treatment and school placement. In addition, sibling interactions are often a focus of treatment during this stage as brothers and sisters may be faced with changes in their status within the family. Finally, planned follow-up contact is scheduled in order to support the family and to evaluate the outcome of treatment.

OUTCOME RESEARCH

An overview of outcome of children in residential treatment has been previously presented (Blackwell, 2002; Blackwell & Vallejos, 2002). Early studies of the effectiveness of residential treatment with children tended to focus on recidivism rates or the child's ability to be maintained at home following discharge (Carter, 1942). Many of these studies viewed the child as chronically disturbed with very limited expectations to function independently. Later studies sought to evaluate more autonomous areas of functioning after discharge, such as school performance, employment, or the quality of adult and peer relationships (Gossett, Lewis, & Barnhart, 1983). Extending beyond externally observable indicators of progress, several more recent studies have sought to asses changes in the internal psychological processes of the child (Zimmerman, Myers, & Epstein, 2001). For example, Zimmerman (2001) found that in a group of 27 children in a residential therapeutic school, 70% achieved higher and more adaptive levels of internalized object representations following two years of care. The children demonstrated more internalized psychological images of others as caring, understanding, and nurturing, while many demonstrated improved self-esteem and greater feelings of mastery in interpersonal relationships.

The study of treatment effectiveness in residential treatment for attachment resistant children is in its infancy. Although many residential treatment centers report conducting follow-up research, most studies are informal, infrequent, or have difficulty exacting any interpretations or conclusions (Mordock, 2002). Three research studies have been conducted at the Villa Santa Maria to determine the efficacy of using Dyadic Developmental Psychotherapy as a model of residential treatment (Blackwell, 2001, Blackwell, 2002, Blackwell, 2003). The first study examined the demographic and clinical characteristics of children treated from 1998-2000. A second study examined the outcome of these children $1^{1/2}$ years post discharge. A third study examined behavioral, self-report, and psychological changes of children treated from 2000 to 2002.

Study One: Descriptive Analysis

Eighteen children, 72% boys, ranging in age from nine to 15 years, were treated at Villa Santa Maria from 1998-2000. They had an average length of stay of 17 months. All exhibited severe externalizing problems such as aggression, and most suffered from internalizing problems such as depression. Over half of the children exhibited risk behaviors such as sexual acting out or suicidal and homicidal gestures.

Family Background	% of Group
Neglect	73%
Physical Abuse	77%
Sexual Abuse	50%
Prenatal Drug Abuse	50%

Treatment History	% of Group
Outpatient Therapy	94%
Hospitalization	61%
Residential Treatment	39%

The typical child had participated in extensive outpatient psychotherapy and had been hospitalized $2^{1/2}$ times followed by brief residential treatment, group home, or foster care before being admitted to Villa Santa Maria. These children suffered from significant psychological problems. Seventy-eight percent were diagnosed with Reactive Attachment Disorder, 61% had Disruptive Behavior Diagnoses such as Attention Deficit Hyperactivity Disorder or Oppositional Defiant Disorder, and 89% suffered from Mood Disorders. Eighty-three percent of the children had been treated with an average of 3.8 psychotropic medications prior to admission.

Study Two: Outcome Analysis

Follow-up data was collected on most of the children from the first study (78%). After approximately $1^{1/2}$ years post discharge, all symptom categories showed progress.

Symptom	ADM %	D/C %
Aggression	100%	21%
Depression	38%	14%
Sexual Acting Out	64%	14%
Homicidal Threats/Acts ·	50%	7%
Suicidal Threats/Acts	30%	0%

All of the children continued to participate in therapy following discharge. However, 50% of the children were not taking any psychotropic medications, while only another 29% were taking only one medication (in contrast to almost all children taking multiple medications prior to admission). Most of the parents described their relationships with their children as generally positive and 93% remained in school. Almost one-third had participated in extracurricular activities.

Study Three: Treatment Effectiveness

Analyses were conducted on 15 children treated at Villa Santa Maria from 2000 to 2002. These children were comparable to the first group. Eighty-seven percent were diagnosed with Reactive Attachment Disorder. A behavioral rating scale, the Devereux Scales of Mental Disorders, a self-report scale, the Reynolds Child/Adolescent Depression Scale, and two measures of personality functioning, the Rorschach and the Roberts' Apperception Test for Children, were administered at the time of admission and approximately after one year of treatment at the Villa Santa Maria. Due to the small number of children, the results would need to be quite robust to be statistically significant.

The Devereux Scales of Mental Disorders showed improvement in all measured areas. Statistically significant positive changes were found in the Total Score, Conduct Problems, Externalizing Problems, and Depression.

Self-report measures were also statistically significant. On the Reynolds Depression Scales, the children's average rating went from 72%, the borderline depressed range, to 48%, the average range. Overall, the children reported fewer feelings of hopelessness, despair, and rejection.

Psychological functioning was assessed through two traditional personality measures: the Rorschach Inkblot Test and the Roberts Apperception Test for Children. Both tests are frequently used to aid in diagnosis and treatment planning. Statistically significant changes were:

- Improved reality testing
- Less distorted reasoning
- Less cognitive confusion under stress
- Healthier perceptions of human interactions
- Trends toward decreased feelings of rejection and depression
- More mature conflict resolution skills
- Improved self-reliance

This research offers substantial evidence that the intensive treatment at Villa Santa Maria, which uses the Dyadic Developmental Psychotherapy model, helps children with comprised attachment to improve their behavioral and emotional functioning. It confirms that the cycle of repeated and costly hospitalizations, ineffective outpatient treatment, and the complex use of multiple medications can be changed with effective treatment. These changes are not only observed on measures of behavioral and psychological functioning, but are also observed by family members as lasting changes in their children.

Dyadic Developmental Psychotherapy in Long-Term Foster Care

CRAIG CLARK

EUGENE: CASE EXAMPLE WHEN DYADIC DEVELOPMENTAL PSYCHOTHERAPY ISN'T UTILIZED

Many years ago, when I first began work as a therapist with attachment disordered children, I attempted to help them deal with the distress they experienced in their relationships with their family, especially their caregivers, with the compendium of skills and techniques that were prevalent in that time. These skills were primarily art and play therapy, interpersonal relational talk therapies of various types, and sand-tray therapy. Even though I worked in a licensed foster and adoptive agency known for its especially good work with children and families, these therapeutic approaches were all we had to offer our young clients and their families. I reflect on this now with some regret because, although the therapy that was provided was better than no therapy, too often our treatment failed to achieve the results that would have given these children a better chance to realize their full human potential. The therapy we utilized helped to maintain children in family placement. It was like dousing water on crises that would repeatedly spring forth like lightening fires during a hot summer. The resulting damage accumulated and scarred the landscape of their lives. We hadn't been able to achieve enough security in the family relationships to soothe the child's fear, anxiety, and anger so that he or she could aspire to the dreams of life that are the fuel of a successful journey from childhood to adulthood. We did not address the underlying trauma, nor did we attempt to develop an attuned primary intersubjective relationship. Fortunately, today we have Dyadic Developmental Psychotherapy, and the potential for healing the psychological wounds of a traumatic childhood are greatly improved.

The following story is representative of a case in which the child received therapy that did not achieve an improvement in attachment style and the consequential effects on social and developmental achievement.

Eugene was removed from his birth family at the age of four due to neglect and physical abuse by his drug-abusing mother. The court record indicates that Eugene was frequently left alone with no food. He was subjected to intermittent physical abuse by his intoxicated mother and was witness to instances of domestic violence perpetrated by the mom's live-in boyfriend. Eugene was initially placed in the children's shelter, where he remained for a few weeks before beginning a series of three subsequent foster placements. The first two placements failed due to the severity of Eugene's emotional needs and the added stress upon the families by the additional placements of his two older brothers. While the first placement lasted for just a few months, it did offer Eugene a family environment that was not institutional as the shelter had been. Since they were eligible for adoption, his county social worker sought out an adoptive family for all three boys.

The home the worker found seemed to fit the bill. The home was not perfect, and the foster mother was a single parent who would be stressed by the child's acting-out behaviors. But she was a trained social worker and her strength, love, and compassion for these children were positive factors. Eugene was an endearingly cute boy with a big smile and handsome features. His big smile seemed to express boundless love and joy. It was only after you got to know Eugene that you discovered his smile was not always an invitation to closeness, but more often a mask for his feelings of anxiety and fear.

Eugene was placed in a long-term foster placement and remained eligible for adoption. The foster mother was a late middle-age, experienced mom who had grown birth children. She was alone in her house and wanted to raise more children. She saw in Eugene the perfect child for her to love. He seemed friendly, healthy, and had a good sense of humor. He did not exhibit many of the unhealthy behaviors of the foster population which she had learned about through her licensing training to become a foster parent. He didn't wet the bed, hoard food, or run away. He wasn't particularly aggressive toward her, but he could be toward her small dog, which he would tease and physically torment. She brought Eugene to me for play therapy once a week. His treatment issues included overly clingy behavior, aggressive behavior towards the dog, nightmares, distractible and hyperactive behavior at home and school, and a lack of emotional connection to the foster mother. His academic performance was poor. He was two grade levels behind and exhibited poor ability to attend to tasks in the classroom. He was not motivated to complete homework or, if he did, he seldom turned it in.

After a year in placement, his foster mother was exasperated with him. During this time, he participated in weekly play therapy sessions. He was a willing participant in board games and kinesthetic activities like ball toss or Nerf® basketball, but was less willing to draw or utilize other expressive art therapy techniques. Mostly he was willing to come to therapy to play with his "nice guy" counselor. Whenever a current topic of concern was presented by the counselor in the therapeutic hour, Eugene would smile and do everything to divert attention away from the topic he found so uncomfortable. At first he would display a big smile and then joke about the problem being discussed; then came denial. Anger followed if the counselor pursued with direct confrontation. At this point, Eugene would become an emotionally disengaged, discouraged youngster who only wanted to get out of the counselors office by any means necessary. Usually this meant a quick dash for the door.

Eugene usually succeeded in using up the therapy hour with a combination of these behaviors, never really allowing himself to explore the pain of his losses, removal from his birth parents, placement and removal from his maternal grandmother, two prior failed placements (including an adoptive placement), and loss of contact with his three other siblings. It was easier for him to run away from the pain of these losses than to risk the chance that he would be further overwhelmed by his own feelings of grief, anxiety, fear, and anger.

We did not have the therapeutic skills of Dyadic Developmental Psychotherapy to create a healing PLACE within which he could be safely held. He had not learned that his feelings could be soothed by trusting in a caring adult. He couldn't tolerate the intense experience of his feelings alone, and he had no one to trust who could help him. Now he was stuck, alone, with his sealed-off memories of an unhappy past. If he was challenged to express his feelings, he became so anxious that he couldn't *tolerate the affect and became fearful of his foster parent and counselor. It seemed a no-win situation to him, so he just tried to avoid it by being a "happy-go-lucky" type of child.*

After several months of play therapy, it was obvious that many of Eugene's issues were not being addressed in therapy. A different approach to treatment was needed to help him resolve the pain from his past and help him heal. I had read a book written by a psychologist from Maine, Daniel Hughes[4], who described a new approach to working with severely damaged children who had backgrounds that included trauma and loss. It was a dyadic model of treatment involving the child's caregivers in the therapy sessions. I decided this was worth a try with Eugene and consulted with his foster mom. She agreed to participate in the session.

The next week, I invited them both to come into the session. The foster mom began to describe a problem she was having with Eugene trying to get him ready for school in the morning. She complained that no matter what she did, he was always off task and late to school. When she started to show some emotion reflecting the level of frustration she felt about the situation, Eugene became very anxious and distracting. He utilized his big smile with both of us and denied that there was a problem at all. Then he tried to pull a game from the shelf in an effort to get us to play with him. I decided to bring him over to sit with me in an attempt to stop his distracting behaviors and help him focus on the topic we were discussing. As I kept him near me, with an arm around his shoulder, he began to cry. The tears rolled down his face, and he felt limp next to me—finally, a genuine display of emotion. He really was a sad little boy, but hid this feeling behind that big smile. This was the first time he felt safe enough to cry and express his sadness. He began to trust the adults in the room enough to share his feelings with us. Being close to his foster mother and therapist and being hugged while we talked helped him set aside the phony demeanor, the big smile, and joking. Perhaps we could have gone on with this form of therapy, but it was not to be. The foster mother sat quietly. Then she said, "If he is going to cry during therapy, I can't stay here. I can't stand to see him crying like that!" With that statement, she rose and left the room.

With this abandonment, so powerfully reminiscent of those that occurred before, Eugene's view of the world as a lonely place where true feelings best not be shared was reinforced. This event highlighted to me the importance of working with the caregiver and developing an attuned, trusting relationship with that person. This mother's difficulty with toler-

---

[4] Hughes, Daniel A. (1997). Facilitating Developmental Attachment: The Road to Emotional Recovery and Behavioral Change in Foster and Adopted Children. Northvale, NJ: Jason Aronson, Inc.

ating her child's display of affect and with providing a secure and safe relationship ended therapy. Had I been more aware of her difficulties, I would have been able to help her manage her own internal conflicts and, I'd like to think, become the parent that Eugene needed.

How would Dyadic Developmental Psychotherapy make a difference with Eugene?

Let's apply some of the approaches used in Dyadic Developmental Psychotherapy to the case of Eugene. He is a child who has suffered multiple abandonments. A goal of therapy would be to establish and augment Eugene's ability to trust his primary caretaker. The foster mother discovers during the therapy session that she doesn't want to see her foster son cry. The feeling is so strong that she declares that she will not remain in the session while Eugene cries, thus replicating the earlier traumatic loss of his parents. This is a good example of why it is so important to assess the ability of the caregiver to provide an attuned relationship within which there is a deep, intersubjective sharing of affect and a well-developed reflective function. If the foster mother had better resolution of her own attachment issues, perhaps she would have been able to develop this therapeutic relationship with Eugene.

Let's assume that in this case the foster mother had some issues similar to the loss issues of Eugene. A preferred approach would be to interview the foster mother before having a session with Eugene and her. In this session we would explore her attachment history and give her the opportunity to become more aware of what might make it difficult for her to engage Eugene in the manner necessary. Had I done this, she possibly would have been able to accept Eugene's display of emotion and then provide empathy for him. The foster mother would have been more emotionally available to Eugene and could have reached out to him emotionally by moving closer to him physically, perhaps placing her arm around his shoulder and then using reflective dialogue to explore the meaning of his tears. If I had developed more of a relationship with her before the session, then she might have been able to offer Eugene her comfort and support, and in so doing, helped him experience his feelings of loss in the context of a loving and nurturing relationship. This might then have allowed us to help Eugene transform his experience of overwhelming loss into one that was intersubjectively shared, reflected upon, and then integrated into a more coherent narrative. It would have become his first step toward experiencing comfort and renewal of closeness in another relationship.

Because she was overwhelmed by her own feelings, the foster mother was not emotionally available to Eugene. Had we continued in therapy, I would have met with the mother to explore what made it so difficult for her. Once we understood that, we then would have needed to explore with Eugene the meaning of this event to help him co-construct the meaning of her actions. Without an opportunity to reflect on the experience and to co-construct meaning, the child would contextualize the episode of his mother leaving according to his previous life experience in similar situations. This is especially important in view of Eugene's past history of multiple placements, intermittent abandonment, and maltreatment by his birth mother.

Another aspect of Dyadic Developmental Psychotherapy that applies to this scenario is the co-regulation of affect. As described by Dan Hughes, "It is an intersubjective experience which involves the active utilization of eye contact, facial expressions, voice prosody, movement, timing intensity and touch."[5] In this case, the mother and therapist would have worked together by accepting the client's emotional state and using soothing vocal tone, nurturing touch, eye contact, and verbal reassurance, resulting in a co-regulation of the client's vitality affect in a continuous dance of communication. The effect of this is to establish for the client a sense of safety so that the themes of shame or fear may be further explored and made sense of.

The foster mother in this case could have been helped to understand and utilize the other aspects of the Dyadic Developmental Psychotherapy approach to help her and Eugene establish the primary intersubjective stance of acceptance, curiosity, empathy, and playfulness, which would have enabled the foster mother and her foster son to co-regulate the negative affect. Once in a more regulated state, we could then explore the meaning of the feelings and the experiences that drove the feelings. In a safe and supportive relationship within the session, Eugene could have come to realize that the foster mother is a different mom than the internalized memory of the birth mom who traumatized him. By utilizing empathy, acceptance, and curiosity, the foster mother could have been able to stay affectively attuned to Eugene during this experience of sadness and grief. She could coregulate his affect by creating a healing PLACE. By utilizing this pattern of attunement, the foster mother, child, and therapist work together to explore past trauma and the resulting damage to the child's development, self-esteem, and self-image.

In this case example, the important steps of engagement, disruption, and repair were omitted. Disruption occurred when the foster mother became uncomfortable and unaccepting of Eugene's tears and his

---

[5] Hughes, Daniel A. (2004). An Attachment-Based Treatment of Maltreated Children and Young People. Attachment & Human Development, September, p. 9.

underlying emotional state. Since the foster mother could not regulate her own affect, she could not help to co-regulate Eugene. She felt helpless to comfort him. She had not been prepared for this experience and chose to leave the session in order to calm herself. The messages to the child in this session probably include: "I want to help you, but your behavior is too upsetting to me. Stop crying, and I'll love you. I cannot tolerate such affect, and neither can you." Eugene may have experienced shame for exposing his feelings while the foster mother may have experienced shame about not being a good enough mother. Eugene once again experiences his world as a place that causes pain, shame, and isolation. The opportunity to heal the attachment disruption is present in this case. Dyadic Developmental Psychotherapy utilizing PACE could have led to repairing the emotionally painful and shaming experiences that were present during Eugene's early childhood.

EUGENE'S ALTERNATIVE STORY, TOM

Let's explore how using Dyadic Developmental Psychotherapy with a caretaker who is effectively prepared and participating in the treatment might proceed and how it will help the client. Tom is an early adolescent by the time he begins Dyadic Developmental Psychotherapy.

Tom was first removed from the care of his birth parents at age three due to neglect, domestic violence, and drug abuse by the parents. The parents would regularly fight in front of their children, and it was during one of these fights that the police were called by neighbors. Tom was taken into protective custody and placed in the children's shelter. After a short stay there, he was given to the care of his maternal grandfather. This proved not to be a good home for Tom. The grandfather regularly drank alcohol to excess and was a contentious and angry person when he was intoxicated. The grandfather believed that many of Tom's behavior problems were due to a lack of discipline by Tom's parents, a mistake which he was determined to correct. Whenever Tom broke a rule or got into some type of trouble, he would be whipped with a belt. Since Tom was young and curious, he often attracted his grandfather's attention and was frequently punished. Some of Tom's behaviors were normal for a child of his age. He would play with his sister's toys without asking, pull open cabinets and empty the contents to see what was there, and go outside exploring when he found a door open. These were all cause for severe physical punishment and stern verbal abuse by the grandfather. Tom learned that the adults in his life couldn't be counted on in positive ways. Tom experienced adults as unreliable, feared, and dangerous people. This contributed to Tom's feeling unloved and unlovable–that at the core, he was a "bad" child. The grandfather constantly complained to the social worker about how much trouble Tom was. Consequently, he was eventu-

ally taken from his grandfather's custody and returned to the biological mother. Tom remained in her care for two years until she relapsed.

Tom was removed and placed in a foster home. By this time he had become more aggressive. He would fight with his foster siblings and with children at school. He was bright, but he didn't apply himself academically and received poor grades. Tom acted as if he perceived the adults in his life as enemies. Tom's sarcastic and aggressive attitude kept well-meaning teachers, foster parents, and therapists at bay.

After another period of placement with his biological mother, Tom stayed with his maternal aunt and was rejoined with a biological sister. By this time, Tom's aggression was too dangerous and he would get into violent fights with his sister. He could no longer be controlled in a home environment. Tom found himself living in a residential treatment facility where the rules were strictly enforced using a behavioral model of treatment.

After two years in residential treatment, Tom's social worker thought his behavior had improved and that he was ready for discharge. She decided to place him in a therapeutic foster family with two other boys his age. During the previous several years Tom had received only behavior modification therapy while in the residential treatment facility. The therapeutic foster home would be his first experience with Dyadic Developmental Psychotherapy. Tom was now 13 years old and very distrustful of all adults.

Tom's new home was managed by experienced foster parents, Sue and Martin. They had raised several foster children and knew that structure was a necessary ingredient to creating a healthy and secure home. The rules were clear and expectations for behavior made explicit the first day Tom arrived. In strange or new situations, Tom could be a cool character. He smiled and was outwardly compliant with his new foster parents. They quickly learned that Tom was a very conniving and manipulative young man. He would not let you know what he was thinking, but he always kept a keen watch on his surroundings. This was something life had taught him in order to stay safe and a step ahead of danger. When Sue and Martin came to my office for the first time, they talked about how hard it was to get to know this boy. Sue was confused by his seeming outward pleasant demeanor and the contrasting angry behavior with his foster brothers when the parents weren't present. Also, there were the reports from his school. He didn't let a day pass without getting in trouble for breaking playground rules, shoving other kids, or walking in late to class after recess. He displayed more passive-aggressive behaviors at school. The teachers were growing tired of his disrespectful attitude. Every day he was sent to the office to talk to the school's guidance counselor. At home, this was causing escalating tensions to build between Tom and his foster parents. They felt powerless because Tom wasn't letting them get emotionally close. He would seek physical hugs from Martin, who would rather be giving them in response to a good feeling about Tom than receiving the clingy hugs that Tom would try to get away with. On the other hand, Tom would resist getting a hug or making eye contact with Sue when she tried to comfort him after another hard day at school.

After a month in placement, Sue and Martin were really struggling to know what to do with Tom. After consulting with the clinical director of the therapeutic foster agency that had placed Tom, the decision was reached to begin Dyadic Developmental Psychotherapy. While Tom had considerable experience receiving therapy in other forms, this would be his first experience with this form of treatment.

The first session was with the foster parents and was used to get a current placement description and to review the case history. Court records and other reports and evaluations were provided by Tom's county social worker. Tom's placement history was reviewed with Sue and Martin and there was a discussion about how Tom's family history, placement history, and academic problems all contributed to making him a challenging young man to deal with. My initial approach was to understand the current situation and how the past was active in the present and to provide support and empathy for Sue and Martin. The therapeutic approach was presented to the foster parents, and Sue was asked if she would agree to attend the therapy sessions along with Tom. She would be working along with the therapist and would take an active role. Sue agreed that she would actively participate in the therapy. She said that she hadn't any experience in therapy herself and that she was a little uneasy because of this. The therapist spent some time in the following sessions describing how therapy would proceed. Sue would use her relationship with Tom to challenge his misconceptions and distorted internal working models about relationships.

ISSUES AND APPROACHES IN TREATMENT: TOM, SUE, AND MARTIN

In this section, I will discuss Tom's issues and goals of treatment and describe how Dyadic Developmental Psychotherapy was helpful in providing opportunities for healing. Let's start off looking at the goals from the perspective of the county social worker. This case includes a history of multiple placements with foster families and failed reunification with the birth mother. There was a two-year placement in a residential treatment facility. The social worker understood the necessity and benefit of finding a secure placement for Tom and felt that a therapeutic foster home was going to provide Tom with his best chance to experience the positive effects of having a family. At the time of placement in the therapeutic foster family, Tom was running out of alternatives because of his serious behavior problems. Tom had become a very aggressive and manipulative child. The reasons he was removed from his foster and birth-family placements included multiple incidences of stealing from family members and repeated aggressive behaviors directed toward peers and adults. Tom would become irritated whenever he didn't get what he wanted, and this often led to aggressive behaviors. His older sister was the target of abuse and suffered serious physical injury when they lived together. He was known to spontaneously slap peers across the face with no obvious provocation. These aggressive behaviors were the primary cause for his placement in a residential treatment facility. The goal of treatment with Tom was to reduce his level of aggressive and oppositional behavior to the point where he could be placed with success in a therapeutic foster family.

From Tom's point of view, he just wanted to go home to his birth mom. Children in the foster system often blame the system, social workers, judges, and counselors for their problems. This was true for Tom as well. He saw his birth mom as the victim of domestic violence and poverty. Through no fault of her own, he now had to endure living apart from her, and he hated those he held responsible. According to Tom, if it weren't for them, he and his mom could make a go of it; no problem.

The mental health report written for the court saw things differently from Tom. It stated that as a result of his many failed relationships with adults and families, he had developed a high level of mistrust and that in order to defend himself, he had to keep people from becoming close to him. He was unable to form attachments with others because his experience told him, he would only end up getting hurt or taken advantage of. He remained withdrawn, emotionally constricted, and angry in response to the neglect and abandonment he had experience during his young life.

Goals of treatment included improving Tom's impulse control and reducing his aggression. This would be achieved by focusing on creating a secure base at home so that his distorted working models and poor affect regulation could be addressed. Therapy would focus on the effects of his past trauma on his current relationships and help him develop a more integrated and coherent autobiographical narrative.

SUMMARY OF TREATMENT

During the initial phase of treatment, Tom was naturally resistant to starting therapy, yet again, with another therapist. He presented as physically aggressive toward the therapist and clearly did not want to participate in treatment. To begin Dyadic Developmental Psychotherapy, Tom was seen alone during the first two sessions. These sessions proved to be very diffi-cult. Tom would present with defensive behaviors to keep me from know-ing much about his feelings. He would joke and distract during the session. If Tom was pressed for an answer, he would move from his pas-sive-aggressive stance to increasingly aggressive behavior. During one such session, I inquired about Tom's previous experiences with therapy. Tom began to make jokes about the therapy he had experience, claiming that, "Those fools don't know how to help me!" When I suggested that Tom didn't trust his previous therapist enough to experience any help from the therapy, he turned toward me and glared at me with piercing green eyes. The tension rose dramatically in the room as Tom rose from his seat and walked in a threatening manner toward me. I maintained an even tone of voice and reassured Tom that I was going to work to make things different and that I respected Tom's feelings about previous trials of therapy. Acknowledging Tom's feelings seemed to calm him, and by the time we were face to face, with me backed into the corner of the office, Tom seemed to realize that this therapy would be different.

The "moment of truth" was past, and the foster mother was asked to join the session. With her there, Tom was able to remain calm and attentive in the session. Was he reassured by her presence? Perhaps at this point in the treatment, he had begun to trust some qualities of his foster mother. She was predictable and naturally very nurturing toward Tom, and he was able to trust that the situation in therapy would remain safe. This experi-ence underscored for me the importance of involving the caregiver in treatment as soon as possible. Because he could experience safety in her presence, Tom was able to relax and become less defensive.

INITIAL PHASE OF TREATMENT

There is an important aspect of the beginning phase of treatment that needs particular attention as the course of treatment depends upon how well this foundation is established. Many parents of attachment dys-functional children with trauma-attachment disorders have begun to doubt their ability to parent. Beyond this, some parents may experience feelings of defeat, disillusionment, frustration, and anger as a result of failed attempts at controlling the child's disruptive behavior. The thera-pist can do much to help these parents regain a sense of equilibrium and the perspective that they have lost. Therapy cannot proceed without helping them to reduce their anger and become assured that the therapy they are about to begin with their child will help relieve their stress, too! The important first step in treatment is to help the parent or caregiver feel more secure in their role.

A single mother sought treatment for her internationally adopted son, age eight. He was very difficult to control, and she worried about his behavior endangering himself or possibly becoming a threat to her or others in the household. She described how she had struggled for the six years they had been together, and now she was feeling that she was not able to control his behavior and keep him safe. Recently, he had run out of the house and into the busy street, unaware of the traffic that could have injured him. More worrisome still was her concern that he would become more aggressive when he was upset and possibly hurt himself or other members of the household. "How can I help him?" she asked. "And what will I do if he needs to be placed in a psychiatric hospital or residential treatment? I can't afford all those bills!" She was letting me know her reality as the parent. She was feeling out of control, powerless, and overwhelmed before we even started treatment. What would she do if therapy didn't help? I could sense the rising panic in her.

It was important for me to help regulate her emotions by giving her time to voice her fears in sessions before we started with her child. She needed me to provide reassurance and information. I did this by suggesting books and referring her to a parents' group and Web sites. She needed to talk about how she felt and then hear that other parents felt the same way. She needed opportunities to explore her family-of-origin relationships with her parents and examine her own attachment style as it had developed in her childhood, because that pattern of attachment would be the model from which she would parent her adopted child and would effect the way treatment proceeded. I provided a supportive environment within which she felt accepted. In effect, my approach with her was identical with the approach we would take with her child, keeping a healing PACE. Although this parent was eager to have her son start treatment and for the egregious behaviors to subside, she soon began to realize that she was receiving some important help in the form of these initial parent sessions. As she was able to access some of the referrals and read more about the issues, she was becoming more relaxed and regaining her confidence.

The goal of these parent sessions is to help the caregiver regain a sense of confidence in their capacity to parent their child. Once this has been accomplished, then treatment can include the child.

Using Dyadic Developmental Psychotherapy in a Therapeutic Foster Home: Back to Tom

There are differences in using Dyadic Developmental Psychotherapy in a therapeutic foster home (contrasted to an adoptive home) that must be addressed if the therapy is to achieve its greatest benefit. From the perspective of Tom, he still has a relationship with his birth mother that is reinforced with regular visitation. Ironically, Tom now feels that he must protect his mother from further harm by a system he perceives as untrustworthy because it jeopardizes his ability to have contact with his birth mother. It seems that Tom feels that the social welfare system's interventions to protect him from abuse are abusive to his birth mother! He is sensitive to perceived criticism of his birth mother and protective of his relationship with her to the point of avoiding any meaningful discussion of their relationship or any comparison to his foster mother. In therapy sessions, attempts to co-construct a cohesive personal narrative that includes Tom's life with his birth mother is made very difficult by his desire to protect her. Tom's relationship with her is an essential core issue that must be explored and the experience integrated into his cohesive personal narrative as part of the therapeutic process that will enable Tom to form a secure, trusting, reciprocal attachment relationship with his foster mother and father.

While Tom struggles with his feelings about his conflicted, dual mother relationships, he is emotionally less available to form good, secure attachments with his birth and foster mothers. There may be times when he feels that he just can't figure out what he feels about his mothers. Due to Tom's internal conflict and all the unanswered questions about his life, he may exhibit symptoms of anxiety, depression, or emotional reactivity that the foster mother wants to help with. As she shows concern for Tom's conditions, he instinctively withdraws from her, knowing from his history that adults who claim they love you often prove to be a disappointment. Because of Tom's history of multiple placements, he interprets his foster mother's nurturing behavior as a sign that his foster placement is in jeopardy. In an attempt to lower his perception of the heightened danger to his ability to stay in a family, he becomes aloof, cautious, and compliant. His foster mother, having desired to help, now experiences Tom's avoidance of her. Because she loves him and wants to care for him, his avoidance is interpreted as distancing or disrespectful and she feels herself getting mad at Tom. Now Tom is picking up on the feeling that he was most concerned about. He experiences his foster mother as unloving because she displays her disappointment or anger. Tom reacts with shame at this moment, experiencing himself as unlovable, and the child's negative experience of attached relationships is reinforced. This cycle of negative self-experience is repeated many hundreds of times and forms the foundation of attachment dysfunction. Dyadic Developmental Psychotherapy is effective in interrupting this cycle by creating a therapeutic dialogue between the child, parent, and therapist that allows the child and parent to experience reciprocal nurturance, building trust in the attachment.

An impediment to the success of therapy is the child's confusion resulting from the parents' different attachment qualities. Emotionally laden experiences with both the foster and birth mothers require that the child react to them differently so that each can receive the correct emotional message back in response. Essentially, the child must learn two sets of stimuli and responses so that he can form an attachment relationship with each care-giving parent. Children who are in contact with a foster mother and a birth mother, for instance, need to maintain two ways to respond to their internal experience of the same feeling and react in either of two learned patterns of response. This need to learn two sets of responses and the ability to correctly react with each mother requires a developmental maturity that is sometimes beyond the child's capability. When the child experiences a failure in the ability of the foster or birth mother to address the child's perceived needs for nurturing care, the child will experience shame. Tom's core schema includes the belief that he is not worthy of love and should not expect it from his foster mother. This feeling is perhaps more deeply experienced in his relationship with his birth mother due to his intense and lengthy history with her. Tom's interactions with either his foster or birth mothers cause him to down-play his true feelings because to expose himself at that level would make him too vulnerable and subject to shame and to the conflicted feelings he has for his foster and birth mothers. Instead of experiencing shame and conflict about these relationships and his life, he displays a false self that is in control and demonstrates a diminished need for nurturance, support, acceptance, or love. The foster mother feels rejection of her overtures of affection, nurturance, care, or love. She experiences Tom as aloof or disrespectful and emotionally distant. She may feel manipulated by what she experiences as Tom's rejecting behavior and begin to respond to him with disregard and defensive callousness in order to protect her feelings from being hurt by his emotional avoidance or reactivity. It is common for both Tom and his foster mother to experience intense feelings of hurt and anger generated between them. These relational transactions, repeated hundreds of times, elicit and reinforce feelings of shame and doubt, further convincing each party that closeness in their relationship is not worth the emotional expense.

Tom, as a foster child, may also hold the common belief that he will someday return to live with his birth mother. Many children believe that they will be able to return to their birth parent after the "trouble" that caused their separation has ceased. In fact, they hear or are told by social workers, judges, and foster and birth parents that they may someday be reunited with their birth family, etc. Tom incorporates this possible scenario as inevitable and internally plans for that wonderful reunification event. This fantasy is incorporated into his personal narrative, which becomes distorted and serves to divert him from taking the risk that he will experience another loss by making a sincere effort to bond with his foster mother.

To further bolster Tom's maintenance of his distorted personal narrative, he tends to idealize his internal understanding of who his birth mother is, eliminating historical facts or diminishing their negative impact on his life. In his memory, he creates the perfect mother image and projects it onto the real person of the birth mother. Imbued with these idealized qualities and fueled by the intense desire to reunite with the lost parental figure, Tom, without being conscious of the process, must keep his internalized view of the foster mother from ever approaching the idealized quality of his birth mother or risk forming too close an attachment bond with her, thus challenging his bond with the birth mother. The event of bonding with the foster mother would cause Tom to experience being loved unconditionally, with the nurturing qualities that he has been missing in his disrupted and previously neglectful caregiver relationships. The reality of the current attachment figure, his foster mother, and the corrective emotional experiences with her cause Tom to begin to internally question the reality of his idealized birth mother. Due to the corrective experience with his foster mother, Tom can more accurately interpret the past in terms of his own pain and loss. This newly developed ability to recognize and feel his foster mother's love for him has prepared Tom to consider a new interpretation that may shatter primary beliefs. How could his perfect birth mother hurt him, now that he has reconsidered the notion that he deserved to be treated poorly? Tom's connection to his foster mother, with the resulting changing interpretation of past abuse, produces anxiety based in fear that he will once again experience feelings of loss and abandonment. Therapy can help through this transition. Tom will need to feel loved, respected, and supported by his foster mother and therapist throughout this process. As he adjusts his internalized view of his birth mother to reflect the historical truths and faces the current reality of who she is, his foster mother may be able to support Tom, accepting the constant, daily care of allowing the attachment bond to develop. Concurrently, Tom will be adjusting his internalized image of his birth mom and become available to establish an updated and potentially more healthy and secure relationship with his foster mother.

During therapy when Tom and his foster mom attempt to explore their relationship through common experiences and issues, at times Tom may evidence his confusion and internal emotional conflict by not being able to put into words what he is feeling or thinking. Externally, Tom is seen and heard by the observer as not answering questions and avoiding confrontation by diversion or diminishment tactics in an attempt to divert the foster mother or therapist's invitation to resolve an issue. Tom's inability to respond verbally may be a reflection of the double bind that he is experiencing with his conflicted feelings of his dual alliance with both his foster and birth mothers.

This is a complicated process that will require many sessions in therapy to work through. In the meantime, Tom will continue to hear his internal voice saying, "No, you're not my real mom!" in response to the nurturing overtures of the foster mom. She will experience his avoiding and rejecting behaviors and remind herself that this is evidence of the healing process. She will gain understanding of her foster son by learning to communicate with him through acceptance, curiosity, and love.

ISSUES IN PROVIDING DYADIC DEVELOPMENTAL PSYCHOTHERAPY IN FOSTER CARE

Foster placements will involve a county social worker who oversees management of the placement. The worker is mandated to insure that the court-dependent children are maintained in a safe home that meets the jurisdiction's standard of care. Social workers are another adult presence in the foster child's life. The social worker makes decisions that effect how the basic needs of the child and foster family are met. In this capacity, the social worker can provide valuable support and assistance to the child in placement. The county is often the source of the money to pay for therapy, and the social worker is responsible for monitoring how well the therapy addresses the needs of the child. The social worker can be viewed as another family member, and an alliance should be formed with the social worker in a similar manner to an alliance with other significant adults in the child's life. In these situations, information required by the court about the child's psychotherapy treatment raises concerns about how the therapist chooses to handle confidential issues. Ethical standards of practice require that a client be informed about the rules of confidentiality before or during the first therapy session. Using the case of Tom as an example, it was explained to him that the information shared with me during his therapy sessions would be kept private except for legally mandated information involving serious harm to himself or an identified other person. Because Dyadic Developmental Psychotherapy is practiced with direct parental involvement in the sessions, no explanation about the usually delicate matter of how information is shared with the parent is necessary. In cases where the child client is a court dependent, the involvement of the court and social worker requires disclosure and discussion with the child and his/her parents.

In Tom's case, he was used to having strangers (social workers, judges, residential treatment center counselors, and others) talk about him, seemingly without any restriction or regard for his feelings or how these disclosures would effect him. From Tom's point of view, there was very little confidential about what happened in therapy. Consequently, his negative belief that adults do not really care about him was reinforced, counter to the goal of increasing trust in his caregivers. As would happen repeatedly during exploration of his understanding of the meaning of significant events, Tom would experience his internal, gut-level distrust of care-giving adults and respond in therapy with little disclosure of his true feelings. The opportunity for integrating a new, co-created meaning of his life experience was avoided.

To break this pattern of response, ample time and focus must be provided in therapy to address Tom's underlying core schema, and internal working models about caregivers and others. Careful attunement to Tom's verbal responses and nonverbal cues by the therapist and foster mother were necessary to help Tom build a trusting, secure attachment relationship. Through the therapeutic co-creation of meaning, within the context of supportive current attachments, an understanding of his past experiences could be explored in emotional safety and nurturing support.

As the therapist, I remained vigilant about how information was handled among the various professionals involved with the case. I communicated clearly with Tom about what information I would share with his social worker and other professionals. He needed reassurance from me that I would not share personal information that was not absolutely necessary to communicate to others. The type of information I shared was usually restricted to evaluation of treatment goals, level of participation by Tom in the therapy, and health and safety concerns as legally mandated. Reassurance was provided to Tom that any concerns he had about confidentiality could be openly addressed. Discussion of this important issue with Tom helped to foster a healthy alliance between us that built trust in our relationship. He could feel that I was looking out for his best interests and that I respected his feelings. I find that offering this open and cooperative process helps the client feel empowered in a healthy way to speak out for what they need. The ways in which I offered positive regard and acceptance of his opinions, feelings, and concerns contributed to his development of a secure, trusting, relationship with me. I grew increasingly predictable in the nature and quality of my responses to his needs. He responded with increasing trust in my dependability and supportive, curious, accepting nature. I was becoming another adult with whom he could build a trusting, secure relationship. Together, Tom and I would continue to co-create a model of a healthy attachment relationship that would form a model to be generalized and applied to other appropriate adult caregivers and would eventually form a healthy model for friendships and romantic relationships as well.

Therapeutic foster care can be a desirable alternative to many other forms of institutional care. The family relationships more closely emulate those found in birth or adoptive families and contribute to the formation of secure attachment relationships. Foster children are maintained in the child welfare system until they are 18 years old or receive a high-school diploma, depending on the jurisdiction. Optimally, this can provide for many years of an emotionally healthy, structurally stable, family-centered environment. In this milieu, the child has the opportunity to form secure attachment relationships and can achieve normal development and emotional maturity.

There are significant challenges and complications to achieving these goals due to the lack of permanence and "ownership" of the child by the family. A child who is placed into a long-term therapeutic foster home can hope to depend on living there until he is 18-years-old. For a child of early age, this would mean over a decade of healthy family life. However, there is a critical lack of security found in foster homes. According to one study, children raised in permanent foster homes were by age 11 significantly more disturbed than either adopted children or children raised with their biological parents.[6] While it is true that many foster families become quite close to their foster children and may extend overtures of a lifelong relationship, there is no legal "tie that binds" them together, and the emotional ties tend to be weaker than in adoptive homes. The permanence of relationship in most adoptive families is due to the legal relationships that are formed by statute and to the emotional commitment that occurs when the decision to adopt is actualized. Adopting is predicated on permanence. Fostering relationships are not of the same design, nor do the parties involved interpret them as permanent.

Foster children continue to experience the effects of dual parent relationships in a more intense manner than do many adoptive children, especially where the court plan dictates regular visitation between child and noncustodial birth parents. A similar effect may be experienced by adoptees that are part of a kinship adoption or extended kinship plan that includes provision for contact with birth parent(s). Children who find themselves with these types of dual parent (foster and birth) relationships struggle with conflicts about the alliances they have with their foster and birth parents. These conflicted alliances are a main focus of

---

[6] Bohman, Michale (1992). A comparative study of adopted children, foster children, and children in their biological environment born after undesired pregnancies, Acta Paediatrica Scandinavica (Suppl. 221), 1-38, 1971. In D. Brodzinsky, M. Schechter, & R. Henig, *Being adopted*, pg. 8. New York: Doubleday.

therapy and take time to resolve. Children who are separated from their birth parents may want to protect the idealized image they hold of those parents, especially those to whom they have formed some type of attachment. They defend against perceived danger of further loss or separation from their birth parent and against challenges to their idealization of that parent. These children may lack the stability of a secure base from which to be able to explore the actual experiences with the birth parent that led to a surrender of termination of parental rights. The child caught in this situation also struggles with defining identity and maintaining normal developmental progress because so much of the child's energy is taken up in attempting to experience safety and security in these primary relationships.

Resolution of these issues is complicated by not having permanent family relationships. Dyadic Developmental Psychotherapy builds on the basic human drive for secure attachment relationships. Where the primary caretaking relationship is well grounded by adoption, the attachment sequence can be fostered through therapy. When there is a question about the ability of the relationship to grow over time, as may be the case in a foster-care relationship, the therapy must address this situation and utilize the positive, nurturing aspects of the foster relationship to establish a new, internalized working model for the child to use. To the degree that the child experiences lack of permanence, and resultant insecurity, and the potential for further experiences of grief and loss, there will be resistance and defense against developing or deepening such relationships.

Dyadic Developmental Psychotherapy in Group Homes

CRAIG CLARK

Group homes offer an alternative placement for children who exhibit behaviors that are considered beyond the capacity of a foster family. Furthermore, there may be children who cannot tolerate the intimacy of a foster family and require a group-home placement and independent living as an alternative. Most group homes have a relatively small number of children who are supervised by an adult staff person. While the supervising staff are often referred to as counselors, they usually have quite limited professional training. Many are young and immature themselves. Although the staff counselor has likely been trained to correctly provide for the physical care of the children assigned to them, they are not trained as therapists and cannot provide that level of treatment. Children in group homes are taught the rules of the house and are expected to abide by them. The model of care is most often behavioral with clear reward-punishment systems. Encouragement is provided through the use of mostly cognitive behavioral interventions, including token economies, assignment of chores for poor behavior, and loss of privileges. Often, psychotherapy is not a component of care in group homes. If therapy is needed or mandated by court order, then it may be of any type or approach that is approved of by the child's social worker.

Children who have attachment disorder need to have therapy that helps them address their underlying beliefs, traumas, and internal working models that prohibit them from forming trusting, secure attachment relationships. The common belief among children who are sent to institutions such as group homes or residential treatment facilities is that they are discarded and unwanted because they are no good.[7] Therapy approaches that do not address a child's feeling of worthlessness cannot hope to accomplish much more than providing assistance for the child to learn rules of behavior so that they may function as members of society and avoid incarceration. Helping a child make fundamental changes that will enable the formation and maintenance of healthy attachment relationships will allow the child to have much more success and happiness in life because they will not only be able to follow the rules of society, but they will also enjoy the benefits and fulfillment that would come from healthy, trusting, and loving relationships with others. Dyadic Developmental Psychotherapy will help the child grow into an adult with the capacity for empathy and self-respect so that the child is able to be a self-regulating, contributing, and functional member of society.

A group home that uses an attachment model of care will operate quite differently from one based on a behavioral model. The attachment group-home model is organized so that it becomes a secure base for the children and allows them to begin exploring the world and relationships from this secure base. Such a model allows the children to regain a sense of direction, heal from their emotional wounds, and achieve developmental and emotional maturity. It promotes establishment of trusting relationships and provides meaningful opportunities for the children to experience reciprocal trust. "This is accomplished by creating an environment in which nurturing and relationships are difficult to resist, confronting behaviors that resist or attempt to reject care and nurturing, and teaching alternate behaviors that are more advantageous to developing relationships and building self-esteem."[8]

---

[7] Cmiel, Kenneth (1995). *A home of another kind: One Chicago orphanage and the tangle of child welfare.* London: The University of Chicago Press, Ltd.
[8] Becker-Weidman, Arthur (2004). Personal correspondence.
[9] ibid.

A group home using Dyadic Developmental Psychotherapy as its model of care uses a team approach in which the youth worker is the primary caregiver for the child. The youth worker provides a nurturing and consistently supportive, emotionally attuned relationship for the child. The primary youth worker is the one to put the child to bed each evening and is there when the child is awakened the next morning. The youth worker also participates in Dyadic Developmental Psychotherapy sessions with the child. Other members of the team include the therapist, primary staff counselor, residence manager, child's teacher, and child's social worker. The basic rules of the house are designed to promote a high level of interaction between the child and the child's primary youth worker. Privileges and opportunities are based on demonstrated attachment behavior and the nature and quality of relationships rather than on achieving points for compliance. The basic rules are:

- You need to ask for everything that you want or need.
- We must know where you are at all times.
- You will not hurt others, and you will not be hurt.

These rules are designed to establish safety and promote close working relationships between the child and his/her primary attachment figures. A primary youth counselor who takes on the parenting role is assigned to the child. This staff attends therapy with the child and collaborates with the parents so that the child effectively has a parenting figure both at home and at the group facility. [9]

The atmosphere of the group home is designed to replicate as much as possible that of a family environment. With a primary attachment figure available to work with the child, behavioral interventions have the feeling of a parent-child relationship. Such interventions contribute to forming healthy attachment relationships with the staff and developing empathy among the residents. Parents, if available, are required to attend training to help them develop an attachment-based parenting approach. This collaborative approach between the primary staff counselor and the parents helps to provide a secure base for the child.

OTHER BEHAVIORAL AND THERAPEUTIC INTERVENTIONS

Group sessions are provided to facilitate problem solving among the staff and residents. Strong emphasis is placed on the interpersonal relationships so residents will establish peer- and sibling-like relationships to further imitate a healthy home environment. Children are encouraged to examine the outcomes of the choices they make. Behavior management is individualized and focused to help the child make healthy decisions. A focus is on how past experiences effect current relationships. The child's affective response and ability to control impulsiveness are monitored and co-regulated by the primary staff counselor and other caregivers.

OTHER TECHNIQUES INCLUDE:

- Time-in with the adult and child in close proximity.

- Meditation or Strong Sitting where the child is assigned a place to sit in a safe area to encourage the child to calm down, think about better responses to problems, and become willing to co-operate with others again.

- Cradling or touch where physical proximity is utilized to help keep an out-of-control child safe and to demonstrate that they can be cared for and kept safe without being hurt.

- Natural and logical consequences are the results of behaviors.

    For example, a child becomes angry and breaks the lamp next to his bed. Now he doesn't have a lamp. This is a natural consequence; break the lamp and there is no light.

    Logical consequences are what parents and parent figures arrange as consequences that make sense based on the behavior demonstrated. This can help develop cause-and-effect thinking. An example is replacing another person's shirt, which you took and threw into the garbage can. The shirt is lost, and you are responsible for replacing it.

    Earned privileges are gained when the child demonstrates that the child can handle the responsibility that accompanies the privilege. An example is gaining access to extra computer time with remembering to complete homework.

- Education opportunities are individualized and offered in a way that the child can take advantage of. They are not placed in a setting that they cannot utilize.

- Family visits are an integral part of the treatment for every child. Parents are trained and supported to offer visits that promote healthy attachment. They are encouraged to use the Dyadic Developmental Psychotherapy model of PLACE. This attachment-based model of treatment significantly differs from the standard treatment afforded in most group homes. The emphasis is placed on the parent/child model and a milieu that facilitates building a close attachment relationship with a primary caregiver.

Summary

Systems and institutions care for children when they cannot live with birth or adoptive families. In this chapter we took a look at how Dyadic Developmental Psychotherapy is practiced in two different residential treatment facilities: Chaddock, located in Quincy, Illinois and Villa Santa Maria in Cedar Crest, New Mexico. When the family has not been involved throughout the course of residential treatment, then follow-up psychotherapy is vital. Ideally, visits home would occur with increasing frequency and be of longer duration as the child progresses. During those visits, the follow-up therapist can begin treatment so there is a smooth transition back into the home.

Next we explored how Dyadic Developmental Psychotherapy is used when working with children in long-term foster care. Children in long-term foster care are not promised adoption, and the course of their treatment is effected by the absence of a permanent attachment figure. Dyadic Developmental Psychotherapy is shown to be useful in helping these children form a securely attached relationship with a primary caregiver through the use of PLACE. The children experience building a securely attached relationship that helps them heal from their histories of neglect, abuse, and abandonment.

Lastly, we briefly applied the Dyadic Developmental Psychotherapy model to group home treatment. Most group homes do not use an attachment model of treatment, and many do not provide psychotherapy in any form on an individual basis. As in the situation of children in long-term foster care, these children may not be in contact with their birth parents or only have infrequent contact with them. Their lives are torn by disruption and chaos, and the failure of their primary caregivers to meet their most basic needs for love and a safe, secure environment has left them with feelings of worthlessness. Utilizing the Dyadic Developmental Psychotherapy approach allows group homes to establish a relationship between a primary attachment figure and child. The basic parenting skills utilized in the therapy are taught to primary care staff and parents. If there are available parents, they form a team with the primary youth worker, the therapist, and other professionals to emulate the qualities of a healthy, well functioning family. Through the use of group therapy, the group home encourages formation of healthy peer relationships that imitate sibling relationships.

In the three settings we have examined—residential treatment facilities, therapeutic foster care, and group homes—Dyadic Developmental Psychotherapy is effective in reestablishing the bond of attachment, providing healing and nurturing experiences to help heal the wounds in cases of historical abuse and neglect, and empowering these children to achieve emotional health and well-being.

CHAPTER 7

Therapeutic Use of Self in Dyadic Developmental Psychology

DAFNA LENDER

"When two people relate to each other authentically and humanly, God is the electricity that surges between them." —Martin Buber

This chapter is primarily about exploring the therapist's use of self when using Dyadic Developmental Psychotherapy in the treatment of traumatized and attachment-resistant children and their parents. Central to the successful implementation of Dyadic Developmental Psychotherapy is the therapist ability to connect emotionally with and support both the parent and the child. In essence, you do with the parent what you want the parent to do with the child: maintain a healing PACE, develop the reflective function to uncover the meaning of an experience and communicate that meaning, and maintain emotional attunement.

Due to the extent of their early loss and conflict, such children have very intense feelings of hurt, frustration, and powerlessness. How then do we tolerate being attuned with such intense feelings? This is the special countertransference issue that we face in using Dyadic Developmental Psychotherapy as compared with other modalities.

Hughes (September 2004, p. 275) explains:

> In this model of psychotherapy, which is so much based on the use of the self within the here-and-now intersubjective space, the attachment history of the therapist is likely to be activated more than it is in other models, and it is even more important that it be resolved. While this activation of the therapist's attachment history may be more likely to occur than is generally the case, and hence may increase the risk of acting out countertransference, the attuned nature of the interactions may also serve as a protective factor against such reactions. Within the ongoing contingency of matched, nonverbal, affective communication, the sensitive therapist is being continuously brought back to the experience of the child. Whereas when the therapist is relying to a much greater extent on more distant representations of the experience, there may be a greater likelihood that the therapist's own attachment history may distort their meaning. Whether this model of intervention causes countertransference distortions to be more or less likely to occur, this issue cannot be ignored

when we are developing a therapeutic alliance with children and young people who have experienced trauma, losses, and extreme negative affective states.

This chapter will address the significant use-of-self issues in Dyadic Developmental therapy and the corresponding challenges and rewards that arise as a result of using our own reactions and feelings in such a primary way. Doing Dyadic Developmental Psychotherapy is exciting and dynamic, but can be anxiety-inducing, so first I speak experientially about what it is like being charged with the task of doing this type of work with these clients. Next I discuss the importance of supervision in order to sort through our own attachment dynamics as they inevitably express themselves in the encounter with the client. I also discuss several unique aspects of Dyadic Developmental Psychotherapy, such as physiologic communication that is involved in doing this kind of work, as well as the challenge of "mind reading" and speaking aloud the unconscious assumptions on behalf of the client. Finally, I talk about such issues of power struggles and how to maintain acceptance as the underlying motivation in the therapeutic encounter.

COUNTERTRANSFERENCE: KEEPING THE FOCUS ON THE CLIENT'S NEEDS

Maintaining an affective tie with the parent and child is the essence of the therapist's job. You have to feel something: responsiveness, sensitivity, acceptance, a deep desire to understand the client. Yet you have to feel without getting overwhelmed by the client's or your own feelings. You must be able to be responsive to the immediate affect and relationship without undue distortions stemming from your own internal working models and states of mind with respect to attachment. In order to do this work, you must be able to tolerate strong affect without becoming dysregulated. You must be comfortable allowing the expression of affect without rushing in to "fix it" or make the client "feel better." It is our capacity to tolerate and contain strong emotions that allows the client to experience strong emotions without becoming dysregulated. The therapist dyadically regulates the level of arousal so that the past trauma can be integrated into a coherent autobiographical narrative.

As therapists, we may run the risk of practicing Dyadic Developmental Psychotherapy because of our own need to control or because of other unexplored attachment dynamics in our history. We must be clear that we are not working through our own problems as we attempt to help these children. Often we may have a desire to be better stewards of a child's inner life than that which we experienced as children. Certainly we can derive satisfaction from being a better steward, and this may be the reason why people become therapists in the first place. However, if our own unmet needs continue to motivate us, then we are at risk of distorting the process due to our own countertransference needs—what we are bringing to the session is impacting the session more than what the child is bringing to the session.

This happened to me with a 14-year-old adopted girl, Monica, whom I'd been seeing for a year in individual therapy. Her relative foster parents would not come to treatment with her because they were busy taking care of five other children. Both foster parents were very young themselves and were preoccupied with financial worries as well as a severely contentious marital relationship. Monica had been neglected by her birth parents, which left her in the care of older sisters who were often abusive toward her. She was separated from her entire family at age eight when the children were removed for risk of harm due to filthy conditions in their apartment, as well as lack of food and heat, and placed in the home of her paternal aunt and uncle.

Monica presented as a brazenly independent girl, showing little affect or concern for any person in particular except her birth parents. She spoke about them in an idealized fashion, recognizing none of their faults which had led to her present situation in foster care. As treatment progressed, Monica spoke about her foster mother's absence from the home and her foster father's disregard for her feelings and needs. I saw this as progress, and provided empathic understanding and intersubjective moments of connection around her feelings of discontent at home. I found myself wishing that she would mobilize toward improved mental health and advocate for her needs more actively. I wanted to empower her to "do something" through providing empathy. The more she spoke of the injustices done to her by her foster father, the more I found myself wishing I could do something forceful to shake him up.

Now, the fact that Monica was being brushed aside, slighted, and left to navigate the world alone was a true misfortune, but what about my powerful feelings that I had to rescue Monica from her situation? In one particular session, Monica told me that her foster father neglected to return a form to school which would have allowed her to participate in a math program that would prepare her for admission to a math and science boarding school the following year. She stated this in a nonchalant way, not showing any disappointment or anger about the matter. I was the one who told her about the program, and had fantasized that Monica could go to boarding school, where she would get an excellent education and at least be sheltered from the chaos and strife in her foster home. I was sure that Monica wanted to participate in this program, and this example of her foster parents' negligence made my blood boil. "What?" I demanded, "He just forgot? Didn't you remind him?" I felt she had disappointed me. Angry at all parties in the matter, I began to lecture Monica about what good parents are supposed to be like, and that her foster father was not providing the kind of care that "good-enough parents" provide. "Monica," I said, "parents are supposed to help you with your interests, not brush you off and forget about your needs." Monica looked surprised, then a flash of shame appeared on her face, her shoulders slumped forward a bit, and she looked away. I could tell that the shame she felt was for disappointing me. Suddenly I realized that Monica's story had revived old feelings about times in my own life when I felt disappointed that my parents had dropped the ball, and having been at those times passive, much like Monica, I was now trying to master my revived feelings of helplessness through rescuing her. Being concerned for Monica's well-being was my role, but at that moment, my break in intersubjective connection with where Monica was in relationship to her foster father's failure closed the door on our being able to explore what the incident meant for her.

Alternatively, in Dyadic Developmental Psychotherapy, we are somewhat at risk of being motivated by the sense of elation, a surge of energy, from helping the client[1]. There is such pleasure when you see that the client is changing and transforming. To quote a fellow Dyadic Developmental Psychotherapist pondering the nature of this work in describing a case:

> *God, this work is so ... what? A 15-year-old, violent, avoidant, antisocial boy with a borderline parent was forced to come in under court order. I did not want to take this case. So I said "Okay, if you ever want to get off probation, let's start the hard stuff: five seconds of eye contact with mom ...." And 15 sessions later he's up to 90 seconds, holding her hand, and telling her his feelings. So I said, "You guys are working so hard and building trust that was never there before—what are you feeling right now?" And this former throw-away, under-socialized client suddenly grins from ear to ear, looks ME in the eye and says, "Joy!" Had to bawl him out for making me cry. God, this work is so ... what?*

Sharing these moments is very powerful. But if sharing these transforming moments is my motive, I'll need the client to make progress, and I'm at risk of rejecting her if she does not. This "high" is transforming for the therapist too, but if in a given moment in therapy, that is my motive—to be transformed by the client—there is a danger that my needs will become the priority. So the question is and will remain: Do I feel I am sufficiently open to feelings in my own life and satisfied with transforming moments in my personal relationships to a) know what it feels like and b) not need

---

[1] In this chapter, I will use the term client to refer to both parent and child.

the client to do the emotional work for me? I must be receptive to my client's transforming moments in order to allow her to have an impact on me, which in turn has an additional impact on the client. An important impact for me as a therapist is the joy of being a good "steward of the client's inner life," whether or not my parents were good stewards for me. In technical terms, one can either have a secure state of mind with respect to attachment or an earned secure status. In either case, one's ability to enter into a healthy and healing state of intersubjectivity with the client depends on the health and security of one's own state of mind with respect to attachment and the degree to which one can experience the current relationship in the current moment without undue distortions.

THE POWER AND PERIL OF FEELING FELT: PRIMARY INTERSUBJECTIVITY

Dyadic Developmental Psychotherapy relies on the therapist's attuned physiological and psychological states to communicate acceptance, curiosity, and empathy for the client's experience. This form of therapy hinges on the therapist's facial expression, voice, cadence, prosody, and pacing; adjusting constantly to the client's nonverbal states in order to provide the client with the experience of feeling felt and engaging in the therapeutic process of co-construction of meaning. There is a special moment when a client produces an image that is emotionally charged and meaningful to the client, whether painful or pleasant, and the therapist latches on to it. Together, both minds are holding on to that image and sharing it; that is the moment of transformation towards emotional integration and healing. Latching on to the client's image is only possible if the therapist is acutely attuned to the changes of the client's tone of voice, body language, and thoughts, so that the therapist can imagine what the client is seeing in the client's mind's eye.

One of these transformational moments occurred when a traumatized mother of an extremely attachment-resistant, 12-year-old adopted boy painfully explained that she no longer knew her role in life now that her son was in residential placement. As she spoke about her feelings of emptiness and confusion about who she was, a painful list of strained or unfulfilling relationships poured from her lips like a whirling pile of autumn leaves in the wind: "I adopted him when he was six, and from the beginning he wouldn't let me parent him, and no one, especially my husband, would believe me that Tom was doing all these terrible things at home. I didn't even believe it, and I blamed myself, just like when I was growing up as a child and I was told that my feelings were nonsense." She looked melancholy and lost, her eyes glistening with tears from the fallout of her years of trauma with her son. Guilt over having "sent her son away" to the residential placement left her questioning what kind of mother she really was. At one moment she said: "I'm just a long-distance caretaker to my son, and I've failed him." Choking back tears, she whispered, "I feel so pained about the fact that I was so relieved he went away ... and I can't see him ever coming back."

At that moment, my mind filled with the knowledge of this woman's sensitive efforts to be a good steward of all her son's needs over the years and her painstaking decision to place him in residential treatment. Yet in her mind she still believed that because her son was unable to attach to her, she was a failure. I leaned in, matching the minor notes in her own thin, pained voice, and said, "You are a mother to your son because you hold him in your mind and you see him for all that he is. That is very painful. It is painful because he is a difficult person who has a lot of needs that he can't let you meet because of who he is. But you are the mom to this boy because you hold him in your heart, and knowing all that you know about him, you have provided him with what you know he needs." As I spoke, quietly, clearly, her eyes grew moist, she nodded her head in small bows of self-acknowledgment, and together, looking intently at each other, we held in our minds the image of her as Mom. For that moment, I joined her in that lonely place of being a parent of such a child, and feeling joined, she settled a little, took in a sigh, and felt held, supported, and understood at a deep level. Both of us sat back in recognition and contentment from the connection. This is an example of primary intersubjectivity.

Maintaining Energy and Focus

The therapist is charged with the task of being present—present in the face of a client's frustration, hurt, and powerlessness, which we invite into the room when we are deeply accepting, curious, and empathic. What lies underneath a client's behavior is shame, pain, and anger that we are making a safe place to explore by directly addressing their history. The rigorousness of the physiologic and psychological demands for awareness and responsiveness from the therapist, coupled with the traumatic content of the client's history, makes for a strenuous, exhilarating, and often fear-inducing experience when I enter a session. It's not unlike skiing down a ski slope whose terrain you know only partially, and the only way to navigate successfully is to stay loose, flexible, and accept the bumps and turns gracefully, all at 90 miles per hour!

There are times when, due to fatigue, worry, or preoccupation with my own life, I dread going into sessions because I fear I will not be up to the task and the client will know it. At such times I feel that I may do damage to the client or myself and there will be a setback in therapy. Oftentimes, once I am "on the slope" and in session with the client, I find I lose some of my anxiety and preoccupation. I am drawn into the client's vulnerability and their eagerness to communicate and connect with me. The dread of going into session is always worse than being present for the client once we are in there together. Once I am in the session, I am often surprised that it is less difficult than I thought it might have been.

There can be a dramatic unevenness to sessions with these clients. During one session, I feel the interaction is smooth as silk: The client's nonverbal communication is transparent to me; I respond; the client relaxes. I have empathy for the parent, we are working together, the parent accepts her child's emotional content, and an intersubjective dialogue begins that is satisfying. We are making meaning.

Then, in the next session, for no discernible reason, the client's behavior seems alien. I lead the client down paths that are just plain wrong, and I am left baffled and frustrated. The parent sits with arms folded, looking scornful and fatigued. I feel trapped in the middle, trying to be present for both and feeling like a failure. At that moment I must stop and make a quick assessment of my motives: Why am I trying to change the child today? What feelings got stirred up in me that make it hard to accept the child where she is today: confused, defiant, grumpy? What might I be picking up from the parent's nonverbal communication that makes me feel like punishing the child? If I cannot figure it out so quickly, then I go back to the four attitudes of Dyadic Developmental Psychotherapy: playful, accepting, curious, and empathic—maintaining a healing PACE. One of those attitudes is bound to be the right fit for whatever the child or parent is giving me, and will be the key to breaking out of the gridlock. I must remember that PACE is enough for now. If I put pressure on myself, then I know the child will feel it and resist. Soon, I will feel like a failure just as the parent does.

Consider a recent experience of this phenomenon. A mom came in with her 10-year-old daughter, Alexis, an extremely sensitive, highly reactive adopted child who was severely neglected for the first four years of her life. One of mom's greatest concerns was that Alexis took everything personally. She was easily frightened and dysregulated by the least sign of discord in her surroundings. Her daughter had been making dramatic progress in therapy. Alexis, her mom, and I shared tremendously powerful moments of meaning-making around her daughter's past history and its effects on her coping styles in the present day. Alexis had recently been placed in a specialized school that was doing a much better job of accommodating her emotional needs than the public school she had attended the year before.

One day, Mom came in for our therapy session angry and activated by a conversation with her daughter's teacher that she had just before coming to my office. Up until that day, her daughter had no behavioral problems at the new school. On this day, however, Alexis had been running around wildly in the classroom and was sent to the social worker to cool down. The reason for Alexis' behavior was that a new girl had joined the classroom who was, according to Alexis, an unremitting bully who took particular pleasure in teasing and hurting Alexis. As a result, Alexis "blew up" and began acting silly, acting out, and getting in trouble. The teacher recommended that Alexis meet with the social worker on a regular basis to help her cope with these situations.

As soon as they walked in to therapy, Mom said, "Alexis, why didn't you tell the teacher when this bully was bothering you?" Her tone of voice was harsh and critical. She began to lecture her: "I've told you that if you don't tell an adult when something is bothering you, then they can't help you." Alexis shrunk into the corner, pillows over her head, unwilling to listen. Joining with mom's frustration, I tried to solicit a response to mom's question.

Alexis whined, "I did try to tell the teacher, but she doesn't always look at me when I raise my hand."

"Why don't you call her name, or get up from your desk to tell her if she's not looking?" Mom demanded.

A long pause ensued before Alexis' red face, buried in the pillows, lifted up just enough to let out a muffled response—"Because sometimes I forget."

Now Mom's anger at her daughter's passivity activates her even more, so she folded her arms across her chest as she leaned back on the couch, distancing herself from her daughter ... and I was caught between mom's anger and the child's wilting shame. Feeling stuck was a sign to me that I needed to take a deep breath and get back on track with acceptance, curiosity and empathy.

"Hold on, Mom," I said to Alexis' mom, reaching my hand out to signal both a "stop" but also to provide a reassuring touch. By this time in treatment, Mom had developed enough trust in me to accept my signal to take a deep breath and keep her own feelings at bay long enough for me to switch gears. Then I turned to Alexis, got down on the pillows where she lay, put my face at her level and said quietly, "Alexis, I wonder what it's like for you when the bully in your class picks on you all the time and the teacher doesn't see it?" Ah, the shift had occurred as I noticed that what I was trying to do was to force Alexis out of a position that Mom and I did not even understand.

An eye peeked out from the pillow as Alexis turned, frowned, and said "Bad!"

"Bad!" I said, matching her affect and tone, "I can sure understand that ...." I repeated the scenario, "The class bully picks on you and when you try to tell the teacher, most of the time she doesn't even see you raise your hand!" Now I was back on track ... getting back in tune with Alexis's feelings and out of the shame she felt and the shame Mom and I inadvertently imposed on her, and into making meaning of what it felt like that she's being bullied and can't get help. I understood how powerless and angry that made her feel. And I can see the connection between these feelings and her experience when she was a baby and needed help and no one came. Then I can have empathy for that, and Mom can see it too, so that we don't just feel that Alexis is stupid or incompetent at advocating for herself. Now with this shared deeper understanding, Alexis and her mother could take a step forward toward healing. Because I was able to feel Alexis' frustrations with her, and was able to link them to her past experience, her mother was able to feel empathy for Alexis' position. I asked mom to let Alexis know that she understood how hard it was for her daughter during those moments in the classroom, and she did, simply, genuinely. It was only then that we were all able to problem-solve with Alexis about strategies for coping with the bully, strategies that Alexis was able to come up with herself, once she knew and felt that her mom and I were really with her in her lonely experience.

USING SUPERVISION TO UNDERSTAND COUNTERTRANSFERENCE ISSUES

Often, it is only through the use of supervision that we can become aware of the unconscious needs that we are attempting to meet through our client. A colleague of mine described working with a boy with whom she was extremely frustrated and the powerful moment of transformation she underwent upon receiving supervision on the case.

The 14-year-old adopted boy was having a hard time at home and school, displaying serious behavior problems, aggressive acting out, and fighting with people. He was resistant to touch and to nurturing and could not show genuine affect. His parents felt frustrated and worried about the direction things were going with their son and came into the session feeling angry and resentful. They felt their son had not been making an effort in any aspect of his life and that he needed to start taking responsibility for his actions. In therapy, the boy began talking about a friend he missed who had moved away, which triggered earlier losses for him. As the therapist spoke to him about his friend and his feelings, the boy felt sad, had tears in his eyes, and was even able to verbalize a few feelings, something he typically could not do. The therapist glanced over at the parents to see if they were picking up on their son's genuine display of emotion. What she saw in their faces was disapproval and disappointment. Sensing the parents' dissatisfaction, the therapist lost her focus on the boy's experience and missed this opportunity for the intersubjective sharing of affect. Because the parents did not see the work their son was doing, the therapist lost appreciation for the boy's work. The therapist had a need for the parents to be pleased and wanted the boy to feel accountable. She then shifted to lecture mode of "taking responsibility for efforts, that he has to change, etc." The therapist was responding to the disappointed parent in her own mind. She never got back the appreciation for the boy's work during that session.

Feeling frustrated that she was not getting through to the boy, the therapist sent her tape for supervision with Dr. Hughes. The first thing that Dr. Hughes said was that he was impressed by the boy and the hard work he had done. This stunned the therapist. Dr. Hughes then pointed out to therapist the many points at which she led the boy in the attuned dance of affective communication: She took him to "sad" and the boy went with her; she took him to feeling playful, and the boy responded in kind. "He followed you," Dr. Hughes said. It was a defining moment for the therapist. The therapist felt shame that she missed the significant work the boy had done, and even was concerned that she may have done harm to the boy. Despite these feelings, the therapist was able to see that the boy was working hard and that they were co-regulating affect and making meaning together. Having recognized the significant amount of work that both she and the boy were doing, the therapist felt freed from the need to please the parents or give them what they thought they wanted. From that moment, the therapist felt liberated to be more present in the session, free from worry about whether the work that the boy was doing was "enough" for the parents. This therapist now knows that every small accomplishment in affective attunement and synchrony such children make in therapy must be explicitly celebrated and reinforced.

AVOIDING THE DANGER OF UNDUE INFLUENCE: PLANTING IDEAS INTO VULNERABLE CHILDREN'S MINDS

Dyadic Developmental Psychotherapy flies in the face of much of what we learned in graduate school about what techniques and interventions to use. It is important to note that we are likely at risk of contaminating the child's psychic process if our own autobiographical narrative is not clear and coherent. Actively using our own affective responses, intentions, and beliefs can be very therapeutic when they accurately reflect what will foster the child's autonomy, safety, and affective development. But when there are gaps, distortions, or inconsistencies in our own narratives, our responses can distort the child's inner life.

This raises the question: Are traumatized children's psyches more vulnerable to outside interference and tampering, and if so, do we run a greater risk of "contaminating" their psychic process? What about the integrity of the child's psychic process? Do we have to worry about "putting ideas into children's heads" regarding the origins of their behaviors? The children with whom we work are young, vulnerable, and closer chronologically to the damaging experiences. Despite this, it is therapeutically warranted to boldly go where no therapist has gone before and state assumptions aloud about the child's unconscious thoughts, and in a sense, to "mind read."

Children who were traumatized in their preverbal years have a somatic memory of the traumatic events that is triggered years later in seemingly incongruent situations with their adoptive parents. For example, Peter, a child adopted from a Peruvian orphanage at age two years, two months, was eight years old when I treated him and had behavioral problems around evening bath time. Peter's behavioral problems began as soon as his parents alerted him to the fact that it was time to go upstairs and take a bath. At that point, he would begin to run around the house, acting wild, knocking things off tables, or hitting his siblings. His adoptive parents, in an attempt to minimize the damage, resorted to chasing him and cornering him in the hallway. At that point Peter would flail, kick, and call his parents names. He was more provocative and dysregulated with his adoptive father than mother, due to the fact that his father got angry at the "disrespect" that Peter was showing him. Peter's father would try to physically maneuver Peter toward the tub, at which point Peter would kick his dad in the groin, or alternatively would position himself in such a way, such as rolling underfoot while naked, that his father would accidentally step on Peter's groin area. This brought the conflict to its highest point of escalation: Peter cries, his father becomes frightened and confused at how things got so out of hand, and Peter's mom comes to rescue them. After this, Peter would dramatically de-escalate and deflate, usually spending time whimpering in bed while his mother soothed him. While Peter cried, he would cling to his mom, mumbling that "it's not fair," "he hurt me," and "I didn't mean it." His dad, feeling guilty, would meekly apologize, but his embarrassment and discomfort at the scene left him feeling upset.

Peter's parents recounted their witnessing of bath time at the orphanage where Peter lived when he was two. All the children had to line up and take a bath in cold, dirty water. They were mechanically lined up and forced into the water without any sensitivity. Peter had open wounds and scabs from mites and bedbugs, and he screamed in fear and pain as the matrons forced him into the tub to scrub him. It is no wonder, then, that Peter became dysregulated around bath time. When he first came to the United States, Peter feared water and taking baths. In response, his adoptive parents engaged in gentle, reassuring attempts to show him that bath time would be different with them, emphasizing clean, warm water and gentle care. Peter learned to acclimate to taking a bath, his wounds healed, and his behavior around bath time improved after several months in the United States.

I asked myself, why this recurrence of hyper-aroused and aggressive behavior during bath time six years later? I made the connection between the frightening and painful experience in Peter's early years to his resistance today. In speaking to Peter about this, I had him sit on the couch between his mom and his dad. I sat across but at an angle from them, and in close enough proximity to touch Peter's arm, foot, or if I leaned in, his head. I spoke in a quiet, almost childlike voice saying, "Peter, I wonder how it must have felt for you when you were a baby, being so small, and not having enough words to say that you were scared of the bath and that you didn't want it. Because, you know, babies aren't supposed to be able to say those things. Their mom is supposed to know those things and take care not to put a baby in cold, dirty water, and to make sure the baby doesn't get bitten by bugs that make big sores on their arms and legs and bellies." Peter curled into the couch, head in mom's arm, legs on dad's lap. He looked at me with pained, saucer eyes, the blue in them so big I could see a whole world in them. Peter frowned and nodded. I continued, "So since you didn't have words back then, you did the only thing you could do! You kicked and screamed! You tried to run away! But you still had to go in the bath and the matrons were gruff and they didn't hold you gently or help you feel safe." Peter's frown got bigger, and for one small millisecond I saw him see himself in the tub with the matron, and then he hid his face inside his mom's arm and whimpered. I stopped. I told Mom to hold her son really close so he would feel her tight hold and know that she wasn't going to let go. I put my arm on his and held it there, steady, saying words of reassurance for a minute, until Peter peeked out of his mom's sleeve.

"Why did they treat me so mean?" Peter moaned quietly.

"I don't know," I whispered gently, and we wondered out loud about the matrons and their situation, and mom and dad joined in to wonder out loud. After several minutes, I met Peter's eyes again, more restored in their gaze, peering into mine, and said, "I wonder, Peter, if when you were a baby and didn't have any words to say 'No!' to the cold, yucky bath, I wonder if sometimes, with your forever family, when it's time for bath, your body still remembers that it was scared, and you start to run and kick and act wild as if you were still in the orphanage!?" My tone was one of curious surprise, questioning, and anticipation. Peter squinted his eyes, held his mom's hand and looked like he was processing what I had said. That made sense to him, I thought, and it did to his parents too. We all held in our minds the picture of little Peter in the dirty, cold bathtub and gave him empathy about how hard that must have been. For a few moments, we paused for a deep intersubjective sharing of affect—a moment of intense primary intersubjectivity.

Later I pointed out to his father how his angry response contributed to the playing out in real life of Peter's traumatized memory. With a more empathic understanding, Peter's father was able to be less authoritarian and confrontational in his approach with his son. Peter's father became more confident and reassuring in his tone when Peter became dysregulated around bath time because he was now able to keep in mind the image of a small, frightened child that was hurt in the bath. He also backed off physically and did not attempt to corral Peter using force. The calmness in his voice was genuine, and Peter sensed it on a physiologic level. This diffused the tension between them. Peter's dad discovered that he was then able to give his son a bath at night without frightening himself or his son. This proved to be a deeply satisfying achievement for both of them.

The dynamics and connections we made based on Peter's history and behaviors were quite straightforward and intuitively easy for the family to understand. What baffled me, however, was Peter's targeting of his father's groin and his positioning of himself over and over to get hit in the groin area himself despite his father's protestations that he did not have any intention of hurting Peter in any way, and certainly not in the groin.

In a subsequent session, I offered in a curious, tentative way to Peter that he may have been hurt by other children or by adults in his groin area or penis in the orphanage, and that his brain had linked being naked and taking a bath with this abuse. Peter responded with a quiet and perplexed look as he lay very still on the pillows by his mom and me. Since Peter neither protested nor resonated with this hypothesis, I went on to say that we know that this may happen in orphanages, and that it's not okay to hurt anyone on their private parts. After a brief moment, I dropped it. I wondered after the session about whether I should have made this inference, as it was not possible for Peter to confirm or deny it. My fear as I was proceeding in the session, one which caused me to hesitate, was that I may have introduced an idea into Peter's narrative that did not exist. I began to think of the many other reasons why Peter might have an issue with injuring or being injured in the genitals, and the burden of the responsibility of helping a child to assemble his narrative weighed heavily on me.

We can never know with certainty what happened to such children, and often there is no way of knowing except through their behavior. Yet their defenses have such convoluted manifestations that suggesting linear connections seems like treading on thin ice. Would it not be safer not to suggest this connection? By keeping to the safe shore, however, we might limit our opportunity to uncover truths about these children's erased lives of trauma. In Peter's case, it helped that I was tentative and curious as I stated my hypothesis. Equally important, I remained highly attuned to the nonverbal responses he had to my statements and reflected on those. I also normalized and gave a rationale for asking the question.

Being attuned to Peter's response, which was one of stillness, a puzzled look, and no apparent interest in exploring the subject further, I did not linger long on this supposition of sexual abuse. By letting the supposition float in the air, I may have laid the groundwork for future work around this subject.

USE OF THE THERAPIST'S PHYSIOLOGIC SELF

In Dyadic Developmental Psychotherapy, establishing and maintaining emotional attunement and connection is achieved through the therapist's physical being and physiologic (rather than verbal/cognitive) communication with the client. Unlike nondirective play therapy and cognitive therapy, attunement communicated through physiologic modes is one of Dyadic Developmental Psychotherapy's primary tools to facilitate the healing process. Physiologic communication means matching the intensity, timing, and shape of the client's physiologic expressions. This type of communication is central to attaining and maintaining regulation of affect. Responding in an attuned fashion to a client's facial, vocal, gestural, or postural communication is how the emotional connection is established (Stern, 1985, p. 147). Physiologic communication also involves physical touch, which is used to give the child comfort and support, and for spontaneous communication of joy—all of which co-regulate various affective states. Whereas in nondirective therapy, physical touch may be limited to a hug at the end of a session, or the rare need for a restraint in case the child becomes aggressive, physical playfulness and affection, as well as physical techniques for re-engagement, are keys to our work. While a naturally talented therapist may intuitively provide this kind of physiologic connection in other modalities such as nondirective play therapy or cognitive/behavioral approaches, Dyadic Developmental Psychotherapy specifically focuses on intervening at this level.

Physiologic communication comes naturally for some and not others. Accuracy in matching a client's affective states is crucial. A client can be put off by a therapist who seems rigid or physically distant and can feel just as uncomfortable if the therapist is overly vigorous in communicating with the child. Establishing physical connection for playfulness, nurturance, and affection, and imparting a sense of safety and connection for regulation of physiologic functions, all have to be taught. It is the rare gift that a therapist would know the use of physical communication without guidelines, instruction, and feedback from a professional trained in this dimension of therapy. Taping oneself and showing one's work to a trained professional or peer consultant, while uncomfortable, is invaluable to learning the use of physical proximity, touch, and other physiologic modes for achieving affective synchrony, such as tone and prosody of voice, affective vitality, and rhythm. I did not really know how to intervene on these levels until I engaged in taped supervision, as well as experiential exercises and role-plays. Without this training, I would be less confident and effective in establishing and maintaining an emotional connection with my clients.

BEING DIRECTIVE VS. BEING IN CHARGE

One of the problems that arise in the course of therapy with an attachment-resistant child is getting involved in power struggles. Often, this can happen both to parents and therapists when they are working with the child. The intention of "being in charge" can pull a therapist into the use of power and power struggles before the therapist knows what is occurring. The goal is to be "directive with empathy." In other words, one accepts what the child is offering in the moment and then begins to lead the child into a deeper intersubjective experience. I accept what the client offers, and am then directive in deepening the experience. The client responds, and based on the client's responses, I continue to pursue my original focus, respond to the client's response, and change direction. We are actively working to get reciprocity so both of us are initiating and responding. The client may avoid this reciprocity and may want to "be in charge." Their stance is not healthy, because authentic human relationships involve reciprocity. So the goal is to maintain reciprocity—with empathy and/or playfulness. The bottom line is that the adult—parent or therapist—must make the decisions that are necessary for safety. But to focus only on that would be to miss the main lesson that the child needs to learn: Reciprocity is better than either parent or child's "being in charge." While at an earlier time it was the only way the child could survive, now that he is in a stable, responsible relationship, it no longer is adaptive.

CHILD'S NEED VS. PARENT'S NEED VS. THERAPIST'S NEED: THE VITAL IMPORTANCE OF ACCEPTANCE

Dan Hughes (September 2004, p. 269) states: "The therapist's intention must be to experience—and communicate—acceptance, curiosity, empathy, and, at times, playfulness for the child's narrative. If the therapist engages in these expressions for another intention—to change the child, the child will be aware of this intention nonverbally and may refrain from joining the therapist's intention and then resist the interaction. When the intention is simply to experience and communicate acceptance, curiosity, and empathy or playfulness, the client is more likely to have a reciprocal intention of experiencing the therapist's intentions."

Acceptance is the underlying motivation that enables the therapist to do everything that she does. It allows her to be curious, to explore without controlling, to provide attunement and connection. Both parent and child need the PACE attitude; sometimes the parent will have to experience it first so that she can then join the therapist in giving it to the child. This issue, however, probably touches the therapist's countertransference issues differently. The countertransference of therapist toward parent is likely to differ from that of therapist toward child. With the parent, the therapist may slip into a "child" mode and try to please the parent. With the child, the therapist may slip into the "parent" mode and enact the therapist's own internal working model of the parent-child relationship rather than respond to this child in this moment. The therapist may be more likely because of her own unresolved issues to focus on the needs of the one, without being aware of the needs of the other. Similarly, she may become an "ally" with one and split off from the other. In any event, what is occurring is that the therapist is acting on an unconscious internal working model that has been activated by some affect or experience in the moment instead of responding to the current affect, relationship, and actual person.

In Peter's case, I was hypothesizing or suggesting that sexual abuse occurred. Peter's parents obviously were not welcoming to the idea that I was suggesting that Peter had endured possible horrors before they adopted him. I could see Peter's mom cringe when I spoke of the possibility, while Peter's father had a skeptical look on his face. When I spoke with each of the parents separately about the topic, neither one revealed any history of sexual abuse or victimization. Did mom's flinching and dad's aloofness cause me to too hastily drop my hunch and move on? Certainly Peter could have sensed that this idea was displeasing to his parents and responded to that by avoiding thinking about it.

This kind of reaction by the parent is to be expected. Even these parents, who are securely and autonomously attached adults, were resistant to sitting with the idea that Peter was possibly sexually abused before they got him. Through curious exploration of this reaction in a separate session, Peter's mom and I were able to uncover the resistance she had toward exploring Peter's possible sexual abuse. I highly commended Peter's mom for being able to do this difficult work. Through curiosity, the meaning of the "resistance" is co-constructed as being a natural and important quality of the therapeutic process. It reflects strength and courage, as well as possible ambivalence about relying on the therapist for comfort and guidance. Peter's mom finally revealed that her family of origin was a conservative, overprotective, and proud lot. She revealed that it was considered a failure on her part that she was unable to conceive children naturally, and there was an expectation that her adoptive children had to "measure up" to the other biologic grandchildren. Furthermore, parents were expected to lift up and motivate their children away from any defect of character. In his grandparents' eyes, Peter had many such defects, ones they believed Peter could overcome if only his parents provided proper discipline. Peter's mom felt at once deficient for not producing children without mental illness and behavioral problems, and at the same time angry at Peter for having so many problems. Uncovering another problem, especially of a sexual nature, imparted an even deeper feeling of anxiety that her son might "not be normal." Having opened up this awareness on this delicate matter, Peter's mom and I continue to use this information to reflect on how difficult it is for her to be sufficiently separate from her own family to allow her son the opportunity to explore all parts of himself. This awareness has assisted Peter's mom in keeping her own family dynamics in check when Peter displays emotions that are uncomfortable for her.

Having grown up with a parent who reacted strongly to any emotional or physical pain I encountered as if it were her own, I know the burden of guilt and concern that a child can feel for causing that parent pain. I was, therefore, able to empathically perceive more clearly the internal experience of the child in this situation. This is an example of positive use of countertransference for understanding my clients. I can resonate with this child's experience because it is familiar to me. It can also tilt me toward identifying with the child and wanting to release the child from the burden of worrying about the mom's needs. However, I have to be able to step back and keep in mind that this child's experience can be different from my own. Certainly, any practicing therapist must engage in this kind of personal work in order to avoid these countertransferential pitfalls.

Summary

Primary intersubjectivity is a valuable key to unlocking the hidden child underneath the trauma. Dyadic Developmental Psychotherapy provides clinicians with the opportunity to use their entire being, psychic and physiologic, to create transforming moments of intersubjective healing to attachment-resistant clients. Dyadic Developmental Psychotherapy raises some potential entanglements for practitioners, as attuning to and containing intense feelings of rage, despair, and hopelessness in such clients can trigger unconscious acting out. This powerful technique, however, can be fine-tuned to become one of the most effective techniques in working with clients who have experienced the damaging effects of early chronic trauma. Healing the whole child demands that we push ourselves to use approaches which when first encountered may not be comfortable or orthodox. Dyadic Developmental Psychotherapy is an invitation to engage in a daring, holistic approach, requiring a level of engagement many therapists initially might find foreign, but when applied with a deft touch, can awaken and heal some of our most wounded souls.

Practical Tips for Working with Children Diagnosed with Reactive Attachment Disorder:
Teachers, Case Managers, Youth Workers, Wrap-Around Staff

ARTHUR BECKER-WEIDMAN & DEBORAH SHELL

"The aim of therapeutic work with shame is that the patient be able to recover and experience the positive nature of the responses that became distorted by shame."
—Diana Fosha, The Transforming Power of Affect

Therapeutic support for families who struggle to parent an attachment-resistant child requires an approach different from other, more common childhood diagnosis. When trying to fulfill your role as a family support worker, skills worker, or case manager, it is imperative that you work closely with the child's parents or caregivers so that you do not undermine or interfere with the basic overall goal: helping to facilitate a primary attachment between the child and the parents.

Adults must set limits, yet attachment-resistant children experience those limits as hurtful. So while setting necessary limits, we must be careful not to replicate the uncaring, harsh, and inappropriate treatment these children have already experienced. At the same time, it is important that we not accept the child's attempts to replicate angry, neglectful, or disrespectful interactions. When working with these children, the adult must be able to maintain and manage the process of interaction between the adult and child by defining the nature and quality of the interaction.

The idea is to manage the process without being controlling. For example, ask questions that reflect your curiosity about the child's behavior or become playful when the child tries to argue; this will help you avoid being controlled emotionally by the child. Use paradoxical interventions. Do not become boxed-in by the child's attempts to control you. When the child chooses not to comply, maintain emotional control by "allowing" the behavior. For example, if the child sits in the wrong chair, you might say, "I'd like you to sit in that chair or your chair." Although it may seem as if the child is in control, unless he controls your emotions and causes you to respond to him with anger, he is not. The attachment-resistant child's weapon of choice is trying to control you by "making" you act as the harsh caregiver.

Begin with the premise that to facilitate an attachment, the parents must be primary in the child's life. The attachment-resistant child must learn how to accept being loved and cherished. He must learn to trust that the parents' decisions are made with his best interests at heart. The parents should be informed about, and approve of, all activities, opportunities, and plans before telling (or asking) the child. Use the same protocol as if you were caregiver to an infant or small child; initiate conversations with the parents to be sure activities are appropriate and approved.

Children with attachment disorders are loners, and if you look carefully, they reveal an underlying belief that they are in charge of themselves. This surface controlling behavior covers a deep fear of intimacy and closeness and a belief that they are unlovable and unloved. This can be mistaken for precocious independence. These children may be very convincing that they can have candy or ice cream, go swimming, or go to the movies. They won't think to have you ask their parent first, nor will they tell you that they've already surpassed the week's candy allowance. These children are opportunistic and have not yet internalized their parent's care and love. Remember that love and care always come with discipline and limit setting. If a child has not yet internalized love, she has not internalized limits, either, and will use every opportunity to advance her immediate gratification. While the child may be chronologically older, many children with trauma-attachment disorders are developmentally at age two or three. It is vital that the child be treated at the child's developmental or emotional age and not according to the child's chronological age.

Another concern is the way an attachment-resistant child can split a team of professional service providers. Some children will demonstrate waif-like innocence and have you confused and half-believing that the parents are mean, power-hungry, insensitive individuals who don't understand their child at all. If you find yourself contemplating how wonderful this child's life could be "if only" the parents would lighten up and give the child more freedom and chances to prove how good the child really is, then stop and reconsider before you undermine the parents' efforts to build an attachment. Instead, help by demonstrating to the child how you defer to the parents' authority. By taking their child's best interests to heart and setting limits, parents demonstrate love. Your primary role is to support the parents. In your professional role, you function to underscore the parents' role as the primary caregiver who knows what is best for the child. Any action that undercuts the parent's authority or central role will ultimately further injure the child's already damaged ability to trust and develop authentic, meaningful relationships.

It can be difficult to imagine life with a child who does not interpret intimate interpersonal communication accurately. The child has the capacity to demonstrate his best behavior while spending limited time with you. This same child, when at home, is frequently disobedient and non-compliant and may use threats as a way to control others. An attachment-resistant child hasn't learned to feel safety in intimate relationships and doesn't accept family as protective and supportive. The child may experience others as motivated solely out of their own selfish interests and see other family members as competitors. Limits seem like punishments because the child experiences relationships through the lens of past maltreatment. Effects of past trauma interfere with current interpretations of daily events. The child may relate events to you with such believable (albeit inaccurate) interpretation that you feel sure this child is not understood and is in the wrong placement. Remember, not only are you getting half the story, but a misinterpreted half at that. The child misinterprets many interactions based on effects of past traumatic experiences. These children don't know, in their hearts, that to have internalized healthy parents means following parental guidelines (ethical behavior, kindness, sharing, honesty) whether near or far from scrutiny.

The helpful service provider communicates with the parents to learn which interactions with the child are preferred. Frequent meetings or phone contact prior to and following your time with the child demonstrate that you are appropriately deferring to the parents' authority and respectful of their healthy choices. Ask ahead of time about snacks, treats, or activities and relate back to the parent what you actually did during your time together. The child may plead and beg for more than was agreed upon, telling you how unfair it is for them. A therapeutic response would involve being non-reactive to the child's feelings of being treated unfairly, not taking sides, and recognizing that the child's difficulty trusting the parents' overall motivation makes it difficult for the child to accept a limit. Remember that by setting appropriate limits, the parents are demonstrating love for the child by taking his best interest to heart. Don't prejudge the parents' limits. They are based on intimate knowledge of the child's capacity to cope with out-of-home activities as well as what is going on within the family throughout the week.

Learning about and understanding how attachment disorders develop is imperative. These children display serious impairment and dysfunctional behaviors based on beliefs founded during critical periods of growth and development. Identity is developed in relation to other's response to our needs. We feel good about ourselves, right, approved of, and secure if our parents have met our fundamental needs in loving ways. Daily care conveys feelings of "you are worth my efforts," which translates into positive self-worth. Attachment-resistant children's needs were not met, for many reasons, yet the outcome is evident. These children suffer from inability to trust that others can and will care for them. Their cause-and-effect thinking is absent, and they may seem not to learn from mistakes. We learn cause and effect largely through consistent and dependable care beginning in infancy. It take lots of patience to convince a child that another human being can be depended upon.

When working with children who struggle with attachment problems, avoid asking them why they misbehave or saying that they should know better. Rather, when you are aware of a breach in appropriate behavior or expectations, try saying "I see you need help with _____." It could be sharing, dividing up the snacks, following rules, speaking respectfully to peers, not kicking your chair, etc. Instead of giving warnings, help the child to comply or stop the activity. Warnings and second chances are not helpful for these children; they often experience these as inconsistent and unreliable adult behaviors. When there is a disruption, you can say to the child, "I see you aren't ready to" do the activity. Use a natural con-sequence, i.e. "Since it took longer than five minutes for you to zip up your pants (brush your teeth, pick up your shoes, etc.), we've run out of time for a story." Then, follow through without argument or becoming emotional. This helps the child realize the interconnectedness of rela-tionships, the larger world's expectations, and the need to comply with rules and limits in order to benefit and contribute. To the uninformed such a response may seem overly strict or rigid. However, keep in mind that due to profound underlying mistrust and misjudgment of other's motives, the child will want to control every aspect of relationships (and people in general); therefore, it is best to react as if the child hasn't yet learned how to respond in appropriate ways to normal, everyday, inter-personal activity. A child diagnosed with Reactive Attachment Disorder often displays misguided beliefs that she can use threats, noncompli-ance, and defiance as weapons to maintain control and to prevent being hurt, even in situations that are inherently benign.

Service providers have large hearts and huge desires to override previous messages, and therefore want to prove to the child that he is lovable. It can be tempting to do too much or to fall into the trap of thinking that say-ing "yes" equals love. When a child whines, complains, begs, and seems to link all happiness to getting his way just this one time, it can feel wrong to say "no." Yet, this is especially the time to avoid indulgences. A thera-peutic message would be that the child is inherently good and lovable even when you say "no." Neglected children never experienced loving lim-its. These children were "allowed" to do whatever they wanted to do, even if what they "wanted" to do was dangerous, such as ride their tricycle in the middle of the street.

Remember, a central concept in working with these children is to be in control of the relationship without being controlling. This applies to parents, teachers, youth workers, and all who come in contact with them. It is vital that you be the one to manage the relationship, setting the rhythm, tone, cadence, and emotional quality. In other words, the relationship must be managed so that the child is responding to you and not the other way around. If the child acts in a way that creates an argument, evokes your anger, or results in your being harsh and punitive, then it is the child who is in control of the relationship. Of course, you can "win" the battle and "make" the child sit, behave, etc., but you are "losing" the battle over the relationship. Your task is to set the terms of the relationship so that the child is responding to you. This does not mean being controlling; far from it. This means being loving and supportive. Not fighting force with force, but facilitating a joining and maintaining an attuned emotionally responsive relationship.

As a simple example, consider the child who asks you to buy some candy. You know the parent does not want her to have candy. If you say "no," you are likely to begin an argument with her. This puts the child in control of the relationship with you responding to the child. If you say, "Well, your Dad said no candy," you may be undercutting the parent or yourself. Again, an argument may ensue with you responding to the child. But, suppose you respond with, "You really like candy; don't you? What do you like about it?" or, "You really want some candy now, are you allowed to have any?" Now the child will be responding to you on your terms. You have acknowledged that the she wants candy and are beginning to explore this. Questions that explore what the child thinks, expects, and feels place you squarely in charge of the relationship without being controlling.

Another method of controlling the relationship without being controlling is to change the terms. For example, while in a doctor's office, you tell the child to sit down. The child says, "NO!" You could say, "Well, what I'd really like is for you to either sit down or stand right now, and if you want, you can walk around the waiting room." You'd be surprised how this simple sidestepping of an argument can flummox the child and result in him sitting down. It is not the response he expects. The child probably expects an argument and fight, which ends with you forcing him to sit or being angry and punitive. Again, attunement would be broken and you would have "won" the battle while allowing the child to be in charge of the relationship and "losing" the bigger issue. The big issue here is not sitting or standing. The big issue is determining who sets the terms of engagement and creating experiences that demonstrate that what you ask isn't so bad.

Most children with attachment issues are in a state of emotional infancy. They require constant supervision and vigilance to prevent disastrous results from their risky behaviors. Again, let the parents be your guide regarding what is appropriate for their child at any given time. When offering choices to the child, a proactive approach reduces the chance for failure or sabotage. For example, if the child begs and says she's ready to ride her bike unsupervised to the neighbor's, she may very well use such an opportunity to defy limits. Then, when she's found two miles away, she'll argue that the limit was unfair to begin with. When she begs to go again and you remind her of the past experience, she'll deny she broke your trust and say the rule was stupid anyway. It is better to provide opportunities she can readily attain and feel approval for making the right decision than to give in to a request for trust she hasn't yet internalized. Once attachments build, so does trust. Once she has begun to internalize her parent's love for her, she will more naturally use her parents for social referencing (i.e. asking before changing locations or visits to friends), as well as present an increased ability to cope with denial without feeling unfairly treated or displaying vindictive reactions.

ACTIVITIES FOR ATTACHMENT-RESISTANT CHILDREN

When considering appropriate interventions to use with attachment-resistant children, think in terms of building a positive identity in conjunction with character development. Some expressive arts activities include making collages with specific themes and then presenting them for parents or friends. Collaborative activities, where you take turns creating, building, and designing, help to build a sense of interdependence. These include:

- Lego® sculptures
- Lincoln Logs®
- Play Dough®
- Clay
- Drawing

- Constructs®
- Blocks
- Finger Painting
- Cat's cradle
- Pat-a-cake

Cooperative games help stress concepts such as win-win by helping each other. What-if stories help build cause and effect thinking. Reading character-building books together with discussions about universal dilemmas, helps develop a sense of connection to others. Making paper dolls, building with Legos®, Lincoln Logs®, or blocks can connect the child to experiences with you as well as increase their basic fund of knowledge through natural interactions. Cutting out magazine photos of people's expressed emotion and then taking turns describing "what happened" can increase interpersonal understanding and help a child to experience being understood by another human being. Reading maps and planning a route to a local destination such as the animal shelter or library can help a child recognize the collaboration and safety of being part of a larger community. Expanding horizons that were narrowly defined helps a child gain coherence and a sense of healthy interdependence. These are just some of the ways service providers can be therapeutic adjuncts and aid in the development of healthy attachments.

TEACHING THE REACTIVE ATTACHMENT-DISORDERED CHILD

As a teacher to a child with attachment problems, you may initially wonder why this child has been reported from prior grades as "impossible," when what you see is a child who is charming, even seeking to hold your hand, climb into your lap, or kiss you. You may wonder what previous teachers did to provoke the behaviors reflected in the prior grade reports. Then, a few months into what you thought was a wonderful relationship, the child begins to act openly defiant, moody, and angry and becomes difficult to handle. Suddenly there is no way to predict what will happen from one day to the next. Knowing that these behaviors stem from the child's internal working model of the world (the lens through which they filter all experience) can help you to avoid common pitfalls. The child's life experience has "taught" her that the world is chaotic and unpredictable and that she does not have the ability to influence outcomes.

Behaviors of attachment-resistant children may include talking out loud in the classroom, not contributing fairly to group work, or conversely arguing to dominate and control the group. Organizational abilities are limited, and monitoring is resented. They often present with cognitive impairments that are more psychologically based than neurologically based. There may be a sense of hypervigilance about them that you initially perceive as a lack of sense of personal space and general "nosiness." They want to know everyone else's business but rarely tell you anything meaningful about their own. There is no apparent sense of conscience, even if someone else is hurt. The child may express an offhand or even seemingly sincere "sorry," but will likely do the same thing again. They act as if they thrive on making you "lose it." What's really going on is that they are trying to modulate the degree of intimacy in the relationship (because intimacy has been hurtful for them in the past). Normal reward and punishment systems simply do not work, and offers of kindness, sympathy, or concern may only exacerbate their poor behaviors.

Attachment-resistant children may deliberately omit parts of assignments even when writing their names just so they are in control of the assignment, not you. When assigned a seat, they may choose an indirect, self-selected path to reach the seat. When given a certain number of things to repeat or do, they often do more or less than directed. They destroy toys, clothing, bedding, and family memorabilia, then feign complete innocence even when the shredded materials are lying at their feet. They destroy school bags, lose supplies, steal food, sneak sweets, break zippers on coats, tear clothing, and eat so as to disgust those around them (open-mouth chewing, food smeared over face). These children sometimes feign fear of parents when in a public place simply for the reactions it elicits from other adults. They are masters at triangulating parents and teachers with any number of half or completely false stories.

These children may slur words just to make you ask them to repeat themselves or speak more clearly. Their speech patterns are often unusual and may involve talking out of turn, talking constantly, talking nonsense, humming, singsong, asking unanswerable or obvious questions ("Do I get a drink any time today?"). They have one pace–theirs. No amount of "hurry up; everyone is waiting on you" will work–they must be in control, and you have just told them they are. If you need the child to finish lunch so everyone can go to the playground, he will eat five times slower than usual. Five minutes later he may be kissing your hand or stroking your cheek with absolutely no sense of having caused the mayhem that ensued from his actions.

Attachment-resistant children often inflict self-injuries, pick at scabs until they bleed, seek attention for nonexistent/minuscule injuries, and yet will seek to avoid adults when they have real injuries or genuine pain. They seem to be "accident-prone" and often have scrapes, bumps, or bruises. They will claim abuse by an adult in order to obtain attention or complain about what other children have done to them. They accept no responsibility for their actions and do not have any sense of why everyone can get so aggravated with them.

These children are in a constant battle for control of their environment and seek that control however they can, even in totally meaningless situations. If they are in control, they feel safe. If they believe adults are in control (even loving and protective parents), these children believe they will not survive. They never learned to trust adults or adult judgment, or to develop any of what you know as normal feelings of security.

WORKING WITH PARENTS OF ATTACHMENT-RESISTANT CHILDREN

You can begin to understand what this child's parents face on a daily basis. Perhaps they adopted the child thinking love would cure anything that had happened prior to the adoption. They may have only recently learned that normal parenting will not work with this child; and worse, much of what they have tried to do for years simply fed into the child's dysfunction.

They may appear frightened, sad, stressed, and lonely. Many parents feel unmerited guilt for their perceived "failure" with their child. The mothers often bear the brunt of the child's actions. The child is often clever enough to make certain none of the difficult behaviors occur in front of the father. Hence even the parents may become triangulated.

It takes a tremendous amount of work and therapy to help these children experience real feelings and learn to trust. Parents who have embarked on this healing journey for their child need support and consistency from other adults who interact with the child. The therapy and home parenting techniques are exhausting and time-consuming, which may be why it seems the parents are not focusing on your goal of home or class work. Do not depend on communicating with the parent through the child. Many parents develop alternative communication methods once they realize why they feel so disconnected to the school—they are not communicating because that is how the child wants it. The child will hide or destroy communications so that it looks like you have an unresponsive parent on your hands.

What can you do as a teacher? Stay in close and regular contact with the parents. Use the phone, e-mail, and regular mail. Often parents appear hostile to outside commentary due to lack of prior support. No one without accurate information really knows what these folks are living with every day. Call them and talk about what you see in the classroom. Ask if they have any other strategies for managing things. Parents who are receiving counseling and therapy with their child will eventually welcome your support to help their child heal. Remember the child's primary objective is to triangulate you from the parents so that the child controls the relationship on his terms, not yours. The child may also seek to triangulate you from other supervisory or authority figures at the school.

BEING THE CHILD'S TEACHER

You are the child's teacher, not the child's therapist, not the child's parent. Remind the child that the parents are where the child can get hugs, cuddles, food, and treats. You will only have responsibility for this child for one school year—understand that this child will consider moving into the next grade as your having abandoned him. The only way to avoid that is to remain in your teacher role and support the process of helping this child learn to be a whole human being as best you can in the time you have. Teachers are left behind each year; it's normal. These children need to learn that lesson.

Make it clear in your interactions with the child that you are in charge of the classroom or activity, and that this is to keep everyone safe. Structure choices so you remain in charge of the rhythm and tone of the relationship. ("Do you want to wear your coat or carry it to the playground?" "You may complete that paper sitting or standing." "You may complete that assignment during this period or during recess.") You are in charge of the relationship; in other words, you want the child responding to you and not the other way around. Remember to keep the anger and frustration the child is seeking out of your voice. Structure and control without threat. Acknowledge good decisions and good behavior. ("I see you made a good choice and finished your homework last night." "So you decided to sit out the game rather than fight with Sally. That's a good choice.")

Utilize consequences for poor decisions and bad behavior. Incomplete homework or the wrong weight jacket for the weather need to be acknowledged. ("I see you chose not to complete the work from this activity period. You may finish it at recess while the other children who chose to finish their work go outside and play. Better luck next time.") Nothing mean, angry or spiteful—just the facts. Remember they have difficulty with cause-and-effect thinking and have to be taught consequences. Standard behavior modification techniques (reward systems like treats and stickers) do not work with attachment-resistant children because they aren't thinking or interacting the way nurtured children do. Their entire being is centered on being in control so they can feel safe. If anyone else is in control, they become anxious and certain they will die—no kidding; it's that serious. Utilization of natural consequences for all behavior helps these children understand that they can have an effect; this will encourage them to trust relationships. A consequence associated with each good behavior and each poor behavior teaches cause/effect and helps the child begin to make predictions about the world's response to their choices. These children will not think of or recognize the effects of their behaviors on themselves or others without your direction.

Be consistent and specific in your expectations. The RAD child will be "good" for you one or two days or even weeks just to watch your incredulity at his or her misbehavior the next time. Refrain from general compliments or admonishments such as, "You're a good boy!" or "You know better!" Be specific and consistent. Confront misbehavior and support each good behavior with direct language. "You scribbled on the desk—you clean it up." "You hit Timmy, so you sit here next to me until I decide you may play again without hitting." "You did well on the playground today; good for you!" "You chose to complete that assignment; that's a good choice! Now you may play outside with the other children who finished their work." Be positive when you can.

Do not accept poor manners or incoherent speech. The child should be able to state personal needs appropriately and make proper requests—not, "I gotta pee," but, "May I please go to the bathroom?" Some children will wet themselves rather than ask appropriately just to upset you and make you think you're responsible for making them stand there too long. Respond by saying, "I see that you wet yourself. That must not feel very good." Offer dry clothing and then go back to whatever you were doing. The child's embarrassment (maybe) or the discomfort of being wet is the natural consequence for the choice (to wet himself rather than ask appropriately), and not having controlled you emotionally will eventually teach the child that it is safe to trust you. If you do not respond harshly, the child will not be able to replicate the maladaptive primary relationship. Do not respond to slurred or incoherent speech. The child will learn it won't work to try to manipulate you into asking for a repetition or clarification. If you want, tell the child you will not respond until you hear the request spoken clearly, and then turn your attention elsewhere.

The child will try to elicit your anger and disapproval, which fits with the child's negative internal working model. Remember, you are in emotional control; you provide the child with appropriate choices based on the child's ability. If the child defaces the school bathroom, the child makes restitution, and supervision is required as a result. Let the child know this is a consequence, not a punishment. He isn't ready to go unsupervised, and that's all.

Use time-in instead of time-out. Use of time-outs replicates rejection, which is why attachment-resistant children isolate themselves from others. The child's internal working model of self as unlovable should not be reinforced. Instead, bring her near the activity and keep her by your side. If you can take the time, speak quietly about how much fun the other children are having and how sad it is that she cannot join in right now. No raised voices, no anger. Don't lose your temper if you can avoid it; remember she is manipulating you to do just that. If you fear you are going to lose it, seek assistance from another adult until you are back in control of yourself.

Time-in enables you to remain in control of the relationship and to facilitate the child's repair of the relationship. It is important that the child has experiences in which she can repair a relationship that has been disrupted by something she did or said. This is how she moves from feeling overwhelming shame to feeling guilt; moving from experiencing the self as unloved, unlovable, and bad, to experiencing the self as loved, lovable, and good despite having done a "bad" thing. This is accomplished by having the child do something specific and concrete to repair the relationship. What the child does is determined by the "victim" and should be something that will make the victim feel better about the child, the relationship, and what transpired. It is not about punishment. If the child likes what is suggested, so much the better. It is more likely that she will do what is asked, and then everyone is a winner. The child has the experience of re-pairing a relationship, and the victim is no longer upset with the child.

For example, Eve, a social worker at a residential treatment center, was working with a teenager, Josh, who concocted an elaborate and false story. Eve believed Josh and spent a lot of time investigating what actually hap-pened in the cottage before Josh finally admitted that he had lied. He "wasted" a large block of her time, and Eve was feeling irritated about that and the fact that he had fooled her, so she had to think of something for him to do to repair their relationship. Eve had Josh sweep the snow off her car each day at 5:00 p.m. for a week, before she left work. Josh really en-joyed this. So much the better! Eve no longer felt irritated with Josh, and their relationship was now back in sync. Eve managed the relationship, and Josh repaired the breach that he had created.

Avoid being alone with the attachment-resistant child. Many of these chil-dren learn (shockingly early in life for some of them) that such situations can be manipulated into an abuse claim for which there is no "witness."

If your classroom is out of control because of this child, get help. Many school counselors and administrators have not had exposure to the RAD diagnosis or how to handle it in schools. Many resources are available. Don't give up. These children are inventive, manipulative, and very much in need of everything you can offer to help them become healthy. Remind the child you will be speaking with their parents on a regular ba-sis. Report to the child's home as often as you can without feeling bur-dened by the effort.

With the right tools and attitude, you can be a valuable part of the pro-cess that will help this child to heal. Remember that what you see in school is only the tip of the iceberg. Family life is terribly threatening to these children, and what the parents have to deal with every day is nearly unimaginable to other uninformed adults. Blaming the family or failing to communicate with them adds to the dysfunction and puts the child at greater risk of never becoming healthy. This child is learning in therapy to be respectful, responsible, and fun to be around. It will take time; it will be an effort. If in the end it is successful, it will be because the adults in this child's life were consistent, and the child decided to work in therapy. Your contribution as the child's teacher cannot be underesti-mated or undervalued. The parents will be grateful for the support, and the therapist will have fewer inconsistent venues to sort out while help-ing the child to heal.

CHAPTER 9

For Parents

MIRANDA RING

"If the child-caregiver relationship is nurturing, reliable and often even joyous, the child's confidence in human relationships as a source of comfort and reciprocity will be strengthened and expanded in spite of the parents' absence. The child will learn that not only are the parents to be trusted but that other people are trustworthy as well."
—Alicia F. Lieberman, The Emotional Life of the Toddler

Parenting a child with attachment difficulties has to be one of the most difficult jobs in the world. Whether you are the adoptive parent of a child with little or poor early parenting or a parent who has recovered from a difficult past yourself and who now wants to build a bond with your child after early neglect or abuse, you may experience a lot of discouragement. The child you are trying to love does not seem to feel your love, does not return that love, and worst of all, may do everything possible to sabotage your best efforts.

The behaviors shown by children with serious attachment problems can be incredibly hard to tolerate. Lying, stealing, manipulating, recoiling from touch or affection are all common. A lack of authentic emotional connection is also common, though it may initially go unnoticed because of the child's skill in superficial charm and manipulation. Eating issues—gorging, hiding food, hoarding food—may be present. Bed wetting, encopresis, and even hiding or playing with feces can be extremely troubling to parents. The child may disrupt normally happy family situations from family dinners to holiday gatherings. The child's intense emotional reactions to seemingly small affronts are probably an everyday event. You may feel jarred and battered by endless demands and tantrums from a small being who seems perpetually discontent. Then again, the opposite may be true: Your child may show very little emotion, as if nothing at all touches him or her.

While attachment-disordered children are on their own emotional roller coaster, one that is often hard to understand, you, the parent, can be in a different kind of emotional tumult, one where you feel equally misunderstood. Friends and relatives may back away, unwilling to put up with your child's behavior, wondering why you don't "do something about it." They may question your faith in the child or your judgment in keeping the child. Finding baby-sitters may be impossible, adding to your own trapped feelings. Other family members can begin to feel neglected, and you may wonder about the fairness of having a child who takes up so much space, especially if you have other children in the home. You may find conflicts erupting with your partner. You may struggle with your own emotions, as the child's distance, sadness, and anger may trigger unresolved feelings from your own past, causing you to react in ways that trouble you. Most devastating of all, you may begin to question your competence as a parent and wonder if you are equal to the task.

Developing–or recovering–your own confidence involves a number of things: 1) coming to understand and empathizing with the feelings that drive your child's behavior; 2) learning a particular set of parenting skills; and 3) getting support for yourself. A therapist experienced in working with attachment disorders can help with all of these.

BUILDING EMPATHY FOR YOUR CHILD

Imagine yourself born–tiny, fragile, and completely dependent–into a family that doesn't care for you. You cry and are not tended to. You are hungry and are not fed. No one smiles at you and touches you gently. Instead, you are ignored, you experience yelling and violence in your environment, and you may even be hit or shaken.

These kinds of experiences are devastating to a baby and interrupt the beginnings of a healthy emotional life. Rather than trust, the child's basic emotion becomes fear. The feelings of physical and emotional need come to evoke anxiety, even desperation. Love and hope become dangerous because hurt and disappointment have been experienced in relation to the child's most beloved people. The result is that a potentially wonderful child is damaged in ways that impair his or her ability to participate in positive, trusting relationships. Caretakers of these children, like it or not, become essential to their recovery.

Dealing with disturbing behaviors is easier when you can empathize with the feelings beneath the behaviors, with the emotions motivating the behaviors. Empathy becomes more possible when you (and the child) come to understand those feelings. So, a significant part of the therapy process is exploring with the child in a nonjudgmental way how the child is feeling when a particular incident and behavior occurred.

In the therapy sessions, the exploration plays out differently from how you might expect. Some children with difficult histories are able to verbalize their feelings, but many are not. A therapist's job is to propose various possible feelings a child might have had, honing in on the ones that the child recognizes as true. If the therapist is perceptive early on, the child begins to feel understood, perhaps for the first time, and begins to learn to express feelings. As the child identifies and expresses feelings, and the therapist and parent empathize with those feelings, a doorway opens to trust.

To illustrate, here is an example from my clinical practice. Jennie, who is a five-year-old girl, lives with her grandparents. Her aunt, who lives nearby, recently had a baby, and Jennie's grandparents were having to deal with very negative behaviors when the baby was around. In therapy, we explored Jennie's feelings about the baby. She thought the baby was cute, but also would start feeling hurt, lonely, and jealous if around the baby for too long. After all, the baby was well loved and cared for, and she had been neglected. The dialogue in therapy went like this:

Me: "How do you like being around Bobby?"

Jennie: (No response)

Me: "He's very little, isn't he?"

Jennie: (A nod)

Me: "I bet a lot of people think he's cute."

Jennie: (A wrinkled face that says, "Yuck;" hides her head)

Me: "Oh, I see. It can be annoying to be around a baby when everyone's talking about (sarcastic edge) how cute they are."

Jennie: (Makes eye contact with me)

Me: "Well, I can understand that. So, I bet sometimes you like being with Bobby and playing with him, and sometimes he really gets on your nerves."

Jennie: (No response)

Me: "Is that true?"

Jennie: (Slight nod)

Me: "Oh, thanks for telling me that. It helps a lot! So, I have an idea."

Jennie: (No response)

Me: "Want to hear my idea?"

Jennie: (Eye contact, curious)

Me: "I really want to tell it to you. I think it'll help a lot. Okay?"

Jennie:	"Okay."
Me:	"Well, when you're visiting Bobby, and you're not enjoying it anymore, and you start feeling jealous and upset, can you tell your grandma?"
Jennie:	(Looks at me)
Me:	"Here's what I mean. Come over here for a minute."
Jennie:	(She comes over)
Me:	"You can whisper in her ear, like this." (I whisper: "I'm having a hard time. Can we go now?")
Jennie:	(She smiles)
Me:	"You try it, with me. Say it in my ear."
Jennie:	(No response)
Me:	"Come on, say it, just to practice."
Jennie:	(Whispers in my ear) "I'm having a hard time. Can we go now?"
Me:	"Great! That was great. You did it. You can do this. So now, during the next week, when you start having a hard time with Bobby, can you tell your grandma just like that?"
Jennie:	(Nods "yes")
Me:	"Great!"

This dialogue in our therapy session introduces the sense that having difficult feelings is okay, not terribly shameful, as an abused or neglected child might feel. It also lets the child know that talking about feelings (rather than "acting them out") might be possible.

The next essential piece of this therapy will be done in Jennie's day-to-day life when the situation arises, and she tells her grandmother (let's call her Jean) how she feels. A lot will depend on Jean's handling that situation with gentleness and skill. Suppose in the week following our therapy session Jennie and Jean are visiting Bobby and his mother. Jennie starts feeling edgy and irritable. Perhaps she expresses this to Jean, or maybe Jean notices the mood change and says, "I see you're beginning to have a hard time. Are you getting some of those feelings we talked about?" Most likely, if asked, Jennie will nod, "yes." (Jennie is probably not even aware of what she is feeling. Having her emotion reflected back to her helps her know what she is feeling by hearing it.)

Jean then has some choices. She can go along with Jennie's sense that it is time to leave. "Okay," she might say, "This is a good time for us to get going." They would say their good-byes and leave, perhaps talking a little about Jennie's feelings on the way home. But suppose Jean is not ready to leave. Suppose they're taking care of Bobby, and leaving is not an option. It is not essential that Jennie's feelings dominate the situation. It is only essential that Jennie is helped to handle the troubling feelings. So, after learning that Jennie is struggling, Jean might say, "Come over and sit with me for a few minutes. Let's take some time out together." She might introduce a toy or activity that she knows will calm Jennie: "I brought your crayons and some paper. Let's take a break and do some drawing." So, Jennie expresses her distress. And her grandmother, Jean, uses her voice, touch, calmness and understanding, and resourcefulness to help her contain those feelings without dysregulating, without "acting out."

While Jennie would start "acting out" when jealous, other children might have different reasons for terrible behavior. Why else might these children "act out"?

1. They are "hyper-aroused." That is, because they are so full of anxiety and fear, their psychophysiology is in "fight or flight" mode all the time. They never really return to a calm state and have trouble regulating their feelings and actions. Clinically, we would say they become "dysregulated."

2. They may have impulses that they cannot manage. Children who have been physically or sexually abused, for example, can find their own sexual or aggressive impulses overwhelming.

3. They have deep feelings of shame. When infants and children are abused or neglected, they feel that the reason is that they are so bad, so shameful. "If I were a better kid, they wouldn't have treated me this way" is a pervasive belief.

4. They are terrified of closeness and of their own needs. They seem to avoid at all costs what they want the most. Feeling close or needing other people brings up tremendous anxiety because of all the times that their early needs were met with indifference or abuse. Either way, having needs and wanting closeness resulted in feeling deeply wounded.

So now, even in a safe, nurturing home, the anxiety aroused by these tender needs and feelings can be overpowering. In other words, current experiences bring up past emotions, and the child begins to perceive the current situation as if it were just like the old one. To end this anxiety, a child may sabotage a potentially good experience or "act out" after feeling close. By "ruining" good things, the child feels less terror.

As you start understanding the child's turbulent, defensive emotional life, it becomes easier to react to the feelings rather than to the behavior. For example, suppose your child is rejecting you. These behaviors—saying "I hate you," recoiling from affection, misinterpreting well-meant gestures—are the very hardest for many parents. Understandably, they can trigger the parents' own insecurity and self-doubt.

A parent who sees beneath the child's behavior will understand that this very limited interpersonal repertoire is the result of devastating early experiences. The parent will not accept the child's limited ability to form positive connections and will keep trying by looking for opportunities, however brief, to be playful and nurturing, the parent will continue to stretch the child's willingness to trust and depend. A sweet bedtime ritual is a good start; touch through games can also lay a foundation, or singing together or playing babyish games (peek-a-boo, hide and seek) can provide the start of intimacy. This ability on your part to respond to the needs and feelings rather than the behavior, as difficult as it is initially, makes you a more stable, empathic parent, which is what your child needs.

PARENTING SKILLS

Even if you have been an excellent parent and raised wonderful, healthy children, parenting a child with attachment difficulties may challenge you. Neglected and abused children cannot tolerate even the mild level of "shaming" that parental discipline often employs. The children already feel so bad, so different, so unloved and unlovable. A show of anger may make the child feel that you hate him, which could result in dysregulation (i.e. tantrum, withdrawal, etc.). So, what is a parent to do?

In attachment-oriented therapy, we talk about an attitude that uses PACE in the therapy environment and PLACE at home. (The "L" added in the home environment is for "Loving.") These are so important that I will discuss separately what each letter stands for.

Playful means using humor, fun, and lightness with the child. In being playful, the therapist may be more physical with the child than you expect—tickling, touching affectionately, or hugging the child—modeling for you how to set that tone with a child who seems distant, controlling, or self-contained. Playfulness makes therapy and home life fun and interrupts some of the sadness and seriousness carried by children who have been neglected or abused. It is nurturing and spirit-lifting for children whose inner lives are heavy, anxious, and depressed.

Accepting means suspending judgment about and deeply accepting the child as a lovable, worthwhile human being. It means accepting the child's feelings and the child's perceptions. A child with such deep feelings of shame and such frequent dysregulation (resulting in anger, tantrums, and other types of "bad" behavior) will only begin to see herself as acceptable when those around her are accepting. When a child begins to accept herself, the quality of relationships with others also changes. There is less defensiveness and need to control. An enjoyable give and take in relationships starts to become possible.

Accepting the child does not mean that you accept all of the behavior. You certainly set limits. In fact, limits allow everyone to feel safe. It means, though, that you continually convey a sense that the child is an okay person, a person whose troubling behaviors make some kind of sense, a person who is worthy of love and care.

Communicating acceptance is closely linked to how "consequences" are given and explained for unacceptable behavior, and to understanding that teaching rather than punishing is the motive. For example, suppose a child is sneaking and hoarding food, and you as a parent begin to worry about insects and rodents in the child's room. You might say (affirming the underlying feelings), "I know you get worried about being hungry. We're not going to let you be hungry here. Ever. But (addressing the behavior) keeping food in your room is going to attract bugs, maybe mice. Yuck! So, to be sure you're not hungry, and to be sure also that we don't have all kinds of critters in your room, here's what I'm going to do. I'm going to leave a big bowl of healthy snacks in the kitchen. You can take some whenever you want to, and I want you to eat food in the kitchen. If I find food in your room, you'll have to spend an extra half-hour helping me with housework."

This way of handling the situation has several implicit messages: 1) I understand and care about your feelings. They don't scare or repulse me; 2) I'm going to take care of you; 3) I'm going to stay in charge of the household, which includes avoiding an invasion of bugs and mice; 4) I'm going to set up a reasonable rule with a consequence if it is broken; 5) The consequence will happen in a loving context, with an implicit message that, "I won't start hating you, won't hit you, won't scream and yell at you, won't stop talking to you. We might even have fun doing housework together. But I have good reasons for my rules, and I want you to obey them."

The *Curious* quality is a constant wondering about how the child feels, how the child makes meaning, and why the child does things. Parents can assume things that turn out to be completely false. Parents often say, for example, that a child is misbehaving to "get attention." Why would a child constantly seek negative attention by behaving in ways that irritate the parents? The answer may be circuitous.

Say, for example, that eight-year-old Joey is afraid of the dark. In his early life, nighttime brought unexpected and frightening intrusions—yelling between his parents, parties with drunk people, strangers occasionally sharing his bed, all before he could speak. Therefore, he does not calm down easily at bedtime. He is ashamed of how fearful he feels, and he is too distrustful to talk about his feelings and ask for help. Yet, he is terrified of going to bed. At bedtime he "acts out," doing everything possible to avoid bed. He whines, he argues, he has tantrums over what seems like nothing. With a "curious" attitude, his parents will try to understand, and help him to understand, what is beneath his dysregulated, irritating behaviors.

If bedtime fears are a major issue, therapy is a good place to address them. Your therapist can help you and your child explore what his or her frightening experiences have been. This knowledge can give you added help in talking about bedtime and planning for it. A bedtime conversation with Joey might sound like this:

Mom: "Bedtime, Joey."

Joey: "No it isn't! I have five more minutes." (Stamps his foot, starts getting upset)

Mom: "Boy, that foot makes a loud noise. Can you do that again?"

Joey: (Scowls)

Mom: "I'm just teasing you." (Smiles, gives him a hug) "I know bedtime is still scary for you. Anything you're extra worried about tonight?"

Joey: "No." (Looks down)

Mom: "Let's see. You might be worried about the dark (questioning) and about monsters under the bed (again, questioning). That's okay. Let's do this. We'll get you into your pj's, read one story downstairs, and then read our other story upstairs. We'll check all the scary spots, and of course we'll bring the flashlight up."

Joey: "Can I have the flashlight in my bed?"

Mom: "Sure you can."

Joey: "Okay."

In this dialogue, Joey's mom is doing several things: 1) Accepting Joey's feelings; 2) Not allowing Joey's oppositional behavior to alienate her; 3) Staying in charge, understanding his feelings, and offering a clear yet flexible plan; 4) Allowing something a little unusual (sleeping with a flashlight) because it works for Joey.

Empathy is the quality of "feeling with" another person, feeling compassion for the pain they suffer and have suffered. Empathy characterizes the stance of therapist and parent that makes it possible for the child to eventually acknowledge deeper feelings of fear, sadness, loneliness, and anger. Because you "feel with" the child, saying kind things when revelations are expressed ("I'm so sorry that happened to you." "That sounds terrible." "That must have been so hard.") the child can start to relax, trust, and share hidden memories and emotions. Empathy involves opening your heart to the child's pain and treating him with reassurance, respect, gentleness.

The place where the parents' emotions extend beyond the tone of the therapy office is in their love for the child. The therapist can feel and communicate acceptance and affection for the child. But it is the parents who show an ongoing day-in, day-out commitment, a deep faith in the child, and the nurturing and caring that help the child gradually come to realize that he is really loved.

But What about the Behavior?

As much as you work to understand your child—and as tender hearted as you are toward her needs—you might still find yourself struggling with behavior that seems endlessly oppositional, manipulative, and angry/ destructive or distant and detached or just confusing (different things at different times). You may feel very much in need of guidance in order to deal with some of the behavior your child presents.

Suppose that Joey's bedtime behavior is much more extreme than what was described earlier. His terror is so great at bedtime that he has a full-blown tantrum, screaming, yelling, kicking. There are a number of ways that you could handle this. Your therapist can be helpful in developing a plan. Regardless of the specifics, however, communicating empathy (rather than anger or rejection) is essential. ("I'm so sorry that you're going through this." "I know how scary this is for you." "It must feel terrible to be that scared." "We're going to help you through this.")

In this approach, difficult behavior is seen as reflecting the child's arrested development and as being an understandable result of trauma and lack of care. Therefore, behavior is approached with a gentle learning model and in a way that builds the parent/child relationship. Humor, affection, surprise, empathy, and a clear sense of when behavior is hurtful to the child or others are the tools of the caregiver. The child is neither punished excessively nor indulged, and the teaching of limits, boundaries, social skills, etc. is always done with love and humor. A child's worth or goodness is never assessed by present behavior, and the cardinal rule is that discipline should never interfere with the relationship you are building.

Again, the empathy, the "feeling with" your child, guides the way in which you handle discipline. Remembering that you're with a young person who has already been badly bruised by life will help you to stay kind and even, despite your own stirred emotions.

That being said, the techniques for dealing with troubling behavior are: 1) natural consequences; 2) keeping the child closer to you; 3) simplifying the child's environment; and 4) understanding the feelings being expressed by the behavior and working skillfully with them. Let's talk about each of these approaches to discipline individually.

NATURAL CONSEQUENCES. When we as adults don't pay our bills, our credit is threatened and our services (electricity, telephone) can be turned off. If we are not reliable at work, we risk losing our jobs. These are "natural consequences." Using "natural consequences" allows life to be the teacher, positioning the parent as an empathic witness and coach. Punishment implies a harshness that is deserved because of bad behavior; natural consequences teach that one's behavior has palpable results. For example, suppose a 10-year-old boy is oppositional at school. He talks back to his teacher, and at times, he strides out of the classroom, slamming the door behind him. The school will respond to this behavior with some disciplinary action which will, most likely, be unpleasant for the child, maybe taking away his recess, for example. That is a "natural consequence" of misbehavior at school. If the parents' response is anger, the boy is alone with his explosive, difficult-to-manage emotions. If, on the other hand, the parents are curious about the situation at school and take the position of wanting to understand and help the child, the boy now has allies as he figures out how to handle situations at school and how to modulate his own emotions.

Here is a second example of natural consequences. Suppose Julie, a seven-year-old girl with poor boundaries, hugs other children indiscriminately. The natural consequence is that children (and their parents) are likely to back away from this child, an experience that may hurt and confuse her. If parents react to this behavior with anger, the girl's already embedded sense of shame is likely to increase, which will not help her social skills. If parents can be on her side, trying to help her figure out how to deal with relationships, then she can, with the sense of safety created by their support, learn to handle relationships more effectively over time. The dialogue in each style might sound like this:

Angry/punishing response:

Parent: "Julie, don't do that. Can't you see that Danny doesn't like it? Take a time-out right now. When you're done, we'll talk about your behavior."

Natural consequences with supportive parent:

Parent: "Julie, come on over here. Let's go for a walk for a few minutes. (They go for a walk, perhaps discussing other things first.) You know, I noticed that when you hugged Joey, he pulled back and got kind of quiet. I wonder why he did that?"

Julie: "I don't know."

Parent: "I have some ideas about it."

Julie: (Says nothing)

Parent: "Want to hear my ideas?"

Julie: "Okay."

Parent: "I think he might have felt uncomfortable."

Julie: (Looks uncomfortable herself, perhaps changes the subject, probably feeling shame.)

Parent: "I think Joey really likes you. But I think that when you're playing together he needs more space."

Julie: (Still looking down)

Parent: "How about saving hugs for Mom and Dad?" (Gives her a hug, demonstrating that the child is loved and lovable, even if the behavior was not)

Julie: (Smiles)

Natural consequences can mean letting the child experience the consequences of his or her actions directly, offering empathy but not coming to the rescue. For example, if a child is irresponsible and loses money, he or she may not be able to buy something at the store. By not stepping in, the parent allows the "natural consequence" to provide a lesson. Likewise, if a child disrupts the dinner table, he or she may be asked to leave the table and finish the meal elsewhere. While parents can remain empathic, this "natural consequence" will teach the child the cost of ruining dinner for other people.

KEEPING THE CHILD CLOSER TO YOU. When a child becomes "dysregulated" (shown by out-of-control behavior), the parents can respond by becoming more protective. Essentially, you are treating the child at the child's developmental level, not at their chronological age. Often children with difficult pasts are developmentally immature. You can choose to react as one would to a two-year-old who is threatening to run into the street: by limiting the child's freedom to get into difficulty, by keeping the child closer. The parent's attitude, again, is very positive, nurturing, accepting. "I see you are having a hard time with .... Come help me work in the garden." Using this tactic, the parent helps the child to be safer while building the parent-child attachment.

Healthy, very young children come and go with parents in a natural way, going out to explore, coming closer to "refuel," to regain a sense of security and balance. With older children whose attachment is damaged, this same strategy can work, though it is more complex. The child must first learn to draw a sense of safety and stability from the parent, a challenge for children with early abuse or neglect. Drawing the child closer when the child is dysregulated helps to create a sense of attachment as "a safe base."

Some parents have found that having the child tutored at home for a period of time is beneficial, enabling them to "keep the child closer" full time. This day-in, day-out contact can allow a trusting relationship to grow more quickly than what might be possible with the child in school. The decision whether or not to devote yourself full time to your child's healing is an individual one. Your therapist can be a helpful consultant if you are considering it.

SIMPLIFYING THE CHILD'S ENVIRONMENT. Children's behavior goes out of control when they can't handle their feelings, especially anxiety, sadness, and anger. These feelings are exacerbated by situations or environments that the child may find difficult. For example, the child may become dysregulated at large family gatherings. Trips to stores may trigger past deprivation and result in endless, highly emotional demands. In these cases, by avoiding the situations altogether—or by making them very short—the child is able to maintain a sense of safety and internal regulation. This experience of success (not "losing it") is very positive for the child, building confidence.

UNDERSTANDING THE FEELINGS EXPRESSED BY THE BEHAVIOR
AND WORKING WITH THEM SKILLFULLY. It is hard to ignore a child's
out-of-control behavior. At the same time, it is essential that you as a parent see the person behind the behavior. Accepting the child as a person, coming to understand the child's feelings, deeply believing that the out-of-control behavior is caused by unmanageable emotions and that these are the legacy of early neglect and abuse: These are core skills and beliefs for parents of children with attachment difficulties. A connected core belief is that with the growth of safety, connection, and trust, these behaviors can change and the child's positive traits can emerge.

Handling the behavior skillfully requires that you, the parent, are able to maintain your own calm and humor when your child is dysregulated. This is extremely challenging for many people. In fact, it may be the most challenging part of this approach to parenting. What often happens in families is that when children are upset, anxious, or angry, parents become upset, anxious, and angry too.

A 10-year-old recently told me that when he was first learning to ride a bike, his mother became so angry that she put his bike in the trash. He said that riding was hard for him at first, and he kept falling off. Maybe he was crying or yelling; I'm not sure. Instead of remaining calm and supporting him, his mother became so angry and frustrated herself that she threw out his bike. What did she communicate by this response? She did not communicate the importance of calming down and trying again with something challenging. She also did not communicate her faith that he would be able to learn to ride with a little more effort.

This boy rescued the bike and, out of sheer fury, taught himself to ride. Now he is a great (and very adventurous) cyclist. With a traumatized or attachment-disordered child, however, this mother's response would likely have had very negative effects. The child might either have given up in despair or railed against the parent, carrying the anger and resentment into other areas of the parent-child relationship. Either way, the task of learning to ride the bike would be lost. A much more centered and supportive response would be needed.

A therapist with experience in attachment work should be able to help you with understanding the meaning behind some of your child's behaviors. Many children I've worked with, for example, get very upset when a parent says "no." If this was interpreted as pure selfishness or even pure stubbornness, a stern parental response would be justified. It turns out, upon exploration in therapy, that the child's meaning is quite different. The child talks about feeling that the parent does not really love them, that the parent does not want them to be happy, that the child is unlovable. So, skillful handling of this negative reaction comes to involve comforting and reassuring the child while maintaining the "no" rather than becoming more angry or emphatic.

Sometimes you can even avoid saying "no" altogether. If the request is okay, but the timing is wrong, you can answer with "Yes, when it's time." For example, it's 9:00 and bedtime for your nine-year-old. She asks to watch TV. You know that if you say "no," there will be a fight and tantrum. Well, you could say, "Sure, sweetie, tomorrow morning after breakfast and before the bus arrives." Another example: Your 15-year-old asks to use the telephone but has still not put the dishes away. You could say, "Sure, you can make your calls as soon as the dishes are put away where they belong."

There is an idea in Buddhism that is relevant to parenting a child with attachment problems. It is called "beginner's mind" or "don't know mind." It is about maintaining a freshness, a willingness to learn and be surprised, a sense that your assumptions may be completely wrong. This mind state is extremely valuable in dealing with your child, whose reasons for doing things may be completely different from what they seem.

THE ROLE OF THERAPY

PARENT-CHILD THERAPY

Therapy designed to strengthen the parent-child bond and to help parent and child understand the child's feelings and defensive/dysregulated behavior can be extremely helpful. The therapy needs to occur in an atmosphere defined by PACE (playful, accepting, curious, empathic). As a parent, you may need some one-to-one time with the therapist to talk through difficulties related to your child's behavior—or even just to vent. Sessions with the child present should never degenerate into complaints about the child. Hearing these will only add to his/her shame.

Several things about attachment-building parent-child therapy may surprise you:

1. There may be more physical contact than you would expect. Nurturing physical contact between you and your child will be encouraged. The therapist may also cradle, touch, or tickle your child or play games that involve physical touch. The goal, as always, is to help your child to relax and build attachment.

2. The therapist will probably seem like more of a "real person" than in many other forms of therapy, taking an active role in sessions, using humor, initiating play, sharing his/her experience, doing "whatever it takes" to engage your child.

3. The therapist may seem not to notice your child's faults and may not react much to things that outrage you. This is because the therapist is always looking for the feelings motivating the behavior, the real child behind the angry/anxious defenses. Hopefully, with the therapist's help, you will come to see that the negative behaviors are not, at the core, what your child is really all about.

4. The therapist will probably be more interested in the meaning of your child's behavior—in understanding his/her emotional world—than in setting limits on it within the sessions (unless, of course, something dangerous is about to occur). This type of therapy can at times seem noisy and frenetic or quiet, meditative, and intimate, depending on your child's responses and needs.

5. Within Dyadic Developmental Psychotherapy, you may be asked to do things that touch deep emotions: Talk with you child about your child's trauma and abuse; talk about your own regrets in regard to your child (i.e. that you were not able to prevent the abuse); talk about the first time you saw your child; talk about your love for your child. You will probably be asked to be vulnerable, to forget (for the moment) all the problems and challenges, and to help your child simply feel valuable and loved.

6. In this approach, the therapist may do a lot of "speaking for" your child and coaching of you. Hurt children often become silent when asked about their emotions. The therapist may explore the child's feelings by saying things like, "I wonder if you felt ..." or "If I were going to speak for you, I would say, 'That hurt my feelings.'" This is not to plant emotions that are not there, but rather to help your child begin to articulate feelings that are there. In coaching you, the therapist is trying to help you to give responses that will be healing for your child.

7. The therapist may be more open in soliciting details of your child's history than you initially find comfortable. The therapist may also choose not to explore certain details, and you might wonder why. These choices are made with specific goals in mind. Children with attachment disorders usually have a very sketchy sense of their own lifelines. Because their experiences have been painful and overwhelming—abuse and/or neglect may have occurred at an early age—they may not remember significant chunks of their lives. Healthy development builds on a coherent sense of one's life. Helping your child construct that narrative is a goal of therapy. At the same time, skillful choices must be made about which details your child is ready or able to discuss.

8. Your child may resist coming to therapy. Even though parts of it are fun, other parts bring up feelings and memories that are hard to handle. The therapist will understand this and in fact, may find ways to play with and use it within sessions.

9. Play is used differently in attachment-oriented therapy than in classic play therapy. In Dyadic Developmental Psychotherapy, play may be used less with young children than you would expect. Even young children will probably be encouraged to find words for their experiences and emotions.

10. Your therapist may suggest some approaches to parenting that are new to you and that, at first, seem strange. The PLACE parenting style, while demanding of parents, is helpful and therapeutic for children with attachment problems. This teaching is not meant as a critique of you as a parent, but rather it aims to help you develop a parenting style that will help your child and your relationship with your child. If you find that certain recommendations fly in the face of your own instincts or are extremely difficult for you, discuss these issues with your therapist.

The structure of therapy includes time just between parent(s) and therapist; time with parent(s), therapist, and child; and may also involve one-to-one time with therapist and child. The therapist may ask to videotape sessions both for review/supervision purposes and, at times, to later share with parents.

Sessions are longer than the usual 50-minute therapy hour. Typically, sessions are 90 minutes to two hours, depending on the therapist and the setting.

Therapy sessions will never, NEVER, seem harsh or disrespectful toward your child or unsupportive of you, the parent.

THERAPY FOR PARENTS

One of the best ways to assess where you might need help is to look at your own "attachment" history. If your own family was stable, loving, supportive—and you felt strongly and securely connected to your parents—you may find that you have the internal resources to cope with this very tough job. If not, which is the case for many people, your child's needs may present you with the impetus to do your own healing. Having difficulties in your own past life with family and relationships does not mean you cannot parent your child. It may mean that your own therapy could be very beneficial in helping you to be as attuned, patient, and loving as you would like. If you find that your child's behavior or feelings trigger strong emotions in you that interfere with your parenting, some parent-only sessions with your therapist may help you to work through the issues you are facing.

A Word about Adolescents

Some people say that adolescence is too late for attachment work, that once a young person hits the teenage years, their pull will be for independence and not for connection. That is not true, and I offer two things to consider:

1. Young people with unresolved attachment issues are much younger emotionally than their chronological age; and

2. The move to independence happens in a much healthier way when there is secure attachment beforehand to a parent or parents. Without that, the internal insecurity/anxiety/anger often pulls the adolescent into trouble as she tries to take on adult challenges.

As with a younger child, working to build a secure connection with an adolescent is a worthwhile undertaking. Most adolescents have a strong wish to "belong" that is focused on a peer group. When earlier developmental needs are unmet, though, the adolescent can be like a younger child in a maturing body. To help the adolescent to catch up emotionally and to insure that she doesn't get into trouble, you might want to deliberately limit time with peers and help the teenager to first develop a sense of belonging in the family. Perhaps a period of time at home, on a full-time basis, with the school providing a tutor, would help the young person to feel connected to you and the other family members. Working together on household activities (cooking, shopping, projects around the house) will also build and stabilize your connection with your child. Your therapist can write the necessary letters to the school explaining that it is a necessary part of therapy that the child be out of school and that you cannot provide home schooling, so that a tutor is provided. While often used with younger children, this intervention may be even more important with teenagers who have had a longer history of maltreatment and impermanence in their relationships.

If successful, your efforts and relationship can have a positive impact for the rest of that teenager's life in terms of the ability to form positive relationships and the confidence to pursue goals that matter to them.

Don't give up on teenagers. The size and behavior can make them seem past the reach of this type of work. On the inside, though, teenagers with unresolved abuse and neglect in their histories are very much in need of connection and nurturing.

GETTING SUPPORT

Parenting a child with serious attachment issues is not something you can do alone. It is too demanding, confusing, and rigorous. Here are some sources of support that can make all the difference:

1. Be sure that you and your partner are supporting one another well, even if it takes couples' therapy to help. Attachment-disordered children can be taxing in ways that strain relationships. To provide a good base for the child, your relationship needs to be strong.

2. If you are a single parent, cultivate supportive friendships. You will need people to talk to about your child and places for your child to be that will give you some respite.

3. Develop a solid relationship with your child's therapist. That person, hopefully, can help you to overcome the sense of shame and failure that parents sometimes feel. A therapist with experience in this area will realize how difficult your task is, that the child's behavior and issues are not your fault. Suggestions on parenting strategies will be meant not as a critique of you but as a way to help you learn the model of "therapeutic parenting" needed by your child. If at any point you feel undermined in any way by your child's therapist, talk with him or her. It may be a misunderstanding that can be easily talked through. You may be confronting things in yourself that are difficult. Still, you should feel understood and supported. If the feeling of distrust persists despite your best efforts to clear the air, consider finding another therapist.

4. Look for other sources of support within your family or community. These may take the form of a support group, respite services, even relevant reading.

5. Many people find that a spiritual path is helpful to them. This may or may not take the form of a conventional religious community. Some type of faith, spiritual nurturing, or inner calm can be extremely valuable to your parenting.

Conclusion

Finally, a word of encouragement. As hard as your child's present dilemmas may seem, all human beings are capable of growth and change. As the parents in the chapter describing their experiences show, significant changes are possible and can occur. Your determination to parent a hurt (and therefore difficult) child is an act of faith. Building your own strategy and skill, keeping your heart open, and finding good support will all contribute to your child's ability to relax, trust, open, and ultimately, heal.

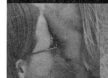

CHAPTER 10

By Parents: The Healing of Three Families

ARTHUR BECKER-WEIDMAN & SUSAN BECKER-WEIDMAN

PARENTS: BETH GREEN, KAREN HUNT, & JODY WALKER

"Parents are like shuttles on a loom. They join the threads of the past with threads of the future and leave their own bright patterns as they go." —Fred Rogers, Mister Rogers Talks with Parents

CHAPTER INTRODUCTION

In this chapter you will read the stories of three families who were desperately seeking help and received Dyadic Developmental Psychotherapy. Each family's story is different: international adoption, domestic adoption, genders, ages, races, and many other differences. But these three families' stories share an apocryphal commonality. Each family had decided to adopt to complete or start a family and entered that process with many hopes and dreams, some of which were quickly shattered. Each family sought treatment and was disappointed by systems and therapists who were not responsive or effective. Each family desperately hoped they could help their child, hoped they could heal their family, hoped that someone would understand.

I had the privilege of working with each family and guiding them on their journey of healing. All of the parents of these families showed a deep commitment to their family and child that allowed them to affectively and effectively create a healing PLACE. They showed me how vital the parents are to treatment and that a better predictor of success is often, but not always, the parents' effectiveness in creating a healing PLACE. From each family I learned something that has enriched my practice and deepened my appreciation for the importance of parents and family in the healing process.

Jody's family showed me how vital it is to revisit trauma and experience the affect associated with the trauma. This reexperiencing is not dysregulating when it occurs in the context of a supportive and attuned therapeutic and family system. This time the child is not alone and can manage the strong feelings without becoming dysregulated and dissociating. As her son reclaimed his past, the range and depth of affect he could experience and express broadened dramatically. She also taught me the importance of attending to the parent's own past history and how this deeply affects the current family and their ability to help the child. She taught me the importance of providing the same level of attunement, intersubjectivity, and acceptance as I want the parents to provide for the child.

Beth's family taught me about the healing power of tenacious love and how important it is that parents allow themselves to feel the child's emotions with the child. Sharing emotions allows the child to feel felt and to know that the feelings can be tolerated without becoming overwhelmed, that strong affect can be healing.

Karen's family showed me the importance of accepting a child with multiple difficulties and the necessity of being thorough in one's assessment so that the various problems are addressed in an integrated manner. The value of persistence, consistency, and deep acceptance were some of the qualities that allowed Karen to help her son heal.

Beth Green's Story   In this section by Beth you will read about an impressive journey. When I was contacted by Beth, the family was living in Europe and desperately wanted help for their daughter. We discussed various options and it seemed that a two-week intensive would be appropriate. However, I was very concerned about follow-up therapy since I will not do an intensive unless there is a follow-up therapist. The two weeks alone are never a complete course of therapy. When Beth made arrangements to remain in the U.S. in the Midwest after the two weeks and followed through on contacting the therapist I referred them to, this was my first inkling of how dedicated and tenacious this mom would be.

When I first met Jerry, Beth, and Anita, I was impressed. Anita was a cute latency-age child with lovely eyes and a friendly but reserved manner. The treatment team and I spent the first hour or so with Beth and Jerry discussing Anita, how we view parenting, and creating the healing PLACE. We found ourselves stressing the importance of attunement and maintaining a positive emotional environment. Beth had read a lot of material, and like some parents, found the literature that describes "what to do" offering the most hope. What she came to realize was that "what" you do is much less important than how you do it.

As therapy progressed, Beth and Jerry's commitment and flexibility became evident. For me, one of the most striking sessions was one in which we had just completed a psychodramatic reenactment of Anita with her foster mother and how Anita may have felt alone, uncared for, and abandoned. The "play" seemed flat with little affect displayed by Anita. After the play, when we all discussed what it was like, Jerry began to cry. He was so sad about how his daughter had been treated and that the family she had been with did not recognize how special she was. He cried because he had not been there to protect her. At this, Anita began to cry and to experience the loneliness and terrible sense of worthlessness she'd felt. This vignette demonstrated for me the vital importance of parents showing their feelings in a session with the child. Anita could allow her feelings to become evident and allow herself to enter into those feelings more deeply when she felt contained by her parents and knew that they felt with her, not for her—that they shared her feelings. In that moment she was again a four- or five-year-old, but this time, she was not alone with her feelings. Her dad reflected back to her what she felt and in that process gave meaning to her experience.

An example of how tenacious and dedicated Beth was to helping her daughter was when we'd discussed how Anita had been kidnapped at a young age (three or four) by her birth parents. We knew nothing about that time period, about nine months. Beth tracked down the FBI agent who was in charge of the case, and although he could not send her any written material, the agent remembered the case and described to Beth what they found when they captured Anita's birth parents. This part of the story was important for Anita, and Beth's persistence was another example of how deeply she loves and cares for Anita.

Beth and Jerry with Anita

We arrived at our decision to adopt due to various factors, but the main ones were exposure to working with troubled youth and the desire to make a difference in the lives of children who simply want a safe, forever family.

You could almost say that our daughter, Anita, was born into foster care. Her birth mom had several children placed in foster homes with relatives at the time of our daughter's birth, and as a consequence, our daughter was not released to go home with her birth mom until Social Services had done a home inspection. After experiencing her first four days of life alone in the hospital, our daughter was released to the care of her birth mom, who, according to hospital notes, never breast-fed her baby. Her birth mom had a history of violent relationships, domestic abuse, and neglect, as well as drug and alcohol abuse.

When our daughter was about 11 months old, her birth mom, together with her boyfriend, regained custody of two of her other children, and thus began a series of life changes. The next year and a half involved several moves and violent events leading up to our daughter's placement in foster care when she was just 2¹ᐟ² years old. Barely five months later, she was kidnapped during a supervised visit. She was recovered by the FBI six months later, returned to

Social Services, and placed in a new foster home. At this point, she was $3^{1/2}$ years old, using a diaper, and barely verbal—grunting and pointing at things she wanted. She made progress in gaining age-appropriate skills in this foster home and seemed well-adapted. She remained there along with her older half-sister, Maria, until placed with us for adoption when she was $7^{1/2}$ years old.

An unexpected call on Christmas Eve set us on a course that would change our lives forever: We had just been matched with our daughter and her older half-sister. After the holidays, we returned to town and contacted our adoption agency for more information about the girls and were very disturbed to find out that one had required X-rays after a violent incident with her foster mother. It was decided that it was best to keep them in the current foster home for a couple of months until they could come to live with us, rather than move them to a new foster home. Our work took us out of town for the next nine weeks, after which we were to begin a visitation schedule. During our absence the girls were informed that they had been matched with an adoptive family and were given the picture albums we'd prepared to introduce ourselves, pets, and home to them. As the time of our return drew near, issues arose with the foster family, leading them to give a 10-day notice to move the girls out. Therefore, instead of a progressive schedule of visits, we ended up meeting the girls for the first time one afternoon and moving them into our home the next. The leave-taking was abrupt and confusing as there were many mixed messages given by the foster family, but their arrival in our home went smoothly considering the circumstances.

In preparing for adoption, we had read many books dealing with parenting, adoption in general, adopting older children, and dealing with grief. Our reading did much to prepare us to be great parents who could understand the unique issues adopted children face. We felt empowered by the information and generally well-equipped to face the challenges.

When the girls first arrived, we allowed them time each day to regress to earlier emotional ages. We wanted to "relive" the years we'd missed together. We bought a bottle for Anita and were surprised when Maria, age 12, wanted one, too. We'd take time bottle feeding them and rocking them like babies. We would often take opportunities to act out what we would have done if they had been with us as babies. These were special moments that Maria really seemed to soak up, but that Anita would often resist, preferring to feed and care for herself.

Reminiscing on what Anita was like in those early days, she could seem like two very different children depending on her audience. When we first met, she was hiding under a table, demonstrating her timid side; however, she could also be very loud and boisterous, demanding everyone's full attention while singing and dancing. More often than not, she was withdrawn and sulky, preferring to spend hours alone in her room or playing by herself. In either mode, she had eyes so deep and haunting, one felt capable of drowning in their empty depths. Physically, she was petite, had an olive complexion, dark brown eyes, and long, dark-brown, curly hair. Intellectually, she was behind many of her classmates in reading, writing, and math skills. While her vocabulary was very limited and grammar quite stilted for her age, I could tell that she was a very smart child from whom little had been expected or required. Socially, she had few friends as she was very bossy and angered easily.

We had expected that Anita would have an initial "honeymoon" period of perfect behavior before feeling safe enough to initiate the grief process. This was, in fact, the case with her older sister, Maria, who had a history of disruptive behaviors, but who was a "perfect" child during her first months in our home. Anita, however, was a fireball of anger when she arrived, and could easily burst into very vocal and physical tantrums. We mistakenly identified this behavior as a healthy sign of grief. We saw no tears from her for a solid two weeks, but experienced a lot of tantrums, attitude, lies, and disobedience—including lying to teachers in attempts to stay after school to avoid coming home. She was oppositional, protesting everything from having her hair brushed to what food she ate. She resisted any physical affection on our part by stiffening her body, pulling away, and screaming that we were hurting her; she didn't, however, seem to mind other adults touching her. She would also hide her pain or physical needs from us, preferring to take care of herself or make her needs known to other adults.

Through play, I encouraged her to act out her feelings. Play with dolls was particularly effective, and my doll was repeatedly drowned, pushed off cliffs, or thrown out in the trash during our play times. I found none of this disturbing as I saw it as a vent for her grief process, which I knew began with anger. Anita also shared her dreams with us, in which we were often portrayed as the bad guys who were eventually killed or accidentally thrown out with the trash. We doubted that she had actually dreamed all of these things, but encouraged her sharing them as a means of processing her emotions. Months went by like this, and her tantrums didn't decrease; in fact, they could last for several hours and were provoked by either the simplest of requests or the answer "no."

At the time, we considered Anita's behavior much healthier than that of her "perfect" older sister, Maria, who was seemingly so well-adjusted. We expected Maria's great behavior to change after the honeymoon was over, and indeed, after six months it altered drastically. She began shoplifting and stealing, hoarding food and hiding it, self-mutilating activities, suicide attempts, threatening to harm Anita, threatening to harm the cats, and running off. These were difficult behaviors, but we were able to be there for her emotionally throughout her fear, anger, and grief.

We firmly believe that Maria was simply giving us her worst to see if we could handle it. Over the months, she was able to open up and share things with me that she had never told anyone before. She was also able to trust us with her tears: something she let us know right off the bat that she would never do. I believe it was very hard for her to handle the love that was growing inside of her because she found it too scary. Because of her age, she had the choice of being adopted or not, and as soon as she found out that she actually had the power to make such an important life decision, she immediately put this power to the test and said "no." I think she wanted us to make her sign the adoption petition, or at least expected us to threaten her or such. We were able to share our tears and sadness as well as our firm belief that she was making a decision she would regret for the rest of her life, but were then able to support her emotionally through the next five months in our home, including making her transition to a subsequent foster home a less abrupt and more positive experience.

It was a difficult time for all of us. Anita was often terrified by what Maria would do next, and at times we wondered if it wouldn't be better for all of us if we asked to have Maria removed from our home. We refused, however, to give up on Maria. We gave her the gift of the only positive leave-taking she had in her life. We believed it would be a life-impacting and positive message to Anita as well: She would know that we were the kind of parents who do not give up on a child when the going gets extremely difficult. We planned a special going away party for Maria, at which we gave her our blessing to bond with her new family, shared our tears and sadness over her departure, and celebrated our special memories together over the past year. She was able to share her feelings with us as well; she used very vivid imagery to express her nearly claustrophobic feeling related to her fear of loving and losing us. For her, it was better not to be loved than to love and experience the fear of heartbreak and loss yet again. She cried openly as the social worker drove her away to her unknown future.

Because we knew that it often takes two years before an adopted child really adjusts and feels part of a family, we probably ignored many signs that Anita needed a different kind of therapy. After a year, we shared some of our concerns with her social worker and our case worker about her progress in bonding, but they pointed to several plausible explanations, assuring us that all adopted children have attachment issues. We easily considered some of her ongoing behavioral issues to be her response to the many months of tumult caused by Maria's dangerous behaviors. After Maria left, we attributed Anita's ongoing issues to her new grief over "losing" Maria. We moved five months after Maria's departure, and knowing that moves can bring up all the emotions surrounding previous moves in a child's life, we again "excused" Anita's issues as understandable. When two years came and went, and I realized that, for all intents and purposes, Anita was essentially the same oppositional, manipulative, and emotionally distant child, I became very concerned.

Because it had more or less been implied by both the social workers and my husband that I was concerned over things that were not real problems, I found it difficult to share my concerns with my husband. We had already been through a lot, and I think emotionally he preferred to believe I had a bad attitude toward our daughter rather than believe that she had any real problem. I could see clearly from my journals that the only things that had changed in two years were that Anita had become more effective in using her "perfect" facade to manipulate adults, and the time she was able to keep composed between her meltdowns (huge temper tantrums lasting several hours) had lengthened to several weeks. Her crazy lying had not been curbed in the least in two years, and in fact, had gotten worse, as had her oppositionalism, constant "forgetting," "accidental" breaking of things, and food stealing. On the flip side, she still had a total absence of any cause-and-effect reasoning, still expressed no physical affection to us and responded with a stiff body when given physical affection, and seemingly had no conscience as she never showed remorse for anything. In any typical day, she would come home with nothing to say. When asked how her day went, she would grunt out "fine" or "good," only for us to find out later from another parent that she had argued terribly with other kids, had provoked trouble on the playground, stolen another's snack, or spread some ridiculous lie about us.

At this point, I began searching the Web to find answers. Other times when I had gone Web surfing, I had not found any sites that helped me with my growing concerns, but at this point, I finally found a site that started to shed some light on our situation. Following links and doing much browsing and e-mailing, I finally began to put things together and realized that Anita's attachment issues were real and serious, and not just a figment of my imagination. Empowered with hard evidence that my intuition was right on, I again presented my concerns to my husband. I ordered some books on reactive attachment disorder, and we soon were in agreement on our need for further therapy.

To return back in time a little, our daughter had been followed by at least two therapists previous to her placement with us to help her in processing her feelings of grief and loss for her birth family and later in regard to losing her foster family in preparation for her adoption into our family, yet we found that at age seven she still had little concept about what was involved in adoption, nor had she made progress in processing her anger and grief. Her first therapist after her placement with us would whisk our daughter away from us and reappear 45 minutes later with a list of suggestions that we should follow to improve our parenting. When she refused to let us participate in any way, or to disclose what was being done behind the closed doors, and persisted with an attitude that clearly placed blame on us as the new parents for all of our daughter's emotional issues, we switched therapists. When we finally found a therapist willing to include us in the therapy sessions, we were only allowed into the therapy room for about the last 15 minutes or so. The therapist even permitted our daughter to sit on one of our laps at times. We had procured a lifebook for our daughter and had asked the therapist to work through it with her to address attachment issues as grief and loss were processed. While this therapist was an improvement over the previous one, we could see how our daughter easily manipulated her, spending lots of time playing or avoiding questions while processing very little. Soon, however, our daughter was released from therapy with an assessment stating that she had made great progress in meeting all of the therapy goals: This occurred after our first 16 months together as a family.

What led us to try Dyadic Developmental Psychotherapy was our desperate desire to see our daughter really and truly heal and become "real." The superficial quality of her emotions and interactions with us was deeply frustrating and profoundly saddening. We felt fairly cynical that any further therapy could help ... unless. Unless it was all that we sensed we needed: a therapist who would build us up as parents in the eyes of our child and treat us with respect, who wouldn't settle for a play session with our daughter, who would allow us to know what happened behind closed doors, who would check things out with us to see if they were true, and who would encourage us in what we were doing right while helping us understand what we needed to change. When we read about Dyadic Developmental Psychotherapy, it sounded like all we had ever wanted; in fact, we'd already been implementing some of the interventions used in this type of therapy, like dramatic reenactments, without realizing that they were a part of this therapeutic approach. So, we were enthused by the possibilities of this therapeutic approach, but were hesitant to get our hopes up again.

We had checked our therapist out via e-mail and online chats, and then asked for a recommendation from an internationally-known therapist who no longer does therapy intensives, and he recommended the very therapist with whom we had been dialoguing. So, with some hope and trepidation, we took the plunge and applied for a two-week attachment therapy intensive. Our therapy experience was exactly as it had been described in the write-up. We were able to observe our daughter in every moment that she was with the therapist(s). Our feedback on our daughter's emotional state as well as on the accuracy of what she relayed was regularly solicited. We were able to have an active part in the progression the therapy took, and were always informed what the therapist's next planned move was in order to get our feedback beforehand. Dyadic Developmental Psychotherapy confirmed the key role we have as parents in our daughter's life, and it powerfully cut through all our daughter's defenses to bring her real needs and wounds to the forefront for true healing.

From the first day, we experienced the amazing difference that this therapy produced in our daughter and our whole family. We observed our daughter's usual tactics to manipulate the therapist and discussion, but smiled as the therapist continued to direct the conversation back to the key issue. In fact, we saw something new: Our daughter was dropping her usually sweet and perfect manners to express a certain amount of anger at someone other than her mom. Wow! As the therapy progressed that day, we also saw another unusual thing: We watched the face of our daughter actually express fear and an almost toddler-like expression as the conversation became truly meaningful. At first, we thought it was a new type of manipulation, but we learned that is was a typical response from kids who had regressed to earlier emotional experiences. The day ended with our being called into the room so that our daughter could be placed across our laps. She was then prompted by the therapist to share several key emotional experiences involving shame or fear. Having just observed the therapists for about two hours, we were easily able to mirror appropriate, quick, and reassuring responses. We then ended with a time of snuggling—something we had often done as a family, but already this time it all felt very different. It was a small start, but was the all-important first successful step so necessary to regain our hope, confidence, and determination.

We experienced a wide range of emotions during therapy. We had to deal with our own sense of guilt and failure as parents. While we knew we had done many good things, we also became painfully aware of ways we may have impeded our daughter's healing. We had to process these feelings and move forward. We were angry at times at the injustices we had suffered previously but had often excused away; the therapy showed us that there were no good excuses and that it was very sad and unfortunate. The therapists displayed the same degree of empathy and understanding with us that they did with our daughter. While we felt guilty about many things, they never blamed us or made us feel guilt or shame. They helped us face our own feelings so that we could help Anita face her feelings. We experienced a deep sense of grief at times as we mourned what could have been had we only known about Dyadic Developmental Psychotherapy sooner. We re-grieved many of our daughter's losses with her as well as our own losses. We felt happiness, relief, surprise, and joy as the barriers that had created so much loneliness and grief were broken down. We also felt hope continually growing—as well as fear at times. We all wondered if the "magic" of therapy would last, but the truth we faced was this: WE were the real magic of the therapy—our family. We had done it! We needed to keep living out what we had learned in confidence and to find the support of a follow-up therapist to help us in maintaining the attitude (PLACE). While we couldn't have done it without the therapeutic team, they couldn't have done it without us. They had shown us the way and gotten us on the right path, and this was very empowering!

Really getting the healing PLACE idea was a process: It was easy to memorize, repeat verbally, and give one's hearty support and approval of the concept, but it was and still IS a very different thing to live it out. Perhaps the most helpful thing I can share about PLACE is a personal experience. A few days into therapy, we were very confused by the amount of fear and grief our daughter was sharing about events for which she had only ever demonstrated anger or rage. Acting on our curiosity, my husband asked Anita to make a "scared" face, then a "sad" face, then an "embarrassed" face, etc. Before therapy, we would have assumed that her response to the request was a manipulative way of refusing to comply as she typically responded in passive-resistive ways to any request. Why might we have mistakenly assumed this? Each face she made looked exactly like the previous. We put her in front of a mirror and had her repeat this exercise. Afterward, we pointed out that we couldn't see a difference between the expressions and began making faces in the mirror above her face as a game to teach her what "scared" looked like. In tense moments, this became a family joke in which one of us would break into an exaggerated "scared" or "sad" face.

What does this experience have to do with the PLACE? Everything! Every face she made was a variation of a mad face. We had a big "aha!" moment in which we realized that our daughter's perpetually mad face wasn't due to its being frozen there, but that she had not learned how to facially express a wider range of emotions yet! In the next months, we would often freeze a video as we watched a movie and play a game to see if she could guess what emotion was being expressed. At first, she was really clueless: Her response was inevitably "mad." We learned a lot about our daughter, and the healing began. She is now very accomplished at reading expressions, all because we were curious, accepting, engaged, playful, and loving.

One big barrier I personally had and still struggle with in keeping the PLACE is that of not assuming that my daughter is pushing me away. I had experienced three years of what I thought were her most energetic attempts to destroy my marriage and destroy me as a person. I was her enemy, and I had to be eliminated or at least be rendered powerless. I had developed many emotional defenses to protect against these heart-wrenching attacks, and I needed to create a habit of new responses which would frame her onslaughts in a new perspective. I needed to replace words such as "attack" and "onslaughts" in my mind with such phrases as "attempts to stay safe" and "survival tactics." As I write this, I realize how far I've slipped in my vigilance in this area—and with a noticeably negative affect on my feelings and interactions with my daughter.

Following this thought, there's a very personal insight that I hesitated to share with the readers, but I believe may help others as well. Because of my faith, I often turn to God in prayer and to His Word for wisdom. I was not brought up to be a person of faith, and in fact, had derided the very idea of God or any concept that couldn't be "proved" scientifically. Sparing the details, God reached out to me in His love and I underwent a dramatic change in my beliefs as I began a personal relationship with Him. This relationship with God is very important to me, and therefore, one in which I've had many struggles: moments of doubt, moments of anger at Him, moments of profound letdown, etc. On a particularly difficult day with Anita, I was praying and going over some Bible promises when God brought me to a passage that speaks about adoption. As I read, I realized how often I had acted toward my Heavenly Father in the same way that Anita was acting toward me. I began asking myself how many times I had pushed God away in anger or fear. How many times had I returned to my birth family, so to speak, discounting the value of my adoption into God's family? How many times had I imagined that life was somehow easier or better before I joined His family? With tears rolling down my face, I realized that in the same way that I would always come back to God feeling like a real creep for my doubts and failings and the unfair things I had said or done to hurt Him, that Anita, too, probably felt very similarly. I always came back to God because I knew the truth: My life had been desperately empty and without meaning before I was adopted into His family. It gave me hope that she too, in those moments of pulling away, would eventually remind herself that her life before adoption into our family was very empty and lonely, and return to reconnect with us. I had to be there with open arms ready to embrace her and reassure her in the same way that my Father is always there to snatch me up into His arms. There are times that I just can't believe that He is ready to forgive me AGAIN, and I need to be assuring Anita of the same thing; I need to be ready to reconnect and not nurse my own hurt and disappointment that's been created due to not seeing her actions through the PLACE filter.

One's therapy expectations must be reasonable. Dyadic Developmental Psychotherapy was not a miracle cure which undid $10^{1/2}$ years of learned perceptions and behaviors on our daughter's part. For that matter, it did not miraculously take away the years of habits we had formed as parents in response to our daughter's behaviors. Nor did it erase the tension or hurts we had felt as a couple in response to behaviors designed to divide and polarize us. So, how did it help? It helped us to see each other in an entirely new light, which helped us to truly understand each other and ourselves: real empathy. We were able to put several principles into practice immediately and live out and enjoy the success immediately, too. These small successes continued to build momentum, giving us a sense of hope for our family's future.

I would like to note something that I believe is very important: For the eight months leading up to the Dyadic Developmental Psychotherapy intensive, we followed the therapeutic parenting guidelines as outlined in Nancy Thomas' book When Love is Not Enough as well as Daniel Hughes' book Building The Bonds of Attachment. Reading these books and putting them into practice brought an immediate change to our household. I would reread Nancy's book each month and brace up my weak areas. The mom time and childlike playing were very powerful in giving us several wonderful memories as mom/daughter. These months of successes and new dynamics gave us much hope and even had us wondering at times whether the Dyadic Developmental Psychotherapy intensive we had scheduled in the meantime was really necessary, *but enough disturbing behaviors would surface to give us a reality check. These books along with online chat sessions and Internet materials were all very helpful in preparing us for Dyadic Developmental Psychotherapy, but I would never exchange these resources for the face-to-face sessions with the therapy team. Being able to relax into the capable hands of the therapists and be a vital part of our daughter's healing without carrying all the weight was of inestimable healing value. For us, it was vitally important to see Dyadic Developmental Psychotherapy in action and take an active role in a supervised setting where we could get immediate feedback and encouragement.*

Our advice to other parents in getting help would be to start by gathering information. There are great books dealing with the subject of Reactive Attachment Disorder that were essential for our success. Nancy Thomas sells cassettes and videos for those parents who don't have the time or desire to read. There are helpful Web sites for quick reading as well as chat rooms for "live" interaction with other parents and the chatroom host. All of these resources should be helpful in finding a Dyadic Developmental therapist as well as preparing the family for the therapy sessions.

A Dyadic Developmental Psychotherapy intensive is not the answer alone. A child must have ongoing, local therapy. It's best to surround oneself with a support team that can help you be the awesome parent you need to be to help your child heal. If you do not have a good hometown therapist or cooperative school system, it will be difficult to keep the gains you've made and continue to progress. Our team was able to find a local therapist for us to do follow-up work. Had they not been able to locate a therapist for us, then they would have helped us find a therapist who would be willing to come with us to the intensive to be trained in Dyadic Developmental Psychotherapy in order to do the follow-up work with us.

If your child has any degree of attachment issues, we doubt that traditional forms of therapy (talk or play) will be of any help to your child. Our child had several traditional therapists through the years and none of them helped in the core issues of bonding and attachment. None of the parenting books we had read did anything to moderate Anita's behavior—and we tried all approaches. A child without attachment knows right from wrong and will consistently choose the wrong unless choosing otherwise will give him or her more power.

Successful parenting after therapy is very difficult without a good support team. One must continue to get lots of rest. Couples need to continue to work together as a united front. Ongoing support by a Dyadic Developmental Psychotherapist is very helpful, even to have nearby for an occasional appointment when new issues surface and it's time for a "tune-up." Since the four months of follow-up therapy, we have not had any type of support system around us—whether scholastic, hometown therapist, or respite care pro-

vider. It's a hard road to travel, and we have experienced times when our whole family has reverted to old patterns.

In terms of parenting after therapy, we're still figuring this piece out. It's a constant flow—or dance, if you will. What works today may not tomorrow, but the principle of remaining in the PLACE is at the base of every approach that works. As time goes by, we find we are able to use the Love and Logic approach more, but in other moments, we find ourselves dealing with a child who's acting emotionally on the level of a three-year-old. The approach needs to be altered to meet the emotional needs at the time, but it's hard to know if something is a manipulative put-on, or a genuine emotional regression.

Now that attachment therapy is over, and Anita is healed, I still have a lot of doubts: I think I need to parent her like any other seventh grader, yet she often regresses emotionally and is so unlike others her age. At times I wonder if we are coddling her too much, especially when I compare ourselves with parents of other children her age. I then remind myself that she isn't like other kids her age, and in fact, often seems to be functioning at a much younger age emotionally. I don't want to smother my kid or teach her to be emotionally dependent on us when emotional interdependence is my goal. I'm constantly reading and seeking help to become an even better parent in this regard, but I've found nothing in writing that describes the average day in the life of a kid a year (or two or three) after attachment therapy. I would really like to see what that looks like. I know what's happening in our house, but I think we can still do better.

Afterward

We have tried to keep track of Maria, who has bounced from foster home to foster home. She is now in high school and gets fairly decent grades when not cutting classes. She has written Anita about twice a year on average. To this day, her only positive leave-taking was from our family.

Anita is now a preteen. Physically, her appearance hasn't changed drastically except for her eyes, which now know how to smile. Socially, she can be very outgoing and loves to be on stage, whether singing or acting. She is learning to curb her bossiness and has grown a lot in the area of friendship skills. Intellectually, she is a very bright student who is at the top of her class. Her personality is still somewhat withdrawn, but she continues to work on sharing her feelings and thoughts. She has learned to enjoy humor and can be quite witty at times. For the most part, she no longer tries to sabotage our family time and generally looks forward to it. She has learned to enjoy surprises. While she continues to struggle with telling the truth, she rarely goes into her crazy lying mode. She still seems to live in fear, but not in that "con-

stantly alert" mode. She has learned to be very careful and considerate of animals as well as feel grief if she accidentally hurts them. She is developing a conscience; she has actually come to us during this past year to admit her own lies and then tell the truth. She has also taken steps in sharing many feelings and events that she had never shared with us (or anyone) before. She still doubts our love for her many times, but she has also learned to let our love into her heart. If you ask her if the very hard work involved in learning how to love has been worth it, she will respond with a very firm "yes." This newfound love still scares her, and she still worries that we will die every time we leave her alone for any period of time, but she will tell you that she would rather love and risk losing the people she loves than never know love at all. And as she tells you this, you will see both the concern and the love very clearly in her now-shining and very expressive eyes.

Karen Hunt's Story

Dima's journey began in a Russian Orphanage. When I first met Dima, Ron, and Karen, I was impressed and saddened by how many failed therapies they'd tried. While it is not uncommon for families to have been through many previous treatments without success, it is still sad to see. This story underscores the importance of persistence and how critical to healing it is to have loving parents who can effectively create a healing PLACE. Karen's dedication is amazing. This story also highlights the importance of having a thorough assessment. Part of the reason Dima had not improved is that he had not received an effective and evidence-based treatment for his problems. Another factor was that several issues had been overlooked, these being his significant sensory-integration difficulties and Bipolar I Disorder.

This story enabled me to reflect on how my practice has changed in the past six years. I now include the parents earlier and more substantively in therapy that I previously did. My focus on parent training is more on attunement, the reflective function, and helping them become "ACE" (accepting, curious, and empathic) parents. Structure is vital to keeping the child and family safe and secure. Structure and limits are important ways to demonstrate care and love by protecting your child. However, it has become increasingly clear that structure is not enough. While structure keeps the child safe and secure, it is contingent on collaborative communication, emotional attunement and intimacy, and a nurturing relationship that heals. Finally, I now put much more emphasis in practice on maintaining attunement with the child, accepting what the child presents, and then using curiosity and much reflection on the current relationship in the immediate moment to uncover the child's internal working models and develop empathy for the child. I now focus more in sessions on how the past remains alive in the present through these internal working models. I also focus more on the parent's reflective abilities and on how their attachment histories affect their current ability to help their child. It has become much clearer that PACE applies to my work with both child and parent. If I can provide an accepting and attuned relationship with the parents, they are better able to do the same with their child.

Dima and Karen worked very hard throughout therapy. Karen's dedication, love, and creativity allowed her to sidestep many power struggles and to keep Dima engaged in a healthy and nurturing relationship, despite his deep fears of intimacy and his negative working models that were evident in his fear, sadness, and anger. This story underscores the importance of a well-developed reflective function and the necessity of empowering parents to see the hurt, scared, and wounded child that is underneath the anger and aggression. It was Karen's ability to look below the behavior to the feelings and trauma that drove or motivated the behavior, to consistently go deeper with Dima, that really facilitated his healing.

Seeing Dima now is a delight. While he still struggles with bipolar disorder, the medication is largely effective. He also continues to have sensory-integration issues, but these are manageable with the interventions suggested by his Occupational Therapist, who is SIPT certified. Dima is a bright, engaged, and affectionate child. His relationship with his mother is clearly secure and loving. When I see him, he displays an appropriate range of affect and the ability to relate on an emotional level with authenticity. I always look forward to seeing Dima and his mom.

Our Journey to Parenthood

Ron and I married in 1985. We were an instant part-time family, with Ron's boys spending several days a month with us. Our plans were to get pregnant the following year so the children would be close in age. With the boys at my side on our wedding day, I knew I was one step closer to the large family of my childhood dreams.

And just as we had planned, I became pregnant right away. Ron was offered a new job and we relocated. Destiny landed me in the hands of a wonderful obstetrician. With my first appointment, he was immediately suspicious of something missed by my former doctor. A biopsy indicated invasive cancer, and in a whirl I found myself in the office of an oncologist/gynecologist. A wonderful, grandfatherly-type man, he guided me through the realities of going from newly expectant Mom to that of a cancer survivor.

I knew immediately that adoption was our answer. I simply wanted a child. A brief look at surrogacy confirmed my resolution that biology was irrelevant. At my six-week post-surgical checkup, I met with the hospital social worker to talk about adoption. She advised me to first take time to grieve and deal with my losses. I went away armed with reading material and information to research, and worked through the grief that reared its ugly head that next year.

It is ironic that my first desire was to adopt a child from Russia. In high school, I had typed a report about Russia for my brother. Those were the days of the Iron Curtain, and I was intrigued by his research on the Russian people. I read the works of Solzhenitsyn and Leon Uris and became more intrigued with the culture.

Ron and I quickly realized that international adoption was out of our financial league and settled into working with an open adoption program. Unfortunately, less than a year later that program folded. Antonio was so committed to helping us form our family that he offered to transfer all of our fees into his international adoption program. Ron and I decided to save for the next year, update our home study, and then pursue international adoption. Meanwhile, I was sad to see his boys getting older without a baby sister.

A few months later, Antonio sent us a video from his newly developed Russia program to give us an idea how international adoption worked. Knowing we weren't ready yet, I satisfied my curiosity by watching the video before Ron got home. And there he was! The connection was immediate. This adorable toddler looked back from the TV screen with a smile that bridged the gap across the Atlantic. Dima was more interested in the "machina" (truck) backing up to the building then being videotaped. Amazing that I would bond so quickly with the oldest child on the video, and a boy to boot. I had thought we wanted to adopt an infant and a girl. Ron came home and in silence I showed him the video. Much to my amazement he commented, "You know, there is something special about that last little boy." We called Antonio and entered the next phase of our journey to expand our family.

Our adventures in bringing Dima home were pretty typical for international adoption. We completed the mounds of paperwork for our petition to adopt an orphan, which was then delayed in immigration. The U.S. Federal Government had shut down for one month the previous November, resulting in a four-month delay in processing our paperwork. It was a cold and snowy April 1st in 1996 when we went to Moscow to meet Dima. Knowing I would need to leave him behind, we soaked up all we could of him in our three days there. Once our petition finished collecting dust in U.S. Immigration, the Russians were in the midst of an election, slowing down work on the Russian end.

Finally, our court date, and by proxy our adoption of Dima was finalized. visas arrived, gifts were bought, bags packed, and airline tickets ordered. And then Antonio called. The policy in Russia had changed and couples could no longer adopt using a tourist visa. Let me tell you, it's no easy feat to get a Russian visa translated in rural Pennsylvania. Amazingly, our journey led us two blocks from our home to a young woman from Ukraine. And yes, we had tourist visas. It was a two-week delay to get the visas straightened out and new travel arrangements made. Finally, we were on our way, and on August 2nd, 1996 Dima was placed in our arms and became part of our family forever.

Dima's Early Years

Dima was born to a single, unemployed woman in a country with no programs to support its poor. She chose to leave him at the hospital. I am sure she hoped that he would be adopted and have a family to fulfill all of her dreams for him. At 2 1/2 months of age, Dima left the hospital and was placed in Orphanage #24, tucked away in a maze of side streets in busy Moscow. Dom Rebyonka (baby house) #24 is home to about 100 children. They are placed in groups of 10 to 12 with one caregiver per group.

We know little of those early, critical years. When Dima came home with us at three years, nine months of age, we were handed a quickly scrawled paper (in Russian) containing his medical records. There was little information of value there. His referral had limited information regarding birth statistics and an undated paragraph describing him. The accuracy of this information is all questionable. We assume that this and the brief two-minute video we have were done around age three when he was placed in the Russian adoption registry.

Dima does not talk much about those early years. Those memories are encoded in the Russian language, which he no longer speaks. What he more likely has memories of are the emotional states he felt when living there. We have never talked negatively about his life in the orphanage. We mostly talked about there being too many babies and not enough caregivers. But there have been hints over the years that his life there was probably not that benign. After completing attachment therapy, Dima has started expressing negative feelings toward what he calls "that place." He has absolutely no interest in ever seeing his orphanage again.

Physical indicators provide us with hints about Dima's early life. Dima had marks on his front baby teeth. The dentist felt this was indicative of a blow to the mouth around the age of 12 to 18 months. Recently my son was evaluated for possible scoliosis, to find that he had an old injury to the growth plate in one hip, deterring that hip's growth. As he's had no such injury since coming home, this must have occurred in the orphanage. Of course, all babies can fall, so it's hard to judge this negatively. Typically the more unexplained injuries a child has, the more likely it is that abuse was the cause. But then, he is also a child with sensory processing difficulties, which can result in increased clumsiness.

Dima reports being "strapped to bed" at night in the orphanage. Attempts to explore this in therapy did not directly point to abuse. He was able to recall that there were several beds in each room and two children to each bed. They had to share a blanket and were often cold at night. They had one toy that they took turns having at night. When discussing this in therapy he began rocking and sucking his fingers. He was obviously flashing back to the orphanage. We are uncertain if he was truly restrained in his bed or if the bedding was tucked in to keep the children warm (which would create the perception of being "strapped" to a three-year-old).

At home, Dima continued to sleep completely hidden under his blankets. Is this a sensory thing, or is it a habit developed years ago to keep himself hidden at night? There are so many questions we will never have the answers to. In an effort to work on his enuresis, I started getting Dima up at night to use the bathroom. He was hysterical at the thought of being out of his bed, and we stopped this after just a few nights. When other parents complain about the troubles they have getting their child to bed, I feel even sadder. I have NEVER had difficulty putting my child to bed, from day one. How does a three-year-old child learn so strongly to stay in bed, that even at age 12 he rarely gets out of bed at night?

Having developed RAD, it's obvious that at a minimum Dima experienced profound neglect, since this diagnosis is very rare in children who are nurtured and well-cared-for. Again, it does not point the finger toward direct physical abuse, but it sure does stack the deck.

I have collected much information over the years about typical life in a Russian orphanage. We will never know how much of this applies to my son or to the orphanage he was in. We thought his caregivers seemed attached to him. They stood in the doorway watching us play with him and beaming with pleasure. When we left to bring him home, Dima became hysterical when he realized he was being put in that "machina" (car). Out of nowhere a woman ran across the parking lot and tore Dima out of his father's arms and rocked and soothed him. She obviously was watching his departure from the window. That spoke attachment to me. At least one person there must have had some level of connection with my son.

I have been told that sexual abuse is rampant in Russian orphanages. Parents have shared stories of adopting babies at six or seven months of age, who later ended up being treated for sexual abuse. We have not seen indicators of such abuse in my son.

Obviously food was in short supply. Dima was anemic upon arrival home, although this might not be rare for a three year old. He was also below the fifth percentile in height and weight. Dima grew 10 inches in his first year home. He's now in the 90th percentile. Once in preschool, just a few months after arriving home, Dima fell carrying his plate of food. He became absolutely hysterical. I would imagine that Dima thought he would be severely punished or that he would get no more food.

We were told that the babies were assembly-line fed in the orphanages. Bottles were propped, and to speed up the process, the ends of the nipples were cut open. I have been told that you can adopt an infant from Russia who has lost their sucking reflex, as they do not need to suck to eat. Dima, to this day, craves oral stimulation. He requires intense oral input and will suck his fingers to obtain this. We provide Dima with significant oral stimulation in his meals by providing chewy, crunchy, or sour (I call him the king of sour) food items at every meal. Dima drinks his beverages through a straw and often chews on gum, mints, taffy, etc. This need could indeed be from a lack of appropriate oral stimulation in infancy. Fortunately, Dima does not have the language delays, speech impediments, or dental/jaw malformations that can come from a lack of oral stimulation in infancy.

In addition to the above, this type of feeding does not promote the Seal-Suck-Breath synchronization essential to good lung development. When the babies nurse, they seal their lips on the bottle/breast, suck, and then take in a deep breath. This deep breath develops the baby's lungs. Dima continues to struggle with asthma at age 12. Again not a certainty, but this medical condition could come from his early years of neglect.

Family Life in the Early Years

At the age of three years, nine months, Dima arrived at the gates of New York City with his little green card. Dima seemed to settle into family life without missing a beat. While still in Moscow, he craved learning the English language. "Etta?" ("What is this?") Dima said repeatedly, as he pointed to everything in site. Dima was like a little sponge, quickly soaking up all he was exposed to.

Three weeks after arriving in America, Dima was enrolled in the Head Start preschool program. Nothing but the best for my boy, and I was impressed with the teaching staff at our local Head Start. I slowly and methodically faded myself away from him at preschool (the behaviorist background in me coming out). I thought I was doing a great job at meeting his needs, and really missed that to Dima caregivers were interchangeable. Me or his teacher—it really didn't matter.

I thought Dima was doing so well that within three months I was back to work. Paying the bills and maintaining our health insurance won out over my desire to stay home with my boy. The wonderful woman from Ukraine who had translated our visas offered to baby-sit. This seemed ideal to me.

Now Dima would be provided with the enrichment of a good preschool environment, have exposure to his culture, continue to hear Russian being spoken with his baby-sitter, and settle into family life with his new mom and dad. We really had an uneventful first year at home. Again, I missed that we were adding yet another interchangeable caregiver into Dima's life.

At a physical the following summer, Dima received the Mantoux test for TB. A positive reaction was confirmed by follow-up testing. Dima's chest X-rays were clear, but the protocol to prescribe INH put his baby-sitter over the edge. Remember, she grew up in communist Ukraine. She KNEW the government (in Pennsylvania the State Health Department follows and treats TB cases) was lying to me when they said he did not have TB and that the antibiotic was precautionary. She KNEW her baby was at risk. In tears she abruptly quit baby-sitting my son. A few months later they relocated, and she was completely out of Dima's life.

By fall, Dima became hyperactive. Within a month, I received a call that he had become aggressive and was terrified to leave Head Start for his new baby-sitter's. In tears, I listened to the Head Start caseworker describe his day. I knew little about Reactive Attachment Disorder at that time, but enough to realize that this was what she was describing. The violence continued at home. At the slightest request, Dima would fly into an hour-plus rage, endangering himself and the adults caring for him. Dima would fight restraint with all his might the entire time. At Head Start, it took two staff members to keep him safe during these rages.

Journey Toward Healing

I feel fortunate that Dima's symptoms were so aggressive. There was no denying his need for help. Had Dima been more passive-aggressive in his behavior, like many other children with reactive attachment disorder, it may have taken me years to recognize his need for treatment. Accepting the need to seek outside help to parent your child is a very difficult decision to make. There is a lot of shame in having an out-of-control child and admitting you cannot manage him.

Just after his fifth birthday, we made an appointment with a local child psychologist. I had consulted with the Parents Network for the Post Institutionalized Child (www.pnpic.org) and realized the importance of "brand-name shopping," as cofounder Thais Tepper liked to say. I thought "child psychologist" was as close to a brand name as we could get in a rural community. Despite my BA in psychology and years of experience in the field of mental retardation, I had no clue about what to expect in a therapist's office.

I never questioned it when the psychologist took my son alone to his office for the evaluation. Three wasted appointments later, he shared the results of IQ testing with my husband and me. We were appalled. We could care less what his IQ was (he was way off the mark, anyhow). We wanted help with his aggression. We left his office angry and depressed. He completely disregarded the literature I had provided on grief and adopted children. He would not support my request for a leave of absence as he "didn't think it was necessary." He diagnosed our five-year-old child with Oppositional Defiant Disorder and suggested medicating him with clonidine. And, "no," he didn't think therapy was necessary. I realized Thais was right; we had failed to brand-name shop.

Many phone calls later, I found a relatively local psychologist who was willing to collaborate with an attachment therapist I had located a few hours away. After an initial consultation with the attachment therapist, we headed to psychologist #2. Within a few appointments, I quickly realized that this wonderful, gentle man was putty in my five-year-old's hands. We walked away from his office with a new set of letters. Now in addition to the label of ODD, my son had received the label of PTSD (Post-Traumatic Stress Disorder).

The attachment therapist we had consulted developed an opening, and we moved onto therapist #3. For the first time, we found ourselves with someone we were confident understood what we were facing. Finally, we realized what the brand name was that Thais had suggested we shop for so many months earlier. The diagnosis was an intense grief reaction and possible RAD. This therapy was like nothing I had ever imagined. My son was held much like a parent would hold an infant. He was confronted with his biweekly woes and screams, kicks, and rages. He calmed and was soothed. I felt so uncomfortable with what I perceive to be all of the pain inside of Dima. After five sessions, therapist #3 relocated. I later learned that this therapy was called Rage Reduction Therapy and was controversial. All I knew at the time was that I had a very ill child and this was the only professional we had yet to encounter who understood his issues. He had explained everything to us, and we agreed to this treatment because it made sense and we had no other options in our area.

The spring of Dima's fifth year was a time of assessment after assessment. I ran from therapist, to audiologist, to therapist, to Occupational Therapist, to therapist, to Neural-psychologist. And each added new letters to our alphabet soup, new diagnoses to research and read about. Dima was diagnosed with a Central Auditory Processing Disorder (CAPD), with significant deficits in processing speech in noise. I could turn him into a textbook case of ADHD simply by taking him to a noisy basketball game. Dima was also diagnosed with Dysfunction of Sensory Integration (DSI), scoring at least two SD's below the mean in almost all measures. The neuropsychological testing indicated probable right hemisphere compromise (which I later learned is com-

mon with profound neglect), although English-as-a-second-language issues may have impacted testing results.

Research led us to therapist #4 and Theraplay® (see footnote 1 on page 27 of this book). I absolutely loved this approach. At almost six years of age, two years after coming to America, my son was officially diagnosed with Reactive Attachment Disorder. I was on a leave of absence and greatly enjoyed being home and implementing the Theraplay games with my son. And Dima seemed to progress. After three great months, at the age of seven, he was deemed to no longer need therapy. I felt like I finally had my son back. His last therapy session was a party to celebrate his success. On the way home, Dima melted down into the ultimate of all rages. And the raging continued for days and weeks on end, worse than ever before. After two years of therapy, my son was sicker then he had been when we started. And he was so violent that I could no longer safely restrain him.

Somewhere else along the way, my son was enrolled in wrap-around services. We received family-based services, then TSS (Therapeutic Staff Support) services to provide a 1:1 for Dima to attend day programs over the summer. We definitely knew this was not a kid to sit in day care or spend weeks on end in unstructured activities. We also knew there was no way a baby-sitter could survive a day with our son without well-trained staff present. In the intake for wrap around, we added more letters to Dima's alphabet soup of diagnosis. I definitely knew that his hyperactivity and attention issues were related to sensory processing deficits and to the RAD, but still the evaluating psychologist added the label of ADHD. More than ever, I wanted to be home with my son. But my employment provided us with access to excellent health insurance. And excellent health insurance provided us with access to excellent specialists for my son's long list of needs. I was torn by this dilemma, but the desire to access good care for my son won out.

Shortly after returning to Theraplay®, I just knew that my son needed something more intense. By now I was better educated on Reactive Attachment Disorder and confident in the appropriateness of this diagnosis. Our earlier experiences in attachment/holding therapy caused me to hesitate. I was well aware of the controversy over this therapy. But I also knew in my heart that my son had no future. I absolutely knew that it would take a miracle to keep him out of jail and that a productive adult life was all but impossible. I had heard Arthur Becker-Weidman speak in the past and had the utmost admiration for him. My husband and I decided to have an evaluation completed by Art and then decide after that what to do.

Dyadic Developmental Psychotherapy

One day, in June 1999, my husband and I entered Art's office, hands full of assessments he had sent to us for completion. I remember sarcastically saying to my husband, "Here's another guy that's going to say Dima has ADHD," since we had checked off so many of the items listed on this assessment. I felt relieved that we wouldn't have to worry about bipolar disorder since only a few items were marked on that questionnaire, and all of those I pretty much chalked up to RAD.

Art confirmed the RAD diagnosis, ruled out ADHD, and felt sensory integration issues were a contributing factor to the behaviors we were struggling with. Much to our surprise, he diagnosed our son with Bipolar 1 Disorder. It took many months for that to sink in, and for me to fully accept the diagnosis and the need for medication. I remember feeling that we were at last on the right path. For the first time since my son had started therapy $2^{1/2}$ years earlier, we were with a therapist who got the full picture. Not a picture I liked, but it seemed that the missing pieces to the Dima puzzle were coming together.

Those first therapy sessions were emotionally intense, more for me than Dima. Dima just wanted to try to find a tactic to manipulate this new therapist. He despised Art from day one, when he quickly realized that this guy had his number. Dima dug in his heels and resolved to wear Art out. My son spent most of those early sessions sitting on the "middle cushion" of the couch in one therapy room, refusing to comply with treatment. Art and I met in an adjoining room, monitoring Dima via closed circuit TV. Initially a second therapist needed to be present to keep an eye on my son, who would attempt to leave the suite in an effort to control the session. Dima's resistance was actually quite beneficial because it provided the opportunity for me to get individualized training with Art on the parenting component of treatment.

Dima made many attempts to create a relationship with me that felt safe to him. For Dima, this meant a relationship with lacked intimacy or dependency and that he could control. He tried to be the one to set the rhythm and tone of our interactions because he was fearful of being dependent on anyone. My role was to show him that he could trust me to not let him get overwhelmed. Through dyadic regulation of his affect, he began to feel more safe and secure in therapy. Put differently, my initial primary task was to create a secure base in therapy so that he could explore his past trauma, internal working models, and relationships.

During those early sessions, in addition to mastering basic attachment parenting concepts, I also learned the basis for attachment disorder and treatment. Prior to working with Art, I had attended several conferences and read many books on attachment. Having a solid foundation in shame and attunement (the dance of joy between a child and mother) were essential to understanding how to help my son. Dima could play the attunement game quite well. Much *of the time he would accept nurturing and fun from me; but kick up his shame, and watch out. Dima would then repel any attempts at nurturing and care as if he were coated with Teflon®. Remembering that my son had an essential absence of self-esteem (much lower than low self-esteem!) helped me get through the rough spots with him. Realizing that he KNEW I was going to abandon and leave him helped me stay empathic and keep my own angry reaction well guarded. Understanding that all his anger and aggression were really a cover-up for shame, fear, and hurt made it much easier to not take his behavior personally.*

I'll never forget one of the early sessions. I was watching Art with Dima via the TV. Dima had actually started to accept the need to lie in Art's arms and talk, but would never let him get very deep. As Art talked with him about how sad it must be to not know how to love his mother, Dima started crying. My heart broke. I remembered telling Art at intake that I KNEW that my son loved me; it was just that the foundation for his love was easily shaken. I KNEW in my heart that genuine love was there. And now I watched my son, crying in his therapist's arms because he did not know how to love anyone, not even me. His emotions were real and raw. There was no con in him for those brief moments. The shock of that realization will stay with me forever. I was grateful to be in another room, watching via TV, so that my much-needed tears could flow unrestrained.

Parents are now more quickly included in therapy sessions than was the case six years ago. We have found that this can often increase the child's comfort level. In addition, I have found that when children see their affect affecting their parent, it intensifies the affect and allows for the reexperiencing of past trauma in a safe environment. The dissociated or split-off affect can more easily be tolerated and integrated because the child is not alone and is supported. In addition, the child is sharing the affect with another rather than having to experience the affect in isolation. Seeing a parent affected by the child's affect makes the experience more real for the child. Just as an infant and young child learn about themselves and what they are experiencing by seeing that reflected in their parent's face, Dima began to learn about who he was by seeing himself reflected in his parents' and therapist's faces.

Art finished with Dima and came over to debrief that session with me. I sat there heartbroken, as Art entered the room cheery and optimistic. He was ecstatic with Dima's response today. Art went on to explain that seeing true emotions so early in treatment was a very good sign. Children with RAD are masters at hiding their emotions, and usually don't give such an early breakthrough. Of course, typical of a child with RAD, Dima then took great care for many sessions to keep those feelings safely hidden away.

When my son entered treatment with Dyadic Development Psychotherapy, I had all but lost hope. He was getting more and more violent and difficult to control. I was facing the reality that my son, age seven, would likely need to be in a residential treatment facility within the next year. This is a reality that chills me to the core to this day. From the very first day with Art, I saw a light at the end of a very long tunnel. I was afraid to hope, and yet afraid not to. We quickly decided to go 100% with Arts recommendations. We could not afford for me to be off work, but I felt my son could not afford for us not to give it all we could.

Dyadic Development Psychotherapy was like nothing we had experienced before. I was never uncomfortable with Art's approach, as I had been with the Rage Reduction Therapy. There was something very beautiful about seeing my son finally accept the need to receive comfort and nurture from someone else. Many times I was also in the treatment room and would get to experience real connection, not the con I had before. While Art was definitely in charge and a firm authority during treatment, it was quite beautiful and calming to watch his interaction with my child. Dima was never forced to face the demons of his past. He was nurtured and helped to feel safe enough to face what he needed to face. At times therapy ended because Dima was not able to summon the strength to do the therapeutic work. He was never humiliated over this, simply understood and empathized with.

I am still in awe of that little boy that was able to take such a gigantic leap in faith and risk learning to love. After all, he had loved once and been wounded to the core by the very people he depended on most. Why should he think I was any different! Why should he believe that I wouldn't walk out on him, just like all of his past "Moms" at the orphanage did! Dima was the one that needed to do the most work. Art and I each had our roles, but without Dima's willingness to learn to love, he would not have made it. Other children are not so fortunate. Their pasts have left scars so deep that they cannot summon the strength to climb that Mt. Everest of pain.

> I remain in awe of Karen's ability to accept Dima and see the emotions below the behavior. This was so important in his healing.

Mastering Therapeutic Parenting

It's funny that a year before working with Art, I had purchased the Anita Thomas book on parenting children with Reactive Attachment Disorder. After first reading it, I thought the book had some good ideas, but seemed a bit too extreme. As my son stonewalled me on the first day of the first procedure we decided to try (thinking time), I quickly decided we were going to follow the full, unabridged version. It was exhausting and draining. Never had being off from work been such hard work. I had to be at my sharpest continually, during all of my son's waking hours.

The first chapter of the parenting protocol requires the primary parent take care of him or herself before beginning the program. There is no way a worn-out, unsupported Mom can orchestrate a healing environment, day-in, day-out, 100% of the time. I could not have done this with the added stress of work and outside responsibilities. I took five months off work and didn't burden myself with expectations of home-cooked meals or a spotless house. My son went to bed early every night, and I got a nice, long soak in a hot tub. I kept well-connected with friends and family over the phone. We lived over two hours from Art's office, fortunately within a reasonable commute of my parents' home. To make the weekly trip for therapy less stressful on me, we stayed overnight at my parents' house. This gave me a capable baby-sitter (after raising six kids, my Mom was well enough seasoned to handle one seven-year-old with RAD). It was refreshing to have someone to visit with, to relax with my sisters, and to attend a support group for parents of children with RAD.

My son's therapist felt a parent should strive for 100% consistency to break through the inconsistency of their child's past. I came close but found perfection almost impossible to achieve. I just did the best I could and many days just hung in there until my son's 7:30 bedtime. I can't tell you how many times I sat at our kitchen counter with the parenting manual in hand, reading and rereading sections while my son was either in his room raging or doing a very passive-aggressive rendition of thinking time. I scoured the pages for answers to turn our stalemate around. As it turned out, time was the only answer. That and sticking to my guns with the parenting protocol. I really tried my best to be extremely consistent in my expectations, although unpredictable with my consequences. It is especially hard to stick with the program when tired or emotionally drained. This goes back to taking care of Mama. I had to take breaks when I needed them, even if it meant my son got 30 minutes in his room to read while I enjoyed a cup of tea. I gave myself a break, and didn't dwell on my mistakes.

Over time and with my stubborn persistence, Dima finally started to come around. I kept his world very small, just him, me, our house, and our yard. Mr. Social got very tired of this small world. In those early days, I believe Dima's biggest motivator was not learning to love me—it was getting back that outside world. I do also believe hidden deep inside him was a tiny little spark in his heart that did want to figure it all out, that did want to know what love felt like.

While my son's initial motives might not have been genuine, like most things, if you fake it long enough it can become real. The therapeutic parenting, coupled with attachment therapy, began to change my son's template of the world. The legacy of neglect is a worldview with a basis in self-preservation. In infancy, my son learned that he was the only person he could count on, for anything. The big people only brought heartbreak and physical pain. He had to control everything and everyone in order to survive and be safe. In the hostile orphanage environment, developing Reactive Attachment Disorder may have been a defense mechanism and perhaps something necessary for survival.

As his world view changed, Dima began to see his early experiences through the eyes of the scared toddler, rather than a rationalizing seven- or eight-year-old. He began to understand that his problems were a natural and normal result of those early experiences, not something that meant he was inherently bad. Dima began to realize that by trying to protect his fragile heart from further damage, he had also hidden it away from love. Dima was guided to see that his new life was different. I was not one of the orphanage moms, and life here was not like the orphanage.

Art used different learning forms in therapy. One that especially helped Dima was the visual presentation of concepts. From drawing out decision trees depicting a long chain of poor choices, to pictures of his heart with a brick wall around it, Dima was able to both see and hear what he was experiencing in therapy. Dima had something to bring home to reinforce the lessons learned that week.

Reading the parenting manual and mastering the techniques were relatively easy. Keeping up with my son's efforts to undermine the techniques, however, were not. Each week, Art and I would discuss the efforts Dima had thwarted in the preceding days. I left each session with several suggestions to handle those situations. Of course there rarely was a repeat performance, almost as if Dima knew I had the ammunition to disarm that behavior.

Each week he came up with some new way to try and break me down. At first, I responded by playing the tapes back in my head, tapes of Art explaining techniques to me, or of other attachment professionals I had heard speak (especially Daniel Hughes, PhD). Then before I knew it, I was just responding. In my gut I knew what to do and just did it.

Mastering the proper attitude was an essential tool to implementing the parenting techniques. Sure, the parenting book thoroughly outlined each technique, but unless done with the correct tone, it would not succeed. Many of us moms refer to this attitude as "Tour Guide Barbie." It was important for my son not to misinterpret any of our interactions. He needed to see me as unconditionally loving in order to heal. Essentially, I just never let any of the child's negativity stick to me. Every exchange, every verbalization was upbeat, engaging, and above all optimistic. I simply talked like I was thrilled

Tone is key in implementing a healing PLACE. "How" you do things is often just as important, and sometimes more so, than the "what" you do. Being accepting, curious, and empathic are essential to helping such a child heal.

The parent becomes a master at emotional judo, never allowing the child to control the relationship by making the parent angry or allowing for the creation of a punitive and harsh relationship. The rhythm and tone are kept healthy and set by the parent.

It is so important not to allow the child to push you away or to create emotional distance. Because of the early maltreatment and how this affects the development of internal working models, many times these children will try to recreate relationships that are similar to those in the orphanage or with the maltreating parents.

to be with him, and as if I knew he was going to do exactly what I requested.

Noncompliance was met with a mere shrug and the mantra-like response of "No problem, honey." No problem for me that is, but plenty of natural learning opportunities for him. I became an expert at doling out natural consequences. Punishment was taboo, as it would only serve to further the gap between my son and me. Rather than punish, I would establish myself as his ally and empathize with the consequences he imparted onto himself. I would express understanding regarding his desires, and confidence that he would soon get strong enough to make choices that would bring these to him. Always with an element of kindness, I would enforce the consequences like a well-trained drill sergeant.

Attunement, play, the dance of attachment or whatever you want to call it is an essential ingredient to helping a child resolve attachment disorder. For many children, it is as difficult as learning to be polite and respectful. Many children are terrified at the idea of trusting a parent enough to play and have fun with them. Fortunately this was a relatively positive area for my son. I greatly enjoyed the attunement piece. Being a craft person, I had oodles of what my husband called "junk" that could be used to create all kinds of interesting things. Dima, being very creative himself, desired to use these materials with me.

This is the essence of attunement.

I became very adept at gauging Dima's reactions and needs, much as the mom of an infant learns her child's cries and mood states. I would provide the regulation of emotion that my son needed, but was unable to provide for himself; again, much like a parent would for an infant. Gradually Dima matured in his ability to self-manage his own emotional states. Helping Dima to label and understand his feelings was another key component of therapeutic parenting. Fortunately, Dima provided many opportunities to address emotional develop-

What Karen is describing is the reflective function. By reflecting back to Dima his experiences and affect, Dima came to understand himself. He began to develop a coherent narrative by seeing himself reflected in Karen's eyes.

ment, especially negative emotions! My son truly saw everything he felt as "mad." Dima was not able to differentiate other emotional states. Another helpful tip was the advice of our first attachment therapist to "think out loud." Dima had not developed cause-and-effect logic in his early life.

He did not understand that when I instructed him to hold my hand when crossing the street, it was because a car could hit him. I had to speak out all of this to help fill in the holes of his early experiences.

We also engaged in many of the Theraplay® games taught in a previous therapy. Theraplay games promote eye contact, touch, respect, following rules, and being nurtured. I was able to take these basic Theraplay concepts and incorporate them into general play with my son. For example, when pushing him on the swing, I would stand in front of him rather than behind, promoting eye contact. I would engage in playful tickling as he would swing toward me. We purchased a hammock and net swing that we could use together to further promote nurturing. I found combining these games with the Anita Thomas parenting program heightened the benefit of both. Of course, without the therapy component my son would likely not have gone very far in his recovery.

As previously outlined, structure is provided for safety. Structure acts to contain the child in a safe and secure setting. Attunement, the reflective function, and nurturing heal.

Therapy opens up the child and addresses the underlying trauma so that a coherent sense of self and autobiographical narrative can develop. Giving meaning to the past and connecting it to the present are elements of therapy.

Reading everything I could get a hold of on attachment greatly helped with understanding my son and how to parent him. I took the low-budget approach and ordered most of the books through my local public library. Most libraries have an interlibrary loan program and can search across the state for a book you are interested in. Over the years I have also purchased many books for my own personal library and often loan these out to other parents. Some material is also available in video form for the more electronic learners.

My background in behavior modification was both a hindrance and a blessing. For years prior to adopting my son, I had seen great success in the use of structured behavior plans with adults and children diagnosed with mental retardation. When my son first started to have problems, I put on the old behavior-specialist hat and went right to work. Before we had hit the first therapist's office, I already knew that reinforcement alone was not going to help my son's behavior. Dima could con a token plan for as long as it suited him, creating a false sense of success, and then just as quickly prove to you that nothing indeed had changed. I had to throw all those years of work-related success out the window and recognize the need to start anew. I had to accept that despite my training and experience, I knew nothing about what was going on with my son. I was failing miserable in the power-struggle war with my son.

Our bedtime tooth-brushing and medication regime best exemplifies the style I used to circumvent power struggles. Prior to bedtime, Dima would dish out his finest noncompliance and refuse to take his asthma medication or brush his teeth. I was eager to try out my new skills. Come evening, Dima, as expected, refused to complete his bedtime routine. A probably too-happy mom assured him this was "no problem, as I stay up quite late and will be happy to wake you up in an hour." One hour later, Dima was awakened and groggy, but still resolved to win this battle. Again I said, "No problem honey. I don't plan on going to bed yet. I can wake you up in an hour." By midnight I was pretty groggy myself. Keeping up the "Tour Guide Barbie" routine was getting tough; I just wanted to go to bed. Fortunately, Dima caved *in, took his medicine, brushed his teeth, and went to bed. Never again did he balk past the first awakening. Generally speaking, I found my groggy child was quite motivated to comply so that he could go back to bed.*

My behavior-modification background was also helpful. I was already well-versed at planned ignoring, so I could pull this off quite well when playing "Tour Guide Barbie." Let me tell you, it's no easy feat to act calm when your seven-year-old is peeing all over your kitchen floor (I had quickly learned to stand my ground on linoleum, not carpet). I learned to welcome these as learning opportunities and the chance to get my entire kitchen floor expertly mopped by my child. I also learned that part of the essence of the parenting attitude is to always remember that the nastier my child is, the more he has been hurt in the past. I made myself see the cries for help in Dima's aggression and defiance. On a side note, the most important thing I learned about enuresis is that vinegar does wonders in cutting the urine odor (so strong in older children). I put a bucket of water in the bathtub with a few cups of vinegar in it for my son to rinse out his sheets and pajamas.

Interesting was the realization that I was indeed doing behavior modification with my son. Granted it was nothing you would find in a traditional text, but if you look at the basic definition of reinforcement principal, it applies to attachment work. Once I understood that my son had an altered view of the world, and once I thoroughly understood things from his perspective, then I was able to apply reinforcement principals based on his template. I had failed previously because I assumed my son was like all other kids, and I reinforced him like all other kids. Indeed, my son was not rewarded by time with me, by trinkets, or by stickers. He was reinforced by power and control. So when I disciplined him and would show my anger or disapproval, I was actually rewarding the very behavior I was trying to stop. He wanted to control my emotions and me. As long as he had the power to get me angry, sad, or upset, then he won. He won no matter what else happened.

During attachment therapy, we attempted to use wrap-around supports so that a TSS (therapeutic staff support) could work with my son for a few hours a day and give me a break. We quickly found out that this was not going to work. The poor TSS was way out of her league and putty in the hands of my 7¹ᐟ²-year-old son. I still think the nature of a wrap-around program has a lot of merit in supporting families parenting children with RAD. But it would take highly trained staff to achieve this.

The Role of Parenting Partners

Oftentimes, attachment therapists will state that the primary parent is the one that needs to do the attachment work with the child. The other parent is mainly there to support the therapeutic parent. While I agree with this, I feel the parenting partner should be involved in the treatment process. Unless both parents get to hear the input of the therapist firsthand, things can get lost in translation. Developing the proper attitude is a very difficult task and all but impossible for some without a therapist's guidance. Both parents deserve the benefit of firsthand support from the therapist. Having both parents present in the therapist's office can provide considerable mileage in undermining a child's efforts at triangulation.

The primary therapeutic parent will feel more supported and understood when their partner takes an interest in being present for treatment. Nothing can tear a relationship apart as quickly as parenting a child with Reactive Attachment Disorder. These children prey on any weakness and are experts at pitting one adult against another. Often they only permit the primary parent to see the depth of their pathology. The other parent sees a darling little angel, and may become critical of their partner. Having both parents on the same page can be a challenge. Resentment can build very quickly when one parent bears the burden of not only managing the pathology but also of resolving it.

In some ways, however, I probably had things easier than my husband. Dima was obsessed with me. He followed me around the house and wanted to be in control of everything I did. Initially Dima had no interest in a father. When with his father, he insisted that Dad do everything exactly as I did. Dima would rage when Dad handled something differently. He absolutely never gave Dad a chance. As our son started to heal, we would set up situations for him to desire being alone with Dad. Initially it would be a trip to McDonalds with Dad or to the park. To this day, Dima still tends to want things done Mom's way, but more like a typical child. There is no longer an obsessive quality to it.

Even though I was off work for five months and home all day, I most definitely did not have time to care for my home as I had in the past. Essentially I did have a job. A job that required me to be my most professional, most therapeutic self. I had to maintain this ability for 15 hours or more each day. I thought being home with my son would give us time to do all of the fun things a working parent never has time to do with their child. I imagined home-cooked meals, baking cookies together, and flowers—not weeds—in my garden. Instead, while I did get to do a lot of fun things with my son, I was emotionally and intellectually drained by the time he went to bed each night. By the way, the kitchen floor did sparkle, while dust bunnies and cobwebs abounded elsewhere. While I had no time to clean, my son loved to pee out his anger and spent many an afternoon moping up my floor!

Parenting a child with Reactive Attachment Disorder is likely to bring out emotions you never thought you would be capable of feeling. It is NOT unnatural for parents of such a challenging child to feel intensely negative emotions toward their child, to wish they had never parented that child, to wish they could ship their child elsewhere. Many parents, at times, have an overwhelming desire to just give up. And all of this then brings on an enormous sense of shame and guilt. After all, parents imagine, I must be some sort of monster to not be able to love my own child. It's common for parents to question their own abilities and parenting skills, despite successfully parenting their other children.

Karen's ability to be open about this was a significant factor in helping treatment move more quickly. The more open a parent can be, the more the parent can use the relationship to explore his/her own thoughts and feelings and family-of-origin issues, and the more easily the parent can implement effective attachment-facilitating parenting methods.

As the parent is better able to do this, so too does the child become better able to do this.

What compounds the pain of parenting such a child is that many times we do indeed make major parenting blunders. We take the bait and take our child's behavior personally. How do you not, when the child you want so much to love is hurling insults, cursing at you, and meets your gaze with an intense look of hatred in their eyes?... a child that never, ever lets you get close, unless it's in public and they want to con? Our children are experts at making us look like the monsters when others are around to observe. Our child can embrace us in a hug. People see a sweet child, hugging their mother. Mom sees the glare in their eyes and feels the chin drill into her shoulder. We get the real kid; the outside world gets the con.

Every parent of a child with Reactive Attachment Disorder whom I have met admits to engaging in discipline tactics they are ashamed of. Many believe they are horrible parents, because sometimes they have reacted in what they perceive to be horrible ways. This compounds the guilt of not feeling love or connection with your child. As a parent, in order to move forward and heal, we have to make peace with ourselves. We have to realize that we are parenting a child who is a pro at pushing buttons. Many of our children could turn Mahatma Gandhi or Mother Theresa into a raving lunatic. We all have our past; we all have our buttons. Our kids survived their early lives by becoming proficient in the study of people. They know what our buttons are before we do. And push them, they do. A key component to parenting a child with RAD is to learn to avoid the battles, to avoid being pushed over the edge, and never to take your child's behavior personally.

Anxiety Disorder, Depression, and Post-Traumatic Stress Disorder are commonly diagnosed in parents of children with Reactive Attachment Disorder.

What makes RAD more challenging than many other behavioral disorders is the often complete lack of connection with one's child. Parents of other children generally get to feel the reciprocity of love. Maybe not all the time, but at least occasionally they will get a glimpse of true love from their child. This is usually absent or a con in children who have RAD. A parent has to face these challenges with a child who has never let them bond, never let them have a sense of connection. Love is definitely a one-way street when parenting a child with RAD. It is very difficult indeed to keep oneself in love with another being whose main goal in life is to destroy any semblance of affection.

Many parents have to play the "Tour Guide Barbie" act and face the intense challenges of the parenting program for a child they are not yet able to love. These parents are the true unsung heroes and have my utmost admiration. I am a lucky one. I had a good first year with my son, a year in which I felt intense love for him, and felt loved by him. (Even though it was a con, I did not perceive it to be at the time). I had a lot of good memories to hang onto during the rough early months of treatment.

Parents of children with significant behavioral difficulties rarely find themselves supported by others. They feel like they are always under a microscope and blamed for their child's problems. Quite often neighbors, fellow church members, school personnel, family, and even friends feel they could do a much better job parenting this child. These folks may feel they are showing empathy and understanding, but I can tell you that a parent of RAD will see right through all that to the blame and criticism. Since we are already blaming ourselves, we are even more sensitive to the perceived blame of others.

Often the well-meaning advice of others is even more hurtful. When we seek support and talk about our kids, many try to normalize what we are saying. I could scream every time someone echoes, "Oh, that's normal; all kids do that." One time I casually commented to a coworker that my son was quite the snot over brushing his teeth the previous evening. When she commented one time too many that all kids do that, I shot back with, "Wow, I didn't realize all kids go into an hour-long rage, physically attack their mothers, and try to kick out a TV set over a request to brush their teeth." I guess she did get it, because after that I felt much more supported when we talked. As parents of such challenging children, we probably should take the time to help family and friends truly understand, before snapping at them as I did. But not all people are open to seeing, believing, or understanding this information. They see a sweet child and find it impossible to believe otherwise.

Then there is the helpful advice-giver. I find this most annoying from professionals who feel they know more about parenting children than the parent does. Often in a patronizing tone, they will try to explain basic parenting principles designed for typical kids. Like I hadn't been there, done that already. Many parents find this quite insulting, as if the advisee feels they could parent our child better. The funny thing is, these same people never offer to take our kiddos for a while and give us a break. I provide myself a fantasy release by imagining the well-meaning advice-giver handling my child for just one hour. Again these people do not mean to be hurtful. They are usually genuine in their desire to be helpful. But to the parent wracked with guilt and self-blame, our sensitivity is heightened.

Usually our children are very well-behaved with others—so well-behaved that it's obviously fake to the parent, but the rest of the world is pretty oblivious to this. They see such a wonderfully charming child that it truly is hard for them to even begin to imagine the horrors that we live with on a daily basis. The things our kids do are beyond imagination. Before parenting a child with Reactive Attachment Disorder, I never would have imagined a healthy child peeing themselves at will or painting their bedroom walls with feces. It is incomprehensible to most that a child could actually kill a large dog with their bare hands, terrorize siblings, or attempt to stab a family member. And yet these are everyday realities in the household of a child with RAD.

Is it any wonder that the parents living in such a war zone end up needing treatment for depression, anxiety, and Post-Traumatic Stress Disorder? It is not that these parents had something wrong with them to begin with. This is what happens to perfectly healthy people in horrible situations. Is it any wonder that many of our marriages end in divorce, and long-term friendships and relationships with family fail?

There is nothing lonelier than parenting a child with Reactive Attachment Disorder. Parents of children with RAD desperately need to connect with other parents in the same shoes. It is all but impossible to fully understand the devastation of this disorder until one has lived with it. During those early days of treatment, I was able to participate in a group facilitated by my son's attachment therapist. I cannot stress enough the value of sitting in the same room with other parents who intimately understand what you are feeling and going through. Until parents are able to comfortably voice fears and worries, those emotions may choke their therapeutic parenting efforts.

Parents can check online for an attachment therapist or support groups in their area by going to www.ATTACh.org. The links from this site can lead one to a wealth of attachment resources from credentialed therapists and agencies to parent support groups. One of my favorite sites is our therapist's site: www.Center4FamilyDevelop.com. There are some great parent e-support groups at sites such as www.thelittleprince.org and www.forums.adoption.com. Some sites have chat rooms and discussion boards open to the general public. Others are restricted to a registered audience, offering some protection to their members. For those who have adopted from Eastern Europe, a good site with many e-lists is www.eeadopt.org.

I participate on several adoption and attachment support lists and find them to be of great value. You can choose to have individual e-mails sent to you (sometimes dozens per day), or have them arrive bundled several at a time. A parent can post a concern or success story on a list and, within a few hours to a few days, have dozens of replies from parents all over the globe. E-support has the benefit of providing immediate relief. Just typing out your concern and knowing help is on the way is cleansing. I also find it helpful for me to provide advice to others. In typing out my replies to their posts, I better formulate and understand the issues myself.

The downside to posting on Internet sites is that your material is available to anyone having access to that list or site. Most choose a pen name to post under to preserve the anonymity of their family and especially their child. Remember, what you are posting is not always complimentary and might not be something you want your mother-in-law or next-door neighbor to know you are writing. Internet groups occasionally experience phenomena of negativism. It seems to be human nature to look at a computer screen and forget that your words go to real live people with feelings and sensitivities. Readers sometimes misinterpret what others have written. Many lists are moderated to help keep this under control. Generally I have found that list-mates work through their misunderstandings to clarify feelings and the posters' intentions. As a participant in e-lists, I find them highly valuable. You come to know the personalities and quirks of individual posters. For many people, electronic support is the only access they have to parents facing the same issues they are. It is important, however, not to immerse yourself into a computer screen at the expense of connections with real, live, soft, and huggable people.

The last type of support I would like to comment on is that of conference support. There are a wealth of conferences to attend on a variety of attachment topics. Initially, I craved information on Reactive Attachment Disorder and other issues related to neglect. Attending a conference provided a nice break away from my son and helped me master the attitude and techniques essential to his healing. Even better, I met many parents, live and in person. I found I did best interacting and mingling when traveling alone to a conference. Parents of children with RAD must have an aura, because we never seem to have any difficulty finding each other. The most dynamic of all conferences is one sponsored each fall by ATTACh (Association for Treatment and Training in the Attachment of Children). In a four-day whirlwind, you can meet hundreds of parents and attachment professionals. In addition to dozens of seminar choices, there are social activities woven into each conference. It is the ultimate experience in knowledge and support I have yet to encounter. Information on the next ATTACh conference can be found at www.ATTACh.org.

Another benefit of attending conferences is the dramatically growing basket of tricks I am developing. Even things that don't work with my son are thrown in there. It may be of benefit to another parent I meet some day. I *see myself as a collector of "tidbits." I love to take little pieces of information and add them to what I already understand. If it doesn't fit, or make sense, I still keep that tidbit. Someday, I may gather another piece that suddenly helps that piece fit into place. The attachment field is a very young field. The knowledge base is growing by leaps and bounds.*

To anyone reading this book who is part of the support network of someone parenting a child with Reactive Attachment Disorder, I say "thank you." Thank you for caring enough about the child's parent to read this material and try to understand. Join your loved one at support groups or read the online posts to further develop your understanding and empathy. Above all, trust what the parent is saying, trust his/her pain. Your support of the parent is the best thing you can do to help that parent's child heal. Your simple acceptance and understanding can renew the parent's strength for yet another day.

Dima's Perspective on Treatment

As I am in the process of writing this, Dima turns 12 years old. He completed therapy with Art, and resolved his Reactive Attachment Disorder 3^1/2 years ago. This section is written by Dima himself.

I don't remember much about my life in the orphanage. I don't know what happened, but for some reason I developed attachment disorder and bipolar disorder. My life was not good before getting help with these. I would steal things and didn't care about other people. I thought it was fun to lie. It was a lot of fun to get my mom upset and get my dad aggravated. If I didn't get what I wanted, I would have a hairy fit.

I remember my first attachment therapist. He would grab me, annoy me, and make me mad. I don't think he helped me. He actually probably made it worse. I really hated him. Then I went to someone who did Theraplay® with me. Theraplay was a lot of fun. I really liked this guy and going to therapy. I think it helped me somewhat with my attachment disorder. But I only felt a little bit safe with my parents. I still felt like I was a rotten kid, and I was afraid my mom would leave me. I really didn't care if my dad was around.

At my first appointment with Dr. Art, I had to draw a stupid picture. I laugh now when I think about my dilemma with my sneakers and Michael, my monkey puppet. I wasn't going to let Dr. Art tell me what to do, so I wouldn't put my sneakers where he told me. It made me mad that I couldn't get him angry. I had to go home in my socks and earn money to buy my sneakers back. Another time I took Michael with me and kept squeaking him in Dr. Art's ear. I was doing it on purpose to try and annoy him. But it didn't work and then Dr. Art took Michael and put him in a desk drawer. Next time I was afraid to ask for him back, but Dr. Art asked if I wanted him and I got him back.

In the beginning I thought Dr. Art was ugly and mean. I only went because my mother made me go. I tried to annoy Dr. Art and make him mad. I thought therapy was a waste of time. I would just make things up to try and shut him up. I had no interest in learning how to love my mother. What really made me mad about Dr. Art was that he had me figured out.

Dr. Art was not like the first attachment therapist. He let me know what he was going to do. He didn't just grab me. Dr. Art didn't force me into a hold and didn't restrain me. He didn't force me to talk about things I didn't want to hear. When I lay in Dr. Art's arms, it felt more like he was keeping me safe.

At first, I thought Anita Thomas was a rude lady to make little children do all that stuff. I hated the parenting things my mom did at home. I didn't want to do things the way Mom was asking because I wanted to do it my own way. I thought that everything my mom said was a waste of time. I thought that what Mom was asking didn't make sense and I didn't trust her enough to do it. Now I think Anita Thomas is a nice lady. I got to meet her at the ATTACh conference in Pittsburgh. I felt nervous meeting her because she knows all about attachment disorder, and I didn't know what to expect. I felt proud telling her that I didn't have attachment disorder any more.

When things started to change, I felt like my heart inside of me was getting warmer. My feelings changed about Dr. Art too. Now I like him and admire him. I think what he has done for me is very good. I finished therapy, and I feel good now. I can actually admit that I have anger and handle my anger better. Now I know what it feels like to love. I feel safe and loved by my parents.

Without therapy I am afraid that my life would be very bad. I am afraid that I might have killed my mom and dad. Before, I thought I was a rotten kid. Now I think I'm a pretty good kid. I have a lot of interests and friends. I'm good at music. I want to be a teacher when I grow up.

School Issues While in Therapy

During those early, critical months of therapy my son was out of school. Dima was home with me 24/7, living in a world totally focused on relationship issues and healing. He had very little contact with the distractions of the outside world in those early months. Despite my son's being in second grade at the time, getting the school to accept this plan and provide a tutor was no problem. Simply presenting a letter of recommendation from Dima's therapist, signed off by his pediatrician, was all it took to get an approval. I've yet to hear a parent of a disruptive child say that the school resisted a plan to get their child treatment, and thus be out of the school for a while.

Once my child returned to school, he did well. We started him back in slowly, one class at a time. Dima initially regressed and struggled with being away from me, but then adjusted and settled in. In all, my son was out of school full time for four months, and it took an additional two months to get him back up to full-time status. One thing to be aware of is that once a child starts back to school for even one class, they are no longer eligible for a tutor. Fortunately Dima returned to school a little ahead of his class. While he had only received tutoring for five hours per week, it was all individualized instruction. Dima was so eager to have this connection with the outside world that he gave me no difficulties over completing the homework he was assigned.

Another key to Dima's success in school is requesting the right teacher. I always request the benevolent dictator, the teacher who definitely knows she is in charge, and has an element of kindness to her approach. My son thrives in this type of academic atmosphere. He also had the benefit of an aide for three years following his recovery from RAD. Our school district assigns all aides as classroom support, not just for an individualized child. They are there to focus on the identified child when the need dictates, but otherwise work with the entire class. While everyone knew the aide was there for my son (including his peers), because the entire class benefited so much from her presence it was not stigmatizing for him. During the days when he was still attachment disordered, the aide deserved combat pay. She was wonderful at managing Dima's behavior and rages calmly and firmly. I think his peers were sadder to see her go at the end of last year than he was. We started fading his aide out over two years. She started providing support in other grades to help weaken my son's dependence on her support. Dima has struggled a little in being more responsible for his own work, but overall has handled the weaning of his aide dependence remarkably well. This year, for the first time, my son attends school without the need for any aide support. We jokingly tease his aide for her demotion back to kindergarten!

I have found that it often takes until late winter for teachers to see the value of my advice. Until they have experienced some trial and error with my child, it is common for many to want to normalize his behaviors. Unless one has actually lived with a child who has RAD or attachment issues, understanding and interpreting our children's behavior is truly impossible. It is contrary to anyone's experience with other children. It is important to not blame the teachers and school for not understanding. Very few professionals have any formal training in the diagnosis or treatment of attachment concerns. Teachers are more likely to receive training in issues impacting many kids, rather than the issues of less than 1% of their school population.

My son has a 504 plan, which is similar to an IEP. A 504 is for kids who do not qualify for special education but have some needs to be addressed. Dima's plan is mainly to address some related disabilities, rather than his mental health needs. I request a late-spring transition meeting to discuss how his plan is working and to fine-tune it. We meet with the current teachers and try to include the following year's teachers. This provides an opportunity for the current teachers to discuss what has succeeded with them and adds some validation to my requests for the next year. I offer the upcoming teachers information regarding my son's multiple diagnoses.

I no longer make copies of packets with articles about all of his pertinent diagnosis, as I had in the younger grades. Experience taught me that many teachers did not look at the articles or value what they had to offer. I now send out a brief letter outlining my son's basic diagnosis and how they impact his schooling and offer to forward more information at the teacher's request. This is followed up with a late-August meeting to review my son's 504 plan just prior to the new school year.

This year is the first time (6th grade) that I did not mention my son's mental health concerns with his teachers, at the principal's urging. While I am not comfortable with this lack of disclosure of some very important information, I am respecting the principal's judgment. It is important to recognize that not all people, including professionals, do well with the knowledge that someone has a mental illness. My son now needs to interact with a team of teachers rather than just one. I have chosen instead to fully inform his main teacher, hoping the others will come to him if they see concerning behavior in my son.

A Word About Co-Morbid Diagnoses and Its Impact on Treatment

Most of the children I hear about who have Reactive Attachment Disorder seem also to collect an alphabet soup of other diagnoses. In the circles of children with a history of orphanage placement, we often talk about a complex of diagnoses, which could be called a Post-Institutionalization Syndrome. Many of these issues are also common in children who have experiences profound neglect early in life.

Often other mental health concerns complicate the diagnosis and treatment of Reactive Attachment Disorder. The chronic neglect and often accompanying abuse that lead many children to develop attachment complications, can lead to a comorbid diagnosis of Post Traumatic Stress Disorder. These children will neurologically link often benign things with their past trauma (perhaps their abuser always wore a certain cologne). Unknown to their adoptive or foster parents, the child will suddenly melt down or dissociate when exposed to this same item. It can be very difficult to differentiate the PTSD reaction from the behavior seen with Reactive Attachment Disorder. Other commonly found comorbid diagnosis include anxiety disorders and childhood depression.

My son was born with the genetic predisposition to Bipolar 1 Disorder. I believe this made him more vulnerable to the impact of neglect. This is not to say that he has bipolar disorder because he was neglected. Bipolar disorder comes as a result of inheritance, much like diabetes, not from neglect. My son was born with a medical susceptibility, which made him more likely to develop RAD and other disabilities associated with neglect (this is a personal hypothesis).

Having untreated bipolar disorder greatly impacted Dima's therapy. Until the mania was under control, he made very little progress. Dima's bipolar manifested itself as a rapid cycling mixed state. His mood was all over the place, especially when he was younger. In a young child, it's almost impossible to differentiate depression from mania from RAD behaviors. I did reach the point where I could differentiate them, but it was more of an art than a science! Once I accepted the bipolar diagnosis and the need to use medication, Dima started to make dramatic progress in therapy. Six months later he was stable enough to complete attachment therapy.

Many children suffering from the legacy of neglect seem to have difficulties with sensory processing. Understanding your child's sensitivities is important to attachment work. A child who is tactilely defensive may find light tough repulsive. Attunement activities that involve such touch will be counterproductive. My son will calm considerably when held in a snug cuddle. To this day he's what we call a "deep-pressure kid." He craves intense input, which has a calming influence on his body. The firmer the hug, the better. We chose to wait until my son completed attachment therapy to start working with an occupational therapist specializing in Sensory Integration. Other parents have had good success with completing OT first, or along with attachment therapy.

A good Sensory Integration-based occupational therapy program will help a parent develop a sensory diet of activities and experiences geared toward the child's individual needs. My son's OT also helped me to understand things like Dima's intense need for oral stimulation. This was actually an asset with attachment parenting. My son desperately wanted the stimulation that drinking from a bottle could provide him. But at his RAD finest, he also wanted to be in control of the bottle. He would attempt to engage in a power struggle to keep me from holding the bottle and thus nurturing him. I simply stood my ground and insisted that the only way he could get the bottle was if I held it. His desire for the oral input won out over his desire to control.

My understanding of sensory integration helped me to create attunement opportunities in which Dima would want to engage. I knew Dima needed cuddle time with me. I never forced this; instead I would sit on the couch with a bottle of milk and wait him out. Dima's turmoil was so obvious. He would pace, approaching and retreating. He was so torn, and it was painful to witness his internal struggle. But Dima's desire to have the bottle would eventually win out over the fear of letting me nurture him. Cuddle time gave me the opportunity to provide the deep pressure input his body needed and the oral stimulation he craved in a wonderfully attuning manner.

The Journey Continues: There is Life After RAD

Developing life after resolving RAD is a gradual process. Just as it takes months, maybe years for a child to heal, it will take many ongoing years for the legacy of neglect to lesson its impact. I'm not sure any child who has significant trauma in his past can have that all simply erased and go on to live life like his more typical peers. I can accept that those first years in Russia will mark my son for life. But that does not mean he's destined to struggle for life. This should not be read with a pessimistic tone, for my intent is to be honest while inspiring optimism. There is life after RAD.

A part of what made transitioning to life after treatment so hard is that nothing is written on this topic. I had many materials to guide me on the journey to resolution, but nothing to guide me into the life of a healed child. I was certain that typical parenting would set my son up for failure, but also sure he no longer needed the intense structure of attachment parenting.

Initially I found it hard to lose that weekly connection with my son's attachment therapist. Art had become my lifeline. While confident in knowing how to handle my son, I was still hesitant to accept that his RAD really could be fully resolved. RAD had controlled so many years of our lives that it was hard to imagine my son being stable for long. But as Dima gradually came to see that he was now different, so did I. And thanks to modern technology, Art is just an e-mail away!

It was also difficult to initially believe that the change in my son was permanent. I kept waiting for the raging to resume. I would hold my breath when he started to get upset. But then I started to notice something that was not obvious to me at first. My son was dramatically different now after a shaming experience. In the RAD days, I would immediately know if he had a bad day at school by his distancing and hostile behavior toward me. Now, if my son struggles with a shaming experience, he is more likely to ask to cuddle or to have a bottle. He turns to me for help, rather than pushing me away.

I have learned to look at Dima's behavior as having multiple layers, much like an onion. On the outside layer is all of the "stuff" typical for his age. When Dima is acting out, I first ask myself, "Is this pretty typical for a 12-year-old?" Many kids at this age start to get a bit mouthy and cocky. While Dima does this, in reality it is less than his peer's parents report. The benefits of the highly structured attachment parenting do pay off into adolescence as our children have better developed abilities to respect adults. Also natural for *a child this age is to start distancing from their parents, and move more toward his peer group. For Dima this is difficult, due to the RAD scar tissue. Recognizing both layers helps us both to move through this normal developmental phase with more ease.*

If I have peeled away the first layer, and ruled out typical childhood issues as the cause of Dima's behavior, then I move onto the second layer. I ask if what Dima is experiencing is typical for many children who are adopted. Dima just had his 12th birthday. For several days leading up to his birthday, Dima was mopey and irritable. Since resolving his attachment disorder, Dima has been freed to think about his birth mother and incorporate the loss of her into who he is. Birthdays, Mother's Day, and sometimes other holidays can be a time to reflect on the lost family. It is a painful, but healthy experience during the journey from adopted child to healthy adult. Dima needs my nurturing and understanding during these times, not discipline and punishment (although natural consequences still have their place). Dima has a pretty box that he uses to collect things in for his birth mom. He makes or buys her cards. He puts in school papers he is proud of. This year, Dima and I have started to write a summary of his previous year, a computer-drafted text and clip art memory of his previous year. One copy is for his Lifebook, the other for his birth mom. Dima talks about wanting to meet her, "once I am grown up." Most important is that Dima and I are not afraid to label his pain and talk about his birth mom.

The final layer I look at when interpreting Dima's behavior is through the lens of disability. Sensory processing deficits can lead to a variety of behavior. Dima's noncompliance in doing homework could just be that he is in sensory overload. Give him a 15-minute break to jump on the trampoline, take the dog for a walk (trust me, with our dog, this is an intense physical workout), or shoot basketballs, and it is amazing how compliant he becomes. Ongoing noncompliance, usually accompanied by a significant downward spiral of behavior and hostility, is a good indicator of mania. For Dima, the best solution to his current level of mania is isolation in his room until the medicine kicks in. It's amazing what a different child I have 30 to 60 minutes later.

I imagine that Dima will always be more sensitive than the average person. I often refer to this as his "RAD scar tissue." Dima still requires the presence of nurturing authority figures in his life. He struggles with a harsh or punitive teacher. But unlike the days of RAD, he now permits me to support him in these struggles. I imagine the dating years will be difficult for Dima. I have seen that the issues any child typically struggles with hit Dima much harder. We are helping Dima to link with naturally occurring resources, such as the guidance counselor at school, in the hopes that he will turn to these supports when he needs them. I jokingly comment that it'll take quite a woman to nurture Dima through a marriage. But the fact that I can visualize him getting married some day is testimony to just how far he has come.

My son still has bipolar disorder. Resolving his RAD has not cured this, nor should it be expected to. As he enters the preteen years and hormonal fluctuations, Dima has had periods of instability and needed medication adjustments common for this stage of life with bipolar. I am ever so grateful to be addressing the more mature mania and depression with a child who is attached. Dima sometimes has to go to his room and ride out the mania until his medication takes effect. With my firmness and insistence, he complies with my request to be by himself until he is able to manage some control over his behavior. Thank goodness I am only dealing with manic-driven manipulation and defiance. Not to undermine how difficult this is to manage, for it is indeed an intense struggle, but I shudder to imagine how much more difficult it would be in combination with RAD.

With ongoing parenting, I also had to recognize my own PTSD, or post-RAD parenting scar tissue. With the reemergence of mania, and the months of medication trials, we have had to manage some very challenging and difficult behaviors. I continue to struggle with accepting that this disorder may result in psychiatric placement if the medications cannot stabilize Dima. I have found myself less able to react and cope then I had when dealing with difficult behavior 24/7. Having a stable child for over three years and then going back to challenging behavior is extremely unsettling. This has nothing really to do with RAD; it is more the reality of life with a youth who has bipolar disorder. But I have also felt that PTSD-type flashback, that kick in the gut, that intense fear I felt four years ago when I feared my son would never get better. Again, reaching out for support, including therapeutic support when needed, is essential to parenting such high-maintenance children.

My son also still has intense sensory needs. Our daily routine is full of occupational therapy and physical therapy interventions from brushing and joint compressions to stretches and push-ups. Dima may not always be keen on completing these activities, but he has enough trust and faith in me to comply. Dima is still not a child to push himself when frustrated, something common with the legacy of neglect. Dima does, however, now have enough faith in me to respond to my encouragement and advice. Yes, he is still a 12-year-old and no little angel. But overall, Dima responds and listens to me better than the average child his age.

Dima is now able to handle the end of the school year in stride. Previously he would struggle with abandonment and loss issues a few months before school let out. Now he eagerly looks forward to the summer break, like any child his age. Dima has also managed with less structure during summer recess. While still attending more summer programming than the typical child, Dima does not need the daily activities of a few years ago. We have gradually reduced his attendance at camps and YMCA programs since he achieved attachment.

This year, I did learn not to push things too far. We planned for Dima to stay at his grandmother's from Tuesday through Thursday for six weeks in order to attend an occupational therapy handwriting camp. By the one-month mark, Dima was very irritable on the ride home. He needed attunement activities to reconnect with me. I started staying at grandma's at least one night with him to ease his way through the last few weeks.

Parenting after the resolution of attachment disorder involves a lot of give and take. I find myself approaching more typical parenting until I see signs of a struggle in Dima. Then I pull back and increase the nurturing and structure. Overall I continue to provide much more of the glue of connection than I would with a typical child. Perhaps that is a mistake; Dima simply needs what all kids need. He needs a mom who is loving, caring, playful, and a consistent authority figure in his life.

Dima is a great joy to be around these days (well, okay—he's 12!). Joking aside, I am able to enjoy my son more than the parent of a typical preteen does. Perhaps my son's sensitivities and need for connection with me contribute to our mutual enjoyment of each other's company. I look forward to watching his future unfold. I am confident now that Dima will be able to become whatever it is that he desires to be (for the moment that is to be a teacher). Whatever it is, he will be better at it than many, as a result of all he has already faced and overcome in his short 12 years.

Jody Walker's Story

When I first met Jody, her spouse, and their son, I have to admit I was a bit intimidated. She was a lioness who'd actively searched for help for her son and was not shy about moving on when it was clear that the treatment wasn't working. She'd done her homework and came with many questions about my background, training, and approach. She'd quickly question anything I didn't make clear. Certainly these are excellent traits and appropriate; it's just not what you see every day.

Their son had a truly horrific history and was very damaged by all he'd experienced. He was a closed, withdrawn, passive-aggressive, withholding child. In other words, he was scared. As I worked with him and his parents began to see the scared, hurt, very sad little boy inside, their empathy and ability to be attuned with him increased dramatically. I remember Jody saying to me after a session, "I can't believe it. He actually looked like a two-year-old for a while. That poor little boy, what he had to go through—my heart really bleeds for him."

Jody's openness in therapy and my ability to enter into both primary and secondary intersubjective states with her son and her helped her do the same with him. As she felt supported, understood, and that I had empathy for her, she increasingly did the same for her son. In addition, this allowed Jody to feel safe and secure enough to be open about herself, her past, and how this was affecting her, and to question my work. This openness in our relationship allowed both of us to help her son.

Now, nearly five years later, I am awed when I see Jody and her family. Her son is a delightful young man, soon to finish high school and enter the military. His grades are outstanding, he has friends, loves his family, is able to share and express emotion, and has deep and authentically meaningful relationships. I am deeply honored that I had the opportunity to be a part of Jody's journey with her family.

My Adopted Daughters

My journey to adoption was an easy step to take because adoption was not a foreign concept to me. I always wanted to give a child a chance, and I always seemed to bring home all the oddball kids or the lost puppy dogs when I was a child. I just knew that I wanted a big family when I grew up, and if adoption could make that dream happen, then that would be an option for me.

I married in my early 20s. The marriage lasted less than two years, but during that time I adopted my husband's two daughters who were five and six. I couldn't have loved them any more if I had birthed them myself.

They did have a lot of behavioral problems. My older daughter would constantly lie, steal, and hit; she always wanted to be in control and would pit her father and me against each other. She wanted to be seen as the "woman of the house." She was very jealous of her little sister and very abusive toward her. She would break her sister's toys and say very demeaning, hurtful things. She did not like my being in her space. Her parental grandparents told her she didn't have to listen to me. This only complicated things more. This child was screaming on the inside for me to love her but was afraid I would leave her. I thought she was just going through an adjustment period and eventually everything would be all right. Heck, what did I know? I was only 24 and still a kid myself.

My younger daughter was very withdrawn, always quiet, shy, and hiding. She clung to me right way, almost like a frightened puppy. I would read to her at night and lie in bed with her until she fell asleep. She was a very fragile child and stole my heart immediately. I sensed she needed to feel I was a real mommy. It became apparent that her extended paternal family treated her differently from my older daughter. She was the spitting image of her birth mother. I felt that might have had something to do with the way she was treated by them; she was often pushed to the side and not spoiled like the older sister.

It wasn't until much later that I discovered that their father had physically, emotionally, and sexually abused both girls. They had definite attachment issues as well. All the signs were there, but neither the professionals nor I had the education at that time on Reactive Attachment Disorder. The girls were only being treated to help them through the trauma of the abuse.

My older daughter told the school and her paternal grandparents that I treated her badly and abused her. For a 6 ½ years old, she was pretty convincing with her accusations. She would claim that I starved her or made her sit in the corner for hours. It was hard for me to bond with her. Every time I would get closer to her, she would push me away. She only let her guard down when she was ill or very tired. This is when I would make my move to get into her heart. When she let me in, I could feel the natural bond taking place and the beautiful loving child within trying to get out. She made my heart melt every time she let me in.

She had a hard time sharing her father with me and would crawl into bed between us every night to keep me away from him. She would have him cuddle her and push me away. At first I thought it was sort of sweet, but after a while, I felt the adjustment time had passed and this child shouldn't be doing this anymore. There were many times that I slept on the couch because her father would not put her back to bed. This went on for at least the first six months of our marriage. At the time, I just thought this was all an adjustment period to having a new mom.

The writing was on the wall, and the marriage was over. It was a nasty, bitter divorce, and the custody battle took a toll on the girls. On one occasion their drunken father came into our home in the middle of the night and violated me. The police were called, and I tried to press charges; however, because we were not legally divorced, they viewed us as a married couple and could not arrest him for sexual assault. He did not hit me, but I had marks on my wrists from being held down by him. This was not considered assault at the time.

One officer had the nerve to say, "Ma'am, do you know how many husbands we would have to put in jail for coming home drunk and wanting to have relations with their wives?" I was furious and sick to my stomach at the same time. At that time there was no such thing as the date-rape law, and the state did not recognize the word "no" between a legally married couple. The police found him passed out in my bed. I begged them to get him out of the house. They woke him up and let him "sleep it off" in his truck that was parked in my driveway! This was devastating. Not only did he violate me, but now my girls had witnessed another act of violence. They saw firsthand how the police couldn't keep us safe.

On another occasion he came home drunk and starting breaking things. He started pushing me around like a rag doll. The children and I hid in their room under the bunk bed. He came into the room and ripped the television from the wall, stating we were not fit to have such nice things. The girls were terrified, and my younger daughter literally wet her pants. He smashed a few more things and then passed out.

We had just moved to a new state. It was the middle of winter, and I did not have a car, so it wasn't an option just to leave with the girls at that particular time. I was scared and needed to make long-range plans for our lives and safety. The girls and I climbed into the bottom bunk to calm down. The girls told me he would spank them a lot when I was working nights. They told me of his weird-smelling cigarettes and all the beer and the people he would have over. They were instructed not to tell me a thing or he would spank them again. He mentally manipulated my older daughter with mind games. He would tell her that she had to love him more because he was her real parent, and I would leave like her first mom did. The girls told me how they witnessed their father hit their first mommy and chase her into the bathroom. They remember her coming out of the bathroom and stabbing their father, result-ing in his fingertip being cut off. Their last memory of that night was Daddy, dripping blood all over the floor, a blood-soaked towel, and their mommy running out the back door into the darkness and never coming home.

Eventually, when I thought it was safe enough, I moved back to my home state to get away from him. The girls were back and forth between two states over the next five years during the divorce and afterward. I did gain full custody, but at a price. I now had two girls that were young teenagers and really having a hard time with bonding. Their aggression toward their birth mother was now showing and growing daily. They blamed her for the bad experiences in their lives, and they took it out on me. They both started pushing me away physically and emotionally. The stealing and lying started up again, and they tried to pit me and my new husband against each other.

My older daughter showed signs of sexual abuse. She cut her hair to look like a boy, ate anything she could get her hands on, and gained a lot of weight. She would openly masturbate in any room and had a strong vaginal odor (which turned out to be an infection). The doctors could not confirm how she obtained the infection or from whom. It was speculated to be assault. During counseling she denied any abuse by her father. The deeper you dug, the harder she defended him. She now stated that he never spanked her or mistreated her at all. She said I was the one abusing her.

Counseling seemed to help for a while, but I felt the therapy wasn't really getting through. It became even harder when our protection order against their father expired. He had accepted a plea, and the charges against him for violating the girls were knocked down to "neglect." He was granted visitation again through the courts. All the work I had put into keeping them safe after he hurt us was now being threatened. He had access to us again, and the girls' behavior took a turn for the worse. They didn't feel safe anymore. It became very hard to parent them.

Average parenting techniques like grounding, restricting privileges, or giving extra chores were not working with my older daughter. She became more defiant in therapy sessions but when she became very upset with her counselor, she would slip and talk about her father's abuse. She starting opening up on the sex abuse, but it was too late. Her father and grandmother gained custody of her, and my younger daughter was granted to me. The judge in her father's state would not accept documentation from our therapist unless she flew to their state and presented it herself. I could not pay for this to happen. All records were thrown out of court as a result. So my older daughter was returned to her father via court order at age 15. She stated that I was the abuser and convinced her father, grandmother, and judge that I was beating her. This was devastating to me, but my hands were tied. She eventually ran away from them, and I have not heard from her since.

My Adopted Sons

My younger girl stayed with me. She did well for the next few years. I remarried and found that I could not conceive, so adoption was the choice for building a family with my new husband. My daughter was fine with my adopting the little 10-year-old boy who came into our lives. She looked at him as if he were my husband's child. She felt that she was mine and didn't really have to share me, and she would stay Mommy's little girl. She was now 14 but very much a little girl emotionally—with the body of a 20-year-old young woman.

She appeared to bond with our son. He did not have Reactive Attachment Disorder, but had suffered a lot of abuse over the last 10 years of his life, and much of it was due to the foster-care system. They seemed to share the common bond of feeling unwanted and not fitting in. She started mothering him and did not feel threatened by his becoming a part of our family.

Things were going so well that we decided to add another child to our loving family. Our new son came to us at age 12. He had been in over 18 foster homes and three pre-adoptive homes. He was a victim of sexual abuse by his mother, father, paternal uncle, and paternal grandfather. He looked like a little old man, carrying the weight of the world on his shoulders. He was overweight and very sad inside. He required a lot of attention. He was jealous of our younger son and tried acting out sexually with him to get a rise out of me. He tried to get my husband and me to argue with him and each other. He would purposely ignore us and then do something sneaky. I had doubts about keeping him. He turned my entire house upside down.

After a year of family counseling to help the family blend, I felt we had everything under control. Things were running smoothly again. The therapist felt each child was feeling secure in his/her role in the family. The boys were getting along and doing well in school. My daughter seemed to adjust to the idea that she had to share me, and her grades were up. We felt like a happy, loving family. So we planned a big family trip to Disney World.

To say the least, it was horrible! My second son could not handle how happy everyone was. He would cause a disturbance whenever possible. I felt as if he were given a time-out at every trash can in Disney World (if not every can, at least every other!) It was the worse six days of my life and a vacation spot that I never wish to visit again. It was the trip from HELL!

After we came home, he was fine again. The therapist said it must have been too much excitement for my son, and he didn't know how to process it. Okay, so now I was feeling like the worst mom on the planet because I took my son to Disney World! She made me feel like I should have known that he couldn't handle it. I found a new therapist for him, and things smoothed out again.

Adding One More

Another year went by, and things were still going along great. We had the opportunity to adopt an infant girl and jumped at the chance. Life seemed like all my dreams were coming true—that is until a few days before the baby came home. My older son didn't say much about adding a new child to the mix, and my daughter was jealous over not being the only girl anymore. My younger son was head over heals in love with the idea of having a baby sister. He couldn't wait to bring her home. The therapist felt things would be fine after an adjustment period with the new baby. She thought the children were just handling their anxiety in different ways. She felt that we could go ahead with the adoption.

So we set up child care for the two days that we would be away to get the baby. The night before we came back home, my daughter ranaway. I came home with a new baby and had to track down a teenage run away. Things were complicated, and I felt that the therapist didn't take this issue as seriously as I did! Months went by with no word from my daughter. The baby was growing, my younger son was in heaven, and my older son was just going with the flow. Then the bottom dropped out!

My older son started showing aggression at school. This was odd for him because he was so good at putting on a show for the teachers. They all thought that he was such a good little boy. I knew his behavior needed special attention, and it wasn't all due to the baby. His therapist didn't seem to be helping. I started questioning if "I" was the problem because I fired so many counselors.

I heard about a doctor who was practicing a new form of therapy. I went to one of his workshops and was sold. I may not have understood everything he was saying, but he was describing my teenage daughter and older son to a T! I set up an appointment and started therapy for my son.

The therapy was hard for me at first. It went against all the traditional parenting methods and contradicted what we learned in foster-care classes. We were told in foster-care classes to always tell the child his birth family loves him. Now I had a therapist telling my son to look at the big picture to see what healthy love is. This therapist wondered aloud with my son whether it was love he had received in his birth home or abuse. At the time this rubbed me the wrong way. How dare it be implied that they didn't know how to love him properly. Every child should feel they were loved. Those were my feelings until I saw how my son started to feel better after processing his birth parents' treatment and lack of proper love. All during traditional therapy, he felt he did something wrong to make his birth family not love him properly and abuse him so badly. Now he had tools to see it wasn't him. Of course it still hurt him, but he was seeing the bigger picture and trying to make sense of it all.

I was also told to let the school handle "school" issues, and if he didn't get his homework done, it was his problem, not mine! I had a hard time with this and was resistant at first. It took me a few weeks to get with the program.

My son started acting out more as I began to learn how to parent him differently. He was loosing the battle of control and wasn't ready to give it up just yet. He was trying to learn new ways to get under my skin but was unsuccessful. His pent-up anger against his birth mother for not protecting him and sexually abusing him was coming at me full force.

His therapy also brought up my own baggage with the abuse I had suffered from my ex-husband. I guess I put that stuff on hold while I tried to get my kids healthy, and now it was slapping me in the face! I found myself relating to my children better because I fully understood how they could be fake and live day by day. Wasn't I doing the same thing by not addressing that I was a victim and that it doesn't just go away? You can hide things so deeply, and it may take a while for them to resurface, but boy when they come up, you feel like a truck has hit you!

During this time we got word from my daughter. She had been house hopping and telling stories to her hosts. We couldn't believe other parents would let this kid live in their homes and not contact us! Turns out she had them convinced that we abused her and she was afraid of me. The families felt they were "saving her." This kid was a great actress! She had everyone fooled for a while. When she outstayed her welcome, the parents started questioning her stories and then called us.

So now I had two children that I knew had Reactive Attachment Disorder. One was in treatment, and the other I was trying to get home so I could put her into treatment. My stress level was on overdrive, and to add to it my husband's new job now required him to travel out of state. The timing couldn't have been any worse! The cloud over me was getting darker and darker. It was harder to deal with each new day, but I had the baby to keep me going. I was definitely feeling depressed. I don't smoke or drink, so that wasn't going to be a way to release my stress. I began to take up remodeling projects. I was getting pretty good at it but then found myself starting and stopping many major projects. I just couldn't keep focused. I'd start painting one room and never finish but would start to paint another. It was crazy. I am usually a very well-organized person and keep things in control, but, wow, I had days when I didn't know who I was. This might sound a bit melodramatic, but this therapy was taking a toll on me emotionally and physically.

I dragged myself to take my son to therapy, but after I got there, I felt happy. I was actually being counseled as well, but may not have realized it at that time. I started to use the baby as part of my son's therapy. He fed her and played with her while I supervised. It helped him to fill the gaps that he missed as a child. I was teaching him to be a future good parent and sharing with him how he should have been treated. I could see that I was becoming the parent he needed, and it was also helping me be a better parent to my daughter from a distance. Things seemed to be getting back on track again. My heart was still broken that my daughter was not home, but at least I knew how to handle her when she tried to manipulate me. My son was really moving along well with therapy, and I started to see him truly begin to have "real feelings" for us and a bit of trust.

Did I say things were going along well? They were, until we found ourselves pulling away from extended family and friends. Many did not approve of our new parenting and thought this "attachment disorder" stuff was a bunch of hogwash. We had grandparents trying to undermine our parenting, so we took a break from seeing them. It killed me to do this, but I had to put my kids first. I still don't socialize with many of our "old crowd" and other family members. They don't seem to fit our new lifestyle, so that's just how it goes. I developed the attitude, "The hell with you; my kids come first."

My husband was quite another story. He had a harder time letting go. He did it, but sometimes falls back into the trap of thinking that the old friends and family will understand and things will get back to how they used to be. Or, our kids are fine now so we don't need to keep doing RAD parenting. I will be very blunt. If your spouse is not on board, then this therapy won't work to the fullest. I still have days when I do average parenting and then have to snap back into "RAD mom" mode. The kids start doing so well that I forget they had issues ... then they backslide. It's like a roller coaster. You go up, up, up, things look great, then ... bam, you start rolling down head first! You get the wind knocked out of you ... and then you start going up and up again.

It does get easier. You begin to see when your child is starting to resort back to old behaviors, and you nip it before the roller coaster has a chance to take the plunge. One of the hardest parts is finding the right therapist. You need to ask around and find someone who is experienced in this type of work. You also need to be willing to take the hour or two or three ride to get to that therapist.

School is another big issue. I chose to put my kids into a small Christian school to help them feel nurtured and so I could have more say about the care they received. Public school was not cooperating and only added to my stress. Home school was suggested, but that was not for me! I just couldn't do it for financial and personal reasons. I needed to work to feel like "me." I needed to have a break, and work was my stress release.

Taking care of myself was and still is a challenge, but I manage to find mental health. I did send my child to camp during the time he was in treatment. I had to, and I did it against my therapist's wishes. I needed those 10 days to sleep, regroup, refuel, and feel like me again!

I feel that all children with RAD will always have scars and will resort back to some old behaviors, even after their hearts have been healed. You as the parent will start to see the child spiral down and will need to get him back to the therapist for what I like to call a "tune-up!" My son has had a few "tune-ups" over the last five years. He worked through his issues in about three or four sessions, and we were sent on our merry way.

As long as you get the mind-set that your child will never be the "average" child, then you will be fine. "Average" children have not been violated sexually, beaten, and tossed from home to home. The average child doesn't have to worry about where his next meal will come from or who will be the caregiver. Our children come with baggage. It is our job to help them take their past and find a healing place to deal with it. No, I don't have "average" children, and I am not an "average" parent. Our family works very hard every day to stay connected and to work through the pain of the past.

Do I feel we are a great family? YES! Would I change a minute of the journey? Well, maybe a few steps. But the journey made my son a loving kid and made me a better parent. So I ask myself again, "Would I change anything?" The answer is NO!

Good luck to you on your journey to healing your child's heart. It is a hard road to travel, and many quit, but if you keep at it, you will find a good resting spot that will be more peaceful!

Okay, so by now you are wondering ... hey, what's going on with her son and daughter? I have not spoken to my daughter in over five years. I heard through the grape vine that I am now a grandmother to a little boy. My heart aches for her daily, and I have come to some realization that she may never come back, but I will not sit by and do nothing. I put ads in the little local paper to wish her "happy birthday" or say "hey, I love you,"–stuff like that. Even if she doesn't see it, a friend will, and it will get back to her. It also gives me peace of mind that I am being a good mom and not turning my back on my child. It is not my fault that she has RAD, and it is not her fault. It just is what it is.

If she called today and needed a place to stay, would I move her and my grandson in? No. I would look for alternative living arrangements for her. I have enough sense to know she is not the little girl I used to know. She is in her 20s now and has learned a lot of street smarts. Bringing her into my home would only disrupt the work I have done with my other children and may not be personally safe for any of us. She is a stranger now, someone we would have to get to know again. I can be a good RAD parent for her at a distance, and if I felt we could move forward with the relationship, then so be it.

My son will be graduating from high school this spring and has enlisted in the United States Air Force. He wants to become a pilot and also have police training. We are very proud of him. He hopes to retire from the Air Force and then work as a police officer. He is dedicated to helping children and does not want another child to suffer the way he did. Who knows, in a few years, he may be the pilot on your vacation flight or the cop who gives you that speeding ticket!

CHAPTER 11

Closing

JESSICA MROZ

"When children feel good about themselves, it's like a snowball rolling downhill. They are continually able to recognize and integrate new proof of their value as they grow and mature."
–Stephanie Martson, Magic of Encouragement

"In healthy families, a baby forms a secure attachment with her parents as naturally as she breathes, eats, and cries. This occurs easily because of her parents' bond with her. The bond guides her parents to notice her feelings and needs immediately and to respond sensitively and fully. Beyond simply meeting her unique needs, however, her parents 'dance' with her. Hundreds of times, day after day, they dance with her.

"There are other families where the baby neither dances nor even hears the sound of any music. In these families, she does not form such attachments. Rather, her task, her continuous ordeal, is to learn to live with parents who are little more than strangers. Babies who live with strangers do not live well or grow well.

"... It is the foster and adoptive parents who come to know and love these children who are leading the way. They are demanding that the professionals with whom they consult truly understand their kids. They also are expecting that their interventions make a difference. They have given their homes and hearts to these tragically isolated and unhappy children. The rest of us need to find ways to help them in their work." –Daniel A. Hughes, Building the Bonds of Attachment: Awakening love in deeply troubled children

Dyadic Developmental Psychotherapy is a unique approach for treating attachment and trauma problems in children, as well as a broad approach to the treatment of adults, individuals, couples, and families. Dyadic Developmental Psychotherapy was developed by Daniel A. Hughes, PhD in order to meet the complex treatment needs of children with serious emotional disturbances. Dyadic Developmental Psychotherapy provides therapists with the unique opportunity to assist traumatized children in forming secure attachments with their caregivers by using the parents as an active ingredient for their child's healing. Through Dyadic Developmental Psychotherapy, therapists are able to help parents and children replicate the parent-child dance in a healthy way that allows the child the ability to integrate his/her past experiences with those of the present and develop a coherent autobiographical narrative.

Those of us who contributed to this book have come from various backgrounds and experiences. Many of us have worked with children with trauma-attachment difficulties using other models and have found ourselves unable to reach many children using those methods. Universally, the therapists who contributed to this book have found that Dyadic Developmental Psychotherapy helps us reach children we could previously not help, frees us to use our self in the treatment that traditional methods frown upon, and help families heal and create healthy attachments with their struggling children. In this book, we share our experiences with Dyadic Developmental Psychotherapy so that other therapists working with these hard-to-reach children will have better access to these effective tools. We have described the development of Dyadic Developmental Psychotherapy, the theoretical background, the practice of Dyadic Developmental Psychotherapy in typical situations, practice with families in which the parent has a history of trauma, use of Dyadic Developmental Psychotherapy with children in alternative placements, and the therapist's use of self. We have also dedicated an entire chapter to describing effective methods to parent children with attachment-trauma problems. There is a chapter providing resources, including useful books for professionals, parents, and children, and we also have a chapter written by three parents about their experiences. This book is a comprehensive description of Dyadic Developmental Psychotherapy and how it applies to working with children with attachment-trauma problems.

DYADIC DEVELOPMENTAL PSYCHOTHERAPY AND RESEARCH

While those of us using Dyadic Developmental Psychotherapy in our practices know based on our clinical experiences that the treatment model works and children are attaching and healing, solid research documenting its effectiveness is essential. Arthur Becker-Weidman, PhD described his research in Chapter One. Dr. Becker-Weidman studied the effectiveness of Dyadic Developmental Psychotherapy with 64 closed cases of children who had been seen at The Center for Family Development with a DSM IV diagnosis of Reactive Attachment Disorder. Becker-Weidman (2005) hypothesized that Dyadic Developmental Psychotherapy would reduce the symptoms of attachment disorder, aggressive and delinquent behaviors, social problems and withdrawal, anxiety and depressive problems, thought problems, and attention problems. The study found significant reductions in all measures in an average of 23 sessions over 11 months. These findings continued for an average of 1.1 years after treatment ended for children between the ages of six and 16 years. Dr. Becker-Weidman's study will be published in the December 2005 issue of Child and Adolescent Social Work Journal, entitled "Treatment for Children with Trauma-Attachment Disorders."

In order to further the credibility of this treatment model, Dr. Becker-Weidman's study will need to be replicated. With the publication of this book, some universal points of Dyadic Developmental Psychotherapy can be agreed upon. While Dyadic Developmental Psychotherapy emphasizes the uniqueness of the individual therapist as well as that of the child and family, certain ingredients of the treatment model can be agreed upon for the purpose of validating research outcomes. Different therapists could then replicate the study in order to corroborate the results. In the Foreword, Daniel Hughes describes the development of Dyadic Developmental Psychotherapy. Within that chapter he identified six factors that "facilitate the ability to develop and maintain a rhythmic emotional dialogue that enables the co-creation of coherent narratives for our clients." These factors could be deemed necessary for consistency among research projects, and the chapters in this book further define each factor. The following are those factors identified by Hughes:

1. Nonverbal communication
2. Follow-lead-follow
3. Connection-break-repair
4. Affect/reflection balance and integration
5. Attitude of Playfulness, Acceptance, Curiosity, and Empathy
6. Parent-child attachment classification congruence

OTHER RESEARCH IDEAS

Research regarding the use of Dyadic Developmental Psychotherapy could be expanded beyond the scope of individual practice. For example, this book could be used as a template for treatment for children in foster care and its effectiveness could be studied. Foster parents could follow the parenting protocol outlined in Chapter Nine, and therapists could follow the treatment described in Chapters Two and Three. Foster parents could be asked to be open about their own attachment histories so that if parenting a child with trauma-attachment problems brought anything up, then the parent and therapist could shift to address these issues. This protocol could be used with children at the initial time of placement into the home, and the children served this way could be compared with those who received the standard treatment procedures.

Chapter Six describes the use of Dyadic Developmental Psychotherapy in alternative settings. The effectiveness of Dyadic Developmental Psychotherapy in these settings could also be studied, using Chapter Six as a template for what Dyadic Developmental Psychotherapy in a residential setting should look like.

DYADIC DEVELOPMENTAL PSYCHOTHERAPY: FOSTER CARE, ADOPTION, AND BEYOND

Many problems in childhood impact or are impacted by the parent-child relationship. Children other than foster and adopted children who have obvious disruptions to their attachment could benefit from Dyadic Developmental Psychotherapy treatment. Oftentimes parents and children have experienced trauma together and would benefit from the joint healing experience Dyadic Developmental Psychotherapy could offer. Children come to treatment for a multitude of identified problems, including oppositional behavior, depression, aggression, and so on. Some of these children are coping with biological conditions, and in such situations, the parent-child relationship often suffers as a result of the child's acting-out behaviors and the parent's inability to respond to the child's behavior as is needed. Others of these children may have experienced forms of traumas that are not early attachment traumas, in that they did not experience abuse, neglect, or inconsistent care from their caretakers in infancy and early childhood. Such children may have lost one parent to death or witnessed a parent's illness or difficulties, or their parents may have divorced. These parent-child relationships may also have suffered due to the parent's struggle to meet the child's need while attempting to manage their own experience. And still other children may present with emotional problems due to inappropriate parenting. In this third situation, parents should first receive their own treatment, but once the parent has addressed his or her own issues and is parenting more effectively, the parent and child could benefit from repair work in order to heal the parent-child relationship, reestablish trust, and decrease the child's need to act out in order to protect him or herself.

Dyadic Developmental Psychotherapy can be applied to adult clients. Examples of applying the attitude and tenets of Dyadic Developmental Psychotherapy were demonstrated in several chapters. In Chapter Five, Deborah Shell focused on working with parents who have themselves experienced trauma. Shell demonstrated how a therapist can use the Dyadic Developmental Psychotherapy attitude of Playfulness, Acceptance, Curiosity, and Empathy with an adult who is struggling with a hard-to-parent child and is having their own trauma history triggered. Dafna Lender's chapter on the use of self also describes work with parents using Dyadic Developmental Psychotherapy. The treatment approach's applicability with adults could be expanded beyond parents of children with attachment-trauma problems. Dyadic Developmental Psychotherapy could be specifically applied to adults who present in a clinical setting for a variety of reasons, including depression, anxiety, and trauma histories. In some situations, particularly those adults with trauma histories, an important figure in the adult's life could also participate in the treatment. This second individual could serve as the client's secure base and be the person who assists in co-creating new meaning and helps the adult integrate their experience into their day-to-day life.

Future publications about Dyadic Developmental Psychotherapy could focus on work with different populations. This would include the children who have not experienced early attachment-trauma problems as well as adults who are not parenting such children.

The Impact of Dyadic Developmental Psychotherapy

Chapter Ten was written by three parents who described their experiences participating in Dyadic Developmental Psychotherapy. Their stories poignantly depict the depth of pain they were in as a family prior to this treatment and the powerful healing impact after getting the help they so badly needed. The following are a few more inspirational quotes from parents and children. The descriptions of dramatic changes in the lives of these individuals inspire us as therapists to continue to strive to improve our methods for helping future families grow and heal together.

Billy, age 7
Billy began treatment when he was disrupting school every day and being cruel to the cat. His stepfather always said he was evil and felt he should be placed out of the home. After six sessions, two with Billy's parents only, his stepfather made a complete change, and Billy's behavior dramatically improved both at home and at school.

Billy's mother reports, "He has more positive interactions and attention and acknowledgment now from his stepfather. I've seen such a change in Billy— even the cat hangs around him now. The cat is even loving him up!"

Melissa, age 11
Melissa used to shut everyone out when she became angry. She would hide away in her room and at times not eat or speak to anyone for days. "I'm happy about my therapy because it helps me even though sometimes I get angry."

Foster/adoptive mother of three children with attachment-trauma problems, including Melissa: "Being in attachment therapy with my kids is probably the most helpful experience in my growing relationship with them. It weekly rekindles the nurturing and caring feelings which sometimes get buried when trying to cope with their trying, angry, manipulative behaviors. It is also a place where I can turn with questions regarding their motives and about my best approach to take with them in day-to-day living. I experienced nothing but frustration when the kids received therapy without me present, as I never knew how to help them cope day to day with the issues which arose during therapy. I also never had the support I needed to stay focused on relationships with them."

Isabella, age 13

Isabella was adopted from an overseas orphanage. She initially presented with wild rages at her parents' efforts to care for her. She had suffered from severe abuse in the first three years of life until her biological parents were jailed. Isabella was developing an antisocial edge with the belief that she always needed to be suspicious of other people and always needed to be calculating to stay safe. Isabella lived with supportive adoptive parents who participated in her treatment. After two years of Dyadic Developmental Psychotherapy, here is Isabella's cautious response to the question, "What has counseling been like for you?"

"The counseling has helped me to contain my anger sort of, to not feel as bad about myself. I feel much better than when I was little. It kind of makes the bad thoughts go away. When I was abused, when I was little—(you [parents] said people abused me)—it brings up bad thoughts because I think of it. Robert helped me make them go away. He's helped me. Dad's helped me. Mom's helped me. I want to be around you guys, and it helps me feel better. It's much better now. I can't explain it."

Ann, age 16

(From © Center For Family Development, www.Center4FamilyDevelop.com, used with permission.)
Ann was adopted into her family when she was 15 after over 10 placements, including three failed adoptions. She was in a Residential Treatment Center when she was 13. Ann lived with her birth mother for her first six years. Ann was abused and neglected. She suffered burns and cuts, the scarring of which is visible today. She cared for her younger siblings. One of her younger siblings drowned in the bathtub.

The following letter is from Ann to her younger brother, Bob, who was placed in a foster home after he was violent toward his pre-adoptive parents. Ann had been in treatment approximately a year when she wrote this letter. She is doing very well in school, has real friends, has learned to love and trust her parents and new siblings, and has made remarkable progress. The letter speaks for itself:

Bob,
I just wanted to write to you and tell you what I think that you should know. Everyone needs a family, too bad we had such an awful one with our birth mom Dee, and we never learned how to love or be loved, but you need a family. I have a great family, and its made all the difference in the world for me. They taught me how to be happy. I know it's hard to trust; but you have to let people take care of you so that you can learn how to love and so that you can be happy. I went through some rough times at home and in therapy. For a while I didn't want to work in therapy or sit in his lap, but then I realized he's really trying to help me and he really has Bob, he taught me to stop running from myself and from others. He taught me to talk about what is bothering me, and he has taught me to love and trust my parents and my family. My parents really love me, and I'm beginning to believe that a lot and it makes me happy. Bob, you can do it too. Go home, listen to your mom and dad, let them take care of you, trust them even though you may not want to but it is for your best, trust me. Listen to them though you don't want to, but they do know what is best for you. Work hard in therapy and listen to Arthur, he can help you, you know why, because if he helped me he can help you out. If you are thinking about Dee let me tell you something, Dee never talked to us, she never took care of us. You have to let people love you, you have to move on with your life, do what is best for you and you know what that means, you are getting older you need to act your age, behave, treat your mom and dad with respect, they love you. Do you love them, do you want to live and be with them. You need to let them into your heart and love, trust me Bob. I love you and I want the best for you. Write back as soon as possible. I Love you!
Your sister, Ann

Bob was only three when he and his older sister, Ann, were removed from their mother's care due to neglect; both were placed in foster care. Bob has been in over a dozen foster homes, had several disrupted adoptive placements, been in several psychiatric facilities and two Residential Treatment Centers. Bob is now living with a therapeutic foster family who is in the process of adopting Bob. Bob had been violent with his foster parents. He'd attacked them, destroyed property, and threatened suicide. Bob had been with them a year. He had been in Dyadic Developmental Psychotherapy for about six months when he wrote this letter back to his sister. Bob is doing very well. He now wants to be adopted, and he is able to talk about his anger, sadness, and grief over his "lost" childhood. He is able to experience hope and joy now in his new home.

Ann,
Hi, how are you? I'm fine. I saw David a few weeks ago and he showed me some pictures of you. You looked great, and very pretty! You looked a lot darker than when I last saw you, you are lucky you must keep a tan, it takes me at least a week to get a little tan and then I lose it again fast if I am not in the sun. Do you tan or does it come naturally when you are out and about doing things?

How are you doing with your family? Is it hard to treat them good? I love my family greatly but it is hard for me to treat them like they deserve. I've had a lot of painful and hurtful experiences with loads of other parents, and that makes it hard for me to believe that these are the RIGHT parents for me! So sometimes I treat them bad but they don't deserve to be treated like they are going to hurt and/or reject me the way our birth mother, Dee, and all the other foster parents did. Over the past 14 months my parents have stuck with me when times have been really rough and even when I have rejected them they have continued to love me, so I know that they have a special place in their hearts for me and only me. I'm not perfect so I still have to work hard not to let my past affect my relationships. I signed an intent to adopt with my parents at the end of June and sometime in September (I don't know exactly when) the adoption placement agreement will be signed. I think it is awesome that it is finally not scary for me to want to be adopted.

It is hard to write to you because most of my good memories of you are set in bad times and in a bad place! But my only good memories when I was little are of you. I remember you holding me and trying to make me feel better when James and David were scaring me and you getting me food when I was hungry. This makes me sad because Dee should have been taking care of you and me and James and David. I also remember you finding me behind the dresser at Jane King's and trying to make me feel better because we had to leave her house. I didn't have anyone else at the time but I had you to make me feel important and I thank you for the only comforting memories I have as a young child. I guess part of what I am also trying to say is that I feel bad that we did not end up together. I think it stinks that we were not able to have any control over our lives or where we ended up. Even though we had no control we both ended up in places where we are happy and have families that love us and I am Very Happy about that.

CHAPTER 12

Resources, Exercises, & Examples

ROBERT SPOTTSWOOD

"Hopefulness is the heartbeat of the relationship between a parent and child. Each time a child overcomes the next challenge of his life, his triumph encourages a new growth in his parents. In this sense a child is parent to his mother and father." —Louise J. Kaplan, Oneness and Separateness: From Infant to Child

CHAPTER INTRODUCTION

When we think back over learning Dyadic Developmental Psychotherapy, we can ask ourselves which resources helped most, and which, if we have found them since, would have helped earlier. Those questions, along with "Yes, but what do I DO?" guide the content of this chapter. Some of the answers come some from books, some from analogies, some from brief session stories (changed to protect the innocent), and some from experiential exercises—things which help convey the idea.

Closing this chapter are two lists: texts by author (in APA format) suggested by our group, and a list of children's books recommended by members of our group. Thank you for the opportunity to share our learning with you.

CO-REGULATION OF AFFECT

"None of us is born with the capacity to regulate our own emotional reactions. A dyadic regulatory system evolves .... The infant learns that arousal in the presence of the caregiver will not lead to disorganization beyond his coping capabilities. The caregiver will be there to re-establish equilibrium." —Peter Fonagy, excerpt from Paper to the Developmental and Psychoanalytic Discussion Group, American Psychoanalytic Association Meeting, Washington, DC, May 13, 1999

Fonagy's words describe the infant's early dependence on adults for help with emotional stability. Some psychoanalysts have done a terrific job defining the variety of results from the infant's earliest attempts to make their dependence work.

When a child cannot yet process their own distress, I try instead to help co-regulate their affect in Dyadic Developmental Psychotherapy sessions. The most useful image to me is one of coming upon a crying infant. In order to soothe the noisy infant, I go half-way up to its energy and noise level–paralleling the energy, intensity and volume and then descending in energy and decibels as I talk and soothe. I match intensity and tone (what Daniel Stern calls the "vitality affect") not the feeling itself ("categorical affect"). "OH BABY, BABY, Baby, Baby, Shhh, it's okay now, there, there, there ...." I repeat the process to let the baby hear the pattern and begin to follow me down. Following this image, the child's affect is dyadically (between two people) co-regulated. I find this is more helpful than telling the child they are "being inappropriate" or that they have "made a poor choice."

Once you have that image, you can picture being in your office and helping pull a child into regulation from any emotional extreme–fear, sadness, anxiety, anger, and, yes, exuberance! The children we see typically have difficulty regulating their affect from either direction. Children who are easily angered are usually children who also have difficulty being joyful without dysregulation.

SUGGESTED READINGS ON CO-REGULATION OF AFFECT

Facilitating Developmental Attachment: The road to emotional recovery and behavioral change in foster and adopted children, Hughes

Building the Bonds of Attachment: Awakening love in deeply troubled children, Hughes

The Developing Mind: Toward a neurobiology of interpersonal experience, Siegel

The Interpersonal World of the Infant: A view from psychoanalysis and developmental psychology, Stern

The Present Moment in Psychotherapy and Everyday Life, Stern

Affect Regulation and the Repair of Self, Schore

Affect Dysregulation and Disorders of Self, Schore

EXERCISE TO PRACTICE CO-REGULATION OF AFFECT

Respond to role-played dysregulation with co-regulation:

1. Pair up and practice some PACE responses* to familiar repeated outbursts. "Why can't I!?" "You don't like me!" "I hate you!" (Those are the outbursts, not the PACE responses.) As you respond, go half-way up to match the child's energy and intensity (aka "vitality affect") then shift gently to normal, as if guiding their lost airplane in from a fog.

2. Take turns being the dysregulated child and the PACE parent/ therapist.

3. Take a moment to comment on what it felt like.

*Here are examples of PACE responses. Make them sarcasm-free (i.e. make them verbally [words] and nonverbally [tone] congruent): "Wow, thanks for letting me know you're having a big feeling!" "I'm sorry this is hard for you. I'll stay with you." "No. I wish I could say 'Yes,' but I know I have to say 'No,' and I'm sad about that, but thanks for asking." "Thanks for helping me understand how hard this is for you." "What's that about? Let's figure it out."

> *"For example, when in a therapeutic relationship, the child is able to reflect upon aspects of traumatic memories and experience the affect associated with those memories without becoming dysregulated, the child develops an expanded capacity to tolerate increasing amounts of affect. The child learns to self-regulate."*
> –Art Becker-Weidman, "Treatment for Children with Trauma-Attachment Disorders: Dyadic Developmental Psychotherapy," Child & Adolescent Social Work Journal 22-6 (December, 2005)

CO-CREATION OF MEANING

This takes place when the adult reflects back to the child the meaning of an interaction or experience so that the child can finally begin to learn to do that for him- or herself.

> *"As parents reflect with their securely attached children on the mental states that create their shared subjective experience, they are joining with them in an important co-constructive process of understanding how the mind functions. The inherent feature of secure attachment—contingent, collaborative communication—is also a fundamental component in how interpersonal relationships facilitate internal integration in a child."*
> –Dan Siegel, The Developing Mind, p 333

> *"The therapist helps the patient [come to] see how necessary his defenses were in the past and how they reflect his strength and ingenuity in coping, while also acknowledging their current negative consequences. As defenses themselves, often a source of humiliation for the patient, are met with empathic understanding, self-blame decreases and self-acceptance increases."*
> –Diana Fosha, The Transforming Power of Affect: a model for accelerated change, pp 248-49

SUGGESTED READINGS ON CO-CREATION OF MEANING

Facilitating Developmental Attachment: The road to emotional recovery and behavioral change in foster and adopted children, Hughes

Building the Bonds of Attachment: Awakening love in deeply troubled children, Hughes

The Developing Mind: Toward a neurobiology of interpersonal experience, Siegel

CO-CREATION OF MEANING: REVISING THE NEGATIVE INTERNAL WORKING MODEL

"I want him to stop ..." "He's got to learn ..." "How can I make him understand?!"

Here's one way. Revise the child's negative internal working model. This model directs the child to respond here and now as if she were there and then when an old script is generated. Either the current situation or current emotion is too similar to something in the past. If the traumatized child could articulate it, their subconscious might say this:

Child: "My foster dad just said 'No TV!' I feel disappointed. I remember feeling disappointed before—when my first parents would leave and not come back for two days! I dreaded that! Now I feel dread again!! Omigod, my foster dad might leave me!!" [crash/steal/lie/rage/etc.]

Parent: "WHY DID YOU DO THAT!?"

Child: (back to consciousness) "I don't know."

— — —

Child: "I totally know from growing up abused/neglected/deserted that I must be a really rotten kid. My new parents think I'm not, but they just don't know me yet. When they find out how rotten I am, they'll hate me. They'll send me away. I can't stand waiting for heartbreak when I know it's coming ... waiting is torture. I'll get it over with! Whatever it takes! I may be no good, but I can at least get it over with!" [crash/steal/lie/rage/etc.]

Parent: WHY DID YOU DO THAT!?

Child: (back to consciousness) "I don't know."

Dyadic Developmental Psychotherapy assumes that clients are always showing us, in the best way they can, the meanings they make of things.

It often helps co-create meanings with them to read their minds, tentatively and with compassion.

Co-Creating Meaning: Brief Session Example

(Nonverbals–children pay attention to nonverbals. The following should be delivered with eye contact, voice modulation, and interested expression.)

"I just thought of something! I may be wrong–you can argue with me–but my guess is that you blew up this morning because your adoption date is next week and part of you may be getting more and more scared that your new parents might change their minds. So maybe you can see how important it is to make sure they know what they are getting into–if they are going to change their minds they should do it now instead of putting you through this wonderful adoption and then changing their minds which would be really, really horrible. (Continue if you see signs you are on target.) Do you think you could possibly look at your new dad now and tell him, 'Dad, I'm really afraid you'll change your mind about adopting me–I blew up this morning because I'm so scared you're going to change your mind.'"

Discussion of Co-creation of Meaning: Reading Children's Cues

"Infants explore the world away from their attachment figures when they feel safe and return to them when they feel threatened or uncomfortable." –Patricia Crittenden, PhD

From birth to age 40 and beyond, children give us mostly nonverbal cues about whether they are heading toward or away from us. When they are feeling safe and secure, they find a way to say, "I need more space; it's time to let go while I explore my world." When they have had enough exploring or become distressed, they give nonverbal cues which say, "Time for home-comfort and loving-up again!" Bob Marvin, at the University of Virginia, refers to this cycle as the child's "Circle of Security."

Parents love knowing the right interpretation of their child's cues. But parents can get anxious anywhere along the circle of security. When they are not certain of how to interpret the cues, parents may attribute negative motives to their child.

"He's just doing it for attention."
"He likes to make me mad."
"He wants to be in control so he never has to share."

Lawyer: "Which parent do you think the children should be with?"

Me: "Either one, as long as they provide therapeutic parenting."

Lawyer: "What's therapeutic parenting?"

Therapeutic parenting is caregiving by an adult who has: 1) a secure state of mind with respect to attachment, 2) the ability to create a healing PLACE in each interaction, and 3) a well-developed reflective function which allows the adult to respond in a therapeutic manner to a troubled child's wildest behaviors. A well-developed reflective function allows co-creation of meaning, in which the adult reflects back to the child the meaning of an interaction or experience so that the child can begin to learn to do that themselves.

> *"The experience of security is the goal of the attachment system, which is thus first and foremost a regulator of emotional experience. In this sense it lies at the heart of many forms of mental disorder and the entire psychotherapeutic enterprise."* –Peter Fonagy

THERAPEUTIC PARENTING AND REPAIRS

"Repairs" are logical consequences with a pro-social spin. Repair teaches the child that there can be disruptions in relationships, and that these disruptions can be fixed. Over time, repeated repair of disruptions enables the child to move from feeling shame (which is about self) to feeling guilt (which is about actions). If I made someone's life harder–accidentally or on purpose–then in the near future, after everyone is calm, I need to do something to make their life easier. Repairs are not punishments, but gifts–helping the child learn a skill which will benefit them for the rest of their relational lives: how to think about and care for the feelings of others.

> "So you're bumming because you swore at your dad? Do you want to ask him what he would like for a repair–something to make his life easier so he'll feel better?"

— — —

> Parent: "Sometimes I get so mad I yell at the kids, and then I feel terrible."
>
> Therapist: "You don't have to be perfect. If you lose your temper you can do a repair later. It really helps them learn it when they see you take time to do a repair to them."

Repairs are rooted in the cyclical rhythm of every relationship: connection-break-repair. If Carl Rogers had used repairs, he would have had "directive" client-centered therapy (like Dyadic Developmental Psychotherapy) instead of non-directive. Repairs allow the therapist to speculate, explore, and push because if you make a mistake you can take time to apologize and fix it before moving on.

Therapist: "Looks like you've had a rough week."

Teen: ("Duh"-like, insinuating tone) "No!!"

Therapist: "Oh, I apologize. I misread your tired look. Thanks for correcting me. Let me make amends by just being quiet with you for awhile."

The motive and methods of nurturing "repairs" are miles from the strict-father model of punitive parenting.

> *"Most of our upbringing [in Sweden, 1920's] was based on such concepts as sin, confession, punishment, forgiveness, and grace, concrete factors in relationships between children and parents and God. There was an innate logic in all this which we accepted and thought we understood. This fact may well have contributed to our astonishing acceptance of Nazism .... In a hierarchical system, all doors are closed."* —film director Ingmar Bergman, in his autobiography The Magic Lantern, pp 7-8

SUGGESTED READING ON THERAPEUTIC PARENTING

Attaching in Adoption, Gray.

Becoming a Family, Eshleman

The Search for the Secure Base: Attachment theory and psychotherapy, Holmes

Mother and Child: Visions of parenting from indigenous cultures, Reynolds

Material World: A global family portrait, Menzel
[Depicts 30 families from as many countries, outside their homes with all of their belongings. Everywhere, humans live in cooperative family groups, some with a lot of stuff to make life softer, others with only each other's softness. –Deb Shell]

"I'm finding that even your parent-oriented handouts from last year and Dan's handouts are beyond the reach of many of my parents. They are too overwhelmed with their own problems and attachment-related issues to be able to make much use of educational materials I try to provide." –e-mail from a therapist colleague

"All parents have issues, and RAD children will find them all."
–Daniel Hughes, PhD

"[Sigh] .... I told him [adopted son, age four] we don't say 'butt' in our house, and now he teases me all day with 'butt' until I want to blow up. I know why–my father was alcoholic and he talked potty talk constantly, and I said my kids would never have to go through that. Now this one does it!" –weary adoptive parent

It is important to recognize and address the parent's issues first, so that they can help their child without becoming reactive or distressed, which they will become at times anyway. I recommend that within a few sessions after the assessment you meet with just caregivers. This is partly to get the history and paperwork done, partly to let the parents ask all their most worrisome questions, and partly to establish a loving conspiracy of adults to work for the child's health. Occasionally you may see so much adult anxiety or disruption of thought or mood that you may suggest attention to the parent or the couple before trying to treat the child. As a construction-contractor dad put it, "Fix the foundation first."

In the early session with caregivers, I try to create a safe, depolarized experience. Each person's motive (wanting the best for the child) is praised. Doing the family history with the parents allows everyone's meaning to make sense given the context of what they knew, how they were raised, etc.

"My dad used to humiliate us in public when we misbehaved. I've always wanted to ask him what the hell he was thinking when he was doing that. Everyone still walks on eggshells around my dad. I'd like to take him out in the woods and tell him, 'Let's put all this bullshit behind us.' But he was a salesman–he can turn any argument on its head and make me sorry for bringing it up." –29-year-old father during adult-session history taking

"Is there enough safety, love, connection, and attunement in the room?" –L. Fisher-Katz, DDP-trained consultant

You give grown-ups PACE so they can give it to children. "It's hard for us to give our children what we got too little of growing up," I tell parents. "That's a big reason that I think you are brave."

Sometimes they reply, "Are you giving us empathy now?"

"Yes, thanks for checking. Is that okay?" (Nobody objects.)

Finally, if adult caregivers don't stick together, children get stuck in the middle. "Children in the middle" feel deeply split in their wish to be loyal and supportive to all their caregivers. Sometimes they act confident and managerial as they try to take sides or address adult needs, but as one consultant says "splitting has an edge to it, and it cuts." (For more on the effects of splitting on individuals, see the works of psychiatrist Otto Kernberg; for the effects of splitting on groups, see William L. White, *The Incestuous Workplace*.)

Harville Hendrix, in *Getting the Love You Want*, suggests that we choose our mate partly in hopes that they will fill our emotional empty places for us. When they don't, he argues, we resent them, and may come to hate them for failing us. If these processes are active in your client's caregivers, they will need compassionate attention and empathy before they can help the child.

> "... selecting a partner is not an easy task: half of adults decide that they selected the wrong person (Bumpass & Raley, 1995), actually an unusually terrible person, and they divorce that person—at substantial physical, emotional, and social cost to us all." –Patricia Crittenden, Transformations in Attachment Relationships in Adolescence: Adaptation versus need for psychotherapy

Suggested Reading on Helping Parents Heal

The Whole Parent: How to become a terrific parent even if you didn't have one, D. Wesselmann [Help for parents who are revisiting their own trauma issues.]

Parenting From the Inside Out: How a deeper self-understanding can help you raise children who thrive, Siegel & Hartzel

Time In Parenting, Clarke

It's Not Fair, Jeremy Spencer's Parents Let Him Stay Up All Night, Wolf [Really helpful for parents of children under age 11.]

Get Out of My Life, But First Could You Drive Me & Cheryl to the Mall: A Parent's Guide to the New Teenager, Wolf

Why Did You Have to Get a Divorce? and When Can I Get a Hamster?: A guide to parenting through divorce, Wolf

Mom, Jason's Breathing on Me!: The solution to sibling bickering, Wolf
[Most parents are good-enough parents but are never told, and so they fear they are something less. Therapist Anthony Wolf writes compassionately and accessibly for parents of children with at least some attachment.]

PLAYFUL, ACCEPTING, CURIOUS, EMPATHIC | OUR THERAPEUTIC STANCE

A good analogy to giving children PACE is Grandma's lap. For our purposes, Grandma is a safe grown-up who helps kids feel safe. In Grandma's lap, a young person can pour their heart out and feel *accepted* without judgment. Grandma is interested enough to be *curious* ("Now what do you suppose that's about?"). She is *empathic* enough to make feelings safe ("Sounds like that was hard for you.") And you can count on Grandma to be gently *playful* so you know you are special to her.

Many parents of troubled children have fished out the behavioral and "choices" pond, finding only diminishing nibbles. But working for a reward or "making good choices" is—bottom line—wanting to please you, the adult who sometimes pays attention. Alienated children often have no concept of pleasing adults. They truly believe from their own experience that they are unpleasing and unlovable to the core.

PACE helps adults go for the feelings beneath the behavior, like seeing the fish below the surface. It helps us give children's feelings the attention they need to be taken care of and move on. PACE is pro-feelings.

BRIEF SESSION EXAMPLE–PACE

Here is an example of using PACE to help not only anxious children, but also their harsh parent, "The Great Santini" himself:

"I asked my husband to come with me, like you said, but he told me, 'I don't need no goddam psychobabble.'" This biological father frequently told his highly anxious children he wished they had never been born.

So mother brought in the three children, while father stayed home. The children (all under age 10) were thrilled when I used PACE. Instead of sarcasm or cynicism I used *playfulness* for fun, *acceptance* of all their ideas and feelings, *curiosity* about their lives, and *empathy* for their difficulties.

"Mom says you had a hard time around school this week? (curious) What was hard about it—did the teacher want you to have too much fun and you had to say 'No way, teacher, that's too much fun?' (playful) No? What happened? Dad yelled at you for report cards? Thank you for helping me understand. (accepting) What was that like for you? (curious) Yes, it must have been really hard. (empathic) How did you deal with that; what did you think? What did you do? Were you sad? Did you get mad? How did you handle it?" (curious—and I did pause for each answer.]

They went home and talked about how nice counseling was. Within three sessions the Great Santini-like father came in from sheer curiosity, scowling and ready to do battle with me. But I gave him the same PACE treatment, giving extra special empathy for his motive of wanting the best for his children. "Oh, I'm glad you could make it! (acceptance) It's so nice to meet you and know that you want the best for your kids. (empathy for motives) Please sit anywhere that looks comfortable." (acceptance, empathy) My nonverbals included a warm voice tone, pumping his hand, patting his shoulder, and smiling broadly. (playfulness, acceptance)

With fathers in particular, it can help to ground the present in the past with empathy and acceptance for their own childhood experiences, which I try to collect in the first session. "Considering your own harsh childhood, you've already left behind some of the brutal family traditions you lived through." Occasionally, I have to bluntly tell a parent to stop something torturous—such as telling his kids he wished they had never been born. But the important element is to have enough empathy for the parent so that you understand the parent's motive—wanting his children to grow up to be strong and self-reliant and to not be victimized like he felt as a child. Good motives, mistaken methods. You give PACE to parents so they can learn to give it to their kids.

Father's guarded defenses soon atrophied for lack of purpose, and he became the family's most enthusiastic fan of counseling, reminding the others when it was Wednesday—counseling night! Needless to say, with both parents supported, supportive, and working together, the children were very ready to relax into being cared for.

Playful

Playful in Dyadic Developmental Psychotherapy means humor you would feel when enjoying a playful infant. For teens I modify this with a little edginess—as if Mr. Rogers meets Seinfeld and good things happen. But talk fast.

Teen: (Sudden outburst after refusing to talk) "God, my teacher is such a psycho; I hate him!"

Therapist: "Your teacher is a psycho ... so that naturally raises the question of whether [caretaker who is present] is more or less of a psycho than the teacher. What do you think?"

Playful ideas to get relationship going with children:

- converse with the child as if the parent were the client
- examine shoes, especially soles
- crack knuckles (research says not related to arthritis)

BRIEF SESSION EXAMPLE—PLAYFULNESS WITH KNUCKLE CRACKING

Once day a seriously antisocial teen was hauled in, and he refused to move. Or look. Or speak. No matter what. (Heck, it worked with every other adult.) Father was busy nailing the coffin lid by urging the boy to talk, to be polite, etc. There was only one thing to do—get seriously playful fast! What to do? (Puzzle, puzzle ...) Then I remembered: He cracked one of his knuckles when he first came in. So I went for that.

Therapist: "Hey, you don't have to talk; in fact I support your not talking right now, but just do me a favor and crack your knuckle once, hey? I mean just once, okay?"

Teen: [zombie]

Therapist: "No? (sigh) I guess I'll just have to crack one for you ..."

There was my excuse to get close and pick up a limp hand. I pretended to fiddle around as if trying to get this large soft hand into knuckle-cracking position, and I kept one eye on his face. Under the pulled-down baseball cap I saw a mouth corner inching into a grin. We had connection!

Then I explained to the wide-eyed father that the real key is to crack all the fingers at once, like a concert pianist. As I fumbled earnestly trying to weave 10 limp fingers together, keeping floppy palms outward, this angry, shame-filled 'tough guy" burst out in belly laughs! Houston, we have relationship.

Suggested Reading on Playfulness

Theraplay, Jernberg & Booth
[Positive parent-child play is one dimension that helps create a secure attachment. One way to learn how to play and bring joy and connection into the lives of the families we work with is through Theraplay.]

 # Accepting

Author Diana Fosha, who does affective work mostly with adults, describes the therapeutic effect of acceptance for clients of all ages:

> *"Not feeling pressured to proceed to any experience before he is ready, the patient feels more in control, less anxious, and has less need to defend. Paradoxically, removing the pressure often leads to therapeutic progress. Saying that it is all right to stay right here often has the paradoxical effect of decreasing obstacles to progress ..."*
> –Diana Fosha, The Transforming Power of Affect: A model for accelerated change, pp 250-251

A simple way to start practicing **acceptance** for difficult thoughts and feelings is to say "thank you" up front.

"You think I'm stupid? Thank you for letting me know ...."

"Wow, you are really angry! Thanks for telling us."

"Thank you for staying quiet and keeping part of yourself safe and private from everyone ...."

Acceptance means accepting the child's emotions, motives, thoughts— and not trying to judge or change them. Therapists like myself who were taught clever/funny jujitsu to "handle resistance" may need to pause and downshift. When resistance is truly accepted, the deepening of connection feels moving–almost something closer to sacred.

Suggested Reading on Accepting

Your Child's Self-Esteem, Briggs
[The best primer for parents learning how to convey unconditional love. Teaches respectful communication. –Deb Shell]

The Transforming Power of Affect: A model for accelerated change, Fosha

Brief Client Story of Accepting All of a Child's Thoughts and Feelings

Sometimes I will labor to make a session emotionally safe, but the child has a hard time getting to safe, perhaps because I am male, or resemble someone who was dangerous. But they are listening. Then the caregiver calls later from home:

> "I had to set a limit on some unsafe behavior (eight-year-old foster son) and he suddenly started screaming, worse than anything I've heard in my life. He screamed—just screams at first, then he screamed, 'I HATE YOU!!!' to nobody in particular. Finally he looked at me and said, 'I'm really angry! I want to be adopted by you and Dad, but my first mom should be doing something to get me back! My first mom isn't doing anything to get me back! I don't want any more moms or dads. Just you and Dad.' Then he said, 'I feel better now,' and out he went to play. I've never heard anything like that from him."

I was grateful that this foster mother was able to *accept* without judgment all of this child's feelings and statements. I try not to imagine her stopping him partway through his processing with, "Mikey! That is not acceptable behavior! You are making a poor choice!"

Brief Example of Accepting a Child's Avoidance

Each session I would sit close to the child and deliver PACE over whatever the week's issues or events had been. But he would make some endless attempt to keep the discussion away from feelings—movies, toys, family birthdays—anything but feelings!

Soon I might say, "This must be really hard for you because you sure are working hard to keep us away from talking about feelings. I wonder what makes talking about feelings so hard?" I accept his not wanting to talk about feelings, and don't make him do it, but I wonder aloud about the difficulty. (Thanks to Art Becker-Weidman for helpful mid-career supervision on this.)

 Curious

In Dyadic Developmental Psychotherapy *curiosity* works best for me when I envision approaching an unhappy infant. Asking questions is less to demand information than it is to demonstrate that the client is important and valuable. It shows that I value what the client thinks and feels and want to take time to know him and his world. The nonverbal message is, "I'm paying attention. I like you. I care about you. I think about your life." A good message for any age, including teens.

"What's that like?" "How come?" "How do you know?" "What's that about? Let's figure it out." "Does anybody know how hard your life has been?" "How did you get by?" "What did you do?"

Curiosity is especially helpful when the child makes distorted statements. Instead of reacting with escalation or (worse) lecturing, we can get curious about the distortion, and what it is like to have it. Practice ahead of time to avoid sarcasm, even accidental.

"My mom hates me."

"Huh. How do you know? When did you find out? How do you handle it? Why do you think she does that?" (very big mystery to kids: grown-ups' motives)

Grown-ups' motives stump most kids. Your curiosity–"Why does she do that?"–can open doors and windows long nailed shut around what meaning the child has made of their caregivers' motives. Their logic may be unsound, but it is their logic and it has allowed them to make sense of the seemingly paradoxical world of grown-ups.

The catch is keeping congruency between verbal and nonverbal message. That is, your curiosity is kind and your tone of voice must convey kindness, avoiding slivers of irony, sarcasm, cynicism, judgment, or "gotcha." These negative attitudes are culturally pervasive, perhaps inherent in a corporate marketing culture. (Anxious people who continually put each other down buy more stuff trying to feel safer.) You may argue–kids often like that–but ask first. "Huh. That makes some sense. Can I argue with you?"

SUGGESTED READING ON CURIOSITY

How to Talk So Kids Will Listen and Listen So Kids Will Talk, Faber & Mazlish [Two moms write from experience.]

 # EMPATHIC

Some believe we learn empathy from surviving our own suffering. A colleague in medical research reports that a very wealthy businessman once agreed to a research interview only after he contracted a life-threatening illness. "I never would have agreed to this interview before," he said.

"Helping others was not important. Then I got sick. You can be very callous about something until it happens to you."

But real empathy for therapists develops after we understand the world of the client, after we have fully accepted the client, her feelings, and her view—and then, using curiosity, understand what it means.

One foster mother called back after a single session—I hadn't met the child yet—to report, "I tried your empathy idea. The next time he started winding up, instead of yelling at him I said, 'I know you had a really hard life in Nevada. But you're with us now, in New Hampshire. You're safe.' Suddenly tears came to his eyes."

SUGGESTED READING ON EMPATHY

Twenty Things Adopted Kids Wish Their Adoptive Parents Knew, Eldridge

How to Talk So Kids Will Listen and Listen So Kids Will Talk, Faber & Mazlish

Between Parent and Child, Ginott & Ginott

BRIEF EXAMPLE OF EMPATHY

An adoptive parent in New York, who organizes RAD parent support groups, gives empathy to other parents:

"We adopted a little boy last July—considered unadoptable due to severe attachment issues. He got much better with nurturing, holding, and lots of structure—in three months we had fallen in love. He is a joy!

"Our first adoptee, Eddie, now 15, continues to make steady but slow gains. He made honor roll all year, is a peer mediator, is active in clubs and sports, is a doting brother to the new one, and is a helpful and loving son. He would definitely be in jail now without all the attachment work. His journey has been long and hard.

"We would be happy to help out anyone we can. It is a pleasure for us to support others!"

EMPATHY—THE QUIZ

1. In session, a young girl pops out with, "You don't know what it was like to put yourself to bed and get your own supper!"

Most empathic response from therapist:

    A. "I know just how you feel. It happened to me once."
    B. "I know exactly how you feel. It happened to me a lot."
    C. "Why, when I was your age ..."
    D. "Um-hmm." [the "Rogers"]
    E. "What is your foot saying?" [the "Perls"]
    F. [with genuine gratitude] "You're right. Thanks for pointing that out. That must have been so hard for you ...." [listen]

2. No matter what you do, a teen tries to not engage. He dysregulates by staring at the clock, asks when we'll be done, etc. Suddenly he sneers triumphantly and drops a bombshell, claiming that his mother, who is sitting in the room, does drugs every day at home.

Most empathic response from therapist:

    A. Turn on parent: "He tells me you're doing drugs every day at home!" (the Split)
    B. Confront teen: "So you're trying to turn me against your mother. In our business we call that splitting." [bad choice]
    C. Call 911. If the statement is true, it's about time somebody caught this mom. If it's false, the kid should witness the natural consequences of lying. Heck, true or false, this family needs shaking up. [the Cop-out]
    D. "I'm really sorry; that must be difficult for you to be around every day."

3. "I hate you."

Most empathic response from therapist:

    A. "Why? What did I say?"
    B. "Same to you only double."
    C. "Hate is such a strong word. Let's be reasonable ..."
    D. "I know exactly where you're coming from ..."
    E. "You need cheering up. May I offer you a smiley-face button?"
    F. "Thanks for letting me know. It's okay to hate me, and I'm sad that I haven't found a way to help that hurts less."

INTERSUBJECTIVITY

"This healing relationship can heal you." –L. Fisher-Katz, DDP consultant

"Connections between minds ... involve a dyadic [two-person] form of resonance in which energy and information are free to flow across

two brains .... There is an overwhelming sense of immediacy, clarity, and authenticity. It is in these heightened moments of engagement, these dyadic states of resonance, that one can appreciate the power of relationships to nurture and to heal the mind."
–Siegel, The Developing Mind (1999), p 337

As Siegel points out, a child uses the caregiver's state of mind to regulate the child's own mental processes. For this reason, significant early neglect and abuse cause difficulty regulating affect plus incoherence in autobiographical narrative–my feelings overwhelm me AND my life doesn't make any sense. Intersubjectivity–rarely associated with therapies focused on behavior or cognition, but core to Dyadic Developmental Psychotherapy, helps the child find safety and inner organization through deep connection, perhaps for the first time. As Siegel has put it, people in connection not only "feel" the other, they "feel felt."

"The attuned resonant relationship between child and therapist and child and caregiver enables the child to make sense (a left-hemispheric function) out of memories, autobiographical representations, and affect (right hemispheric functions)."
–Art Becker-Weidman, "Treatment for Children with Trauma-Attachment Disorders: Dyadic Developmental Psychotherapy," Child & Adolescent Social Work Journal 22-6 (December 2005)

Brief Session Story–Intersubjectivity

An eight-year-old severely neglected "wild child" in foster care began raging in my office when I talked about how hard his life had been, how no one seemed to know just how hard, and how sad I felt thinking about his life. When he saw a tear in my eye as I spoke, he suddenly stopped avoiding my eyes, stopped yelling angry statements at me, dropped his defenses for about 20 seconds and stared deeply into my eyes. While he was quiet and our eyes were locked I poured in empathy for his hard life, using both verbal (words) and nonverbal (sad tone and tears.) At last, totally calm, he looked away. He talked about something mundane, and we played a board game and chatted about nothing in particular. The next day he finally wanted to talk to his father on the telephone. He told his father he loved him.

"When we look at a baby and talk to it and play with it, we are doing exactly what the baby needs to survive and grow."
–Greta Spottswood, medical student/parent educator

Brief Session Story–Achieving Intersubjectivity with Eye Contact

Early in my Dyadic Developmental Psychotherapy training, a 13-year-old violent avoidant antisocial fellow was forced into counseling under court order. At that time I did not want to take this case–it looked like what I used to call "hopeless"–but for a number of reasons I agreed. So I said "Okay, if you ever want to get off probation let's start the hard stuff: five seconds of eye contact with Dad." Fifteen sessions later he's up to 90 seconds and telling Dad his feelings. So I said, "You guys are working so hard, and building trust that was never there before–what are you feeling right now?" And this former throw-away, violent young person suddenly grins from ear to ear, looks ME in the eye and says "Joyful!"

Exercise in Conversational Intersubjectivity
(Try this in supervision or with a trusted person.)

Do a "flat-face" exercise of your own. Talk for two minutes to a friend, telling them about something that happened recently–nothing big. Somewhere in the middle have your friend drop their eyes to the floor and make no response for 20 seconds. Then they come back to paying attention. You keep talking. After the exercise talk about what it felt like trying to continue telling your story while being ignored. What did the listener feel? Switch roles.

Suggested Reading on Intersubjectivity

Facilitating Developmental Attachment: The road to emotional recovery and behavioral change in foster and adopted children, Hughes

Building the Bonds of Attachment: Awakening love in deeply troubled children, Hughes

The Developing Mind: Toward a neurobiology of interpersonal experience, Siegel

The Interpersonal World of the Infant, Stern

NONVERBALS

Reading the Nonverbals of Others

One of the laws of interpersonal communication is that we are never NOT communicating. A brief example follows.

Father, daughter (age 12), and new stepmother arrived for their first session. Before I could stop him, Father directed the child, as parents sometimes do, "Tell us all about your feelings." Does anything bring on opposition quicker? But Daughter DID tell us all about her feelings: She immediately began a physical assault on Stepmother. Thinly disguised as a game, she poked, jabbed, and threatened Stepmother around Father's useless objections. Stepmother smilingly obliged, threatening the daughter back in an unequal hierarchy of worthlessness.

The embarrassed father repeatedly told the daughter, "Tell us about your feelings!" until I said, "She is," and pointed out the barely hidden rage at Stepmother.

Father later informed me Stepmother had recently begun displaying a host of shaming attitudes toward his daughter. I began this case by working with the adults first.

OUR OWN NONVERBALS

MIRRORING: Many readers are familiar with the old training exercise of pairing up and taking turns copying as best we can the expressions and actions of the other. It has a reassuring subconscious effect which conveys useful messages apart from words.

EXERCISE IN NONVERBAL MIRRORING

Sometimes when we are talking with an adult who endlessly argues with us, our first thought is that they aren't listening to our brilliant ideas. Our second thought is that they probably think we're not listening to their brilliant ideas, which frankly shine a little less than our brilliant ideas. Next time this happens begin casually mirroring their body language as you listen. You will soon notice that a connection is present, as if you are dancing together without talking about it.

SUGGESTED READING IN NONVERBAL COMMUNICATION

The Developing Mind: Toward a neurobiology of interpersonal experience, Siegel

The Present Moment in Psychotherapy and Everyday Life, Stern
[Specifically suggested for nonverbal communication with voice—especially his thoughts on matching vitality affect with rhythm and intensity.]

Brief Session Story about Nonverbal Mirroring

A severely narcissistic teen (with a very sad history) comes in with her exasperated mother. Ninety-nine percent of her loud chatter is cognitively distorted and emotionally pumped. Mother is quickly and effectively annoyed. I suspect this helps daughter feel safer by distracting everyone from her painful early life. When I try to ask about, that she brushes me off with interruptions and distractions—faster than I can respond. She clearly has her black belt in verbal martial arts. Emotional connection on a verbal level appears blocked.

I find it helps to sit near her, listen intently, and slowly mirror her posture, her limb positions, the attitude of her head and neck, her expressions. In my mind I think, "I am listening. I want to understand so much. I will try to be you so I can understand better." Her rapid-fire chatter slows, her eye contact (to see whether someone is paying attention) increases, and she begins to relax. Soon I get a word in edgewise. Gradually we start a dialog.

It is up to the therapist to stop mirroring when the connection is concluded. As an end in itself, mirroring is a questionable goal.

Example of Mirroring from the Child

Especially delightful is when the child decides to mirror everything YOU say and do. Since we learn what we practice, you can now help them practice words for their inner life:

> "[Sigh] My life has been so hard! When I was a baby nobody took care of me. Now it's really so hard to trust grown-ups! I wish I could ask Julie [caregiver in the room] for help with my big feelings! But I am so afraid if I ask, she'll give up on me. I'm afraid she'll say I'm not worth loving. I want so much to say, 'Please don't give up on me, Julie! Please don't stop loving me!'"

Tone of Voice

Quickly, what is the difference between saying, "I couldn't care less!" and "I could care less!" While literally reading the exact opposite of each other, the statements are used interchangeably to mean, I don't care! How can this work? They are both used in the same contexts and with the same tone of voice. In other words, they deliver the same nonverbal message. Because we listen to nonverbals more than verbals, the message "I don't care!" is all we hear.

Exercise in Nonverbal Communication—Eye Contact

Pair up and try eye contact for five seconds, 10 seconds, 20, and finally 30. Remember you can blink, smile, or whatever—this is not a staring contest. After each attempt take a moment to share what feelings were noticed by each person.

Coherent Autobiographical Narrative Making Sense of the Child's Life Story

"The conflict between the will to deny horrible events and the will to proclaim them aloud is the central dialectic of psychological trauma ... far too often secrecy prevails, and the story of the traumatic event surfaces not as a verbal narrative but as ... protean, dramatic, and often bizarre symptoms ..."
—J. Herman, Trauma and Recovery

With just the adults present, I do a deep family history. Give each parent sincere admiration for what they survived in childhood. Give empathy around how hard it is to give children playfulness, acceptance, or empathy which we were never given. "One of the hardest things is to give our kids emotional support which we rarely received."

If both parents are present, they usually enjoy it if you interview each one about the other's family of origin. Comfort level rises and they are more easily engaged with the therapy for their child.

Did he [father] have brothers and sisters? How many? What number was he? Are his parents still living? Still married? How old was he when they broke up? How did his parents handle their conflicts? What was that like for him growing up?

You can stop along the way if discussion takes off. More impressions. If you have only one parent present, just ask them the questions, giving PACE as you go.

Perhaps less important than the details laid out in a family history/genogram is the cohesion which the story provides to the child's life. One of the therapeutic goals is to let the chaotic, painful life of the child have enough story to be tell-able without having protective blank spots or other dysregulation emerge.

The grisly details ("the pornography of the real" as some wise woman renamed television news) need not dominate the story of a child's hard life. Instead of saying, "When you were four you lived in Dallas where your aunt and uncle hit you every day," you can talk about connecting pieces, even adding a therapeutic marker for them. "Then when you were four you moved from Bar Harbor to Dallas, where you were abused until you were five, when you moved to Granddad's in Chicago. That was a hard time in Dallas. I really, really wish I had known you then. I could have gone to Dallas and told them you were a good little girl and that they needed to treat you nice!" The child can now think about Dallas and find connection, both with the rest of her life, and with your wish to be there with her.

> *"I don't understand emotions."*
> —struggling father of a challenging five-year-old adoptee

Sometimes dads wonder what to say to kids. Ask kids anything about their memories, experiences, or emotions. These are the ingredients of our autobiographical narratives, where our lives begin to make sense and become cohesive stories.

SUGGESTED READING ON COHERENT AUTOBIOGRAPHICAL NARRATIVE

Genograms in Family Assessment, McGoldrick

The Whole Parent: How to become a terrific parent even if you didn't have one, Wesselmann

Trauma and Recovery, Herman

Healing Trauma: Attachment, mind, body, and brain, Solomon & Seigel [Contributors include Allan Schore, Bessel van der Kolk, Mary Main, Robert Neborsky, Francine Shapiro, and Diana Fosha.]

Ainsworth, M. (1967). *Infancy in Uganda; infant care and the growth of love.* Baltimore: Johns Hopkins Press.

Ainsworth, M. (1978). *Patterns of attachment: a psychological study of the strange situation.* Hillsdale, N.J.: Lawrence Erlbaum Associates; New York: distributed by Halsted Press Division of Wiley.

Barkley, R. A. & Benton, C. M. (1998). *Your defiant child: Eight steps to better behavior.* New York: Guilford Press.

Becker-Weidman, A. (2005). Treatment for Children with Trauma-Attachment Disorders: Dyadic Developmental Psychotherapy. *Child & Adolescent Social Work Journal* 22-6.

Bergman, I. (1994). *The magic lantern: An autobiography.* New York: Penguin.

Bowlby, J. (1975). *Attachment and loss, vol.2.* New York: Basic Books.

Bowbly, J. (1990). *A secure base: Parent-child attachment and healthy human development.* New York: Basic Books.

Briggs, D. C. (1970). *Your child's self-esteem.* New York: Doubleday.

Carey, W. B. (1997). *Understanding your child's temperament.* New York: Macmillan.

Clarke, J. I. (1999). *Time-in: When time-out doesn't work.* Seattle, WA: Parenting Press.

Cline, M. D., Foster, W. & Fay, J. (1992). *Parenting teens with love & logic: Preparing adolescents for responsible adulthood.* Colorado Springs, CO: Pinon Press.

Crittenden, P. M. (1995). Attachment and psychopathology. In S. Goldberg, R. Muir, & J. Kerr (Eds.), *Attachment theory: Social, developmental and clinical perspectives* (pp. 367-406). Hillsdale, NJ: Analytic Press.

Crittenden, P. *Transformations in attachment relationships in adolescence: Adaptation versus need for psychotherapy.* Retrieved November 20, 2004, from http://www.patcrittenden.com/m_adult.php.

Daniel, S. J. (1999). *The developing mind: Toward a neurobiology of interpersonal experience.* New York: Guilford Press.

Dozier, M., Stovall, K.C., & Albus, K. (1999). Attachment and psychopathology in adulthood. In J. Cassidy & P. Shaver (Eds.), *Handbook of attachment* (pp. 497-519). NY: Guilford Press.

Dozier, M., Stovall, K.C., Albus, K.E., & Bates, B. (2001). Attachment for infants in foster care: The role of caregiver state of mind. *Child Development, 70,* 1467-1477.

Eldridge, S. (1999). *Twenty things adopted kids wish their adoptive parents knew.* New York: Dell Publishers.

Faber, A. & Mazlish, E. (2002). *How to talk so kids will listen and listen so kids will talk.* New York: HarperCollins.

Federici, R. S. (1998). *Help for the hopeless child: A guide for families* (with special discussion for assessing and treating the post-institutionalized child). Alexandria, VA: Dr. Ronald S. Federici and Associates.

Fonagy, P. (1999). *Transgenerational consistencies of attachment: A new theory.* Paper to the Developmental and Psychoanalytic Discussion Group, American Psychoanalytic Association Meeting, Washington, D.C., May 13, 1999.

Ginott, H. G., Ginott, A., & Goddard, H. W. (Eds.). (1969). *Between parent and child: The bestselling classic that revolutionized parent-child communication.* New York: Three Rivers Press.

Gray, D. D. (2002). *Attaching in adoption: Practical tools for today's parents.* Indianapolis, IN: Perspectives Press.

Greene, R. (1998). *The explosive child: A new approach for understanding and parenting easily frustrated, chronically inflexible children.* New York: Harper Collins.

Herman, J. (1997). *Trauma and Recovery.* New York: Basic Books.

Holmes, J. (2001). *The search for the secure base: Attachment theory and psychotherapy.* London: Brunner-Routledge.

Hughes, D. A. (1999). *Building the bonds of attachment: Awakening love in deeply troubled children.* St. Northvale, NJ: Jason Aronson.

Hughes, D. A. (2000). *Facilitating developmental attachment: The road to emotional recovery and behavioral change in foster and adopted children.* St. Northvale, NJ: Jason Aronson.

Hughes, D. (2002). *The psychological treatment of children with PTSD and attachment disorganization: Dyadic developmental psychotherapy.* Manuscript submitted for publication.

Hughes, D. (2003). Psychological intervention for the spectrum of attachment disorders and intrafamilial trauma. *Attachment & Human Development, 5,* 271-279.

Jernberg, A. M. & Booth, P. B. (1998). *Theraplay: Helping parents and children build better relationships through attachment-based play.* San Francisco: Jossey-Bass.

Kranowitz, C. S. (2003). *The out-of-sync child has fun: Activities for kids with sensory integration dysfunction.* New York: Perigee.

Kranowitz, C. S. & Silver, L. B. (1998). *The out-of-sync child: Recognizing and coping with sensory integration dysfunction.* New York: Perigee.

Lakoff, G. (2004). *Don't think of an elephant: Know your values and frame the debate.* White River Junction, VT: Chelsea Green Publishing.

Levy, T. & Orlans, M. (1995). Attachment theory and assessment. In C. A. McKelvey (Ed.), *Give them roots, then let them fly: Understanding attachment therapy* (pp. 36-53). Evergreen, CO: Attachment Center Press.

Lyons-Ruth, K. (1996). Attachment relationships among children with aggressive behavior problems: The role of disorganized early attachment patterns. *Journal of Consulting and Clinical Psychology 64,* 64-73.

Lyons-Ruth, K. & Jacobvitz, D. (1999). Attachment disorganization: Unresolved loss, relational violence, and lapses in behavioral and attentional strategies. In J. Cassidy & P. R. Shaver (Eds.), *Handbook of attachment: Theory, research, and clinical application* (pp. 520-554). New York: Guilford Press.

Lyons-Ruth, K., Alpern, L., & Repacholi, B. (1993). Disorganized infant attachment classification and maternal psychosocial problems as predictors of hostile-aggressive behavior in the preschool classroom. *Child Development 64,* 572-585.

Main, M. & Cassidy, J. (1988). Categories of response to reunion with the parent at age six: Predictable from infant attachment classifications and stable over a one-month period. *Developmental Psychology, 24,* 415-426.

Main, M. & Hesse, E. (1990). Parents' unresolved traumatic experiences are related to infant disorganized attachment status. In M.T. Greenberg, D. Ciccehetti, & E.M. Cummings (Eds.), *Attachment in the preschool years: Theory, research, and intervention* (pp. 161-184). Chicago: University of Chicago Press.

McCreight, B. (2002). *Parenting your adopted older child: How to overcome the unique challenges and raise a happy and healthy child.* Oakland, CA: New Harbinger Publications.

McGoldrick, M. (1986). *Genograms in family assessment.* New York: W. W. Norton & Co.

Menzel, P. (1994). *Material world: A global family portrait.* San Francisco: Sierra Club Books.

Osofsky, J. D. (Ed.). *Infant Mental Health Journal.*

Payne, R. (2003). *A Framework for understanding poverty.* Highlands, Texas: aha! Process, Inc.

Reynolds, J. (1996). *Mother and child: Visions of parenting from indigenous cultures.* Rochester, VT: Inner Traditions Intl Ltd.

Schore, A. N. (1999). *Affect regulation and the origin of the self: The neurobiology of emotional development.* Hillsdale, NJ: Lawrence Erlbaum Associates.

Schore, A. N. (2001). The effects of a secure attachment relationship on right brain development, affect regulation, and infant mental health. *Infant Mental Health Journal, 22,* 7-66.

Schore, A. N. (2001). The effects of early relational trauma on right brain development, affect regulation, and infant mental health. *Infant Mental Health Journal, 22,* 201-269.

Schore, A. N. (2003). *Affect regulation and the repair of the self.* New York: W.W. Norton & Co.

Siegel, D. J. (1999). *The developing mind: Toward a neurobiology of interpersonal experience.* New York: Guilford Press.

Siegel, D. J. (2002). Toward an interpersonal neurobiology of the developing mind: attachment relationships, "mindsight," and neural integration. *Infant Mental Health Journal, 22,* 67-94.

Siegel, D. J. & Hartzel, M. (2003). *Parenting from the inside out: How a deeper self-understanding can help you raise children who thrive.* New York: J. P. Tarcher.

Solomon, J. & George, C. (Eds.) (1999). *Attachment disorganization.* New York: Guilford Press.

Solomon, M. F. & Siegel, D. J. (2003). *Healing trauma: Attachment, mind, body, and brain.* New York: W.W. Norton & Company.

Sroufe, L. A. (1996). *Emotional development: The organization of emotional life in the early years.* New York: Cambridge University Press.

Steele, H. (Ed.). *Attachment and Human Development.* Quarterly journal. Online version available.

Stern, D. (1985). *The interpersonal world of the infant: A view from psychoanalysis and developmental psychology.* Philadelphia, PA: Basic Books.

Stern, D. (2004). *The present moment in psychotherapy and everyday life.* New York: W.W. Norton & Co.

Thomas, N. L. (1997). *When love is not enough: a guide to parenting children with RAD-reactive attachment disorder.* Glenwood Springs, CO: Families by design.

Thomas, N. L. (Writer). (1999). *Rebuilding the broken bond* [Motion picture]. (Available from Nancy Thomas, P. O. Box 2812, Glenwood Springs, CO 81602).

Van der Kolk, B. A., McFarlane, A.C., & Van der Hart, O. (1996). A general approach to the treatment of post-traumatic stress disorder. In B. Van der Kolk, A.C. MacFarlane, & L. Weisaeth, (Eds.), *Traumatic stress: The effects of overwhelming experience on mind, body, and society* (pp. 417-440). New York: Guilford Press.

Vermont Adoption Consortium. (2003). *Vermont adoption handbook.*

Walker, B., Goodwin, N.J., & Warren, R.C. (1992). Violence: A challenge to the public health community. *Journal National Medical Association, 84,* 490-496.

Wesselmann, D. (1998). *The whole parent: How to become a terrific parent even if you didn't have one.* New York: Plenum Publishing Corp.

Wolf, A. (1991). *Get out of my life, but first could you drive me & Cheryl to the mall: A parent's guide to the new teenager, revised and updated.* New York: Farrar, Straus & Giroux.

Wolf, A. (1996). *It's not fair, Jeremy Spencer's parents let him stay out all night!: A guide to the tougher parts of parenting.* New York: Farrar, Straus & Giroux.

Wolf, A. (1998). *Why did you have to get a divorce? And when can I get a hamster?: A guide to parenting through a divorce.* New York: Farrar, Straus & Giroux.

Wolf, A. (2000). *The secret of parenting: How to be in charge of today's kids—from toddlers to preteens—without threats or punishment.* New York: Farrar, Straus & Giroux.

Wolf, A. (2003). *Mom, Jason's breathing on me!: The solution to sibling bickering.* New York: Ballantine Books.

RESOURCES FOR CHILDREN

Appelt, K. (2000). *Oh my baby, little one.* San Diego, CA: Harcourt.

Barrett, J. D. (1989). *Willie's not the hugging kind.* New York: Harper Collins.

Barrett, J. (2001). *Things that are most in the world.* New York: Scholastic, Inc.

Biderman, D. (1983). *The book of kisses.* Book Sales.

Brown, M. (1988). *Dinosaurs divorce.* Boston, MA: Little Brown & Company.

Brown, M. W. (1942). *The runaway bunny.* New York: Harper Trophy.

Crasny, L. & Brown, M. (1988). *Dinosaurs divorce.* New York: Little Brown & Co.

Crooke, T. (1994). *So much.* Cambridge, MA: Candlewick Press.

Harris, R. (1996). *It's perfectly normal: Changing bodies, growing up, sex and sexual health.* Cambridge, MA: Candlewick Press.

Hazen, B. S. (1992). *Even if I did something awful.* New York: Aladdin Library.

Hoban, R. (1996). *The little brute family.* Elgin, IL: Sunburst.

Joose, B. (1998). *Mama do you love me?* San Francisco: Chronicle Books.

Kuchler, B. L. (2001). *Just moms: A mother by any other squawk, cheep, yip, or mew is still as sweet.* Minocqua, WI: Willow Creek Press.

Lee, D. (1999). *Because Brian hugged his mother.* Nevada City, CA: Dawn Publications.

Lender, D. (2000). *Little heroes #3: From across the seas.* Chicago, IL: National Training Institute.

Long, S. (1996). *Hush, little baby.* San Francisco: Chronicle Books.

McBratney, S. (1994). *Guess how much I love you*. Cambridge, MA: Candlewick Press.

McCourt, L. (1997). *I love you stinky face*. New York: Troll Associates.

Mcmullan, K. (1996). *If you were my bunny*. New York: Scholastic Press.

Menzel, P. (1994). *Material world: A global family portrait*. San Francisco: Sierra Club Books.

Minarik, E. H. (1992). *Little bear*. New York: Harper Collins Juvenile Books.

Minarik, E. H. (1979). *Little bear's visit*. New York: Harper Trophy.

Modesitt, J. (1996). *I love you the purplest*. San Francisco: Chronicle Books.

Modesitt, J. (1999). *Mama, if you had a wish*. New York: Simon & Schuster Books for Young Readers.

Nichols, M., Lacher, D., & May, J. (2002). *Parenting with stories: Creating a foundation of attachment for parenting your child*. Deephaven, MN: Family Attachment Center.

Numeroff, L. (1998). *What mommies do best/What daddies do best*. New York: Simon & Schuster Books for Young Readers.

Penn, A. (1993). *The kissing hand*. Washington, D.C.: Child Welfare League of America.

Pringle, L. (1993). *Octopus hug*. Honesdale, PA: Boyds Mills Press.

Ross, D. (2000). *A book of hugs*. New York: Harpercollins

Schlein, M. (2000). *The way mothers are*. Morton Grove, IL: Albert Whitman & Co.

Scott, A. H. (1972). *On mother's lap*. Winnipeg, MB: Clarion Books.

Tafuri, N. (1998). *I love you, little one*. New York: Scholastic Press.

Taylor, A. (1999). *Baby dance*. New York: Harper Festival.

Thompson, R. (1998). *Foo* (Jesse adventure series). Vancouver, BC: Annick Press.

Vincent, G. (2000). *A day, a dog*. New York: Front Street Press.

Walvoord Girard, L. (1984). *My body is private*. Morton Grove, IL: Albert Whitman & Co.

Walvoord Girard, L. (1991). *Adoption is for always*. Morton Grove, IL: Albert Whitman & Co.

Walvoord Girard, L. (1992). *We adopted you, Benjamin Koo*. Morton Grove, IL: Albert Whitman & Co.

Wyeth, S. D. (1998). *Something beautiful*. New York: Doubleday books for young readers.

References

Ainsworth, M., Blehar, M., Waters, E., & Wall, S. (1978). *Patterns of attachment.* NJ: Lawrence Erlbaum.

Allan, J. (2001). *Traumatic relationships and serious mental disorders.* NY: John Wiley.

Andrews, B., Varewin, C.R., Rose, S., & Kirk (2000). Predicting PTSD symptoms in victims of violent crime. *Journal of Abnormal Psychology, 109,* 69-73.

Archer, C., & Burnell, A. (2003). *Trauma, attachment and family permanence: Fear can stop you loving.* London: Jessica Kingsley Publishers.

Bailey, B. (2000). *I love you rituals.* New York: Quill.

Becker-Weidman, A. (2005). Treatment for children with trauma-attachment disorders: Dyadic developmental psychotherapy. *Child & Adolescent Social Work Journal, 22-6.*

Blackwell, S. (2001). *Villa Santa Maria Program Report 2000.* Unpublished manuscript.

Blackwell, S. (2002). *Villa Santa Maria Clinical Program Report 2001.* Unpublished manuscript.

Blackwell, S. (2003). *Villa Santa Maria Clinical Program Report 2002.* Unpublished manuscript.

Blackwell, S. & Vallejos, A. (2002). *Residential treatment: For referral to outcome.* Paper presented at the 2002 ATTACh Conference, Orange County, CA

Bowlby, J. (1975). *Attachment and loss, vol. 2.* NY: Basic Books.

Bowlby, J. (1980). *Attachment, separation, and loss.* NY: Basic Books.

Bowbly, J. (1988). *A secure base.* NY:Basic Books.

Carlson, E.A. (1988). A prospective longitudinal study of disorganized/disoriented attachment. *Child Development, 69,* 1107-1128.

Carlson, V., Cicchetti, D., Barnett, D., & Braunwald, K. (1995). Finding order in disorganization: Lessons from research on maltreated infants' attachments to their caregivers. In D. Cicchetti & V. Carlson (Eds), *Child Maltreatment: Theory and research on the causes and consequences of child abuse and neglect* (pp. 135-157). NY: Cambridge University Press.

Carter, A. (1942). The prognostic factors of adolescent psychoses. *Journal of Mental Sciences, 88,* 31-81.

Cicchetti, D., Cummings, E.M., Greenberg, M.T., & Marvin, R.S. (1990). An organizational perspective on attachment beyond infancy. In M. Greenberg, D. Cicchetti, & M. Cummings (Eds.), *Attachment in the preschool years* (pp. 3-50). Chicago: University of Chicago Press.

Dozier, M. Stovall, K.C., Albus, K.E., & Bates, B. (2001). Attachment for infants in foster care: The role of caregiver state of mind. *Child Development, 70,* 1467-1477.

Dozier, M., Stovall, K.C., & Albus, K. (1999). Attachment and psychopathology in adulthood. In J. Cassidy & P. Shaver (Eds.), *Handbook of attachment* (pp. 497-519). NY: Guilford Press.

Fahlberg, V. (1990). Residential treatment: A tapestry of many therapies. Indianapolis, IN: Perspectives Press.

Finzi, R., Cohen, O., Sapir, Y., & Weizman, A. (2000). Attachment styles in maltreated children: A comparative study. *Child Development and Human Development, 31,* 113-128.

Fosha, D. (2000). *The transforming power of affect: A model for accelerated change.* NY: Basic Books.

Gauthier, L., Stollak, G., Messe, L., & Arnoff, J. (1996). Recall of childhood neglect and physical abuse as differential predictors of current psychological functioning. *Child Abuse and Neglect 20,* 549-559.

Glasser, W., (1988). *Choice theory: A new psychology of personal freedom.* NY: Harper-Collins.

Gossett, J., Lewis, J. & Barnhart, F. (1983). *To find a way: The outcome of hospital treatment of disturbed adolescents.* NY: Brunner/Mazel.

Gray, D. (2002). *Attaching in adoption.* Indianapolis, IN: Perspective Press.

Greenberg, M. (1999). Attachment and psychopathology in childhood. In J. Cassidy & P. Shaver (Eds.). *Handbook of attachment* (pp.469-496). NY: Guilford Press.

Hesse, E. (1999). The adult attachment interview. In J. Cassidy & P. Shaver (Eds.), *Handbook of attachment.* NY: Guilford Press.

Hughes, D. (1997). *Facilitating developmental attachment: The road to emotional recovery and behavioral change in foster and adopted children.* NJ: Jason Aronson.

Hughes, D. (1998). *Building the bonds of attachment: Awakening love in deeply troubled children.* NY: Guilford Press.

Hughes, D. (2002). *The psychological treatment of children with PTSD and attachment disorganization: Dyadic developmental psychotherapy.* Manuscript submitted for publication.

Hughes, D. (2003) Psychological intervention for the spectrum of attachment disorders and intrafamilial trauma. *Attachment & Human Development, 5,* 271-279.

Hughes, D. (2004). An attachment-based treatment of maltreated children and young people. *Attachment and Human Development* Vol 6, No 3 (September 2004) 263-278.

James, B. (1989). *Treating traumatized children: New insights and creative interventions.* Lexington, MA: Lexington Books.

Jernberg, A., & Booth, P. (1999). *Theraplay: Helping parents and children build better relationships through attachment-based play (2nd Ed.).* San Francisco: Jossey-Bass.

Loeber, R. (1991). Antisocial behavior: More enduring than changeable? Special section. *Journal of the American Academy of Child and Adolescent Psychiatry, 30,* 393-397.

Lyons-Ruth, K. (1996). Attachment relationships among children with aggressive behavior problems: The role of disorganized early attachment patterns. *Journal of Consulting and Clinical Psychology 64,* 64-73.

Lyons-Ruth, K., Alpern, L., & Repacholi, B. (1993). Disorganized infant attachment classification and maternal psychosocial problems as predictors of hostile-aggressive behavior in the preschool classroom. *Child Development 64,* 572-585.

Lyons-Ruth K. & Jacobvitz, D. (1999). Attachment disorganization: unresolved loss, relational violence and lapses in behavioral and attentional strategies. In J. Cassidy & P. Shaver (Eds.) *Handbook of attachment.* (pp. 520-554). NY: Guilford Press.

MacMillian, H.L. (2001). Childhood Abuse and Lifetime Psychopathology in a Community Sample. *American Journal of Psychiatry, 158,* 1878-1883.

Main, M. & Cassidy, J. (1988). Categories of response to reunion with the parent at age six: Predictable from infant attachment classifications and stable over a one-month period. *Developmental Psychology, 24,* 415-426.

Main, M. & Cassidy, J. (1988). Categories of response with the parent at age six. *Developmental Psychology, 24,* 415-426.

Main, M. & Hesse, E. (1990). Parents' Unresolved Traumatic Experiences are related to infant disorganized attachment status. In M.T. Greenberg, D. Ciccehetti, & E.M. Cummings (Eds.), *Attachment in the preschool years: Theory, research, and intervention* (pp. 161-184). Chicago: University of Chicago Press.

Main, M. (1991). Metacognitive knowledge, metacognitive monitoring, and singular (coherent) vs. multiple (incoherent) models of attachment. In C. M. Parkes, J. Stevenson-Hinde, & P. Marris (Eds.), London: Routledge.

Malinosky-Rummell, R. & Hansen, D.J. (1993). Long term consequences of childhood physical abuse. *Psychological Bulletin 114*, 68-69.

McEwen, B. (1999). Development of the cerebral cortex XIII: Stress and brain development – II. *Journal of the American Academy of Child and Adolescent Psychiatry, 38*, 101-103.

Minde, K. (1993). Prematurity and serious medical illness in infancy: Implications for development and intervention. In C. Zeanah, Ed., *Handbook of infant mental health*, NY: Guildord.

Mordock, J. (2002). A model of milieu treatment. *Residential Treatment of Children and Youth, 19(4)*, 39-59.

O'Connor, T., & Zeanah, C., (2003). Attachment disorders: Assessment strategies and treatment approaches. *Attachment & Human Development, 5*, 223-245.

Porges, S. (2003). *Psychological Science Agenda*, 15, 9-11.

Prino, C.T. & Peyrot, M. (1994). The effect of child physical abuse and neglect on aggressive withdrawn, and prosocial behavior. *Child Abuse and Neglect, 18*, 871-884.

Quay, H.C. & Peterson, D.R. (1983). *Interim manual for the revised behavior problem checklist*. Coral Gables: University of Miami Press.

Randolph, E. (2000). *Randolph Attachment Disorder Questionnaire, 3rd Ed.* Evergreen, CO: The Attachment Center Press.

Randolph, E. (2000). *Manual for the Randolph Attachment Disorder Questionnaire, 3rd Ed.* Evergreen, CO: The Attachment Center Press.

Robins, L.N. (1978). Longitudinal studies: Sturdy childhood predictors of adult antisocial behavior. *Psychological Medicine, 8*, 611-622.

Robins, L. & Price, R. (1991). Adult disorders predicted by childhood conduct problems: Results from the NMH Epidemiological Catchment Area Project. *Psychiatry, 54*, 116-132.

Schore, A. (2003). *Affect dysregulatioon and disorders of the self.* NY: Norton.

Schore, A. (2003). Early relational trauma, disorganized attachment, and the development of a predisposition to violence. In M. Solomon & D. Siegel (Eds.), *Healing trauma: Attachment, mind, body, and brain* (pp. 107-167). NY: Norton.

Schore, A. (2001). The effects of early relational trauma on right brain development, affect regulation, and infant mental health. *Infant Mental Health Journal, 22*, 201-269.

Schreiber, R. & Lyddon, W. J. (1998). Parental bonding and current psychological functioning among childhood sexual abuse survivors. *Journal of Counseling Psychology, 45*, 358-362.

Siegel, D. J. (1999). *The Developing Mind.* NY: Guilford Press.

Siegel, D. J. (2001). Toward an interpersonal neurobiology of the developing mind: Attachment relationships, "mindsight," and neural integration. *Infant Mental Health Journal, 22* (1-2), 67-94.

Solomon, J. & George, C. (Eds.) (1999). *Attachment Disorganization.* NY: Guilford Press.

Stern, D. (1985). *The interpersonal world of the infant.* New York: Basic Books.

Teicher, M.H., Ito, Y., & Glod, C.A. (1996). Neurophysiological mechanisms of stress response in children. In C.R. Pfeffer (Ed.), *Severe stress and mental disturbances in children* (pp. 59-84). Washington, D.C.: American Psychiatric Press.

Tizzard, B. (1977). *Adoption: A second chance.* London: Open Books.

Tyrell, C., Dozier, M., Teague, G.B., & Fallot, R. (1999). Effective treatment relationships for persons with serious psychiatric disorders: the importance of attachment states of mind. *Journal of Consulting and Clinical Psychology, 67,* 725-733.

Van der Kolk & Fisler (1996). Dissociation and the fragmentary nature of traumatic memories: overview. *British Journal of Psychotherapy, 12,* 352-61

Walker, B., Goodwin, N.J., & Warren, R.C. (1992). Violence: A challenge to the public health community. *Journal National Medical Association, 84,* 490-496.

Wolkind, S., Hall, F., & Pawlby, S. (1977). Individual differences in mothering behaviour. In P. Grahm (Ed.), *Epidemiological approaches in child psychiatry* (pp. 107-123). New York: Academic Press.

Zimmerman, D., Meyers, P., & Epstein, R. (2001). The Rorschach evaluation of object representation and therapeutic change is group care. *Residential Treatment for Children and Youth, 19(1),* 59-88.

The publisher would like for you to know that Deborah Shell and Art Becker-Weidman are available to provide workshops and training on a variety of topics for therapists, child welfare workers, educators, residential treatment staff, and other care providers. They can provide training on such topics as:

1. The development of attachment and the effects of maltreatment on child development.

2. Dyadic Developmental Psychotherapy.

3. Assessment, diagnosis, and treatment of children with Reactive Attachment Disorder.

4. Effective methods of educating children with trauma-attachment disorders.

5. Effective parenting approaches to use with attachment disordered children.

6. Treating children with trauma-attachment disorders in residential settings.

They are available for one-day or multi-day workshops and training programs. Contact Wood 'N' Barnes Publishing at 800-678-0621 or 405-942-6812 for more information.

716-810-0790

5820 Main St Suite 406
Williamsville NY 14221

ARTHUR BECKER-WEIDMAN, PhD, directs the Center for Family Development in Williamsville, NY, providing evaluations and treatment for trauma-
attachment disordered children, consulting with Departments of Social
Services, residential treatment centers, and mental health clinics in the
U.S. and Canada, and providing training workshops for therapists in the
U.S. and Canada. He is an Adjunct Clinical Professor at the State University of New York at Buffalo, has published over a dozen papers, and has
presented at numerous local, regional, and international professional
meetings. E-mail: Aweidman@Concentric.net
Web site: www.Center4FamilyDevelop.com

fax 716-636-6243

CRAIG CLARK, MA, LMFT, is a private marriage and family therapist specializing in trauma and attachment issues with adults and children. In
addition to clinical practice, he is core faculty at John F. Kennedy University Graduate School of Professional Psychology in Campbell, CA, and Director of their School-Based Counseling Program in Cupertino, CA.

DANIEL HUGHES, PhD, is a clinical psychologist who has specialized in the
treatment of children and youth with trauma/attachment problems for the
past 20 years. He has written books and articles about his interventions
and conducts seminars and trainings for therapists in the U.S., UK, and
Canada. More recently he has expanded his work into the attachment-
focused model of family therapy. E-mail: Dhughes1060@adelphia.net

DAFNA LENDER, MSW, LCSW, is the Training Director at The Theraplay
Institute in Wilmette, IL, where she trains therapists, coordinates clinical
services, and practices Theraplay. Dafna also has a private practice in
Chicago. Dafna's main area of expertise is in combining Dyadic Developmental Psychotherapy and Theraplay to enhance the therapeutic effects of both modalities and improve the quality of lives of children and
families with attachment issues. Dafna's other area of interest is in the
treatment of children who have neurological problems as a result of prenatal substance exposure. E-mail: dafna@theraplay.org

JESSICA MROZ, MSW, LCSW, is in private practice in Oak Park, IL. Jessica
specializes in treating children with trauma-attachment problems and
their families, and with children from birth to age three. Jessica is also a
Certified Theraplay Therapist and trainer with the Theraplay Institute.
Jessica has presented at national and international conferences on topics
pertaining to attachment.

MIRANDA RING, PsyD, is a child/family clinical psychologist who works at the Edmund Ervin Pediatric Center of MaineGeneral Medical Center in Waterville, ME. Her works involves treatment of children (and their families) presenting with a wide range of issues including anxiety, depression, aggression, and divorce as well as trauma and attachment concerns. She is also a clinical supervisor and chairs a team in Education and Training at the Pediatric Center.

PHYLLIS RUBIN, CCC-SLP, PsyD, is a clinical psychologist and speech-language therapist in private practice in Oak Park, IL. Her specialty is treating children and families with trauma-attachment issues as well as children from birth to age three. A Certified Theraplay Therapist and Trainer with the Theraplay Institute, Phyllis has presented on Theraplay nationally and internationally, is co-author of Play With Them: Theraplay Groups in the Classroom, and has written book chapters on Theraplay. She is also EMDR trained.

DEBORAH STIEGLITZ SHELL, MA, Licensed Clinical Mental Health Counselor, currently works as an outpatient therapist at Northwestern Counseling and Support Services, Inc., a community mental health center in northern Vermont. She provides therapy for children and families, specializing in attachment and trauma issues as well as relationship concerns with individuals and couples. Although her formal training spans three decades, beginning with concentrations in art/pottery and culminating in a Master's in Counseling from Johnson State College, VT, her interest in attachment-style parenting began nearly 30 years ago and has led to extensive work as a leader with La Leche League, International and later as developer of a resource center for homeschoolers. She has written articles for unschooling publications and has contributed to books about homeshcooling. Her best and most informative teachers have been her children. E-mail: debshell_vt@yahoo.com

ROBERT SPOTTSWOOD, MA, Licensed Mental Health Counselor, directs North Star Counseling Services, Inc. in Springfield, VT (802-885-3670). He works with children and famlies on a wide range of issues, including foster, adoption, trauma, and attachment. He sees children only with a caregiver to work with relationally, and is particularly interested in affect and building social supports for parents.

SUSAN BECKER-WEIDMAN, MSW, LCSW is Director of Adoption Services at the Center For Family Development in Williamsville, NY. She provides home studies, post-placement supervision, and adoption training for families wishing to adopt locally and internationally. She also provides evaluations and treatment for older teenagers and young adults with adoption-related issues.

SCOTT L. BLACKWELL, PhD, is the Chief Clinical Officer at the Villa Santa Maria. As a psychologist in private practice, he specializes in the evaluation and treatment of children, adolescents, and families. Dr. Blackwell is also a Clinical Adjunct Professor at the University of New Mexico School of Medicine, Department of Psychiatry.

KAREN DOYLE BUCKWALTER, MSW, LCSW is the Director of Treatment Services at Chaddock in Quincy, IL. She has been a leader in the development of Chaddock's Integrative Attachment Therapy Residential Treatment Program and is a trainer and Supervisor for the Theraplay Institute in Chicago. She is a frequent presenter and has conducted training for both national and international audiences.

BETH GREEN is an adoptive parent. E-mail: bethgreen@hotmail.com

JODY HANSEN-WALKER, has been a therapeutic adoptive parent since 1987, and licensed foster parent since 1995. She is a Family Support Specialist for the Center for Family Development in Buffalo, NY specializing in attachment parenting techniques. She also runs the Post Placement Department for Adoption Star Inc. in Buffalo, NY providing guidance to birth mothers after placement of a child.

KAREN A. HUNT, is a parent whose youngest child, adopted at age four, has been successfully treated for Reactive Attachment Disorder via Dyadic Developmental Psychotherapy. Presently a MSW student at the University of Pittsburgh, she anticipates graduation in December, 2005. Karen is employed as a caseworker, serving individuals diagnosed with developmental disabilities, and provides online support to adoptive parents (as Dima's mom).

JOSEPH MCGUILL is Executive Director of Villa Santa Maria in Cedar Crest, NM. He began his career as a child-care worker at the Villa in 1981. Under his direction, the Villa became licensed to provide mental health services and rehabilitation for children in 1992. The implementation of the Attachment Model as the foundation of treatment is the most recent shift in the Villa's therapeutic history.

MICHELLE ROBISON, MSW, LCSW is the Associate Director of Clinical Services at Chaddock in Quincy, IL and is a Certified Theraplay Therapist. In addition to her work as a clinican, she has played a significant role in the development and implementation of Chaddock's attachment-based services, including the Integrative Attachment Therapy Program. She has also provided training on both a local and national level.